THE WILSON–JOHNSON CORRESPONDENCE, 1964–69

The Wilson–Johnson Correspondence, 1964–69

Edited by

SIMON C. SMITH
University of Hull, UK

ASHGATE

© Simon C. Smith 2015

All rights reserved. No part of this publication may be reproduced, stored in a retrieval system or transmitted in any form or by any means, electronic, mechanical, photocopying, recording or otherwise without the prior permission of the publisher.

Simon C. Smith has asserted his right under the Copyright, Designs and Patents Act, 1988, to be identified as the editor of this work.

Published by
Ashgate Publishing Limited
Wey Court East
Union Road
Farnham
Surrey, GU9 7PT
England

Ashgate Publishing Company
110 Cherry Street
Suite 3-1
Burlington, VT 05401-3818
USA

www.ashgate.com

British Library Cataloguing in Publication Data
A catalogue record for this book is available from the British Library

The Library of Congress has cataloged the printed edition as follows:
The Wilson–Johnson Correspondence, 1964–69 / edited by Simon C. Smith.
    pages   cm
Includes bibliographical references and index.
1. Johnson, Lyndon B. (Lyndon Baines), 1908–1973 – Correspondence. 2. Wilson, Harold, 1916–1995 – Correspondence. 3. United States – Foreign relations – Great Britain. 4. GreatBritain – Foreign relations – United States. 5. United States – Foreign relations – 1963–1969. 6. Great Britain – Foreign relations – 1964–1979. I. Smith, Simon C., 1967– editor.
E183.8.G7W67 2015
327.7304109'046–dc23   2014039122

ISBN   9781409448082 (hbk)
ISBN   9781409448099 (ebk–PDF)
ISBN   9781472406347 (ebk–ePUB)

Printed in the United Kingdom by Henry Ling Limited, at the Dorset Press, Dorchester, DT1 1HD

Contents

Acknowledgements   *vii*
Note on Sources   *ix*
Abbreviations   *xi*

Introduction   1

1   Labour's Return to Power, Nuclear Sharing, Rhodesia, and the Escalation of the Vietnam War, March 1964–March 1966   33

2   Dissociation, NATO, and the Continuing Crisis in Rhodesia, March 1966–January 1967   127

3   The Wilson–Kosygin Talks, Crisis in the Middle East, the Defence Review, and the Devaluation of Sterling, January–December 1967   195

4   Withdrawal from East of Suez, Wilson's Visit to Moscow, Gold and Monetary Crises, Vietnam Peace Initiatives, and the End of the Johnson Presidency, January 1968–January 1969   255

Dramatis Personae   *299*
Further Reading   *311*
Index   *317*

Acknowledgements

I would like to thank the staff of the National Archives (Kew), the Bodleian Library (Oxford), the US National Archives (College Park), and the LBJ Library (Austin) for their assistance in researching this volume. I would also like to record my gratitude to Michael and Judith Thornhill for their hospitality during the Oxford phase of my research.

Note on Sources

The most complete class of documents dealing with the Wilson–Johnson correspondence is to be found at the LBJ Library in Austin, Texas: NSF, Head of State Correspondence, boxes 9–11; NSF, Special Head of State Correspondence, box 56. Correspondence between Wilson and Johnson is also scattered through the records of the Prime Minister's Office (PREM 13) at the UK National Archives, Kew Gardens, the US National Archives, College Park (RG 59, Lot Files: Presidential and Secretary of State Correspondence with Heads of State), and Harold Wilson's papers at the Bodleian Library, Oxford (MS. Wilson c. 1576–1589). Some of the messages have been published in the volumes of the *Foreign Relations of the United States* for the Johnson years, especially: *FRUS, 1964–1968*: Volume V: *Vietnam, 1967* (Washington, DC: United States Government Printing Office, 2002); *FRUS, 1964–1968*: Volume VIII: *International Monetary and Trade Policy* (Washington, DC: United States Government Printing Office, 1998); *FRUS, 1964–1968:* Volume XII: *Western Europe* (Washington: United States Government Printing Office, 2001); *FRUS, 1964–1968*: Volume XIII: *Western Europe Region* (Washington: United States Government Printing Office, 1995); *FRUS, 1964–1968*: Volume XIX: *Arab-Israeli War 1967* (Washington: United States Government Printing Office, 2004); *FRUS, 1964–1968*: Volume XXIV: *Africa* (Washington, D.C.: United States Government Printing Office, 1999). A handful of messages have also been reproduced in Wm. Roger Louis and S. R. Ashton (eds), *East of Suez and the Commonwealth* (London: TSO, 2004) and in George C. Herring (ed.), *The Secret Diplomacy of the Vietnam War: The Negotiating Volumes of the Pentagon Papers* (Austin: University of Texas Press, 1983). Other sources used in this study (archival, printed primary, and secondary) are to be found in the notes that accompany the Introduction and individual chapters. A brief guide to further reading has been provided at the end of the study.

Abbreviations

ABM	Anti-ballistic Missile
ANF	Atlantic Nuclear Force
ASPAC	Asian and Pacific Council
ASW	Anti-submarine Warfare
BAOR	British Army of the Rhine
BST	British Summer Time
CAB	Cabinet
CENTO	Central Treaty Organization
CINCPAC	Commander-in-chief, Pacific Command
DM	Deutschmark
DMZ	Demilitarized Zone
DRV	Democratic Republic of Vietnam
EEC	European Economic Community
EFTA	European Free Trade Association
EURATOM	European Atomic Agency Community
FBI	Federation of British Industry
Fed.	Federal Reserve
FCO	Foreign and Commonwealth Office
FRG	Federal Republic of Germany
FRUS	Foreign Relations of the United States
G10	Group of Ten
GMT	Greenwich Mean Time
HMG	Her Majesty's Government
IMF	International Monetary Fund
LBJ	Lyndon Baines Johnson
MDAP	Mutual Defense Assistance Program
MLF	Multilateral Force
MIT	Massachusetts Institute of Technology
NATO	North Atlantic Treaty Organization
NLF	National Liberation Front
NSF	National Security File
OAU	Organization of African Unity
OECD	Organization for Economic Co-operation and Development
PKI	Indonesian Communist Party
POL	Petroleum, Oil and Lubricants

PREM	Prime Minister's Office
RAF	Royal Air Force
SAC	Strategic Air Command
SACEUR	Supreme Allied Commander Europe
SACLANT	Supreme Allied Commander Atlantic
SEATO	Southeast Asia Treaty Organization
SPD	Social Democratic Party of Germany
TNA	The National Archives, Kew
UAR	United Arab Republic
UDI	Unilateral Declaration of Independence
UN	United Nations
USAF	United States Air Force
USSR	Union of Soviet Socialist Republics

Introduction

I was glad to learn from Dean [Rusk] that you find our exchanges and messages useful. I most certainly do.[1]

As rancher no less than as President, I count it a rewarding day which brings a good letter from you.[2]

On hearing that Harold Wilson's Labour Party had secured victory in the 1964 General Election, President Lyndon Baines Johnson wrote to the new Prime Minister assuring him that 'I look forward to the continuation of the close and friendly cooperation, based on mutual confidence and respect, which has bound our countries so closely and for so long' (4). Wilson reciprocated these warm sentiments, informing Johnson that 'I shall look forward to continuing the close and confidential communication which you have already begun and which has existed between successive presidents of the United States and prime ministers of the United Kingdom' (5). So began a long-running correspondence between Wilson and Johnson that lasted for over four years until the latter's departure from the White House in January 1969 and yielded nearly 300 messages, some just a few lines, others running to many pages. In March 1966, US Ambassador in London, David Bruce, recorded that 'we receive almost daily copies of messages passing between the Prime Minister and the President. Their tone is cordial to the point of being on both sides effusive'.[3] That the high hopes for 'close and friendly cooperation' between Wilson and Johnson were sorely tested by a multiplicity of domestic and international problems is widely recognized. The effect of these challenges on the relationship between Britain and America in general, and Wilson and Johnson in particular, however, is a contested issue.

---

[1] Message from Wilson to Johnson, 10 June 1966, LBJ Library, NSF, Head of State Correspondence File, Box 10, United Kingdom: Prime Minister Wilson Correspondence, Volume 5 [2 of 2], no. 165.

[2] Message from Johnson to Wilson, 12 Feb. 1969, TNA, PREM 13/3006.

[3] Raj Roy and John W. Young (eds), *Ambassador to Sixties London: The Diaries of David Bruce, 1961–1969* (Dordrecht: Republic of Letters Publishing, 2009), p. 249 (diary entry for 3 March 1966). In response to a parliamentary question regarding his consultations with Johnson over Vietnam, Wilson confirmed that 'I am in close touch with President Johnson on a wide range of subjects, including Vietnam' (*Parliamentary Debates (Hansard): Commons, 1966–67*, Volume 751, 26 Oct. 1967, col. 555).

Even before Wilson had become Prime Minister, US Secretary of State Dean Rusk had warned Johnson that Wilson was 'not a man of strong political convictions' and that 'somehow, he does not inspire a feeling of trust in many people'.[4] While recognizing that the Wilson–Johnson relationship had its 'ups and downs', the Deputy Chief of Mission at the US Embassy in London during the Johnson presidency, Philip Kaiser, recalled that overall the two men established only a 'shaky rapport'.[5] In a similar vein, US Under Secretary of State George Ball mused that Anglo-American relations in the 1960s were 'seriously impeded by the fact that President Johnson and Prime Minister Wilson were temperamentally poles apart and did not basically like each other'.[6] Ball also recalled that Wilson was 'too ordinary, too much like other politicians with whom LBJ had dealt, and Johnson took an almost instant dislike to him'.[7]

As regards historical interpretations, Paul McGarr observes that 'although they enjoyed a healthy and workmanlike relationship, Wilson's mendacity and inveterate sponging undoubtedly irritated the American President'.[8] Melissa Pine suggests that Wilson's bid for British membership of the EEC may have been influenced by his 'poor relations with Johnson and inability to act as mediator between the US and the USSR'.[9] Sylvia Ellis, moreover, contends that 'there was no chemistry or ideological common ground between Wilson and Johnson'.[10] Compared with earlier relationships between prime ministers and presidents (Churchill–Roosevelt, Macmillan–Eisenhower, and Macmillan–Kennedy) and later ones (Thatcher–Reagan[11] and Blair–Clinton), Ellis insists that the one between Wilson and Johnson was 'indeed cool'.[12] In Ellis' interpretation, it was

---

[4] Philip Ziegler, *Wilson: The Authorised Life* (London: Weidenfeld and Nicolson, 1993), p. 221.

[5] Philip M. Kaiser, *Journeying Far and Wide: A Political and Diplomatic Memoir* (New York: Charles Scribner's Sons, Maxwell Macmillan International, 1992), pp. 209, 230.

[6] Jonathan Colman, 'Harold Wilson, Lyndon Johnson and Anglo-American "summit diplomacy", 1964–68', *Journal of Transatlantic Studies*, 1, 2 (2003): 132.

[7] George W. Ball, *The Past Has Another Pattern: Memoirs* (New York: Norton, 1982), p. 336.

[8] Paul M. McGarr, *The Cold War in South Asia: Britain, the United States and the Indian Subcontinent, 1945–1965* (Cambridge: Cambridge University Press, 2013), p. 278.

[9] Melissa Pine, *Harold Wilson and Europe: Pursuing Britain's Membership of the European Community* (London: Tauris Academic Studies, 2007), p. 181.

[10] Sylvia Ellis, 'Lyndon Johnson, Harold Wilson and the Vietnam War: A *Not* So Special Relationship?', in Jonathan Hollowell (ed.), *Twentieth-Century Anglo-American Relations* (Basingstoke: Macmillan, 2001), p. 200.

[11] The closeness of the Thatcher–Reagan relationship has recently been subjected to scrutiny – see Richard Aldous, *Reagan and Thatcher: The Difficult Relationship* (London: Arrow Books, 2013); Andrea Chiampan, 'Running with the Hare, Hunting with the Hounds: The Special Relationship, Reagan's Cold War and the Falklands conflict', *Diplomacy and Statecraft*, 24, 4 (2013): 640–60.

[12] Ellis, 'Lyndon Johnson, Harold Wilson and the Vietnam War', p. 200.

Wilson's public distancing of his government from the decision of the Johnson administration to bomb Haiphong and Hanoi in June 1966 that marked a parting of the ways. 'The public act of dissociation', she asserts, 'condemned Wilson to the ranks of other critics in LBJ's mind; Wilson was now a suspicious and unreliable character'.[13] Drawing on Richard Neustadt's celebrated work, *Alliance Politics*,[14] in which he argues that, paradoxically, misapprehensions are more likely between countries that enjoy close relations since more is expected of one another, Ellis points out that 'at no time was this more apparent than during the Vietnam War'.[15] Indeed, she posits that while the Johnson administration 'hoped and expected, and at times almost demanded, loyalty and support from Britain', it remained during the Wilson government a 'reluctant and unconvinced ally on Vietnam'.[16]

John Young remarks that over Vietnam Johnson 'personally became resentful of what he saw as a lack of co-operation from the Prime Minister'.[17] Young also argues that 'the President never looked forward to meetings with the new British Prime Minister and his growing obsession with the Vietnam War meant that he judged Wilson largely on the refusal to commit even a token force of British troops to the conflict'.[18] Similarly, Peter Jones contends that the relationship between Wilson and Johnson was a 'poor one', adding: 'the unwillingness of Wilson to offer tangible support to the American effort in Vietnam and the British Prime Minister's insistence on attempting to find a basis for a negotiated settlement were major causes of aggravation'.[19] Jim Tomlinson, moreover, records that there was 'considerable fury in the Johnson administration' when Wilson equivocated over support for US policy in Vietnam.[20]

While recognizing that initially Wilson and Johnson were 'effusive in their reciprocal praise of each other', Ritchie Ovendale notes that the two men 'viewed

---

[13] Sylvia Ellis, *Britain, America, and the Vietnam War* (Westport, CT.: Praeger, 2004), p. 275.
[14] Richard E. Neustadt, *Alliance Politics* (New York: Columbia University Press, 1970).
[15] Ellis, *Britain, America, and the Vietnam War*, p. xvii.
[16] Ibid.
[17] John W. Young, 'Ambassador David Bruce and "LBJ's War": Vietnam viewed from London, 1963–1968', *Diplomacy and Statecraft*, 22, 1 (2011): 86.
[18] John W. Young, 'David K. E. Bruce, 1961–69', in Alison R. Holmes and J. Simon Rofe (eds), *The Embassy in Grosvenor Square: American Ambassadors to the United Kingdom, 1938–2008* (Basingstoke: Palgrave Macmillan, 2012), p. 157. See also, John W. Young, *David Bruce and Diplomatic Practice: An American Ambassador in London, 1961–9* (New York and London: Bloomsbury, 2014), p. 179.
[19] Peter Jones, *America and the British Labour Party: The 'Special Relationship' at Work* (London: Tauris Academic Studies, 1997), p. 172.
[20] Jim Tomlinson, *The Labour Governments 1964–70*: Volume 3: *Economic Policy* (Manchester: Manchester University Press, 2004), p. 38.

one another with some suspicion'.[21] In particular, Ovendale suggests that Johnson thought Wilson was 'only too keen to cross the Atlantic to bolster his domestic position'.[22] Moreover, Robert Hathaway contends that 'Wilson and Johnson re-directed British-American ties into the less personal, more distant character that would mark the relationship for much of the following two decades', concluding that 'Wilson and Johnson never hit it off'.[23] Similarly, Alan Dobson asserts that 'Wilson did not have a good relationship with President Johnson'[24] and that the 'rapport between Wilson and Johnson was never close enough to paper over widening cracks in the Special Relationship'.[25]

In the opinion of Wilson's former private secretary, Michael Palliser, there was something of a 'Walter Mitty quality' in the Prime Minister in that he believed his relationship with Johnson was better than it was.[26] In a similar vein, Minister of Housing, Richard Crossman, poured scorn on what he perceived to be Wilson's overblown account of his encounter with Johnson in December 1964, remarking that it had been 'extremely funny, but I fear the humour was entirely unconscious'.[27] John Young bluntly argues that from the outset Wilson had 'high hopes of establishing a close relationship with the White House, but Johnson never showed any sign of reciprocating'.[28] In Rajarshi Roy's interpretation, Anglo-American co-operation in the economic field came about despite, not because of, close relations between Wilson and Johnson. He concludes that Johnson authorized financial assistance to Britain for fear of the repercussions of the devaluation of sterling on the weak dollar 'even though he patently held the British Prime Minister and his economic policy in such low regard'.[29]

---

[21] Ritchie Ovendale, *Anglo-American Relations in the Twentieth Century* (Basingstoke: Macmillan, 1998), p. 136.

[22] Ibid.

[23] Robert M. Hathaway, *Great Britain and the United States: Special Relations since World War II* (Boston: Twayne Publishers, 1990), pp. 76, 77.

[24] Alan P. Dobson, 'Labour or Conservative: Does it matter in Anglo-American relations?', *Journal of Contemporary History*, 25, 4 (1990): 402.

[25] Alan P. Dobson, *The Politics of the Anglo-American Economic Special Relationship 1940–1987* (Brighton: Wheatsheaf, 1988), p. 211.

[26] Thomas Alan Schwartz, *Lyndon Johnson and Europe: In the Shadow of Vietnam* (Cambridge, MA: Harvard University Press, 2003), p. 306, note 34.

[27] Richard Crossman, *The Crossman Diaries: Selections from the Diaries of a Cabinet Minister, 1964–1970* (London: Hamish Hamilton and Jonathan Cape, 1979), p. 50.

[28] John W. Young, 'The US embassy in London and Britain's withdrawal from East of Suez, 1961–69', in John W. Young, Effie G. H. Pedaliu, and Michael D. Kandiah (eds.), *Britain in Global Politics*: Volume 2: *From Churchill to Blair* (Basingstoke: Palgrave Macmillan, 2013), p. 140.

[29] Rajarshi Roy, 'The Battle for the Pound: The Political Economy of Anglo-American Relations, 1964–1968', PhD thesis, London School of Economics, 2000, p. 325.

Contrasting the relationship between Wilson and Johnson with that of their predecessors, David Bruce's biographer, Nelson Lankford, has observed that 'gone was the personal chemistry that helped Macmillan and Kennedy smooth over differences'.[30] Alex Spelling, moreover, argues that Wilson and Johnson had a 'turbulent partnership', which he contrasts with the smooth relationship established by the British premier with LBJ's immediate successor, Richard Nixon.[31] John Dumbrell has gone so far as to claim that 'LBJ was certainly contemptuous of the British Prime Minister'.[32]

George Brown (Foreign Secretary, 1966–68) was particularly sceptical about the Wilson–Johnson relationship, stressing in his memoirs that 'the Prime Minister's hot line to President Johnson was not as reliable as it ought to have been. I think the fact of the matter was that Mr Johnson didn't really like the Prime Minister much.'[33] Wilson's ministerial colleague, Edmund Dell, was equally contemptuous, remarking of the Prime Minister that 'when, as he frequently did, he informed the House of his latest conversation with President Johnson, his critics would wonder whether there had, in fact, been anyone listening at the other end of the telephone'.[34] Former US Ambassador in London, Raymond Seitz, commented that 'Johnson could 'barely conceal his disdain for Harold Wilson. He once referred to him as "a little creep"'.[35] In response to one of Wilson's frequent requests for a meeting, Johnson is alleged to have exploded: 'we got enough pollution around here already without Harold coming over with his fly open and his pecker hanging out, peeing all over me'.[36] On another occasion, Johnson confessed that if he had to 'get sick and leave town' in order to avoid a meeting with Wilson, 'he would do it'.[37] In his diary, Ambassador Bruce, confided that 'the President has an antipathy for the Prime Minister … .

---

[30] Nelson D. Lankford, *The Last American Aristocrat: The Biography of David K. E. Bruce, 1898–1977* (Boston: Little, Brown and Company, 1996), p. 328.

[31] Alex Spelling, '"A Reputation for Parsimony to Uphold": Harold Wilson, Richard Nixon and the Re-Valued "Special Relationship"', *Contemporary British History*, 27, 2 (2013): 192–213.

[32] John Dumbrell, 'Sentiment and the US–UK relationship, 1960–1990', in Antoine Capet (ed.), *The "Special Relationship": La Relation Speciale" entre le Royaume-Uni et les Etats-Unis* (Rouen: University of Rouen, 2003), p. 131.

[33] George Brown, *In My Way* (London: Victor Gollancz, 1971), p. 146.

[34] Cited in Dominic Sandbrook, *White Heat: A History of Britain in the Swinging Sixties* (London: Abacus, 2006), p. 384.

[35] Jonathan Colman, *A 'Special Relationship'? Harold Wilson, Lyndon B. Johnson and Anglo-American Relations 'at the summit', 1964–68* (Manchester and New York: Manchester University Press, 2004), p. 1.

[36] John W. Young, *Twentieth-century Diplomacy: A Case Study of British Practice, 1963–1976* (Cambridge: Cambridge University Press, 2008), p. 133.

[37] Colman, 'Harold Wilson, Lyndon Johnson and Anglo-American "summit diplomacy"', p. 137.

He believes Wilson, for his own domestic political purposes, wishes to capitalize on a supposed close relationship with Johnson which is non-existent'.[38]

At other times, however, Johnson could be effusive in his praise for the British Prime Minister. Despite an initial reluctance to schedule a meeting with the Prime Minister against the backdrop of the 'dissociation' controversy,[39] Johnson relented and took the opportunity during an informal lunch towards the end of July 1966 to liken Wilson's 'gallant and hardy leadership' to that of Winston Churchill during the Second World War.[40] Two months earlier, the *Sunday Times* Washington correspondent, Henry Brandon, conveyed to Wilson, following a private conversation with the President, that 'he went out of his way to emphasise how much he enjoys communicating with you and reading your personal messages. He also seemed gratified that the drafting betrayed your own pen'.[41] Brandon concluded: 'I am certain that you are the only foreign statesman who has succeeded in establishing this kind of rapport – and personal relations matter a great deal with this President'.[42] Johnson himself is purported to have said of Wilson: 'I really do like that man'.[43] Referring to the British premier following discussions in Washington on 16 December 1965, Johnson professed that he 'considered his conversation with Wilson today the most satisfactory he had ever had with a foreign president or prime minister, and ... voiced a sympathetic feeling about Wilson'.[44] Wilson's Cabinet colleague, Barbara Castle, moreover, declared that he 'developed a close friendship with President Johnson'.[45] Summing up, nonetheless, Jonathan Colman concludes that 'the personal relationship between Wilson and Johnson cannot be described as "special", although their mutual dealings were unlikely to prosper when British weakness was felt so painfully in Washington'.[46]

---

[38] Roy and Young, *Ambassador to Sixties London*, p. 199 (diary entry for 22 March 1965).

[39] Letter from Dean to A. M. Palliser, 22 June, 1966, TNA, PREM 13/1274.

[40] Harold Wilson, *The Labour Government 1964–1970: A Personal Record* (London: Weidenfeld and Nicolson, 1971), pp. 264–5. Wilson admitted that he had feared his dissociation from the bombings of Hanoi and Haiphong would earn him the 'frozen mitt from the President' (ibid., p. 263).

[41] Letter from Brandon to Wilson, 24 May 1966, TNA, PREM 13/1064.

[42] Ibid.

[43] Colman, *A 'Special Relationship'?*, p. 116.

[44] Roy and Young, *Ambassador to Sixties London*, p. 233 (diary entry for 16 December 1965).

[45] Barbara Castle, *The Castle Diaries, 1964–70* (London: Weidenfeld and Nicolson, 1984), p. xiv.

[46] Colman, *A 'Special Relationship'?*, p. 179. Colman also opines that 'it is plain that Johnson was not an enthusiast for Anglo-American relations or for seeing Wilson; the suggestion that he once described him as "a little creep camping on my doorstep" is plausible' (Colman, 'Harold Wilson, Lyndon Johnson and Anglo-American "summit diplomacy"', p. 145).

Carl P. Watts, by contrast, argues that Wilson 'largely succeeded' in establishing a good working relationship with Johnson.[47] Saki Dockrill, moreover, asserts that it is 'premature to argue that Wilson and Johnson did not forge a "special relationship". On the contrary, the Wilson–Johnson association demonstrated how close Anglo-American interests became as a result of financial considerations and the Vietnam War'.[48] H. W. Brands is particularly keen to stress the rapport between the two men, arguing that 'Johnson found Harold Wilson a man after his own heart. On Wilson's visits to Washington the two politicians would dismiss their advisers and talk shop – Johnson relating his experiences as head of America's more-progressive major party, Labourite Wilson speaking from a similar position in British politics'.[49] Political scientist and adviser to President Johnson, Richard Neustadt, concluded following a visit to Britain in 1965 that Wilson's 'emotional commitment to the U.S. link is strong and he personifies it in LBJ'.[50] He added that the Prime Minister saw himself as a 'small king on a tight-rope looking toward the big king with the power and leeway to extend a steadying hand'.[51] During a visit to Austin two years after Johnson's retirement, Wilson recalled that he had had 'five years of close and intimate working with a great Texan', adding: 'At a time when Britain and the United States faced deep economic and international problems, it was a great and rewarding experience to be dealing with the first ever really Texan President'.[52]

As regards Anglo-American relations more generally, the Wilson–Johnson era has been seen as a period of decline. The American Ambassador in London, David Bruce, memorably remarked in May 1967 that the 'special relationship' amounted to little more than 'sentimental terminology'.[53] In the aftermath of Britain's decision to withdraw from 'East of Suez' by the end of 1971, the US Defense Secretary, Clark Clifford, baldly noted that 'the British do not have the resources, the backup, or the hardware to deal with any big world problem … they are no longer a powerful ally of ours as they cannot afford the cost of an

---

[47] Carl P. Watts, 'The United States, Britain, and the problem of Rhodesian independence, 1964–1965', *Diplomatic History*, 30, 3 (2006): 463.

[48] Saki Dockrill, *Britain's Retreat from East of Suez: The Choice between Europe and the World?* (Basingstoke: Palgrave Macmillan, 2002), pp. 5–6.

[49] H. W. Brands, *The Wages of Globalism: Lyndon Johnson and the Limits of American Power* (New York and Oxford: Oxford University Press, 1995), p. 87.

[50] 'Round-up on trip to England', Memorandum for McGeorge Bundy from Neustadt, 9 Aug. 1965, LBJ Library, National Security File: Name File, Box 7, Neustadt memos, No. 3.

[51] Ibid.

[52] Remarks of Mr. Harold Wilson before a Joint Session of the Texas Legislature, 3 May 1971, LBJ Library, National Security File: Special Head of State Correspondence File, Box 56, United Kingdom [1 of 4], no. 2a.

[53] Ellis, *Britain, America, and the Vietnam War*, p. 251.

adequate defense effort'.[54] The Foreign Office itself conceded that the East of Suez decision had engendered a feeling in many Americans that Britain was 'the sick man of Europe who lost his nerve and chickened out of his responsibilities',[55] while an FO mandarin painfully observed: 'Americans are: resentful of our failure sufficiently to support the anti-communist crusade, especially against Red China and in Viet-Nam; frightened by our withdrawal from Asia; contemptuous of our economic and financial difficulties and diminished power-influence'.[56]

Following this line reasoning, John Dumbrell has argued that the '1967–70 period saw a general cooling of Anglo-American relations'.[57] In an even more downbeat assessment, Dumbrell has noted that 'US–UK relations soured dramatically in the later years of the presidency of Lyndon Johnson over London's refusal to send troops to Vietnam, over the 1967 devaluation of the pound, and over London's decision ... to end military commitments East of Suez'.[58] Reviewing the relationship between Britain and America at the time of Wilson's failed peace initiative towards Vietnam in early 1967, Dumbrell and Ellis admit that 'we are struck by the intensity of Anglo-American antagonism'.[59] Colman, furthermore, contends: 'It is evident that by 1968 Washington felt less regard for Britain's capabilities than it did four years earlier, and in that sense the "special relationship" suffered a major blow'.[60] Colman also draws attention to Johnson's comment that it was no longer worth spending two days with a British Prime Minister since the UK 'was not that important anymore'.[61] For John Subritzky, a weakening of Anglo-American relations was evident even earlier. 'In 1965', he

---

[54] Summary Notes of the 587th Meeting of the National Security Council, 5 June 1968, cited in *FRUS, 1964–1968*: Volume XII: *Western Europe* (Washington, DC: United States Government Printing Office, 2001), p. 626. As early as July 1965, Francis Bator of the National Security Council had warned that 'anything which could be regarded as even a partial British withdrawal from overseas responsibilities is bound to lead to an agonizing reappraisal here' (Diane B. Kunz, 'Cold War Dollar Diplomacy: The Other Side of Containment', in Dianne B. Kunz (ed.), *The Diplomacy of the Crucial Decade: American Foreign Relations During the 1960s* (New York: Columbia University Press, 1994), p. 95).

[55] Jonathan Colman, '"Dealing with Disillusioned Men": The Washington Ambassadorship of Sir Patrick Dean', *Contemporary British History*, 21, 2 (2007): 262.

[56] Minute by D. J. Swan, 4 Dec. 1967, TNA, FCO 7/771.

[57] John Dumbrell, *A Special Relationship: Anglo-American Relations in the Cold War and After* (Basingstoke: Macmillan, 2001), p. 154.

[58] John Dumbrell, 'Personal Diplomacy: Relations between Prime Ministers and Presidents', in Alan P. Dobson and Steve Marsh (eds), *Anglo-American Relations: Contemporary Perspectives* (London and New York: Routledge, 2013), p. 85.

[59] John Dumbrell and Sylvia Ellis, 'British Involvement in Vietnam Peace Initiatives, 1966–1967: Marigolds, Sunflowers, and "Kosygin Week"', *Diplomatic History*, 27, 1 (2003): 147.

[60] Colman, *A 'Special Relationship'?*, p. 170.

[61] Jonathan Colman, 'The London Ambassadorship of David K. E. Bruce during the Wilson-Johnson years, 1964–68', *Diplomacy and Statecraft*, 15, 2 (2004): 335.

argues, 'all the Wilson government could offer of real value to him [Johnson] were troops in Vietnam, but this was something they were not prepared to do. Given these circumstances, Anglo-American relations clearly became less intimate, even strained, during the second year of Johnson's presidency.'[62]

C. J. Bartlett characterizes the Wilson–Johnson era as the 'weakening relationship',[63] while John Dickie claims that it marked the 'lean years of the almost forgotten friendship'.[64] John Young, moreover, concludes that under the post-1964 Labour government 'It would be pointless to deny that, in Washington's eyes, Britain was becoming less important as an ally'.[65] He adds that there was 'undoubtedly a decline in the value to the United States of the "special relationship"'.[66] As regards British perceptions, Tore Petersen argues that Wilson's Labour government merely paid 'lip service' to close Anglo-American relations and a continued British role East of Suez, but ultimately 'did not care much for either'.[67] Referring to the apparent weakening of Labour's commitment to a world role, Matthew Jones notes that 'one can also detect some resentment on the part of American observers, that after earlier promises to remain east of Suez, the British might now be using the threat of a withdrawal to extract more guarantees from the Americans over the position of sterling'.[68]

Alan Dobson produces perhaps the most lugubrious interpretation, arguing that at the close of the 1960s 'the special relationship was looking less special than it had at any time since the late 1920s'.[69] For Ben Pimlott, the devaluation of sterling on 18 November 1967 was something of a watershed. In the wake of this dramatic event, he argues, 'it was clear that the relationship between Wilson and Johnson, between London and Washington, had been seriously devalued –

---

[62] John Subritzky, *Confronting Sukarno: British, American, Australian and New Zealand Diplomacy in the Malaysian-Indonesian Confrontation, 1961-5* (Basingstoke: Macmillan, 2000), p. 158.

[63] C. J. Bartlett, *'The Special Relationship': A Political History of Anglo-American Relations since 1945* (London and New York: Longman, 1992), pp. 107–26. Bartlett does note, however, that 'Co-operation continued to flourish between diplomats, members of the armed forces, and between sections of the bureaucracies' (ibid., p. 123).

[64] John Dickie, *"Special" No More: Anglo-American Relations: Rhetoric and Reality* (London: Weidenfeld and Nicolson, 1994), pp. 133–43.

[65] Young, 'David K. E. Bruce', p. 165.

[66] Young, *David Bruce and Diplomatic Practice*, p. 199.

[67] Tore T. Petersen, *The Decline of the Anglo-American Middle East, 1961–1969* (Brighton: Sussex Academic Press, 2006), p. 2.

[68] Matthew Jones, *Conflict and Confrontation in South East Asia, 1961–1965: Britain, the United States, and the Creation of Malaysia* (Cambridge: Cambridge University Press, 2002), p. 292.

[69] Alan P. Dobson, *Anglo-American Relations in the Twentieth Century: Of Friendship, Conflict and the Rise and Decline of Superpowers* (London: Routledge, 1995), p. 137. Dobson also argues that 'In the mid-1960s the Special Relationship was more facade than substance' (Dobson, *The Politics of the Anglo-American Economic Special Relationship*, p. 211).

not to be restored in full until Thatcher, Reagan and the Falklands. East of Suez rapidly became a thing of the past, and the elaborate house of cards on which the special relationship between Democratic America and Labour Britain had been built, simply collapsed'.[70]

More recently, the residual and enduring elements of the 'special relationship' in the Wilson–Johnson period have been highlighted. Thomas Schwartz, for instance, records that

> there was an extraordinary degree of interaction, involvement, and influence between the U.S. and British governments during this period, with intense U.S. involvement in such matters as the British budget process and subsequent reciprocal British influence, especially on U.S. approaches to the alliance .... To an extent much greater than many have thought possible, both Johnson and Wilson compartmentalized their relationship and learned to live with their differences over Vietnam and to work together effectively in matters where they shared a similar outlook.[71]

In keeping with Schwartz' analysis, James Ellison, focussing on the Gaullist challenge to Western unity in general and NATO in particular, questions the notion that US–UK relations were eroded in the Wilson–Johnson era: 'The striking degree of Anglo-American cooperation in seeking a resolution to the 1966 NATO crisis provides a cautionary tale about over-generalisation. Ironically, given his well chronicled animus towards the Anglo-Americans, de Gaulle created the conditions in which US–UK cooperation was able to flourish'.[72] More specifically, Ellison observes that 'the Anglo-American relationship was never stronger than when common bonds were born from a common opponent. De Gaulle was such an opponent'.[73] Placing the Wilson–Johnson relationship in a wider context, moreover, Ellison points out that the more 'considered' view of the Johnson–Wilson era 'fits with the recent analysis of the Kennedy-Macmillan

---

[70] Ben Pimlott, 'Courting the President: Wilson and Johnson in the 1960s', in Capet, *The "Special Relationship"*, p. 191.

[71] Schwartz, *Lyndon Johnson and Europe*, pp. 232–3. Despite claiming that 'Anglo-American relations were strained for much of the Johnson years', Sylvia Ellis is in broad agreement with Schwartz's more positive interpretation of LBJ's European policy, arguing that 'regardless of his obsession with the Vietnam War, Johnson was able to pay sufficient attention to transatlantic relations as to be able to steer the Atlantic alliance through some very stormy waters' (Sylvia Ellis, 'A Foreign Policy Success? LBJ and Transatlantic Relations', *Journal of Transatlantic Studies*, 8, 3 (2010): 253, 248).

[72] James Ellison, *The United States, Britain and the Transatlantic Crisis: Rising to the Gaullist Challenge, 1963–68* (Basingstoke: Palgrave, 2007), p. 70.

[73] James Ellison, 'Dealing with de Gaulle: Anglo-American Relations, NATO and the Second Application', in Oliver Daddow (ed.), *Harold Wilson and European Integration: Britain's Second Application to Join the EEC* (London: Frank Cass, 2003), p. 184.

relationship;[74] if their days were not as "golden" as previously thought, then it is possible to see the 1964–68 period as less of a trough if the peak prior to it was not quite so high.[75]

Referring specifically to high-level Anglo-American discussions on Rhodesia shortly after Labour's return to office in October 1964, Carl P. Watts remarks: 'These talks demonstrate the continuing importance that London and Washington attached to Anglo-American consultation and cooperation, which contradicts the view that there was nothing left of the special relationship by the time that Wilson came into office.'[76] While recognizing that there were more areas of dispute between London and Washington at the end of the 1960s than at the beginning, Andrew Priest insists that the 'US–UK relationship during the second half of the 1960s cannot be dismissed as unimportant and while the strains must be acknowledged, so must the achievements'.[77] As regards achievements, Kristan Stoddart focuses on the restoration and maintenance of Anglo-American nuclear cooperation, which he presents as a 'central feature of their wider "Special Relationship"'.[78]

The correspondence between Wilson and Johnson, given its scale and extent, provides a valuable source to shed light on the contested interpretations of both the Wilson–Johnson relationship and the Anglo-American 'special relationship' during their overlapping terms in office. Although Wilson undoubtedly put more store by the messages he received from Johnson than vice versa, it would be misguided to follow George Brown's line that 'the hot line from No. 10 that went allegedly directly to the President was inclined to go instead to Mr Rostow'.[79] Wilson's messages were passed to the President, even when he was at his Texas ranch, and while his replies were normally drafted by his National Security Advisers, often with some State Department input, he did not merely rubber-stamp the correspondence issued in his name, making personal interventions, especially is cases where there was disagreement between the White House and Foggy Bottom.[80] Wilson had a more direct hand in drafting his messages to

---

[74] In particular, see Nigel J. Ashton, *Kennedy, Macmillan and the Cold War: The Irony of Interdependence* (Basingstoke: Palgrave Macmillan, 2002); Nigel J. Ashton, 'Harold Macmillan and the "Golden Days" of Anglo-American Relations Revisited, 1957–63', *Diplomatic History*, 29, 4 (2005): 691–723.

[75] Ellison, *The United States, Britain and the Transatlantic Crisis*, pp. 199–200.

[76] Watts, 'The United States, Britain, and the problem of Rhodesian independence', p. 449.

[77] Andrew Priest, *Kennedy, Johnson and NATO: Britain, America and the Dynamics of Alliance, 1962–68* (London: Routledge, 2006), p. 159.

[78] Kristan Stoddart, *Losing and Empire and Finding a Role: Britain, the USA, NATO and Nuclear Weapons, 1964–70* (Basingstoke: Palgrave Macmillan, 2012), p. 8.

[79] Brown, *In My Way*, p. 146.

[80] A metonym for the State Department.

Johnson and often adopted a colloquial tone, sometimes to the dismay of those around him.[81]

The correspondence between the two men was dominated by a number of key issues, of which the state of the British economy was one of the most persistent and formed the subject of the first major piece of correspondence between the two men shortly after the election of the Labour government in October 1964. Wilson reported that the deficit was much worse than expected, amounting to as much as £800 million for the current year (6). In outlining the measures to tackle the problem, Wilson implicitly ruled out devaluation. Johnson wished Wilson 'every success in your effort to protect the pound' and subsequently offered to help stabilize sterling by supporting Prime Minister's intention to draw on the IMF (7 and 12).

Britain's economic problems had a direct impact on its pretensions to maintain its position as a major world power. Meeting at Chequers on 21 and 22 November 1964, leading ministers associated with defence questions agreed to place a ceiling on defence expenditure of £2,000 million at 1964 prices until the end of the decade. Despite the freezing of defence expenditure, Wilson still felt able to tell the Commons that 'whatever we may do in the field of cost effectiveness ... we cannot afford to relinquish our world role – our role, which, for shorthand purposes, is sometimes called our "East of Suez role"'.[82] Wilson's apparent commitment to the world role pre-dated the election of his Labour government. As Leader of the Opposition, he had assured Johnson that Britain would continue its 'active support of US efforts to maintain worldwide security'.[83] This chimed with the Johnson administration's conception of Britain's international persona and responsibilities. Secretary of State for Defence, Denis Healey, informed the Cabinet on 11 December 1964 that the Americans wanted Britain to 'keep a foothold in Hong Kong, Malaya, the Persian Gulf, to enable us to do things for the alliance which they can't do. They think our forces are much more useful to the alliance outside Europe and in Germany.'[84] Following his first summit meeting in Washington (7–8 December 1964), Wilson himself reported that 'President Johnson and his colleagues had been particularly insistent on the value of the world-wide military role played by the United Kingdom.'[85] Expressing admiration for the way in which the US had 'shouldered the military, political and economic burdens of the defence of

---

[81] Roy and Young, *Diaries of David Bruce*, p. 272 (diary entry for 29 June 1966).

[82] Dockrill, *Britain's Retreat from East of Suez*, p. 2.

[83] P. L. Pham, *Ending 'East of Suez': The British Decision to Withdraw from Malaysia and Singapore, 1964–1968* (Oxford and New York: Oxford University Press, 2010), p. 17.

[84] Kathleen Burk, *Old World New World: The Story of Britain and America* (London: Abacus, 2009), p. 618.

[85] Conclusions of a meeting of the Cabinet, 11 Dec. 1964, CC (64) 14th conclusions, TNA, CAB 128/39.

liberty all over the world', Wilson assured Johnson following his Washington trip that 'I personally have always believed that Britain had an equally essential role to play, complementary to yours, if smaller in scale, exploiting our particular advantage as the centre of the Commonwealth and as a member of all three regional alliances and the fact of the British presence from Gibraltar to Singapore, no longer for imperial purposes but simply to help keep the peace, to promote a stable and just order and to be ready to respond to United Nations calls' (16). Differences over extra-European affairs, however, caused the first real spat between Wilson and Johnson.

Wilson had already politely, but firmly, rejected Johnson's suggestion of inviting Sukarno to Washington on the grounds that such an invitation would represent a 'heavensent triumph' for the Indonesian President who was engaged in a bitter 'confrontation' with the new British-backed state of Malaysia (22). More serious divisions were to emerge over the mounting crisis in Vietnam. Fearing that Johnson might succumb to the 'hawks' and escalate the conflict, even to the extent of using of nuclear weapons, Wilson phoned the President on 11 February 1965. In response to Wilson's suggestion of an urgent meeting in Washington, Johnson, who had already expressed his scepticism about such an encounter to the British ambassador, Lord Harlech, thundered: 'we ought not to run back and forth across the Atlantic with our shirttails hanging out'.[86] 'Why don't you run Malaysia and let me run Vietnam?', Johnson declared.[87] Providing a hint to the source of his frustration, the President expostulated: 'As far as my problem in Vietnam we have asked everyone to share it with us. They were willing to share advice but not responsibility' (24). Ambassador Bruce subsequently wrote that Johnson regarded 'attempts on the part of the British to insinuate themselves into Vietnamese affairs as irrelevant and impertinent',[88] while Johnson's National Security Adviser, McGeorge Bundy, described Wilson's phone call as 'outrageous'.[89] Summing up, Sylvia Ellis contends that after the 11 February conversation 'Johnson, a president who favoured telephone communication, did not want to talk to Wilson unless it was absolutely necessary'.[90] It would be misguided, nonetheless, to suggest that one telephone call, however fractious, precluded a cooperative and constructive

---

[86] *FRUS, 1964–1968*: Volume II: *Vietnam, January–June 1965* (Washington: United States Government Printing Office, 1996), p. 231. The British version of the conversation is reproduced in this volume (see 24). Wilson's own account can be found in *The Labour Government*, p. 80.

[87] *FRUS, 1964–1968:* : Volume II: *Vietnam, January–June 1965*, p. 231. In the British version of the conversation, Johnson informs Wilson: 'I won't tell you how to run Malaysia and you don't tell us how to run Vietnam' (24).

[88] Roy and Young, *Diaries of David Bruce*, p. 199 (diary entry for 22 March 1965).

[89] Ellis, *Britain, America, and the Vietnam War*, p. 51.

[90] Ibid.

relationship between Wilson and Johnson, even on the vexed and intractable question of Vietnam.

Towards the end of July 1965, Johnson provided Wilson with an update on US policy towards Vietnam, informing him of likely increases in US forces stationed there (38). Wilson supported American moves with the comment: 'In the face of the persistent North Vietnamese refusal to negotiate, I can see no alternative to your policy of strengthening your forces in South Vietnam in order to demonstrate to Hanoi the futility of their dreams of military victory' (40). At the beginning of 1966, Johnson enthused that 'it has been a great help to have your staunch support on Vietnam throughout these last months, and with some hard decisions right ahead of us, I want to be sure that you have a full picture of our thinking' (84). In particular, Johnson provided a detailed explanation of his intention to resume bombing of North Vietnam following a Christmas suspension and assured Wilson that 'when we do make the decision on the timing of the resumption of the bombing, I will make sure that word gets to you at once' (84). Johnson was as good as his word, giving Wilson advance notice of the recommencement of bombing and adding: 'I want you to know above all how grateful I am for the firm support that you and your government have shown throughout the Vietnam conflict as well as during this suspension. Your assurance that you will support us firmly in the present hard decision to resume is another encouraging proof of the depth of our understanding' (88). Referring to the political difficulties, not least within the Labour Party itself, which Wilson's broad diplomatic support for the US administration's Vietnam policy produced, Johnson remarked: 'I continue to admire enormously your fortitude and skill in dealing with your opposition' (90). The President was also appreciative of Wilson's attempts to persuade the Soviets to re-convene the Geneva conference[91] during his visit to Moscow in February 1966 (92). 'Your continuous and constant interest', gushed Johnson, 'gives me strength and I send my thanks and the gratitude of my countrymen' (92).

Reporting on his talks in Moscow, Wilson admitted that it was 'to quote the Iron Duke, hard pounding' (99). He was also candid enough to admit that 'on Vietnam, we made, as expected, absolutely no progress at all'. Johnson, nevertheless, thanked Wilson for the 'splendid account of your talks in Moscow', adding that 'they are a frustrating lot, but we must keep hammering away. And right now, you are in a better position to do so than I' (102). Johnson concluded by emphasizing 'how much I appreciate your readiness to keep in close touch on the many problems which confront us. It is of great comfort to me, and a good thing for our countries, the Alliance, and the world'.

---

[91] Britain and the Soviet Union had been co-chairmen of the Geneva conference, which had ended the first Indo-China war in 1954.

Presidential approbation was also forthcoming with respect to Wilson's role in the resolution of the dispute between India and Pakistan over the Rann of Kutch territory in 1965.[92] 'We all admire', waxed Johnson, 'the great skill and patience shown by you and your people in helping to bring about a peaceful settlement between the two great countries of the subcontinent' (32). Moreover, Johnson was fulsome in his raise for Wilson's discussions with Ayub Khan in December 1965, which preceded the Pakistani president's visit to Washington later in the month. Wilson had impressed upon Ayub American concerns about Pakistan's evident drift into the Chinese orbit (64), prompting Johnson to remark: 'The vigorous way you dealt with the matter will make my job much easier' (65).

As regards the looming crisis in Southern Rhodesia in the course of 1965, stemming from mounting evidence of the white minority government of Ian Smith's intention to make a unilateral declaration of independence from Britain, Johnson assured Wilson that 'we agree that the Southern Rhodesian affair could quickly become a calamity, with potentially serious damage to Western interests. We also agree that deterring Smith from any fateful step is by all odds the best course open to us' (49). Johnson also offered to approach Smith directly which he did through the US Consulate General in Southern Rhodesia. In this message he stressed US support for the efforts of the British government to find a solution agreeable to the population of Southern Rhodesia as a whole, and expressed his view that UDI would be a 'tragic mistake'.[93] Replying to Wilson's concerns that President Kenneth Kaunda of neighbouring Zambia might be tempted to close the border with Rhodesia which could in turn 'ruin Zambia without overthrowing Smith' (80), Johnson subsequently assured Wilson that he was 'weighing in at Lusaka in an effort to steady Kaunda' (82). Wilson continued to keep Johnson abreast of the unfolding drama in Rhodesia (121, 124), while Johnson expressed his appreciation for Wilson's 'constant thoughtfulness' (122) and provided encouragement for the British premier's efforts to kick start negotiations with Ian Smith (125).

At the end of February 1966, Wilson had given Johnson advance notice of his intention to hold a general election. Anticipating that the Conservatives would 'make an appeal to the latent anti-Americanism amongst some of our electorate', Wilson jocularly suggested to Johnson 'I might suggest to you that we should have a row in order to help me', adding: 'but quite honestly I cannot think of anything to have a row about' (100). On a more serious note, Wilson

---

[92] Rusk informed Johnson that Wilson and his officials had 'worked like Trojans, under the most complicated and frustrating circumstances' to restore peace to the Indian sub-continent (McGarr, *The Cold War in South Asia*, p. 310).

[93] Telegram from the Department of State to the Consulate General in Southern Rhodesia, 29 October 1965, *FRUS, 1964–1968*: Volume XXIV: *Africa* (Washington, DC: United States Government Printing Office, 1999), p. 831.

warned Johnson that 'you may find me, if driven, taking a slightly anti-German line' (100). The possible repercussions of carrying out this threat were increased by General de Gaulle's decision, communicated to Johnson on 7 March 1966, that France would be withdrawing from the integrated command structure of NATO and requesting NATO forces to leave French soil. Johnson immediately contacted Wilson, reminding him that 'Germany lies at the heart of the problem of maintaining a safe and healthy Europe' and observing: 'I feel that the crisis precipitated by the General should lead both sides in Britain to refrain from any comments in the campaign that might give aid and comfort to the General in his attack upon the great post-war structure of defense which we have all built together' (103). In a further message, Johnson emphasized that 'our best hope of security in the future is for our two countries to work with the Germans in a meaningful partnership. We must avoid the rankling discrimination that has caused so much grief in the past' (112). As the crisis following de Gaulle's demarche unfolded, Johnson again impressed upon Wilson that 'we cannot risk the danger of a rudderless Germany in the heart of Europe', concluding: 'I am sure that the one best hope of stability and peace lies in the inclusion of Germany in a larger European unity, in which any latent nationalistic drives can be submerged. I am sure, also, that you and your country hold the key to this possibility and that you can play a role of great leadership in Europe' (129). It was with relief, therefore, that Johnson received word of Wilson's meeting with German Chancellor Erhard which the British premier described as marking a 'high-point in our relations with Germany' (131). Johnson responded that it was 'really good and strengthening to know that your meeting with Erhard went well' and expressed particular satisfaction that 'you and Erhard had a good talk about your EEC situation' (132). In the next sentence, nevertheless, Johnson raised an issue – namely the bombing of oil targets near Hanoi and Haiphong – which was to lead to palpable strain in his relationship with Wilson.

The day after the Labour Party was returned to office with an increased majority Johnson congratulated Wilson on his 'sensational victory' and declared: 'It's comforting to me to know you are still at the British helm. I feel better about the future' (117). A note of discord over Vietnam was soon sounded, nonetheless. Although he appreciated Wilson's efforts to stop British flagged vessels from calling at North Vietnamese ports, Johnson pointed out that since 25 January 1966 six British flagged ships had called compared with only three from other free world nations. 'So long as the trade persists', he cautioned, 'there is danger that the Congress may try to tie the Administration's hands in helping out on Rhodesia' (123). Towards the end of May, Ambassador Bruce was authorized to inform Wilson of American intentions to bomb oil installations around Hanoi and Haiphong. Wilson immediately told Johnson that 'any bombing of either of these cities would create a situation where we would have to dissociate ourselves from the action taken' (130). He also pleaded with Johnson 'to reconsider whether this action, whatever its results in terms of immediate military advantage, is worth the candle' (130). Despite Johnson's sending Colonel Bernard Rogers to London to brief Wilson about the proposed action, the Prime Minister remained sceptical, opining: 'I am bound to say that, as seen from here, the possible military benefits that may result from this bombing do not appear to outweigh the political disadvantages that would seem the inevitable consequence' (134). Elaborating his argument, Wilson ventured that the bombing would only be justified if the Americans and South Vietnamese government were fighting a 'declared war on a conventional pattern'. However, Wilson proceeded to point out that 'since you made it so abundantly clear ... that your purpose is to achieve a negotiated settlement, and that you are not striving for total military victory in the field, I remain convinced that the bombing of these targets without producing decisive military advantage, may only increase the difficulty of reaching an eventual settlement' (134). Wilson did subsequently assure Johnson that 'the bombing will not affect our general support' (136).

National Security Adviser Walt Rostow was unimpressed by Wilson's argument about a 'declared war', dismissing it as 'Oxford debating and unacceptable in my view'.[94] Johnson was more conciliatory, conveying his hope that Wilson would 'find a way to maintain solidarity with us on Vietnam' (138). Johnson's blandishments were in vein. In a Commons statement on the bombing on 29 June, Wilson informed the House that when 'President Johnson informed me that the United States Government judged it necessary to attack targets touching on the populated areas of Hanoi and Haiphong, I told him that, while we naturally accepted his assurance that these attacks would be directed specifically against the oil installations and that everything possible would be done to avoid harm to the civilian population, we should, nevertheless, feel bound to reaffirm that we must dissociate ourselves from an action of this kind'.[95] He added, nevertheless, that the United States was 'right to continue to assist the millions of South Vietnamese, who have no wish to live under Communist domination, until such time as the North Vietnamese Government abandon their attempt to gain control of South Vietnam by force and accept the proposals for unconditional negotiations which have repeatedly been put forward by the United States as well as by Britain and the Commonwealth'.[96]

In a lengthy message to Johnson shortly after his Commons statement, Wilson wrote: 'I am being pressed to acknowledge that the logic of disagreeing

---

[94] Memorandum from Rostow to the President, 3 June 1966, LBJ Library, NSF, Head of State Correspondence File, Box 9, United Kingdom: Prime Minister Wilson correspondence, Volume 4, no. 3.

[95] *Parliamentary Debates (Hansard): Commons, 1966–67*, Volume 730, 29 June 1966, col. 796.

[96] Ibid.

with this particular operation would be a total denunciation of the whole of your Vietnam policy. This I have firmly rejected, not only because I distrust the motives of those who put this argument forward, but because their argument itself is balls' (142). With more than a note of self-justification, Wilson went on characterize his dissociation statement as 'the price I have to pay for being able to hold the line in our country where the public reaction is very widespread even if, as I have said, it stems from widely differing motives' (142). Johnson was clearly less than impressed by Wilson's rationalization, declaring: 'Your message gave me the picture of your political problem and how you intend to deal with it. My problem is not merely political. I must also convince Hanoi that the will of the United States cannot be broken by debate or pressures – at home or from abroad' (143). He also intoned that 'we must and will continue to apply hard military pressure'. Wilson dutifully promised Johnson that during his forthcoming visit to Moscow it would be his purpose to make 'absolutely clear to the Russians my firm belief that you mean business and intend to continue applying hard military pressure, however long it takes' (144). He also assured the President that 'if they think they can drive a wedge between you and me, they are sadly mistaken'. Referring subsequently to the talks themselves, Wilson reported to Johnson that 'I have left him [Kosygin] in no doubt that nothing is going to turn up from me, in terms of a withdrawal of British support from your policies' (145). In justifying to his Minister for Technology, Frank Cousins, why he had not taken a firmer stance with the US over Vietnam, Wilson pragmatically noted: 'Because we can't kick our creditors in the balls'.[97]

Despite the tensions caused by 'dissociation', Wilson's visit to Washington at the end of July 1966 was an unexpected success and belies Sylvia Ellis' assertion that Johnson viewed the British premier as a 'suspicious and unreliable character' post dissociation. The British Ambassador in Washington, Sir Patrick Dean, reported that 'the personal rapport between the President and the Prime Minister was reaffirmed and I have no doubt that the President genuinely enjoys seeing the Prime Minister and talking about their mutual problems'.[98] Accounting for Johnson's positive attitude towards Wilson, Dean emphasized that 'the negative aim of ensuring that HMG ... do not withdraw their general support for the United States over Vietnam and in relation to Southeast Asia generally, acquired an almost dramatic importance when the President began to reflect seriously upon the potential consequences of Britain drifting seriously out of line'.[99]

In the aftermath of the summit meeting, Johnson informed Wilson that 'I fully understand your anxiety to complete the steps necessary to deal with your

---

[97] Ziegler, *Wilson*, pp. 228–9.
[98] Colman, *A Special Relationship?*, p. 117.
[99] Ibid.

balance of payments problem. We put the safeguarding of Sterling high on our list of priorities and, as you know, I admire the sturdy measures you have taken so far to put your house in good order' (155). Referring to Wilson's attempts to offset the foreign exchange costs of maintaining the British Army on the Rhine through securing higher contributions from the German government, however, the President requested that 'steps to stop the outflow of foreign exchange must always be measured against the cost in terms of defense and foreign policy' (155). Wilson's threat to reduce or withdraw British forces stationed in Germany unless satisfied on the offset question alarmed Johnson who warned that 'the proposals you are considering with respect to the BAOR be carefully handled or they may start the unravelling of our Western defenses. De Gaulle's abrupt action in pulling his own forces out of NATO was a brutal blow at the solidarity of the Alliance, and there could be great danger from further withdrawals that are not related to a common plan' (155). Johnson subsequently offered $35 million in orders from the United Kingdom to forestall any precipitate British action on BAOR and to ensure that Wilson would 'stay with us and the Germans in completing this fundamental review of the military, political and financial basis for the US–UK presence in Germany, making no change in your troop and supply dispositions there until after the completion of the review, and then that you will concert with us on any such changes in the light of that review' (169). Although Wilson sought clarifications on this offer, he did agree to continue tripartite negotiations with the Americans and Germans and pledged to 'make no changes in our troop supply dispositions in Germany before the end of June 1967' (173).

As regards British European policy, Johnson warmly welcomed Wilson's announcement in November 1966 to make an application for Britain to join the EEC with the comment that 'your entry would certainly help to strengthen and unify the West. If you find on the way that there is anything we might do to smooth the path, I hope you will let me know' (169). Johnson had earlier assured Wilson that he could 'depend on our full support' in the ongoing crisis in Rhodesia (162). Wilson responded by acknowledging that 'you have given us such staunch support throughout this Rhodesian business, and despite the misgivings that I know many of your people have felt' (174). The year ended on something of a high note,[100] Johnson recalling that 'during the past our two

---

[100] 'Dissociation', however, evidently still rankled with Johnson. Averell Harriman told Ambassador Dean that 'if governments who were not directly engaged in Vietnam wished to retain influence with the President, who would be under continuous and increasing strain from the hawks to spread and intensify the war, it was most important that those governments should not "dissociate" themselves from the President. "Dissociation" was in any case an unfortunate word and had had an unfortunate effect … . Those who dissociated themselves from the President could not expect to have much influence with him' (Letter from Dean to Sir Paul Gore-Booth, 29 Dec. 1966, TNA, PREM 13/1917).

countries have cooperated closely, as friends and allies, in the cause of world peace. I know that we shall continue this work together in the years ahead' (178). These high ideals were soon to be tested by the vexed question of Vietnam.

From the outset, Wilson had been keen to broker peace in Vietnam. While recognizing that the Prime Minister was 'undoubtedly motivated by a genuine desire to end the bloodshed', Kevin Boyle notes that Wilson 'understood that a cessation of hostilities would reduce the possibility of another run on the pound, give him freedom to reduce troop levels east of Suez and undercut his critics at home'.[101] Wilson's efforts, however, were dismissed by Johnson as a case of 'Nobel Prize' fever.[102] Foreign Secretary George Brown's attempts to mediate during a visit to Moscow in November 1966 were undermined by Washington's failure to put HMG in the picture regarding a mission by the Polish member of the International Control Commission, Lewandowski, to explain to Hanoi the terms under which the United States would cease the bombing of North Vietnam. During a conversation with David Bruce on 10 January 1967, Wilson grumbled: 'it was most unsatisfactory that the Poles should have known what was going on whereas the Foreign Secretary was "put in to bat" in Moscow without complete knowledge'.[103] Musing on the US role in the failure of Brown's mission to Moscow, Wilson's private secretary, Michael Palliser, minuted: 'All in all, a rather gloomy story of muddle, lack of confidence and incompetence. I think the Foreign Secretary will have a pretty good reason to feel aggrieved at the way he has been treated'.[104] An even gloomier story was provided by events surrounding the visit of Soviet Premier, Alexei Kosygin, in the first half of February 1967.

With the Lewandowski affair firmly in mind, Wilson had impressed upon the Americans, through Ambassador Bruce, the need to be kept 'completely in the picture before the Kosygin visit'.[105] As a result of Wilson's concerns, Johnson sent Chester Cooper to London to place Wilson in a 'knowledgeable position to deal with Kosygin' (181). Wilson subsequently thanked Johnson for the 'admirably full briefing' Cooper had provided (182). The apparent concord soon dissolved into acrimony and mutual recrimination.

---

[101] Kevin Boyle, 'The Price of Peace: Vietnam, the Pound, and the Crisis of the American Empire', *Diplomatic History*, 27, 1 (2003): 45.

[102] Ibid., p. 46. A useful summary of Wilson' peacemaking efforts is provided by Panagiotis Dimitrakis, *Failed Alliances of the Cold War: Britain's Strategy and Ambitions in Asia and the Middle East* (London: I.B. Tauris, 2012), pp. 111–12.

[103] Record of conversation between the Prime Minister and the United States Ambassador at No. 10, Downing Street at 12.10 p.m. on Tuesday, 10 January 1967, TNA, PREM 13/1917.

[104] 'Vietnam', Minute from Palliser to the Prime Minister, 4 Jan. 1967, TNA, PREM 13/1917.

[105] Wilson, *The Labour Government, 1964–1970*, p. 346.

On 12 February, Wilson undiplomatically started his message to Johnson with the expostulation: 'You will realise what a hell of a situation I am in for my last day of talks with Kosygin' (190). The main cause of the Prime Minister's dismay was the alteration by Washington of the text passed to Kosygin from 'the United States will stop bombing North Vietnam as soon as they are assured that the infiltration from North Vietnam to South Vietnam will stop', to 'the United States will order a cessation of bombing of North Vietnam as soon as they are assured that the infiltration from North Vietnam to South Vietnam has stopped'.[106] Quite apart from the embarrassment of already having presented Kosygin with the original version, the crucial change of tense in the revised one meant that, as Cooper recognized, 'what we would be saying to the North Vietnamese was that a bombing cessation would be directly conditional on their stopping infiltration – a proposition Hanoi had thrown back at us time and time again'.[107] In a draft letter that was ultimately never sent, Wilson complained: 'As things stand he [Kosygin] will either conclude that I am not in your confidence or that you and I have pulled a very fast one on him'.[108] In a separate draft message, also not despatched, Wilson warned of the 'difficult political situation in Britain as well as in the United States if he [Kosygin] is able to make capital out of his assertion that he knows for certain that North Vietnam would be ready to stop the war if you stopped the bombing and that you alone aided and abetted by your British stooges stand in the way of peace'.[109]

In a hastily convened meeting at 10 Downing Street, Wilson told Cooper that he could 'only conclude that Washington did not know what it was doing from one day to the next, or that Washington knew what it was doing but did not wish to keep the British informed, or that Washington was consciously trying to lead him up the garden path by tightening its negotiations posture while letting the British proceed on the basis of an assumption that Washington was in fact ready to reach a settlement'.[110] Clearly getting into his stride, Wilson proceeded to remark that he 'felt that he had been made a fool of by Washington

---

[106] Dumbrell and Ellis, 'British Involvement in Vietnam Peace Initiatives, 1966–1967', pp. 137, 138.

[107] Ellis, *Britain, America, and the Vietnam War*, p. 228.

[108] Draft message from Prime Minister to President, undated, TNA, PREM 13/1918.

[109] Draft message to the President from the Prime Minister, 11 Feb. 1967, TNA, PREM 13/1918. The draft message gained some notoriety as a copy was found by a member of the Diplomatic Service on 17 February on the counter of the Bank of Scotland's Regent Street Branch. Investigation revealed that it had been left there by C. M. MacLehose, Foreign Secretary George Brown's Principal Private Secretary (see TNA, PREM 13/1788). MacLehose, who was described by Brown as a 'hell of a good fellow', avoided serious censure and in fact was appointed Britain's Ambassador to South Vietnam later in the year.

[110] Memorandum for the Record, February 11, 1967, cited in *FRUS, 1964–8*: Volume V: *Vietnam 1967* (Washington, DC: United States Government Printing Office, 2002), p. 136.

and that his credibility (which he had built up with great effort over the last 20 years) was now badly damaged'.[111] He concluded his diatribe by claiming that he had been 'betrayed' by Washington.[112] Johnson responded by coldly observing: 'I really do not believe that the matter hangs on the tense of verbs' (192).[113] When Cooper himself protested to Washington, Walt Rostow fumed: 'Well, we don't give a goddam about you and we don't give a goddam about Wilson'.[114] In his memoirs, Cooper recalled that 'ten years before, during the Suez crisis, I had had a ringside seat at a major Washington-London squabble. Once again I sensed Anglo-American relations dissolving before my eyes'.[115] Wilson's Principal Private Secretary, Michael Halls, admitted that there had been a 'blazing row between 10 Downing Street and the White House'.[116] The Executive Secretary of the Department of State, Benjamin Read, depicted the transatlantic understandings regarding the timetable and conditions for a US cessation of bombing as 'hopelessly garbled'.[117]

Explaining the American approach to the Wilson–Kosygin talks, Cooper noted that Washington saw them as essentially a 'sideshow'.[118] Johnson himself recollected that 'Wilson seemed to feel that he and the Soviet leader could serve as mediators and bring about a settlement of the war. I doubted this strongly.'[119] At the time, Johnson wrote to Wilson: 'I'm always glad to know that you are in my corner but I would have some difficulty, in view of my responsibilities and problems here, in giving anyone a power of attorney' (192). The President subsequently characterized the Wilson–Kosygin deal as a 'pure phoney'.[120] By

---

[111] Ibid.

[112] Ibid. The Foreign Office recorded that Wilson and Brown had made it 'quite clear that the United States Government had placed them in an acutely embarrassing position with Mr. Kosygin' ('The Kosygin Visit: A Study in Anglo-American Relations', Memorandum by the Foreign Office, February 1967, TNA, FCO 73/137).

[113] Referring in his memoirs to the alteration in tenses, Rusk mused: 'personally I don't think the change was that big a deal. Had Hanoi been seriously interested in talks, this kind of misunderstanding could have been ironed out' (Dean Rusk, *As I Saw It* (London and New York: W. W. Norton and Company), 1990), p. 470).

[114] Ziegler, *Wilson*, p. 325.

[115] Chester L. Cooper, *The Lost Crusade: The Full Story of U.S. Involvement in Vietnam from Roosevelt to Nixon* (London: MacGibbon & Kee, 1971), p. 363.

[116] Jonathan Colman, 'Lost crusader? Chester Cooper and the Vietnam War, 1963–68', *Cold War History*, 12, 3 (2012): 441.

[117] Transcript, Benjamin H. Read Oral History Interview I, 1/13/69, by Paige E. Mulhollan, p. 13, LBJ Library.

[118] Ben Pimlott, *Harold Wilson* (London: BCA, 1992), p. 464.

[119] Lyndon Baines Johnson, *The Vantage Point: Perspectives on the Presidency, 1963–1969* (London: Weidenfeld and Nicolson, 1971), p. 253.

[120] Recordings and transcripts of telephone conversations: March–June 1967 chrono file: June 1967: President Johnson to Senator J. W. Fulbright, 19 June 1967, 10:57pm, LBJ Library.

contrast, Wilson declared in his memoirs that a 'historic opportunity had been missed'.[121] At the time, Wilson lamented to Sir Patrick Dean that 'Kosygin's visit had provided a great opportunity to create the basis of confidence which was essential if a settlement was to be achieved'.[122]

In a less than flattering biography, Andrew Roth argued that 'it was his efforts to save President Johnson's scorched bacon in Vietnam which showed Prime Minister Wilson in his most Mitty-like role'.[123] Certainly Sylvia Ellis contends that the Wilson–Kosygin episode demonstrates that Anglo-American relations by 1967 were 'nowhere near as intimate as Wilson liked to claim or, indeed, believed'.[124] Jonathan Colman goes so far as to assert that 'Wilson's treatment by the White House led him to question the value of his relationship with Johnson and Britain's ties with the United States'.[125] There is some justification in this analysis. Despite a lengthy post-mortem with Walt Rostow on the still-born peace initiative,[126] Wilson remained dissatisfied. He wrote to Johnson referring to an 'unresolved problem between us' and requested that Ambassador Dean call on the President to discuss the problem and to 'examine what can be done to resolve the misunderstanding that arose between us and to make sure that there is no question of a similar situation arising in the future' (197). Johnson readily agreed to meet with Dean (198), assuring the Ambassador that he 'certainly valued' his 'close relationship' with Wilson.[127] He also agreed that 'no action taken by either side must be allowed to damage the usefulness of this relationship in any way'.[128] Despite Dean's realization of the need to reassure Wilson that 'there was not any deliberate intention on the part of the President

---

Benjamin Read of the State Department also opined that the British 'didn't come close' with the Kosygin initiative (Transcript, Benjamin H. Read Oral History Interview I, 1/13/69, by Paige E. Mulhollan, p. 13, LBJ Library).

[121] Wilson, *The Labour Government 1964–1970*, p. 365. This was a sentiment that Wilson had also felt at the time – see 'Anglo-American Relations over Vietnam', Minute from Palliser to the Prime Minister, 17 Feb. 1967, p. 6, TNA, PREM 13/1918. The *Observer* reported that 'Mr Wilson's standing here with the Administration has declined sharply over the past few weeks. This is a result of what is regarded as his grossly exaggerated account of how near to success he came in his efforts with Mr Kosygin to achieve peace in Vietnam' (*The Observer*, 5 March 1967, TNA, PREM 13/1905).

[122] Note of a conversation between the Prime Minister and Sir Patrick Dean on the afternoon of Thursday, March 30, 1967, TNA, PREM 13/2458.

[123] Andrew Roth, *Sir Harold Wilson: Yorkshire Walter Mitty* (London: Macdonald and Jane's, 1977), p. 51.

[124] Ellis, *Britain, America, and the Vietnam War*, p. 240.

[125] Colman, *A 'Special Relationship'?*, p. 121.

[126] Record of a conversation between the Prime Minister and Mr. Walt Rostow at No. 10 Downing Street at 5.30 p.m. on Friday, 24 February 1967, TNA, PREM 13/1918.

[127] Letter from Dean to Wilson, 10 April 1967, TNA, PREM 13/2458.

[128] Ibid.

to mislead you or put you in a false position',[129] relations between Prime Minister and President remained strained.

During discussions with Johnson in Washington in early June 1967, Wilson referred to the events of the previous February as a 'shambles', stressing 'the possible grave consequences and the need to ensure that it did not happen again'.[130] As regards the longer term consequences of the failed peace initiative, the State Department's assistant secretary for Far Eastern affairs, William Bundy, suggested that it had 'great significance as a source of lasting distrust and feeling of misunderstanding on both sides, between the President and Wilson. If they were not too well off before, they were infinitely worse after this'.[131] Another US official recounted: 'I'm afraid on this occasion the two of them just didn't interrelate at all. It wasn't a case of a special relationship, there just was no relationship'.[132] Controversy over Britain's strategic position 'East of Suez' placed further strain on relations between Washington and London.

Reflecting US views, Ambassador Bruce remarked: 'the appearance of being deserted ... in the midst of our Vietnamese involvement, by a Government assumed to be our most reliable ally, headed by a Prime Minister who had repeatedly declared himself an "East of Suez Man"[133] was unwise, provocative, and absolutely unacceptable to us'.[134] When he visited Washington towards the end of July 1966, Wilson had assured Johnson that Britain would remain East of Suez.[135] Unrest on the Labour backbenches following the publication of the Defence White Paper in early 1967,[136] however, led to a further review of British defence policy. Getting wind of this, Johnson wrote to Wilson that 'it is of utmost importance that we have an opportunity to talk before decision is finally made' (202). Johnson subsequently confessed to being 'much preoccupied with your East of Suez decision', adding: 'It just does not seem to me that this is the time for Britain to make or to announce a decision that it is sharply reducing its presence in Southeast Asia. I do hope that you can find some way to put this matter off for a time and not take a step which would be contrary to your and our interests and to the interests of the free nations of Asia' (217). Despite Johnson's interventions, Wilson informed him on 13 July 1967 of his government's decision to withdraw from British bases in Singapore and Malaysia by the mid-1970s. Although recognizing that this would be 'unwelcome news' to the President,

---

[129] Ibid.
[130] Record of conversations between the Prime Minister and the President at the White House, 2 June 1967, TNA, PREM 13/1919.
[131] Ellis, *Britain, America and the Vietnam War*, p. 240.
[132] Pimlott, *Harold Wilson*, p. 465.
[133] See Roy and Young, *Ambassador to Sixties London*, p. 249 (diary entry for 27 Nov. 1964).
[134] Colman, *A 'Special Relationship'?*, p. 138.
[135] Pham, *Ending 'East of Suez'*, p. 120.
[136] Ibid., pp. 137–8.

Wilson emphasized his conviction that 'if this country is in the future to be the same kind of effective partner for her friends and allies in the world as she has, I hope, been in the past, the political and economic realities must be faced and not fudged; and, in particular, that our essential objective of building an unshakeable economic base for Britain is the right one not only for this country but for all our allies as well' (218). Referring to East of Suez at a press conference shortly afterwards, Johnson stated: 'we have expressed ourselves as very hopeful that the British would maintain their interest'.[137] Ongoing pressure on sterling, which culminated in the Wilson government's announcement on 18 November to devalue, placed renewed pressure on the East of Suez commitment.

Initially, Wilson reassured Johnson that 'provided, as we confidently believe, the pound can now again become a strong currency and our economy forge ahead in the new circumstances, we shall be able to maintain, both in Europe and East of Suez, the policies set out in our defence White Paper as I explained them to you at our last meeting' (230). Referring to devaluation in his memoirs, Johnson memorably recorded that 'it was like hearing an old friend who has been ill has to undergo a serious operation. However much you expect it, the news is still a heavy blow'.[138] In his despatch to Wilson following devaluation, Johnson declared: 'If it is a comfort to you, I can tell you that my faith is deep that the British people have the will and the means both to pay their way and to continue to play the part they must in the world' (232). Underlining the value which he placed on Britain's continuing world role, Johnson thanked Wilson for the 'the strong cooperation so generously given by you and your government' in helping to prevent the outbreak of hostilities on Cyprus towards the end of 1967 (234). Following their meeting in Melbourne for the funeral of Australian premier Harold Holt in December, Johnson told Wilson that he was 'heartened to have the chance of another candid exchange with the partner who brings strength to my purpose and brightness to the prospect of peace' (236). In addition to giving details of measures to improve America's balance of payments position, Johnson's lengthy New Year message recalled that 'it has been a year in which our close consultation and collaboration have helped produce a number of memorable achievements', the maintenance of security in Europe being especially highlighted (238). This note of harmony was soon to be broken by the decision of Wilson's Cabinet at the beginning of 1968 to accelerate the withdrawal from East of Suez.

Referring to the impending withdrawal from East of Suez, Sir Patrick Dean warned that 'the timing could hardly be worse, with the President on the threshold of an election year ... preparing a state of the Union message in

---

[137] *Public Papers of the Presidents of the United States: Lyndon B. Johnson 1967: Book II* (Washington: United States Government Printing Office, 1968), p. 705.

[138] Johnson, *The Vantage Point*, p. 315.

which he will have to justify the extent of his foreign commitments in the face of doubt and criticism'.[139] The ambassador also highlighted that the Johnson administration 'will not be sympathetic to decisions which appear to be at the expense of the free world', and that this reaction would be intensified by the growing conviction that it was being 'confronted with faits accomplis, with no provision for substantive consultation'.[140] The accuracy of Dean's observations was soon borne out.

On 11 January, George Brown informed Dean Rusk of British intentions to bring forward Britain's departure from the mid-1970s to 1971.[141] Johnson immediately gave notice to Wilson that 'I cannot conceal from you my deep dismay upon learning this profoundly discouraging news. If these steps are taken, they will be tantamount to British withdrawal from world affairs, with all that means for the future safety and health of the free world. The structure of peace-keeping will be shaken to its foundations. Our own capability and political will could be gravely weakened if we have to man the ramparts all alone' (240). In a further missive, the President stressed that 'accelerated British withdrawals from its Far Eastern bases and from the Persian Gulf would create most serious problems for the United States Government and for the security of the entire free world. Americans will find great difficulty in supporting the idea that we must move in to secure areas which the United Kingdom has abandoned' (241). Wilson remained unmoved, underlining that 'it is absolutely clear to us that our present political commitments are too great for the military capability of the forces that we can reasonably afford, if the economy is to be restored quickly and decisively; but without economic strength, we can have no real military credibility' (242). Despite Johnson's dire warnings of the consequences, Wilson also relayed the Cabinet's conclusion to cancel the order for 50 American F111 aircraft. 'The British people were sick and tired of being thought willing to eke out a comfortable existence on borrowed money', he bluntly informed Johnson (242).

Speculating on Wilson's likely reception in Washington during his forthcoming visit, Ambassador Bruce mused: 'the Prime Minister will find himself regarded as a man with whom Lyndon Johnson would not wish to go [with] to a water hole. This expression comes from the old days in the West when a great mark of confidence was to have a friend protect you from attack when you went to draw water in enemy Indian country'.[142] As regards the drafting of Johnson's toast to Wilson, Bruce confessed that the 'difficulty is how to couch

---

[139] Telegram from Sir Patrick Dean to George Brown and Sir Paul Gore-Booth, No. 115, 9 Jan. 1968, TNA, PREM 13/2081.

[140] Ibid.

[141] Memorandum of conversation, 11 January 1968, cited in *FRUS, 1964–1968*: Volume XII: *Western Europe* (Washington, DC: United States Government Printing Office, 2001), p. 604.

[142] Roy and Young, *Diaries of David Bruce*, p. 353 (diary entry for 16 January 1968).

the Presidential language so as to butter up the Prime Minister and Mrs Wilson as guests, without being fulsome over his policies. One point is agreed – Wilson should not again be favourably compared with Winston Churchill'.[143] Johnson subsequently told Bruce that his talks with Wilson had been 'satisfactory, and without rancour, although he had spoken sternly about British plans for a withdrawal from the Far East and Middle East'.[144]

A National Security Estimate on the UK dating from March 1966 had declared that Britain would have to 'uphold most of its commitments if it is to retain its intimate links with the US'.[145] In keeping with this sentiment, Johnson stated following the East of Suez decision: 'when our common interests shrink, the flow of communications and common business shrink'.[146] Although there was a flurry of correspondence in the spring following the President's announcement of his intention to curtail the bombing of North Vietnam (257–63), and again in the autumn amid fears about the French economy and a possible devaluation of the Franc (269–75), messages between Wilson and Johnson were fairly infrequent and perfunctory in the course of 1968. In the estimation of John Dumbrell, by 1968 'the personal diplomacy between Downing Street and the White House had virtually broken down in the wake of the British devaluation and Far East troop decisions'.[147] The reduction in the Wilson–Johnson correspondence, nevertheless, is also explicable in terms of the running down of the Johnson presidency following his affirmation on 31 March that he would not be seeking another term as US president.

In his final message while Johnson still occupied the White House, Wilson interestingly chose to focus on the President's domestic, rather than his foreign policy, achievements (278). In his own final missive as President (280), Johnson admitted that there were places in the world, most notably Vietnam, where the policies of Britain and America threatened to diverge. He also referred to the continuing problems of achieving Western European unity and the fact that both Britain and America had been 'hampered by balance of payments problems in a world which has not yet created a kind of cooperative international monetary system which it needs'. 'But through all this', pronounced Johnson, '… we have managed to understand one another, to help one another whenever it was possible, to make it as easy as possible for one another when circumstances did not permit complete accord'. He also assured Wilson that 'I shall be looking for you in the days ahead – at the Ranch and on the podium at the University

---

[143] Ibid., p. 357 (diary entry for 6 February 1968).

[144] Ibid., p. 359 (diary entry for 8 February 1968).

[145] 'The United Kingdom: Problems and Prospects', National Intelligence Estimate, No. 21–66, 10 March 1966, p. 9, LBJ Library, NSF, National Intelligence Estimates, Box 5, '21, United Kingdom'.

[146] Colman, A 'Special Relationship'?, p. 174.

[147] Dumbrell, 'Personal diplomacy', p. 89.

in Austin'[148] and 'cheering you on as you continue to bear the heavy burdens of responsibility'.

In sum, the correspondence between Wilson and Johnson largely confirms the view that the two leaders were able to compartmentalize their relationship and not allow differences, especially over Vietnam, to overshadow or overwhelm their ability to work together in areas of common interest, most notably those connected with European security. The fact that it was issues stemming from the non-European world which engendered the greatest friction between Wilson and Johnson fitted a pattern in Anglo-American relations after 1945. Reflecting this phenomenon, President Dwight D. Eisenhower memorably told Prime Minister Churchill that 'although we seem always to see eye to eye with you when we contemplate any European problem our respective attitudes towards similar problems in the Orient are frequently so dissimilar as to be mutually antagonistic ... . The conclusion seems inescapable that these differences come about because we do not agree on the probable extent and importance of further Communist expansion in Asia'.[149] Wilson's immediate predecessor, Alec Douglas-Home, moreover, succeeded in alienating Johnson over his handling of the export of British buses to communist Cuba.[150] During talks with Douglas-Home's Foreign Secretary, R. A. Butler, towards the end of April 1964, Johnson emphasized the 'deplorable effect' on Anglo-American relations of the British government's attitude towards trade with Cuba.[151] As late as 1968, a British official confessed that Johnson remained 'obessional about Cuban buses and in any conversation with anybody about Britain they always come up'.[152]

Even with respect to the thorny question of Vietnam, nevertheless, relations between Wilson and Johnson were by no means characterized exclusively by division. In June 1965, for instance, McGeorge Bundy told the President that 'it remains a fact that every experienced observer from David Bruce down has been

---

[148] In 1971, Wilson controversially visited ex-President Johnson which provoked the *New Statesman* to declare: 'Even today it is doubtful if he has begun to understand the enormity of the affront he has delivered to the British Left' (Ziegler, *Wilson*, p. 390).

[149] Message from Eisenhower to Churchill, 29 March 1955, cited in Peter G. Boyle (ed.), *The Churchill-Eisenhower correspondence, 1953–1955* (Chapel Hill and London: University of North Carolina, 1990), p. 204.

[150] See Christopher Hull, '"Going to War in Buses": The Anglo-American Clash over Leyland sales to Cuba, 1963–1964', *Diplomatic History*, 34, 5 (2010): 812–13; Andrew Holt, 'Sir Alec Douglas-Home, Lyndon Johnson and Anglo-American relations, 1963–64', in Catherine Hynes and Sandra Scanlon (eds), *Reform and Renewal: Transatlantic Relations during the 1960s and 1970s* (Newcastle upon Tyne: Cambridge Scholars Publishing, 2009), pp. 31–3.

[151] Andrew Holt, *The Foreign Policy of the Douglas-Home Government: Britain, the United States and the End of Empire* (Basingstoke: Palgrave Macmillan, 2014), p. 36.

[152] Jonathan Colman, *The Foreign Policy of Lyndon B. Johnson: The United States and the World, 1963–1969* (Edinburgh: Edinburgh University Press, 2010), p. 73.

astonished by the overall strength and skill of Wilson's defense of our policy in Vietnam and his mastery of his own left wing in the process. This support of the UK has been of real value internationally – and perhaps of even more value in limiting the howls of our own liberals.'[153] In March 1966, moreover, Ambassador Bruce noted that 'the President is clearly grateful for the support given him by the PM on Vietnam'.[154] Johnson himself recorded how 'heartened' he was by the success of Wilson (and George Brown) in 'holding the line so well' when the Labour Party conference in October 1967 rejected the leadership's policy on Vietnam, including broad support for American policy. 'I think you understand how much it matters that the government of the country which means most to us, aside from my own, is lending its support for what we all know is right, despite the storms around us', he enthused (227). The President also expressed his gratitude for Wilson's preparedness to 'seize with both hands' his initiative announced on 31 March 1968 for a severe curtailment of US bombing of North Vietnam coupled with a renewed search for peace (261). Towards the end of his presidency, Johnson informed Wilson that 'I believe you know how much I have treasured our ability to communicate with candor and confidence over these years. No problem was so grave that its burden was not eased by a back-channel message from the Prime Minister' (277). He also confessed that 'our personal association has been a source of special gratification to me. We have achieved much together, and what we have not finished we have started in the right direction' (279).

While Johnson's messages to Wilson often belie the negative portrayals of his attitude towards the British Prime Minister, Wilson's communications with Johnson, despite frequently being obsequious, even unctuous, do reveal a more hard-nosed approach to the President than has perhaps been recognized.[155] During the so-called 'gold crisis' of March 1968, for instance, Wilson warned Johnson that 'if in the interests of urgency and speed you take a decision which puts us in immediate risk it is vital that we are covered by you during the days immediately ahead ... . Alternatively we would have to take urgent action to protect ourselves which could only have the effect of dumping the whole speculative burden back on the dollar' (254). In this sense, the Wilson–Johnson correspondence supports those who question the hegemonic status of the US within the post-war Anglo-American relationship.[156] Indeed,

---

[153] Subritzky, *Confronting Sukarno*, p. 156.

[154] Roy and Young, *Ambassador to Sixties London*, p. 249 (diary entry for 3 March 1966).

[155] A CIA evaluation produced shortly after Wilson became Prime Minister observed: 'He is above all a pragmatist, well aware of the realities of power. His commitment to close Anglo-U.S. relations is not based solely on sentiment' (W. Taylor Fain, *American Ascendance and British Retreat in the Persian Gulf Region* (New York: Palgrave Macmillan, 2008), p. 143).

[156] Dumbrell, *A Special Relationship*, pp. 2, 13, 14; Dobson, *Anglo-American Relations in the Twentieth Century*, pp. 97, 99; Dobson, 'Anglo-American Relations and Diverging Economic

Wilson was prepared to clash with Johnson and withstand his famous powers of persuasion in order to pursue perceived British interests, whether over Vietnam, devaluation, or British defence and global strategy. Equally, Wilson did succeed in maintaining a workable relationship with Johnson, the only real exception being the immediate aftermath of the failed talks with Kosygin towards the beginning of 1967.

There is little evidence, nonetheless, that the Prime Minister's personal diplomacy enjoyed much traction with the President. His efforts to influence Johnson over Vietnam – with respect to the initial escalation of the conflict in 1965, the American bombing campaign, and much-publicized peace initiatives – proved forlorn. Moreover, Wilson's attempts to secure commercial advantage in the US marketplace for British manufacturers, especially those in the aircraft industry, were unsuccessful (94, 102, 223, 226). Equally, and despite the inequality in the relationship, Johnson proved largely ineffective in swaying Wilson, whether with respect to defence reviews, devaluation, or Britain's policy East of Suez. In this sense the personal diplomacy of both the President and the Prime Minister yielded limited results. Whatever the warmth of the relationship between the two men, this could not overcome entrenched policy positions or the pursuit of perceived, and often contrasting, national interests.

As regards Anglo-American relations more generally during the Wilson–Johnson years, it is difficult to gainsay that they were placed under particular strain by the miasma of Vietnam,[157] as well currency instability and balance of payments problems. They also fell foul of exaggerated expectations on both sides which divergent interests left unfulfilled.[158] The Wilson government's decision to withdraw from East of Suez, for instance, led to American accusations

---

Defence Policies in the 1950s and 1960s', in Jonathan Hollowell (ed.), *Twentieth-Century Anglo-American Relations* (Basingstoke: Palgrave, 2001), p. 162; Dobson, 'The USA, Britain, and the Question of Hegemony', in Geir Lundestad (ed.), *No End of Alliance: The United States and Western Europe: Past, Present and Future* (Basingstoke: Macmillan, 1998), pp. 134–58; Michael Kandiah and Gillian Staerck, '"Reliable Allies": Anglo-American Relations', in Wolfram Kaiser and Gillian Staerck (eds), *British Foreign Policy, 1955–1964: Contracting Options* (Basingstoke: Macmillan, 2000), p. 144; Glen O'Hara 'The Limits of US Power: Transatlantic Financial Diplomacy under the Johnson and Wilson Administrations, October 1964–November 1968', *Contemporary European History*, 12, 3 (2003): 257–78.

[157] Former Private Secretary to the Secretary of State for Foreign Affairs (1963–65) and Ambassador in Washington (1979–92), Sir Nicholas Henderson, recalled that the Wilson government's refusal to get involved in the Vietnam war placed 'tremendous strain' on Anglo-American relations (Gillian Staerck, 'The role of the British embassy in Washington', *Contemporary British History*, 12, 3 (1998): 117).

[158] Richard E. Neustadt explored this phenomenon with respect to the earlier Suez (1956) and Skybolt crises (1962) in Anglo-American relations – see Neustadt, *Alliance Politics*.

of being 'double-crossed'.[159] Ambassador Dean recalled that the East of Suez decision had been 'deplored' by the Johnson administration 'as yet another defection from the shared responsibilities of the Western Powers'.[160]

Nevertheless, co-operation by no means came to an end. While Dean Rusk noted in mid-1968 that operationally Britain and America were working on 'fewer real problems', he did concede that 'Close bilateral relations with the British, however, will certainly continue'.[161] Although writing before the twin shocks of the devaluation of sterling and the announcement of the drawdown East of Suez, Ambassador Dean presciently observed that 'our "connexion" with the United States is something that neither we nor the Americans have created artificially but something organic arising from the facts of "life itself" as the Russians would say. It follows from this that it is something which cannot be abolished overnight by some act of policy, even if we wished to do so'.[162] Dean added that 'the Americans have no intention of dispensing with us nor any wish to do so'.[163] Even in the aftermath of the East of Suez decision, Thomas L. Hughes of the State Department's Intelligence and Research Bureau asserted: 'At bottom, the most concrete proof that the US and the UK are each other's favoured partner is found in the fields of nuclear weaponry and intelligence. Each government provides the other with material and information that it makes available to no one else.'[164] A contemporaneous State Department assessment, moreover, observed: 'The special relationship has been pronounced dead as often as Martin Bormann has been reported alive … . Indeed, perhaps the best evidence that it is still alive is the fact that its detractors feel obliged to re-announce its death every few months.'[165] An assessment produced by the US Embassy in London in June 1968 noted that, despite sterling devaluation and the decision to withdraw from East of Suez, 'it would be a mistake to … write off the UK as a US ally … Even in her reduced circumstances, Britain remains the European power most engaged in world affairs.'[166]

At the end of 1968, Ambassador Bruce insisted that, for the US, the 'special relationship' remained 'advantageous'. Of all our allies', he continued, 'Britain

---

[159] 'Anglo-American relations', Minute by Palliser, 17 Jan. 1968, TNA, PREM 13/3016.

[160] Letter from Dean to Stewart, 7 Feb. 1969, TNA, FCO 63/334.

[161] Summary Notes of the 587th meeting of the National Security Council, 5 June 1968, cited in *FRUS, 1964–8*, Volume XII: *Western Europe*, p. 625.

[162] Letter from Dean to Gore-Booth, 25 Oct. 1967, TNA, FCO 7/771.

[163] Ibid.

[164] Jonathan Colman, '"What now for Britain?": The State Department's Intelligence Assessment of the "Special Relationship", 7 February 1968', *Diplomacy and Statecraft*, 19, 2 (2008): 355.

[165] John W. Young, *The Labour Governments 1964–70*: Volume 2: *International Policy* (Manchester: Manchester University Press, 2003), p. 22.

[166] Young, *David Bruce and Diplomatic Practice*, p. 10.

is still the most powerful and most important, still a considerable factor on the world stage, and the support it gives us in our foreign and security policy objectives is of a value which it is hard to overstate.'[167] During the farewell visit of Ambassador Dean to the White House in January 1969, Johnson stated that he had 'always had a special place in his heart for Britain' and had 'always found that the British Ministers and the British people had a sympathetic and understanding attitude towards the United States'.[168] In his own final message to Wilson as President, Johnson asserted: 'I shall always treasure our connection and continue to believe that the special ties between Great Britain and the United States will survive and retain their value as we struggle to build the structure of stable peace' (280).

---

[167] Priest, *Kennedy, Johnson and NATO*, p. 152.
[168] Letter from Dean to Gore-Booth, 13 Jan. 1969, TNA, FCO 63/353.

Chapter 1

Labour's Return to Power, Nuclear Sharing, Rhodesia, and the Escalation of the Vietnam War, March 1964–March 1966

1. Message from Wilson to Johnson, 4 March 1964[1]

I should like to thank you again for so kindly receiving me on Monday.

It was a great pleasure and honour to meet you and I appreciate the time you gave to our meeting, as I know how tight your daily schedules must be.

I found our talk most stimulating.

I need hardly tell you how much my wife, Mary, and Giles[2] enjoyed their time with Mrs. Johnson and the fact that they were able to meet you later.

You were both most kind and made our trip a memorable one.
With every good wish,
Yours
    Harold Wilson

P.S. I have of course made no outside reference to the subjects of our talk. If I was reported as having made references to Cuba in my press conference this was because I answered questions, but in a British context—not in that of the conversation in the White House.

2. Message from Johnson to Wilson, 9 March 1964[3]

Thanks very much for your note of March 4.[4] Our talk was a great pleasure for me, and Mrs. Johnson and I very much enjoyed meeting Mrs. Wilson and Giles.

---

[1] LBJ Library, NSF, Head of State Correspondence File, Box 9, United Kingdom: Prime Minister Wilson Correspondence, Volume 1 [2 of 2], no. 101.

[2] Harold Wilson's son.

[3] LBJ Library, NSF, Head of State Correspondence File, Box 9, United Kingdom: Prime Minister Wilson Correspondence, Volume 1 [2 of 2], no. 99.

[4] See 1.

The papers here treated your visit in the most friendly way, and I am particularly grateful for the care and restraint with which you stated your position on sensitive issues.
Sincerely,
 LBJ

3. Record of a telephone conversation between Johnson and Wilson at 7.45 p.m., 16 October 1964[5]

President Johnson telephoned at 7.45 this evening to offer his best wishes and congratulations to the Prime Minister on his appointment. The Prime Minister thanked the President and said that the election had been close: he was now in the process of forming his administration. The President said that he had sent the Prime Minister a telegram of congratulations,[6] the text of which he would release in Washington if the Prime Minister agreed. The Prime Minister said that he had no objection.

The President said that they would have to meet with each other as soon as possible but that he had much business in hand in the U.S. at the moment. It was agreed that the President and the Prime Minister would get in touch later.

The President said that he had made a statement about the Chinese bomb.[7] The Prime Minister said that H.M.G. would probably be putting out a statement the following day.

The Prime Minister concluded by sending his best wishes to the President for the forthcoming Presidential Elections.

4. Message from Johnson to Wilson, 16 October 1964[8]

My warmest congratulations on your election victory.[9] As you enter the great office of Prime Minister, I want to extend my best wishes for success for you and your government and the people of the United Kingdom. I look forward to the continuation of the close and friendly cooperation, based on mutual confidence and respect, which has bound our countries so closely for so long.
Warmest personal regards,
Sincerely,
 Lyndon B. Johnson

---

[5] TNA, PREM 13/110.

[6] See 4.

[7] China conducted its first nuclear weapons test on 16 October 1964.

[8] LBJ Library, NSF, Head of State Correspondence File, Box 9, United Kingdom: Prime Minister Wilson Correspondence, Volume 1 [2 of 2], no. 96.

[9] Labour secured 317 seats, the Conservatives 304, and the Liberals 9.

5. Message from Wilson to Johnson, 17 October 1964[10]

Dear Mr. President,

Thank you very much for your message[11] and for your telephone call yesterday evening.[12] Ever since we met in March I have looked forward to working with you in the many common pursuits to which our two countries are committed.

I was particularly glad to see what you said about relations between the United States and Britain and this gives me a chance, on my side, to assure you that my colleagues and I are convinced that close friendship and co-operation between us is just as essential now as it has been in the past.

There are many urgent things to discuss. My colleagues and I are about to start on a thorough review of defence and foreign policy questions after which I hope we can respond to your invitation to get together. I hope our two countries will be closer than ever before in United Nations affairs and that we can work together to strengthen the Alliance. The maintenance of the North Atlantic Treaty, signed as it was by the last British Labour Government, which also took the first steps in post-war European co-operation, and our support for the other alliances for the defence of the free world, are vital for both of us.

I shall look forward to continuing the close and confidential communication which you have already begun and which has existed between successive presidents of the United States and prime ministers of the United Kingdom. I hope too that there may be an opportunity before too long for us to meet to review together many questions of mutual concern.

With warmest personal regards,
    Harold Wilson

6. Message from Wilson to Johnson, 24 October 1964[13]

My first task on forming my administration has been to undertake with my senior colleagues a thorough review of our present financial and economic situation.

We knew, while in opposition, that the position was deteriorating: but we deliberately refrained from turning it into a major election issue in order not to undermine confidence.

Now that we have examined all the facts I find the situation is even worse than we had supposed. In brief, we are faced with a probable deficit on external

---

[10] LBJ Library, NSF, Head of State Correspondence File, Box 9, United Kingdom: Prime Minister Wilson Correspondence, Volume 1 [2 of 2], no. 94.

[11] See 4.

[12] See 3.

[13] LBJ Library, NSF, Head of State Correspondence File, Box 9, United Kingdom: Prime Minister Wilson Correspondence, Volume 1 [2 of 2], no. 92.

account for this year which may be as high as 800 million: and a suspected deficit, for next year, if we do nothing about it which, while much less, would still be quite unacceptable.

My colleagues and I have therefore determined to take firm remedial measures. In deciding on our programme of action we have been guided by two main purposes. First, to avoid a repetition of the stop and go policies which have plagued the steady growth of the British economy since the end of the war. Secondly, to ensure that the short term measures which are necessary to meet the immediate situation should not hamper our action to get the balance of the economy right for the longer term.

We have considered and rejected two alternative courses of action: the first, with all its repercussions on the international exchanges, will be obvious to you, and this we have rejected now, and for all time: the second, an increase in interest rates, I am against in principle both because of its restrictive effect on the economy and because of its impact on your own problems, especially at this time. Our immediate situation has to be dealt with by means which we would, of course, have preferred to avoid both for the sake of the British public at home and our friends overseas.

On Monday, the government will be telling the nation what the situation is and announcing an eight point programme to set the economy moving on the right lines.

1. Steps to reduce imports from all sources by imposing a system of temporary charges on all imports, with the exception of foodstuffs, unmanufactured tobacco and basic raw material.
2. Plans to increase exports, including a scheme for relieving exporters of some part of the burden of indirect taxation which enters into the cost of production of exports, improved export credit facilities, the establishment of a Commonwealth exports council, co-operative selling arrangements for small firms.
3. Consultation with both sides of industry on plans to increase productivity and to evolve an incomes policy related to productivity: a price review body to be established.
4. A policy to make it easier for workers to change their jobs in accordance with the needs of technological progress.
5. A policy to foster more rapid development in the under-employed areas of the country.
6. A strict review of all government expenditure. The object will be to relieve the strain of the balance of payments and release resources for more productive purposes by cutting out expenditure on items of low economic priority such as prestige projects. The government are

communicating to the French government their wish to re-examine urgently the Concord project.
7. The social programmes of the government to be unfolded in the Queen's speech.
8. Consultation with the international monetary fund on the use by the United Kingdom of its drawing rights.

I have thought it right to let you know what we propose in advance of any public statement, first because I set great store by close and continuing co-operation with the American administration over the whole international field, and also because my colleagues and I are most grateful for the co-operation we are receiving in these difficult times from the United States authorities. Some of the measures we shall have to take will hurt, but I can give you my assurance that not only are they temporary and not intended to be protectionist, but we consider them essential if we are to have a strong economy as a basis for playing our proper part in international affairs.

We have sent Sir Eric Roll to explain these measures in more detail to members of your administration.

The Foreign Secretary will be in Washington this coming weekend and will be able to put our action in the economic field into the perspective of our general approach to international problems.

7. Message from Johnson to Wilson, 24 October 1964[14]

Thank you for your message[15] giving me the outlines of your new economic program and for the further details given us today by Eric Roll.

While we always regret the recourse to restrictive measures I fully recognize the need for strong action in defense of sterling. I welcome your assurance the import surcharges are temporary in nature and will be removed as soon as your balance of payments permits.

I am also most pleased at your desire to avoid recourse to higher interest rates.

I wish you every success in your effort to protect the pound. Success in this effort will reinforce the position of the whole free world.

---

[14] LBJ Library, NSF, Head of State Correspondence File, Box 9, United Kingdom: Prime Minister Wilson Correspondence, Volume 1 [2 of 2], no. 90.

[15] See 6.

8. Message from Wilson to Johnson, 27 October 1964[16]

Very many thanks for your prompt and helpful reply to my message about our economic situation.[17]

Our plan has now been launched, and it has, on the whole, been very well received both at home and abroad.[18] People seem to think it a sensible start to a vigorous attack on our problems. As a result, sterling is already strengthening and the stock market is more than steady. There have, of course, been some squeals from overseas, but these are mostly for the record.[19]

Without your sympathetic understanding and the co-operative attitude of your Administration as demonstrated in Mr. Dillon's statement, we should have had a much more difficult task ahead of us. Naturally this makes us all the more determined that the dislocations caused by our policies should be removed as soon as possible. Once again may I say how much I appreciate what you said and I at least realise that this was not easy in the middle of an exhausting election. Thank you very much.

9. Message from Wilson to Johnson, 4 November 1964[20]

My heartiest congratulations on your splendid victory. May I send you, both personally and on behalf of the British Government, our very best wishes to you and your Administration.

I look forward to working closely with you over the whole range of our common interests. I know that we will be able to continue that tradition of co-operation in the task of bringing peace and prosperity to mankind which has characterised Anglo-American relations for so long.

---

[16] TNA, PREM 13/109.

[17] See 7.

[18] In an effort to curb imports, Wilson's government decided to impose a surcharge on a range of products.

[19] In fact, there was strong resentment among Britain's EFTA and Commonwealth partners, Jamaican Prime Minister Alexander Bustamante expostulating: 'On behalf of my government and my people I protest most vehemently' (Philip Ziegler, *Wilson: The Authorised Life* (London: Weidenfeld and Nicolson, 1993), p. 192).

[20] TNA, PREM 13/97.

10. Message from Johnson to Wilson, 10 November 1964[21]

I deeply appreciate your warm message of congratulations on my return as President. The close ties between the United States and Britain have benefitted our two peoples as well as the cause of peace and freedom and it will be my endeavor to continue and add to our effort in [sic] behalf of these common goals.

I am certain that our forthcoming talks will be most useful and I look forward to welcoming you to Washington.

With warm personal regards,
Sincerely,
 Lyndon B. Johnson

11. Message from Wilson to Johnson, 19 November 1964[22]

I feel sure that I ought to let you know that we are facing a serious situation on sterling. The pound has been under strong pressure for several days, and although the last two days were better, we cannot be sure that this improvement will continue. The pressure is coming from a number of sources, including the Continent, and probably for a variety of motives.

We intend, as you know, to draw at the beginning of next month enough of our I.M.F. standby to repay the short term credit we have received from the Federal Reserve and the other central Banks. We might perhaps then expect to have a little over £3000 million left in our standby. We shall also have reconstituted the swap facility with the Federal Reserve; the other central Banks also may be willing to give further short term assistance, though this cannot be certain in present circumstances. But, if the run on sterling continues at anything like Monday's rate, we shall have exhausted the credit facilities at present available to us in a matter of weeks. We are being advised that, if we raised the Bank rate this week, we should probably halt the drain. But we are very reluctant to do this since it would run counter to the long-term polices we are developing for dealing with our basic economic problems; and I have no doubt that these are on the right lines and will be successful if only they are given time to work.

Moreover, I believe that an increase in our Bank rate would be as unwelcome to you as it would be to us. Am I right in thinking this? Of course, if you are intending shortly to raise your own discount rate for your own reasons we shall reluctantly have to follow you; and I would hope that we could then make this a

---

[21] TNA, PREM 13/97.
[22] LBJ Library, NSF, Head of State Correspondence File, Box 9, United Kingdom: Prime Minister Wilson Correspondence, Volume 1 [2 of 2], no. 87a.

concerted operation. But if, as I believe, this is not in your mind, we for our part will do our best to withstand the pressure.

In any event, however, recent experience has shown that, if we are to outmanoeuvre the speculators in the short term and to give our longer term policies the chance to mature, we need substantial reinforcement for sterling as rapidly as possible. We therefore have it mind to approach the I.M.F. for a further standby of £1,000 million; and we shall greatly value your support. In order to take the necessary soundings Sir Eric Roll is returning to Washington today. We will be able to give you, if you wish, a fuller explanation of our thinking; and I shall be most grateful if you can let me have your reactions as soon as possible.

12. Message from Johnson to Wilson, 19 November 1964[23]

Thank you for your frank exposition of the problems you are facing with sterling.[24] You can be sure of our deep interest in your efforts to maintain its integrity.

As to your Bank rate, we recognize that this is a decision you must take based on your views of what is necessary for the defense of sterling. We agree with your concept that more fundamental attacks on the basic problems of your trade deficit are preferable to early and indiscriminate use of Bank rate.

As for our own discount rate, this is a matter for our Federal Reserve Board which, as you know, Congress has made independent in this regard of the Executive Branch. However, I am informed that they do not feel that our domestic economy requires any increase in our discount rate.

We will of course be glad to give all the help we can to Sir Eric Roll in his efforts to obtain an additional IMF standby. I think it is essential to continue the close cooperation between our people on all aspects of your current problem, and I will fully inform you in advance should there be any modification of our present situation.

13. Message from Wilson to Johnson, 8 December 1964[25]

Dear Mr President,

As you know, it has been the practice, whenever the office of United States President or British Prime Minister has changed, to reaffirm the Understandings

---

[23] LBJ Library, NSF, Head of State Correspondence, Box 9, United Kingdom: Prime Minister Wilson Correspondence, Volume 1 [2 of 2], no. 85a.

[24] See 11.

[25] LBJ Library, NSF, Head of State Correspondence File, Box 9, United Kingdom: Prime Minister Wilson Correspondence, Volume 1 [2 of 2], no. 78.

between our two governments with regard to consultation on the use of nuclear weapons.

You were good enough to confirm these Understandings in a letter to my predecessor dated February 28 of this year. You enclosed a Memorandum setting out in terms similar to the assurances given by President Kennedy to Mr. Macmillan in 1961.

Sir Alec Douglas-Home replied to you, on March 12, that this Memorandum correctly represented the British position.

I should like to suggest that, following my assumption of office, the Understandings be reaffirmed in the usual way. If you agree, I should be most grateful if you could confirm that your letter to Sir Alec Douglas-Home of February 28, together with its enclosure, still represents the position of the United States.

As you recalled in your letter of February 28, both our governments have notified the North Atlantic Council, on the use of nuclear weapons anywhere in the world.

Yours sincerely,
Harold Wilson

14. Message from Johnson to Wilson, 8 December 1964[26]

Dear Mr Prime Minister:
I agree that it is appropriate, following your assumption of office, that we should reaffirm together the Understandings of our two governments with regard to consultation in the use of nuclear weapons. I wish now to confirm this agreement for my part as it is set forth in my letter of February 28, 1964, to Sir Alec Douglas-Home, together with its enclosure. These documents still represented the position of the United States Government, and I understand from your letter of December 8, 1964, that this Understanding is also acceptable to you and your Government.
Sincerely yours

---

[26] LBJ Library, NSF, Head of State Correspondence File, Box 9, United Kingdom: Prime Minister Wilson Correspondence, Volume 1 [2 of 2], no. 76.

15. Message from Johnson to Wilson, 9 December 1964[27]

Dear Mr. Prime Minister:

As you leave the United States, I want to tell you what a pleasure it was for me to meet you with these past two days.

This opportunity for a comprehensive exchange of views on the great issues facing us, our allies, and the other nations of the world, was most useful. I felt this meeting was in the best traditions of the constructive working relationship between our two countries.

I look forward to a continuation of these discussions between our two governments, along with those of our allies, to assure that we are doing everything possible to strengthen peace and security for all.

Mrs. Johnson joins me in sending our warmest best wishes to you and Mrs. Wilson.

Sincerely,
LBJ

16. Message from Wilson to Johnson, 9 December 1964[28]

Thank you so much for your letter[29] delivered to me this afternoon through your Ambassador in Ottawa. I come away from Washington most grateful for the warmth of your welcome there and much encouraged by our talks together.

We in Britain have long admired the way in which successive United States Administrations since the war have shouldered the military, political and economic burdens of the defence of liberty all over the world. I personally have always believed that Britain had an equally essential role to play, complementary to yours, if smaller in scale, exploiting our particular advantage as the centre of the Commonwealth and as a member of all three regional alliances and the fact of the British presence from Gibraltar to Singapore, no longer for imperial purposes but simply to help keep the peace, to promote a stable and just order and to be ready to respond to United Nations calls. It was a cause of much satisfaction to find in Washington that we saw eye to eye on these matters. I was also gratified to find that both of us viewed the Atlantic Alliance as the essential element in our national safety and that both of us sought to bring cohesion to it by sound and rational plans for the organisation, management and control of

---

[27] LBJ Library, NSF, Head of State Correspondence File, Box 9, United Kingdom: Prime Minister Wilson Correspondence, Volume 1 [2 of 2], no. 73a.

[28] LBJ Library, NSF, Head of State Correspondence File, Box 9, United Kingdom: Prime Minister Wilson Correspondence, Volume 1 [2 of 2], no. 71a.

[29] See 15.

nuclear forces at our disposal. I was glad to feel that you considered our ideas on this subject a useful addition to the common pool of allied thought.

May I once again express my warmest gratitude for the support my Administration has received from yours in its first weeks in office, and my renewed thanks to you and Mrs. Johnson for all our hospitality. My wife joins me in sending our best wishes to you both.

Yours very sincerely,
Harold Wilson

17. Message from Johnson to Wilson, 21 December 1964[30]

Thank you once again for the handsomely framed autographed photograph which you presented during your recent visit to Washington. I am delighted to have this impressive reminder of the occasion and of the pleasure I had in meeting with you.

With appreciation for your thoughtfulness and best personal regards,
Sincerely,
Lyndon B. Johnson

18. Message from Johnson to Wilson, 18 January 1965[31]

I have received, through the British Embassy in Washington, the copy of your book, "The Relevance of British Socialism," which you very kindly wished me to have. I am delighted to be able to add to my personal library this inscribed copy of your most interesting study of the policies and goals of the Labor [sic] Party.

With appreciation for your thoughtfulness and every good wish for the coming year,
Sincerely,
Lyndon B. Johnson

---

[30] TNA, PREM 13/97.
[31] TNA, PREM 13/679.

19. Message from Johnson to Wilson, 24 January 1965[32]

Dear Mr Prime Minister:
I extend our deep sympathy on the death of Sir Winston Churchill. We have admired, respected and loved him as a great leader, parliamentarian and champion of the free. The American people have always had a special affection for him and were pleased and honored by his willingness to become an honorary citizen of our country. This passing is a great loss to all of us and we all mourn his death.
  Lyndon B. Johnson

20. Message from Johnson to Wilson, 25 January 1965[33]

Dear Prime Minister:
I am writing to share some thoughts about the worsening situation in Indonesia, and to invite your comment on possibilities that have occurred to me here. As you will judge from the contents of this letter, the thoughts expressed have been very closely held within my government, and I am sure the same will be true in yours.

Sukarno's withdrawal from the UN does not seem to us too serious in itself, and indeed may get him into serious difficulties during the year as he attempts to exert influence through the proposed Afro-Asian Conference. It is already clear that it has, if anything, worsened his standing in this circle.

Nonetheless, the recent events in Indonesia, both military and political, clearly point to the possibility of increased military action against Malaysia and of a further swing to the left in the internal political balance. Even though these latter tendencies may have been checked for the moment, the power of the PKI seems to be growing steadily, whether because Sukarno actually encourages this or because he no longer has full control. Even if his health should hold up, the prospect seems to be that the left will gain steadily. If he should die or become incapacitated, the left is now in a strong position to move to take over. In short, Indonesia seems to be moving rapidly toward more aggressive policies externally and toward communist domination at home.

As you know, we have never been hopeful that negotiations or discussions with Sukarno would produce lasting solutions and get him back to work solving his serious economic problems and bringing the left under control. Nonetheless,

---

[32] LBJ Library, NSF, Head of State Correspondence File, Box 9, United Kingdom: Prime Minister Wilson Correspondence, Volume 1 [2 of 2], no. 68
[33] LBJ Library, NSF, Head of State Correspondence File, Box 9, United Kingdom: Prime Minister Wilson Correspondence, Volume 1 [2 of 2], no. 64.

I feel strongly that we cannot let Indonesia continue along its present path without exhausting every possible measure to turn it from catastrophe. Even if we are unsuccessful, we would have made every last effort we could make to prevent it.

Two possibilities have now occurred to me that might just help. One would be to take advantage of Sukarno's now-repeated statement that he would accept the findings of any four-power Afro-Asian Conciliation Commission. This has been stated in terms of findings of such a Commission with respect to the sentiments of the inhabitants of Sarawak and Sabah. It carried also the implication that he would accept a call by such a Commission for the cessation of Indonesian aggressive activities—infiltration in Borneo and the sporadic raids now being conducted against Malaya itself. I do not think we can now expect the Philippines to play a useful role in resuming the negotiating track that broke off in Tokyo last June. The Thai seem equally disillusioned. However, the Japanese have retained some modest influence in Djakarta and might be prepared to undertake a quiet initiative in this direction. During my recent talks with Sato, it was clear that they were quite willing to do whatever might be helpful, although I most specifically did not urge that they take on this particular job at the moment. I wonder now whether this may not be worth a try.

I see all the difficulties, and of course the Tunku is quite right in insisting that actions are needed rather than words on the Indonesian side. But it seems to me that there is just enough hope in the recent indications to warrant another try.

My second idea is a much more far-reaching one, and I am sure you will not misunderstand my purpose in putting it forward for your reaction. Plainly, it would require the closest consultation with you and careful preparations with the Tunku.

Briefly, it has long been my judgment that Sukarno set great store by his personal relationship with President Kennedy. The rapport which appears to have existed between the two men did not change the basic direction of Sukarno's policy, but was certainly of value as a point of contact with the Indonesian President and may have had some moderating effect on his actions. Sukarno's personal vanity is maddening; but it may be a possible handle that might be turned to use. I have never met Sukarno and there is the possibility that we could use an official visit to the United States as a tactic to appeal to this vanity and at the same time provide an opportunity to divert him from his current path. The invitation in itself would confront him with a dilemma. His vanity and an acute sense of Indonesia's importance in the world would argue for acceptance of the invitation. The PKI would probably oppose the visit with every resource at its disposal. We might, therefore, drive a small wedge between Sukarno and the PKI, and his acceptance of the invitation would be from the outset some indication of his receptivity to the counsels of moderation. I have already told Sukarno, through Ambassador Jones, that I would be prepared to receive him—as I would any other foreign Chief of State in a like situation—if he should come to New York in connection with a reopening ceremony at the Indonesian pavilion at the New York World's Fair. Such an occasion would not arise before late April or May in any event, however, and I do not believe it could well serve as the occasion for really tough and serious discussions.

Accordingly, I have given thought to the possibility that I might invite him to visit the United States and to see me in the fairly near future, on the basis of what we would call an official visit, with some ceremony but with the greatest possible stress on direct discussions.

Again, I am well aware of the difficulties surrounding such a proposal. We would have to take every possible measure to be sure that it was not understood as an attempt by the US to obtain a compromise of the Malaysian dispute at the expense of the legitimate interests of Malaysia. Rather, we would make clear that our objective was quite simple—to have the opportunity for personal discussion and to stress our well-known view that it is in Sukarno's and Indonesia's own interest to call off confrontation of Malaysia and to turn the attention of Indonesia to the solution of its tremendous economic and political problem. You can well see that it would be essential from my own standpoint to make this position entirely clear to Congress and to our own public opinion, which would undoubtedly have great initial difficulty in understanding the purpose of the invitation.

There are many other arguments which I need not review with you in detail.

I re-emphasize my awareness of all the considerations arguing against this proposal, and recognize that it may prove as fruitless as other past efforts have been to change the course of Sukarno's policies. Nonetheless, Sukarno is today Indonesia, and I believe we should explore every possible avenue to reach him and influence him as a man.

I should be most grateful for your comments and counsel.
Sincerely,
Lyndon B. Johnson

21. Message from Wilson to Johnson, 26 January 1965[34]

Dear Mr. President,
My colleagues and I send you our warmest thanks for your kind message of sympathy on the death of Sir Winston Churchill.[35] It is a comfort to know that

---

[34] LBJ Library, NSF, Head of State Correspondence File, Box 9, United Kingdom: Prime Minister Wilson Correspondence, Volume 1 [2 of 2], no. 62a.
[35] See 19.

his fellow citizens in America share both our sorrow and our loss and our pride in his achievement. His life is an inspiration to us all.

Harold Wilson

22. Message from Wilson to Johnson, 29 January 1965[36]

Thank you for your letter of 26 January.[37] I am grateful to you for explaining your thoughts on Indonesia to me so explicitly and I will try to do the same in return.

Let me say at once that I believe our political objectives in this part of the world to be identical: what we both seek is peace in the area between a prosperous Malaysia and a non-Communist Indonesia. Let me say too that I fully understand your preoccupation with the prospect of a Communist Indonesia, either through the Government putting itself in pawn to the Chinese as Subandrio seems to be doing in Peking, or through the PKI taking over if and when Sukarno dies. These broader considerations are always present in my mind whenever, as all too frequently happens, the problems and decisions in connection with confrontation cross my desk.[38]

Our general view is simply this. We are, as you know, totally committed to the defence of Malaysia and intend to fulfil that commitment. We have at the moment about 50,000 troops in South-East Asia, 8,000 of them in Borneo. At the same time, this quarrel with Indonesia is none of our choosing and we have no wish to prolong it a day longer than is necessary, nor to deal with Indonesian incursions with force stronger than is necessary. It is against this background that I would like to tell you how I see the more immediate problems.

In the first place, I wonder whether there are not one or two instances where our reading of the situation in Indonesia/Malaysia differs from yours. While I agree with you that Sukarno's intemperate withdrawal from the United Nations is liable to weaken Indonesia's standing in neutral (and more particularly Afro-Asian) circles, I doubt whether we need to be too pessimistic about the likelihood

---

[36] TNA, PREM 13/429.
[37] See 20. This letter was actually dated 25 January.
[38] Wilson is referring to the 'confrontation' between Indonesia and the new British-backed state of Malaysia which had come into existence on 16 September 1963 and included the disputed Borneo territories of Sabah and Sarawak. The confrontation formally came to an end on 11 August 1966 against the background of discreet British diplomacy, especially following an attempted coup in Indonesia in October 1965 which presaged the decline of Sukarno's influence and the rise to prominence of conservative figures in the Indonesian army led by General Haji Muhammad Suharto (see Sue Thompson, '"The Greatest Success of British Diplomacy in East Asia in Recent Years"? British Diplomacy and the Ending of Confrontation, 1965–1966', *Diplomacy and Statecraft*, 25, 2 (2014): 285-302).

of an early increase in military action against Malaysia. Certainly the Indonesia forces in Kalimantan and Sumatra have recently been heavily increased; this puts them in a position in which they could step up "confrontation" but the reinforcements we have sent out to the Far East should ensure that anything Sukarno is likely to throw against Malaysia within the foreseeable future can be dealt with as effectively as earlier raids have been. I am confident that he is fully aware of the certainty of military disaster if he were to let military action escalate. As you know, two years of confrontation have cost Indonesia 1,000 casualties against 150 to British and Malaysian forces and have achieved no military success whatsoever. Nor do I believe that the authority we have recently given the Commander-in-Chief in Malaysia to try to inhibit Indonesian concentrations near the frontier in Borneo will lead to any escalation in itself. If there is any sign of this we shall go very warily indeed. All in all we think we can hold the present military position without any radical change until Sukarno dies or is incapacitated; then, of course, a new situation will arise.

Which brings me to the question of the Indonesian Communist Party (PKI). There is no doubt that the PKI have strengthened their position recently at the expense of their political opponents, although not necessarily, so far, at the expense of the army. But we believe that the PKI owe these successes primarily to Sukarno's support. He is backing the PKI fully because they share his desire to keep up pressure on the West, but also because his own ideas have moved steadily leftward for many years. In our view, Indonesian support for North Viet-Nam and North Korea is no mere tactical manoeuvre, but reflects Sukarno's own views. At present, however, the PKI need Sukarno more than he needs them. We do not believe that the PKI's position will look so strong if Sukarno dies or gives up within the next year of two. On the contrary, though the immediate successor might be a compromise candidate backed up both Army and PKI, we think any coalition of this kind would be short-lived and that the Army should eventually win the ensuing struggle for power. Although therefore, Sukarno's death would probably not of itself put an end to confrontation, a situation would arise in which there was a very much better chance that saner councils would prevail. Only if Sukarno retains power for some years longer and is thus able to continue his policy of strengthening the PKI, would we expect him to be succeeded by a Communist Government.

In these circumstances, I wonder whether there is really any prospect at all of persuading Sukarno to "bring his Left under control." He has no reason to fear the PKI himself and we have seen no sign that there is any other Indonesian leader or grouping whom he would prefer as his successor. So why should he make trouble for himself in this direction or risk the new-found friendship with China which is so gratifying to his self-esteem?

Nevertheless, I agree entirely that we must exhaust every possibility of a peaceful settlement; so long, of course as this is consistent with Malaysia's security and territorial integrity. Any attempt at a solution which compromised Malaysian territorial integrity would simply encourage Indonesia to push ahead with foreign adventures even more enthusiastically than hitherto. But provided we can avoid this snare a Japanese initiative might well be worth trying even if the omens are not at present particularly favourable. In this connection you will know that Mr. Kosho Ogasa is already in Djakarta on what he has described as "a mission to find out what ground exists for mediation," and that the Malaysian Ministry of External Affairs has quoted the Tunku as telling a Japanese correspondent that Malaysia would welcome any move from any country if it would help bring about a peaceful settlement. These developments seem to be entirely in line with what you have in mind and we will gladly let the Tunku know our views. I can assure you we shall not stand in the way of any reasonable proposals that may emerge.

At the same time, we cannot overlook the fact that any proposal for a reascertainment in Sabah and Sarawak would create very great difficulties for the Malaysian Government. The local leaders in Sabah and Sarawak (whose relations with the Federation Government are always a little prickly) would immediately suspect the Tunku of being prepared to sacrifice them and their people to appease Indonesia. There can, of course, be no question about what the verdict would be if there were an impartial enquiry, but this might not in the event be easy to achieve. For instance I suppose that the Afro-Asian Commission might either recommend a plebiscite or undertake the reascertaiment itself. The first would open up prospects for Indonesian bribery and mischief-making which we can be sure they would utilise to the full. The second would be asking the Tunku to give up the firm basis of the existing U Thant verdict in his favour. In return for which, what prospect would there be that Sukarno would be willing to accept an unfavourable verdict, any more than, despite his Manila undertakings, he was willing to accept the verdict of the Michelmore Mission[39] in September, 1963?

I would be less than frank with you, however, if I were to conceal that I am very unhappy about the proposal to invite Sukarno to Washington in the near future. Such an invitation would be a heavensent triumph for Sukarno after a year of setbacks everywhere. Even if he chose to reject is [sic] publicly, it would allow him to convince the Indonesian people that his tactics had paid dividends and that the "old established forces" (as he calls us) had lost their nerve. And would the effect be confined to Indonesia and confrontation? Would not China and North Viet Nam draw similar conclusions about Western unity and resolution in South East Asia? As you recognise, this would be a very difficult

---

[39] Led by Lawrence Michelmore (the American Deputy Director of the UN Office of Personnel), the Mission derived from an earlier meeting between the Tunku, Sukarno, and Philippines President Diosdado Macapagal in Manila which decided to ask the UN to ascertain the degree of support for Malaysia in Sabah and Sarawak.

proposal to put to the Tunku, and while the controlled Press in Indonesia were writing up your invitation as a triumph, I cannot see how it would be possible to contain the disillusionment and anger that it would cause in Kuala Lumpur and Singapore. After all, it is only a week or so since Sukarno finally broke with the United Nations and incurred the displeasure of virtually every free country in the world. How will it be possible to ask him to Washington in circumstances that do not suggest a measure of acceptance and approval for Indonesian policy? Certainly this is how an invitation would present itself to public opinion here and we should have to face some very outspoken criticism of the United States both in Parliament and in the Press. This in turn would be interpreted as a major breach in Anglo–American solidarity on policy in South East Asia. I recognise that these objections might seem less insuperable if there was a serious chance of Sukarno calling off "confrontation" as the result of such a visit. But is there in fact any chance of this? Sukarno is not an economist and has gloried, apparently sincerely, in what he supposes to be Indonesia's ability to do without Western aid. If, as seems probable, he knows he has not long to live, he is unlikely to retreat from the "heroic" pose he has adopted for the sake of an economic security that means little to him. The face of the stabilization plan, blithely sacrificed two years ago on the altar of "confrontation," surely proved once and for all how Sukarno weighs the relative merits of prosperity and military adventure. Of course not all prominent Indonesians see eye to eye with him on this, but how much has Sukarno ever listened to their advice?

All in all, while I share your concern that we should not overlook any reasonable steps with the object of a fair settlement, I do earnestly hope that on reflection you will decide not to invite Sukarno to Washington as proposed. As I see it, not only would this be a set-back for Malaysia internationally and a serious blow to Malaysian morale, but I am convinced that the overall effect on Sukarno, on Indonesia and on the Western position in South East Asia as a whole, would more than offset any good that could be done by negotiations with a man as crooked and irrational as Sukarno.

Please forgive this forthright expression of my feelings, but I am fortified by the conviction that we are both groping for the same solution to this intractable problem. We look forward to discussing this subject with Dean Rusk while he is here. Meanwhile, may I say once again how grateful I am to you for consulting me in this way.

23. Message from Johnson to Wilson, 1 February 1965[40]

Dear Prime Minister:
I sincerely appreciate your warm good wishes on my inauguration. We have many common tasks ahead, and I look forward to our continued close cooperation in dealing with them. Mrs. Johnson joins me in sending you and Mrs. Wilson our best wishes.
   Lyndon B. Johnson

24. Record of a telephone conversation between Wilson and Johnson, 11 February 1965[41]

President Johnson: I don't think that we need to get too excited about it at the moment. They have been, we think, playing with the situation there.
Prime Minister: We are facing quite a serious situation with Parliament and public opinion on both sides of the House and I have got to face the House of Commons tomorrow afternoon, Thursday.
Johnson: I have the same over here. We have it last week with committed troops to Malaysia. These folks get a little excited if things go wrong.
P.M.: Our problem is that every nation in the world is making a statement. India and France have taken the initiative. The U.S.S.R. were saying last week they would be accepting responsibility as Chairmen. It is very difficult here for us to be saying nothing at all except that whatever the U.S. decides to do we shall go along of course. The feeling is that we tag along afterwards. If I were to come on Thursday, that is what my colleagues would like me to do, it would look too dramatic. The feeling is that I should come over as quickly as possible.
Johnson: That would be a serious mistake. I would have been dashing over there every week looking over your shoulder and advising you. I would not get upset, keep a normal pulse and I would wait until I was called upon to do something and consider it on its merits.
P.M.: My point is that assuming you were going to do something about this we are afraid ...
Johnson: It would be very measured and very reasonable action.
P.M.: As far as whatever you do [is] measured, we shall back you straight away and say this was right and measured and the right response. This is the line we took on Monday. We are under very strong pressure from both sides of Parliament about the long term solution. I would like to suggest that as opposed to coming on Thursday or Friday ...

---

   [40] Bodleian Library, Oxford, Wilson Papers, MS Wilson c. 1578, folio 40.
   [41] TNA, PREM 13/692.

Johnson: I think a trip, Mr. Prime Minister, on this situation would be very misunderstood and I don't think any good would flow from it. If one of us jumps across the Atlantic every time there is s critical situation, you and I will be flying over when Sukarno jumps on you and I will be giving you advice.

P.M.: We do not want to dash over. We just want to talk.

Johnson: We have got telephones! I tried to be very co-operative on the IMF when you were here and you know what I have gone through as a result of that. I did not think it would help the discussions with our Allies.

P.M.: We do not want to come and plead with you to be peacemakers, we want to come and find out what you feel about things.

Johnson: Well we can telegram that now and it will tell you just what you want to know.

P.M.: But we have had to face some very strong criticism that we have not been taking the initiative in calling a Conference. So far as any talks are concerned we do like to know what you think.

Johnson: I will tell you the exact situation as I see it on classified cable.[42] I do not want to heat up the situation that involves your country, whether monetary, Malaysia or whatever it is. I know you don't want to do the same here. Let me send you the exact situation on classified cable so that you can say you have been in touch and asked our views and we have given them.

P.M.: So far as Malaysia is concerned ...

Johnson: As far as my problem in Vietnam we have asked everyone to share it with us. They were willing to share advice but not responsibility. Let me send you the exact situation as I view it in classified cable. You could show this cable to your colleagues and then you could cable back to me with whatever suggestions you have.

P.M.: I cannot show it to the House of Commons, that is my trouble.

Johnson: You would not want to use me as an instrument to deal with the House of Commons.

P.M.: The problem here is of course that on Monday afternoon that they do not accept the co-chairmanship position and are taking a very definite interest in it. The problem is with escalation ...

Johnson: I have met escalation in many places and I take it in my stride and I do not think our personal visits would do anything but dramatise and heat it up.

P.M.: That is on the assumption that things die down.

Johnson: The President of America rushing to the U.K. to ask their advice might just look overdramatic in the eyes of the world.

P.M.: You give me your views in a classified telegram.

---

[42] See 25.

Johnson: If you have got any suggestions on it, any improvements, we would be glad to have them as always as a true ally, and carefully consider them and try to act in harmony with them.

P.M.: We have given 100 percent support of the action you have taken.

Johnson: You have your hands full in Malaysia.

P.M.: We have got 50,000 troops there.

Johnson: We are going to support you all the way. We have been content to try to assume our responsibilities in Vietnam and now that things look a little bit dark we do not want to appear that we are desperate and it is all very critical, and I do not see that any good would flow from talks.

P.M.: We don't like it in Malaysia …

Johnson: I won't tell you how to run Malaysia and you don't tell us how to run Vietnam. Do you want me to come over …

P.M.: We are the only country in the world who has not made any comment on this.

Johnson: You make whatever is required for your future. If you want to help us some in Vietnam send us some men and send us some folks to deal with these guerrillas. And announce to the Press that you are going to help us. Now if you don't feel like doing that go on with your Malaysia problem.

P.M.: We have said that we are 100 percent with the U.S. on this in spite of serious pressures and attacks. The next thing that will happen is that the Russians will take the initiative on conference and the line we will take is that we are not interested in this as you are.

Johnson: I think we can agree on that and let me send you a cable and we will consider your views as we always do. We understand the problems you have as I tried to indicate when you were here. I want you to talk about the MLF. I tried to hold my real views until you had talked to the Germans. I had very strong views on that and I did not want to be domineering.

P.M.: I am going to meet the Germans but the problem there is they are not going to say anything until the Elections are over.

Johnson: I talked to them yesterday and they say they are waiting on you.

P.M.: Erhard was here last week.

Johnson: Their ambassador was here yesterday and says they are looking forward to you going. I told them I did not want to be suggestive or overpowering and I tried to be persuasive and let everyone form their own opinion. And I told you I was awaiting the result of your visit.

P.M.: I have spoken to Erhard and I shall be seeing him again in 2 or 3 weeks time and I shall be very happy to send you a telegram as far as the ANF and the MLF are concerned. I will let you have my assessment then.

Johnson: I said yesterday that I had understood and that we had been willing to postpone them and not go ahead. I said we were waiting for you.

P.M.: So far as that is concerned there is only one thing they are interested in at the moment and this is reunification, where you are taking exactly the same line as we are. I am not prepared on that issue to raise their hopes.

Johnson: David Bruce is here and will be returning at the end of the week. I will give him a memorandum on Vietnam and he will let you have it. Say you have had an extended conversation with me and that Mr. Bruce is bringing you a personal message from me fully outlining the various problems of the world in which we are vitally concerned, on which we are allies.

P.M.: I assure you that we will be helpful. We will look into that and let you have our views. I think I will indicate that as far as this is concerned we are standing by you throughout. The feeling is that as far as this is concerned the only country that has got nothing to say is Britain.

Johnson: We are having murder there overnight and we have lost 30 to 40 people today and we shall lose a good many more tomorrow. And we want to join with any of our allies to come and help us.

P.M.: It is because of our concern, that we heard of tonight, that I telephoned my ambassador and speak to you. Whatever response, and that is not easy, we shall support and stand firmly by whatever action you take.

Johnson: Every time they murder our people we are going to react promptly and measuredly. I know that is what you would want to have us do. Wherever you have your problems, whether it is Malaysia ...

P.M: Whatever measured response you take tomorrow we shall be backing that too. We have been extremely loyal allies on this matter and that will be the position tomorrow. The situation is growing. You have got India making speeches and France; and the Soviet Union is going to intervene.

Johnson: I have not considered any of them as anxious to share the responsibilities of the world with me. I have never seen India take up arms. I do not know why that is disturbing.

P.M.: They are making statements on it. They are all taking initiatives and saying that we should join with them as co-chairman and it very difficult to ...

Johnson: You are quoting India to me as one of the reasons for being disturbed. Why are you so concerned?

P.M.: I am relying on their public statements which I suppose they stand by. All I say here is that in any situation where you have got over their opinion as expressing a view we have stood by simply loyally.

Johnson: I think that is generally true of most of the free world. I don't want you to get excited. When you have trouble with Malaysia I do not ring up my ambassador and come rushing over to see you.

P.M.: All I want to do is to reassure the House of Commons. Do you think I can do this on the basis of a transatlantic call in the middle of the night?

Johnson: You were the one who placed the call.

P.M.: I have got to be able to tell them.

Johnson: You needn't say it was the middle of the night.

P.M.: May I come to a serious point. I have said it to David Bruce in whom we have the fullest confidence. If the point arises where you want a conference we are prepared to go into this conference with you. We shall not take an initiative in that and this we have told you.

Johnson: I think we may well reach that point and we shall have to see what flows from the activities out there. We are not going to be provocative or belligerent; we are not going to be domineering; and we are not going to throw our weight around. But if they come in the middle of the night and kill all my men our response will be prompt, adequate, measured. That is what I expect you to do wherever your people are and in that response you have our full support.

P.M.: We have given our full support on this matter and if you do it tomorrow we will give it to you again. I should be glad in this memorandum that you are going to send to us, whether by David or by telegram, if you would give us your view on the long term situation. We are not getting any backing from your people about the trouble we are facing with Spain on Gibraltar.

Johnson: We are pretty well occupied.

P.M.: We are facing a hell of a problem in Gibraltar with the Spaniards[43] who are treating our people abominably.

Johnson: What do you think I ought to do then?

P.M.: You do just what we are doing on Vietnam; say that whatever we are doing you will back. But I won't press it on you this time. Goodnight Mr. President.

Johnson: Goodnight Mr. Prime Minister.

25. Message from McGeorge Bundy to J. O. Wright for the Prime Minister, 11 February 1965[44]

The President has asked me to send you at once the following account of the situation and our current plans. In daylight hours, February 11, U.S. and Vietnamese air units will strike two targets in southern part of North Vietnam. These targets will be army barracks, clearly associated with infiltration program of Hanoi. These strikes will be in areas where air reaction is unlikely. Operation has been designed under President's personal and careful supervision to be prompt, adequate and measured.

---

[43] A handwritten note at the bottom the page recorded that Wilson had said: 'a lot of bloody fascists.'

[44] LBJ Library, NSF, Head of State Correspondence File, Box 9, United Kingdom: Prime Minister Wilson Correspondence, Volume 1 [2 of 2], no. 57.

We have carefully considered the fact Kosygin is in Asia and present operations are ordered only because after very grave provocations of recent days, failure to react could be dangerously misunderstood by friends and adversaries alike.

We estimate Soviet reaction, to date, as very moderate in light of competition among communists. Reaction from Peking is strong in words, but not clear in action. It is an [sic] Hanoi that provocations appear to be deliberately planned, and we currently expect more outrages before there are less.

The President remains determined to give all necessary replies while keeping it clear at all times that he desires no wider war and that root cause of entire situation is in systematic campaign of aggression by force and fraud against South Vietnam under direction of North Vietnamese leadership.

Announcement of operation is expected to be in approximate following terms about 0800 Washington time:

"On February 11, U.S. air elements joined with the South Vietnamese air force in attacks against military facilities in North Vietnam used by Hanoi for the training and infiltration of Viet Cong personnel into South Vietnam. These actions by the South Vietnamese and United States governments were in response to further direct provocations by the Hanoi regime, beyond those actions reported to the press on February 7. Over the past several days, a large number of South Vietnamese and U.S. personnel have been killed in an increasing number of Viet Cong ambushes and attacks. A district town in Phuoc Long province has been overrun, resulting in further Vietnamese and U.S. casualties. In Qui Nhon there has been an explosion in quarters used by U.S. enlisted men, resulting in an as yet undetermined number of dead and injured. In addition, there have been a number of mining and other attacks on the railway in South Vietnam as well as assassinations and ambushes involving South Vietnamese civil and military officials. The United States Government has been in consultation with the government of South Vietnam on this outbreak of new aggressions and outrages. While maintaining their desire to avoid spreading the conflict, the two governments felt compelled to take the action described above."

The President will discuss whole situation fully with Ambassador Bruce before his return to London and asks me to repeat that he welcomes consultation by cable and telephone at any time the Prime Minister thinks it useful. He assumes Prime Minister will protect confidential information in these exchanges, but is glad to have it known that he and Prime Minister are in closest communication.

26. Message from Wilson to Johnson, 11 March 1965[45]

When we last spoke on the telephone,[46] I said that I would let you know how I got on during my visit to Berlin and Bonn which has just taken place.

As it turned out, it was a very good thing that my trip should have started with the visit to Berlin. This enabled me to make an act of presence in the city and to make a speech re-affirming British determination, together with our allies, to safeguard the freedom of city. The demonstration and the speech acted as a useful curtain raiser and set the tone for my subsequent talks in Bonn with the Federal Chancellor.

My talks with Erhard covered four main points:

(1) The nuclear organisation of the Alliance
(2) Re-unification
(3) European problems including measures to improve the cohesion of the continent and bring EFTA and E.E.C. closer together, and
(4) The offset agreement

In addition I had a private session with him, as between two retired or reformed economists, on the British economic situation. This gave a chance for me to say what I thought about Rueff and all his works and for Erhard to say that he totally disagreed with de Gaulle about the gold standard.[47] Erhard indicated clearly, without actually committing himself, that we could expect German support when we apply for our fund drawing later in the year.

As to nuclear matters, it soon became very clear that whatever Schroeder's view might be, Erhard was not going to have anything to do with nuclear matters this side of the German elections. It is clear that the only way that Erhard can preserve his relationship with de Gaulle and the unity of his party is by putting nuclear matters on ice for the time being. When I told Erhard that I assumed he wanted the M.L.F. and A.N.F to be a sort of sleeping beauty he did not disagree. The wording in the communiqué represents the compromise between the British desire not to lose momentum and the German wish to forget about it for the time being. I would judge that there is no progress to be made on this until after the German elections.

The one thing that the Germans were really interested in, again for electoral reasons, was some demonstration of public activity to which they could point

---

[45] LBJ Library, NSF, Head of State Correspondence File, Box 9, United Kingdom: Prime Minister Wilson Correspondence, Volume 1 [2 of 2], no. 51.
[46] See 24.
[47] In February 1965, de Gaulle expressed interest in returning to the gold standard and announced his decision to exchange dollars for gold.

on the re-unification front. I made it quite clear that, in practical terms, re-unification can only come as a result of a period of detente with the Soviet Union and could not be made a condition for detente: and in agreeing to remit the matter to the Ambassadorial Group, I was careful not to commit myself to any specific project. Although the Germans would like progress in time for the NATO Ministerial Meeting in May, they may be able to live with a minimum of demonstrable activity on the subject with their Western allies.

On the economic organization of Europe, I found Erhard equally concerned as I was myself to prevent the further division of Europe by allowing the gulf between the Common Market and EFTA to widen. He is a strong proponent of liberal outward-looking policies, and, privately, indicated that as an economist, he did not think much of the present agricultural arrangements of the Common Market. It was however a price that had to be paid. I am myself instituting a study here of ways and means of mitigating the effect of present divisions and hope to come up with some useful ideas.

We had some very tough sessions on the offset agreement but since you have yourselves virtually equipped the German armed forces, there does not seem to be much for us in that line. However Erhard undertook to issue a directive to his people to try harder and the fact of the directive was written into the communiqué. We shall give them a couple of months and then if necessary send the chief secretary, who is a very tough character, back to Bonn to re-negotiate the whole process. We left the Germans in no doubt that if we did not get satisfaction on this point, we should be forced to agonizing re-appraisals.

All in all the talks were tough but constructive. The visit was well worthwhile and has, I hope, generated the right sort of atmosphere for the Queen's state visit in May.

27. Message from Wilson to Johnson, 16 March 1965[48]

May I add my warm thanks and congratulations to the countless others you must be receiving for your courageous stand before Congress over Selma.[49]

Though this is in one sense a domestic American matter, the problem of race is one that faces all of us who care for the future of mankind, since it is one that could divide the world more bitterly than ideology. What you have said

---

[48] LBJ Library, NSF, Head of State Correspondence File, Box 9, United Kingdom: Prime Minister Wilson Correspondence, Volume 1 [1 of 2], no. 49.

[49] Selma, Alabama, was considered one of the most oppressive cities in the South with only 1 per cent of potential black voters registered. On 7 March, some 600 protestors were confronted by state troopers amid much violence. Before Congress on 15 March, Johnson described events in Selma as 'a turning point in man's unending search for freedom' and called for a voting rights bill which eventually passed into law on 6 August 1965.

and done will encourage men and women far beyond the borders of the United States and will give the free world the inspiration it needs to tackle this, perhaps toughest and most tragic of all the world's problems.

28. Message from Johnson to Wilson, 24 March 1965[50]

I am slow sending a proper acknowledgement to your helpful message of March 11 about your visit to Chancellor Erhard.[51] I am very glad to have your account of this meeting, and we agree that the visit was a real success. The Germans clearly liked what you said and did in Bonn and Berlin, and the atmosphere created by the meeting should help in the growth of the close and effective relations between the United Kingdom and the Federal Republic which are so important to the future of both Europe and of the Atlantic world.

On nuclear matters I share your view that the Germans do not want to do anything serious between now and their election. I think it is wise, however, to use these intervening months for a very careful review of this whole problem, so that we can be ready to move ahead in whatever way seems most likely to be effective after September. You can be sure that we will be interested in taking a strong and active part in such discussions, just as we shall be ready to carry our full share of responsibility in working out the best possible means of concrete progress after September.

Your understanding with the Chancellor on procedural arrangements for reunification is clearly a useful step. There now seems to be general agreement for consideration of the German proposals in the ambassadorial group. I have myself assured the German ambassador that we will deal sympathetically and constructively with any suggestions that can advance a sound German settlement. I think that with care we can find a way of meeting their legitimate interest without the disadvantages of seeming to advance wholly unrealistic proposals.

On the economic organization of Europe, we of course share your concern over protectionist and inward-looking tendencies. We will be very much interested in any ideas and suggestions that you and your people may come up with for dealing with these tendencies and of narrowing the gap between the common market and EFTA. I talked to Hallstein last week and I told him directly of the importance which we attach to progress in the Kennedy round in agriculture as well as in industry. This is not a matter merely of narrow economic self interest—it is near the center of our effort to expand the sense of partnership of the Atlantic community.

---

[50] LBJ Library, NSF, Head of State Correspondence File, Box 9, United Kingdom: Prime Minister Wilson Correspondence, Volume 1 [1 of 2], no. 47.

[51] See 26.

I am not surprised that you had tough sessions on offset payments. We have had some of those ourselves. On the other hand, it is good to know that the German government does not share the monetary notions of the French, and I was glad to learn of Erhard's preliminary attitude toward your coming fund-drawing. As you know, we are acting energetically to improve our own balance of payments, and we know how important a topic this will be for you too in the coming weeks.

I look forward to your visit in April, which, I understand will follow the talks you will be having with General de Gaulle.

Lyndon B. Johnson

29. Message from Johnson to Wilson, 24 March 1965[52]

Thanks very much for your generous message about my address to Congress.[53] You are certainly right when you say that this is only part of world-wide problem, and while of course we must deal with it here as an American matter, I myself am struck by the degree to which our people recognize more and more that our progress on this front is a matter of more than national importance.

Lyndon B. Johnson

30. Message from Wilson to Johnson, 5 April 1965[54]

Dear Mr. President,

I thought you might be interested to have a brief account of my Paris trip. On the whole it went very well, and I found the General, although running true to form on the basic political issues, very friendly and forthcoming. I think that he was anxious to minimise the areas of disagreement and to concentrate on making progress on those topics where we can broadly see eye to eye.

The organisation of NATO, including nuclear sharing, was not of course one of these topics, and you won't be surprised to have seen from the communiqué that we had to confine ourselves to discussing our respective points of view about the security of the West within the framework of the Alliance. I don't think we can look for any significant shift in French policy in this field in the foreseeable future. As regards the Middle East and Africa, however, we found ourselves

---

[52] LBJ Library, NSF, Head of State Correspondence File, Box 9, United Kingdom: Prime Minister Wilson Correspondence, Volume 1 [1 of 2], no. 43.

[53] See 27.

[54] LBJ Library, NSF, Head of State Correspondence File, Box 9, United Kingdom: Prime Minister Wilson Correspondence, Volume 1 [1 of 2], no. 40; TNA, PREM 13/1196.

in more agreement on the need to try to reduce the Arab–Israeli tension, to counter Sino-Soviet penetration of Africa and so forth. It may be significant that the French now seem ready to resume the periodical discussions at expert level which we used to have on these topics, and I hope that, if these talks start again, it may be possible to find out rather more clearly what the French intentions on these areas really are.

We discussed the Vietnam situation in some detail. But here again of course it was essentially a matter of examining differing points of view which showed no real signs of being nearer each other at the end of our meeting than at the beginning. Couve was particularly unyielding in his talks with the Foreign Secretary, but we made it no less clear that in our opinion there could be no question of merely pulling out of the area and that, as co-chairman of the 1954 conference[55] we had a definite part to play and were determined to do whatever we could (e.g. by Patrick Gordon-Walker's mission) to promote what the communiqué called a lasting and peaceful settlement.

We had several interesting discussions at various levels about economic affairs. Was very grateful to you arranging for Kermit Gordon to be in London when we came back: and I have given him today a full account of our Paris talks which he will be able to pass on to you. Perhaps all I need say now therefore is that the main features of those talks strengthen the British economy without devaluing the pound and that on their side they gave us pretty categorical assurance that, when we go to the IMF in May, they will associate themselves with the raising of the necessary funds. This does not commit them of course as regards the amount, the conditions and so forth: but I took it as a good sign that they were prepared in principle to recognise our need for a breathing space and to commit themselves to support us. We also had some very interesting exchanges about possible ways of reforming the international monetary system. Here again both sides stated their position on lines with which you will be familiar: and there was not much sign of any change of heart among the French. But they were clearly divided among themselves on the question of the gold standard and I think that I managed to shake them a bit on this issue. Kermit Gordon will be able to tell you more about this. It will be interesting to see how the French will now behave both at the I.M.F. meeting on the U.K. drawing and at the discussions (for which they hope to be ready soon after that meeting) about changes in the international monetary system.

I think that in some ways the most valuable parts of our discussions were those which dealt with the possibilities of cooperation between Britain and France in various technological fields, including aircraft. I could not say too much to de Gaulle about our recent examination of the TSR2 and the TFX, since our decisions here are technically a budget secret, which we cannot reveal

---

[55] The Geneva Conference which ended the First Indo-China War (1946–54).

until the Chancellor of the Exchequer opens his budget on Tuesday. But I was anxious that there should be no subsequent Nassau-type misunderstanding between de Gaulle and ourselves,[56] and I therefore let him know that we had it in mind to take an option on the TFX, but that we were anxious at the same time to explore the possibilities of future cooperation with France as regards aircraft. There are some signs that the press may get this wrong and may suppose that we have an Anglo-French aircraft in mind as a replacement for the TSR2; but we shall, of course, take the first opportunity after the budget to dispose of this misunderstanding and make it clear that any new Anglo-French aircraft will be for a different purpose and will belong to a subsequent generation. I was interested to find that de Gaulle agreed that the concept of Anglo–French collaboration in this field made sense in terms of the enlargement of the market which is essential if these very specialised resources are to be deployed in the most economic way. And this is true, of course, not only of aircraft but also of such other technologies as computers, electronics and so forth. I think he also realised, although he was careful not to say so, that the argument in favour of Anglo–French cooperation in these fields is not merely economic and that, if this collaboration becomes a reality, it will represent a genuine beginning in the process of creating functional links between the two camps into which Europe is divided. If to this extent it contributes to a healing of the breach, I know that you will be no less pleased than ourselves.

Yours sincerely

Harold Wilson

31. Message from Johnson to Wilson, 7 May 1965[57]

I want to thank you for the gifts which you very kindly brought for me on the occasion of your recent visit to Washington.

I am so pleased to have the bell from the ship "Resolute" which played such a fascinating part in the history of Anglo–American relations during the last century.[58] I am most grateful to you, and to Admiral Wright, for returning

---

[56] Wilson is referring to President Kennedy's offer of Polaris missiles to the British at the Nassau conference at the end of 1962, an offer subsequently extended to, and rejected by, de Gaulle. The Nassau agreement was one of the factors in de Gaulle's vetoing of the British application to join the EEC.

[57] Bodleian Library, Oxford, Wilson Papers, MS. Wilson c. 1578, folio 149.

[58] HMS Resolute was one of the four relief ships which played a part in the Arctic search for Sir John Franklin's missing expedition. She was abandoned in the ice to the west of Barrow Strait in May 1854 and in September of the following year was found drifting in pack ice off Baffin Island by a US whaling vessel. She was subsequently refitted at US government expense and returned to Queen Victoria in December 1856. Rear Admiral Noel

this unique symbol of the truly close relationship that exists between our two countries.

Please accept my thanks also for your thoughtfulness in wanting me to have the handsome raincoat, as well as the attractive and useful piece of luggage.

With appreciation and best personal regards,
Sincerely,
Lyndon B. Johnson

32. Message from Johnson to Wilson, 30 June 1965[59]

Congratulations on your success in working out a solution to the Rann of Kutch dispute.[60] We all admire the great skill and patience shown by you and your people in helping to bring about a peaceful settlement between the two great countries of the subcontinent.

33. Message from Wilson to Johnson, 5 July 1965[61]

Thank you for your message about the Rann of Kutch.[62] We have all been most grateful for the helpful understanding your people have shown throughout these prolonged negotiations. We look forward to working out in close co-operation with them further steps to encourage India and Pakistan towards a settlement of other outstanding problems.

Wright suggested that the bell from HMS. Resolute be presented to President Johnson, an idea that Wilson accepted with the comment: 'the bell itself will be an admirable symbol of the link between our two countries, as well as our two navies' (Letter from Wilson to Wright, 15 Jan. 1965, TNA, PREM 13/507). The bell from Resolute was presented to Johnson during Wilson's visit to the US in April 1965. Wilson subsequently informed Wright that the President was 'delighted to have it and was, I think, greatly interested in the story of its history which you let us have' (TNA, PREM 13/507, Letter from Wilson to Wright, 3 May 1965).

[59] LBJ Library, NSF, Head of State Correspondence File, Box 9, United Kingdom: Prime Minister Wilson Correspondence, Volume 1 [1 of 2], no. 37.

[60] The Wilson government had played an important role in mediating an end to fighting over the disputed Rann of Kutch territory which straddled the Indian state of Gujarat and the Pakistani province of Sindh. It was less so later in the year when Indo-Pakistan hostilities broke out over Kashmir (see Jonathan Colman, 'Britain and the Indo-Pakistan conflict: The Rann of Kutch and Kashmir, 1965', *Journal of Imperial and Commonwealth History*, 37, 3 (2009), 465–82).

[61] LBJ Library, NSF, Head of State Correspondence File, Box 9, United Kingdom: Prime Minister Wilson Correspondence, Volume 1 [1 of 2], no. 34a.

[62] See 32.

34. Message from Wilson to Johnson, 6 July 1965[63]

We shall be giving your people here our views of the Commonwealth Prime Ministers' meeting,[64] but I thought it might be useful if I were to send you direct my own personal impressions.

It was a good meeting in the sense that we had this large and very varied gathering of heads of government discussing a great many contentious issues in an atmosphere which was at times very outspoken but always remained friendly. I hope that it may have done something to widen the horizons of some of our newer colleagues to the broader problems of the world, and to lead and encourage them towards moderate points of view. Bob Menzies was, as ever, a tower of strength.

The main subjects engaging the meeting were of course Vietnam and Rhodesia.

I was glad that you were able to welcome the meeting's decision to set up a mission on Vietnam. Like you, I was not very optimistic about this even when I launched the idea, and the reception it has had in Moscow and Peking has not been encouraging. But I think that whatever the ultimate outcome it was well worth while doing.

Within the Commonwealth, some of the African members have been deflected from extreme ideas. Nkrumah, for example, readily agreed to serve on the mission and has been surprisingly moderate. As a member of the mission he is likely to be careful in his utterances on Vietnam in future. Abubakar is very sound. Closer contact with the realities of the situation will be valuable for all the members of the Commonwealth who are not already involved in Vietnam. We may benefit later from widening their knowledge of the problems.

Abroad we have managed to demonstrate once again that it is the Communist countries, not the United States and South Vietnam, which are opposed to a peaceful settlement. Your Baltimore speech last April[65] and repeated offers of discussions since then have been crucial in this respect. Moreover we have driven a small wedge between Hanoi and Peking on this issue. Nearly two weeks have passed without the North Vietnamese imitating the Chinese example of final and formal rejection. Hanoi is obviously receiving conflicting advice from Moscow and Peking and is temporising accordingly. This leaves the door slightly

---

[63] LBJ Library, NSF, Head of State Correspondence File, Box 9, United Kingdom: Prime Minister Wilson Correspondence, Volume 1 [1 of 2], no. 32.

[64] The meeting took place at Marlborough House, London, between 17 and 25 June 1965.

[65] During a speech at John Hopkins University on 7 April, Johnson declared: 'it should also be clear that the only path for reasonable men is the path of peaceful settlement ... . We will never be second in the search for such a peaceful settlement in Viet-Nam' (*Public Papers of the Presidents of the United States: Lyndon B. Johnson, 1965: I* (Washington, DC: US Government Printing Office, 1965), p. 396).

ajar and until it is shut we shall keep the mission in being and be ready to act when possible. You know of our other activities.

The Rhodesian problem continues to cause us great anxiety and is a very difficult one. We came under very heavy pressure, and not only from the Africans, at the Commonwealth Prime Ministers meeting, but I think that there is an increasing realisation of the difficulties of the problem. I found it desirable to offer to consider promoting a constitutional conference if our negotiations with Smith do not progress satisfactorily. Fortunately Smith did not react too badly to this and we shall continue to pursue our negotiations with him. But I cannot pretend that these hold out great hope of success, or that any solution to which we will agree will be likely to be acceptable to the Africans. The situation therefore remains potentially dangerous.

We had discussion of economic and development matters which I hope may prove helpful. We also set up two new Commonwealth bodies following last year's decision—the Secretariat and the foundation, the first a governmental and the latter an autonomous body to promote unofficial professional contacts especially with the newer countries. I hope that these will, in their different ways, help to promote the development of the modern Commonwealth.

We also managed to deal with the Rann of Kutch and to get more general support for Malaysia than at one time looked possible.

A subsidiary bonus was having no fewer than thirteen Afro-Asian heads of government present in London when the news from Algiers came though.[66] The news made a tremendous impact and the unanimous decision of all 13 not to go to Algiers must have played its part in getting the whole thing called off to the discomfort of the Chinese who were lobbying at Marlborough House like mad. We played it very cool and let them make up their own minds. I think this helped us in what was one of the major underlying issues of the conference—our struggle with China for the soul of Africa.

Altogether I think, as I told the House of Commons, the meeting has given a sense of purpose and a new sense of unity in diversity. I believe that the Commonwealth—the world in microcosm—has a great role to play in taking the sting out of the major problems that lie ahead of us in international life: the terrible problems of race and poverty. Certainly we in Britain intend to do all we can to enable it to play that role modestly but effectively.

---

[66] During the Commonwealth meeting news emerged of the ousting of Algerian President, Ben Bella, in an army coup. He was to have hosted a conference of non-aligned nations.

35. Message from Johnson to Wilson, 8 July 1965[67]

I want to thank you for your helpful message about the Commonwealth Prime Ministers' meeting.[68] I am glad to know that it was a good meeting, and I agree with you that the proposal for a mission on Vietnam has demonstrated once again that it is the communist countries that are not interested in a peaceful settlement at present.

I am sorry that you are having continuing troubles with Rhodesia, but I share your view that the Algiers postponement is useful to us all.

In addition to your message, I have had a good talk with Bob Menzies, and I am grateful to you both for keeping us so fully informed about the work of the meeting.

36. Message from Wilson to Johnson, 14 July 1965[69]

I should like to send you this personal message to say how much we have been shocked at the sudden death of Adlai Stevenson.[70] He was a personal friend of mine over many years and I never visited the United States without going to see him. He came to visit me at Chequers only last Saturday and I was impressed once again by his wit, his wisdom and his friendship for this country.

His sudden death was a blow to us all. The news came through just as I was leaving for a meeting of the parliamentary party and when I made the announcement it was greeted with a stunned silence. Before we went on to business a resolution of sympathy was passed.

We are putting out a government statement but I wanted you to know that this is no formal matter. We feel the loss as deeply as you do.

37. Message from Johnson to Wilson, 14 July 1965[71]

I am most grateful for your personal message about Adlai Stevenson.[72] It has been a great shock to all of us, and we shall deeply miss his company and counsel

---

[67] LBJ Library, NSF, Head of State Correspondence File, Box 9, United Kingdom: Prime Minister Wilson Correspondence, Volume 1 [1 of 2], no. 29.

[68] See 34.

[69] LBJ Library, NSF, Head of State Correspondence File, Box 9, United Kingdom: Prime Minister Wilson Correspondence, Volume 1 [1 of 2], no. 26.

[70] Stevenson died in London on 14 July 1965.

[71] LBJ Library, NSF, Head of State Correspondence File, Box 9, United Kingdom: Prime Minister Wilson Correspondence, Volume 1 [1 of 2], no. 24.

[72] See 36.

in all our work for peace. I know how firmly he believed in the friendship of our two countries, and it is good to have your personal words of sympathy, as his friend and ours.

38. Message from Johnson to Wilson, 25 July 1965[73]

I have asked my Ambassador to bring you my frank assessment of the situation in South Vietnam.

In recent months open aggression against the people and government of Vietnam has increased and very heavy strains have been placed upon the South Vietnamese armed forces and the South Vietnamese people.

In this same period, as you know, repeated and imaginative efforts by many governments including your own have been unsuccessful in moving this problem to the conference table because of the determined and rigid opposition of Hanoi and Peiping.

I have been reviewing this situation during the last few days in the light of up-to-date reports from my most trusted associates. While final decisions have not been made here, I can tell you that it now appears certain that it will be necessary to increase United States armed forces in South Vietnam by a number which may equal or exceed the 80,000 already there.

In making this additional commitment, I shall be considering additional decisions, and my Ambassador will be in touch with you on these as soon as they are developed.

I want you to know that as we make this major additional effort we will also continue to make every political and diplomatic effort that we can to open the way to a peaceful settlement.

We will also continue to use every care and restraint to ensure that the fires of war do not spread on the mainland of Asia. Our objective remains the end of external interference in South Vietnam so that the people of that country can determine their own future.

In this situation I must express to you my own deep personal conviction that prospect of peace in Vietnam will be greatly increased in the measure that the necessary efforts of the United States are supported and shared by other nations which share our purposes and our concerns. I know that your government has already signalled its interest and concern by giving assistance. I now ask that you give a clear signal to the world—and perhaps especially to Hanoi—of the solidarity of international support for resistance to aggression in Vietnam and for a peaceful settlement in Vietnam.

---

[73] LBJ Library, NSF, Head of State Correspondence File, Box 9, United Kingdom: Prime Minister Wilson Correspondence, Volume 1 [1 of 2], no. 20.

I have asked my Ambassador to make himself available to you for consultation as to the types of additional assistance you might provide and for liaison with the South Vietnam Government.

39. Message from Wilson to Johnson, 29 July 1965[74]

Dear Mr President

You will have heard by now of the measures which we introduced on Tuesday with the object of steadying confidence. They have already had some effect and I hope that it will continue.

Politically this has been a very difficult operation indeed. Deferment of important social projects, introduction of building licensing, tightening up of hire purchase terms and exchange control, and so on, make a tough package. Many of my colleagues were resistant to what I considered necessary and since the announcement there has been a lot of unrest among our supporters in Parliament and outspoken opposition by Trades Union Congress. The support of the Confederation of British Industries and the recognition by our *Financial Times*, with its specialised readership, that the measures showed the Government's determination to put the strength of sterling before politics, are things that count both ways for a Labour government—particularly when it is far from certain that there is a case on objective economic grounds for more than a minor degree of deflation. But I am determined to face up to our overriding problem of maintaining confidence to the limit.

Unfortunately there may be more breakers ahead. For example a single month's bad trade figures could cause a dangerous run.

Beyond this I am very concerned about the wider outlook for international liquidity, and in particular by the French veto on Secretary Fowler's call for an international monetary conference. If this is carried any further we shall have a situation in which the French will be trying to blackmail the rest of the free world in a matter vital to economic expansion.

I know how deeply pre-occupied you are with Vietnam, as I am with Aden and Malaysia, but I believe that these economic problems, and in particular the threat that hangs over us, are also of great importance for the free world and that we must keep in close touch on them. Sir Burke Trend will be explaining our position in more detail to Mr Bundy and we shall always be ready, at whatever level is appropriate, to get together with you.

With all good wishes,

Harold Wilson

---

[74] LBJ Library, NSF, Head of State Correspondence, Box 9, United Kingdom: Prime Minister Wilson Correspondence, Volume 1 [1 of 2], no. 18.

40. Message from Wilson to Johnson, 2 August 1965[75]

I am most grateful for your personal message about Vietnam received on 26 July[76] and for all that your government have done over the last few months to keep us informed of your assessment of the situation in Vietnam and of your intentions in coping with that difficult and dangerous problem. I have followed with admiration the careful balance you have throughout maintained between determined resistance to aggression and patient insistence on your readiness to negotiate an honourable settlement.

In the face of the persistent North Vietnamese refusal to negotiate, I can see no alternative to your policy of strengthening your forces in South Vietnam in order to demonstrate to Hanoi the futility of their dreams of military victory. I wish there was more we could do to help you, but I need not remind you how far our contribution to international peacekeeping has already overstrained our resources and our economy.

Moreover, I should be loath in present circumstances to run the risk of spoiling any chance we may have of fulfilling the functions which we originally accepted as co-Chairman of the Geneva Conference and have more recently tried to develop afresh by means of the Commonwealth initiative.

This was our position when you first raised the matter with me last December and its advantages for both of us seem to me to be just as valid, if not more so, today.

But I can assure you that Her Majesty's Government are determined to persevere in their support for American policies which I believe to be in the interests of peace and stability in the world at large, no less than in South East Asia. Our solidarity with you on this issue is nowhere better understood than in Hanoi, whose leaders, in common with other communist governments and their sympathisers, never cease to reproach us with it. Nevertheless, I am urgently examining the feasibility of doing something to make still more manifest our support for your patient and courageous policy in Vietnam.

41. Message from Wilson to Johnson, 5 August 1965[77]

SACLANT has recently proposed to Her Majesty's Government that United States nuclear depth bombs, destined for release in an emergency to maritime aircraft of the Netherlands, should be stored in the special ammunition store

---

[75] LBJ Library, NSF, Head of State Correspondence File, Box 9, United Kingdom: Prime Minister Wilson Correspondence, Volume 1 [1 of 2], no. 14a.
[76] See 38.
[77] Bodleian Library, Oxford, Wilson Papers, MS. Wilson c. 1581, folios 122–3.

at St. Mawgan in Cornwall. Similar weapons for release to United States and British aircraft are also to be stored there.

Release of these nuclear weapons in an emergency for use by United States and British forces based in the United Kingdom would be the subject of a joint decision taken by the President and the Prime Minister in accordance with the terms of the understanding, as amended, which were confirmed by your letter of December 8, 1964.[78] I am proposing that we should tell SACLANT that we have no objections to the proposed storage of United States nuclear weapons at St. Mawgan for Netherlands forces—or for the forces of other members of the North Atlantic Treaty Organisation. We should do this on the assumption that these weapons would not be released in advance of the joint decision on release to United States and British aircraft. I should be grateful for confirmation that this assumption is correct.

Yours ever,
Harold Wilson

42. Message from Wilson to Johnson, 5 August 1965[79]

My dear Mr. President,

In your letter of December 8, 1964, in reply to my letter of the same date,[80] you reaffirmed the understanding between our two Governments set out in the memorandum enclosed with your letter of February 28 to Sir Alec Douglas-Home with regard to consultation on the use of nuclear weapons.

Since that time the deployment of United States nuclear depth bombs to the United Kingdom, for use in an emergency by the United States and British maritime aircraft, has become imminent. These aircraft are assigned to SACLANT, and will not therefore be included within the scope of existing understandings, unless these are amended. Paragraph 3 of the memorandum provides for amendment from time to time. I accordingly propose that the following amendments to the memorandum should be made:

i) Paragraph 1: line 7
   1. Delete "SACEUR-assigned forces in the United Kingdom" and substitute "forces in the United Kingdom which are assigned or earmarked for assignment to a NATO commander."

---

[78] See 14.
[79] TNA, PREM 13/3129.
[80] See 13 and 14.

ii) Paragraph 3: line 4
4.   Delete "SACEUR-assigned forces (strike squadrons) based in the United Kingdom" and substitute "forces based in the United Kingdom which are assigned or earmarked for assignment to a NATO commander."

Since these two amendments will cover all United States forces which may be based in the United Kingdom and assigned to a NATO commander in the future, the footnote to paragraph 3 of the memorandum will no longer be relevant and I suggest that it be deleted. This deletion would not prevent the amendment of the Murphy-Dean Report[81] from time to time should that be considered necessary.

For convenience I enclose a revised text of the Memorandum incorporating these amendments.

Yours ever,
Harold Wilson

Memorandum: Understandings with the British on the use of British bases and nuclear weapons

1. Our understanding on the use of the British bases is that the President and Prime Minister will reach a joint decision by speaking personally with each other before certain forces equipped with U.S. nuclear weapons and operating from bases in the United Kingdom will use nuclear weapons, namely SAC, British Bomber Command,[82] forces in the U.K. which are assigned or earmarked for assignment to a NATO Commander and U.S. Polaris submarines in British territorial waters. The basic understanding is contained in the communiqué of 9 January, 1952 covering the Truman–Churchill talks:

"Under arrangements made for the common defence, the United States has the use of certain bases in the United Kingdom. We reaffirm the understanding that the use of these bases in an emergency would be a matter for joint decision by His Majesty's Government and the United States Government in the light of circumstances prevailing at the time."

Procedures for carrying out this basic understanding were agreed upon in the Murphy-Dean Agreement of June 7, 1958, which was approved by the President and Prime Minister.

---

[81]   The Murphy-Dean Report of 7 June 1958 had established the principle of high level consultation in advance of US nuclear weapons based in the UK being used.

[82]   Excluding aircraft of such Command equipped with British nuclear weapons.

The covering document, the Report to the President and the Prime Minister, repeats almost literally the language of the Truman–Churchill communiqué:

"2. The basic understanding between the United Kingdom and the United States Governments, regarding the use of bases in the United Kingdom by United States forces, provides that such use in an emergency shall be a matter for joint decision by the two Governments in the light of the circumstances at the time."

2. There is a second, more general understanding with the British that we will consult with them before using nuclear weapons anywhere, if possible. The basic understanding on this point is contained in a memorandum of conversation of a meeting between the President and Eden on 9 March, 1953. Eden had asked for an assurance of consultation by the President with the Prime Minister prior to U.S. of any nuclear weapon.

"He (the President) said that the United States would, of course, in the event of increased tension of the threat of war, take every possible step to consult with Britain and our other allies."

The President reaffirmed this understanding when he wrote to the Prime Minister on October 27, 1960, in connection with the Holy Loch berthing:

"With reference to the launching of missiles from U.S. Polaris submarines, I give you the following assurance, which of course is not intended to be used publicly. In the event of an emergency, such as increased tension or the threat of war, the U.S. will take every possible step to consult with Britain and other Allies. This reaffirms the assurance I gave Foreign Secretary Eden on March 9, 1953."

3. It should be noted that the agreement for joint decision by the President and the Prime Minister does not extend to all U.S. forces under SACEUR and SACLANT but only covers those forces based in the United Kingdom which are assigned or earmarked for assignment to a NATO Commander. The other U.S. nuclear forces under SACEUR and SACLANT would only be covered by a more general understanding to consult if time permits.

43. Message from Wilson to Johnson, 18 August 1965[83]

As you can imagine, my colleagues and I have been giving the most careful consideration to the implications for our future policy of the secession of Singapore from Malaysia.[84] Our first conclusion was that, before we attempted to make up our minds, we needed to discuss the whole problem fully and

---

[83] LBJ Library, NSF, Head of State Correspondence File, Box 9, United Kingdom: Prime Minister Wilson Correspondence, Volume 1 [1 of 2], no. 9c.

[84] Singapore seceded on 9 August 1965.

frankly with your Government and with the Governments of Australia and New Zealand. The new situation that has been created affects us all and, if Britain has to take new measures to meet it, these should clearly first be discussed and agreed with our friends.

I think this is too complex a problem for discussion in an exchange of messages. If this is agreeable to you, I should like to suggest a quadripartite meeting in London, at which each Government would be represented by senior officials familiar with the political and strategic problem of South East Asia.

We are urgently analysing the problem and its possible implications for future action and aim to complete our study by the week beginning 30 August. I suggest that our officials should assemble in London on 1 September. If we can, we will let your people have a memorandum in advance of the meeting.

In order to avoid arousing suspicion, it will, I suggest, be important that this meeting of our officials should be kept entirely secret.

I hope this proposal will commend itself to you. I am writing similarly to Sir Robert Menzies and Mr. Holyoake.

44. Message from Wilson to Johnson, 24 August 1965[85]

My dear Mr. President,

Mary[86] joins me in sending you our warm personal good wishes for your birthday.

While on holiday here in the Isles of Scilly I have diverted myself by reading Theodore White's book on the 1964 campaign.[87] While no doubt there must be many points which from your greater knowledge seem to you to be wrong or misdirected, I found the book most impressive and giving a powerful sense of a superb campaign, brilliant political strategy, and a great degree of warmth and vision of oratory.

Again our sincere birthday wishes and Happy Returns.
Yours very sincerely,
 Harold Wilson

---

[85] LBJ Library, NSF, Head of State Correspondence File, Box 9, United Kingdom: Prime Minister Wilson Correspondence, Volume 1 [1 of 2], no. 7.
[86] Wilson's wife.
[87] See Theodore White, *The Making of the President 1964* (London: Cape, 1965).

45. Message from Johnson to Wilson, 30 August 1965[88]

We agree that a discussion with your government and with the governments of Australia and New Zealand of the separation of Singapore and Malaysia would be useful at this time. We propose therefore to send to the quadripartite talks, which we understand will be held in London in early September, Mr. Samuel D. Berger, Deputy Assistant Secretary of State for Far Eastern Affairs, and another officer from that bureau. We agree entirely that speculation on the meeting would be most undesirable and hope that it can be kept secret.
Lyndon B. Johnson

46. Message from Johnson to Wilson, 30 August 1965[89]

Thank you very much for your personal note about my birthday.[90] I am grateful for your warm good wishes, and I am glad that you are getting a little time off.
Mrs. Johnson joins me in warm regards to you both.

47. Message from Wilson to Johnson, 6 September 1965[91]

Many thanks for your message of August 30.[92]

I am most grateful to you for sending State Department officials to London for talks with the Australians, New Zealanders and ourselves about the situation created by the separation of Singapore from the Malaysian federation.

It is because such important and far reaching issues are involved that we have been clear throughout that decisions on them can only reached by a process of full and frank consultation with our three allies. We therefore took the initiative in suggesting that the first stage should be exploratory talks by officials. In these talks our officials have emphasized that this is the basis on which we wish to proceed.

The officials had a meeting on Friday at which our people gave an exposition at some length of the various factors affecting the situation as we see them, and they will be meeting again tomorrow, Tuesday. We shall wish to review matters

---

[88] LBJ Library, NSF, Head of State Correspondence File, Box 9, United Kingdom: Prime Minister Wilson Correspondence, Volume 1 [1 of 2], no. 3.

[89] LBJ Library, NSF, Head of State Correspondence File, Box 9, United Kingdom: Prime Minister Wilson Correspondence, Volume 2 [2 of 2], no. 154.

[90] See 44.

[91] LBJ Library, NSF, Head of State Correspondence File, Box 9, United Kingdom: Prime Minister Wilson Correspondence, Volume 2 [2 of 2], no. 152.

[92] See 45.

in the light of the further clarifications afforded by the official talks and we hope thereafter to be able to explain to your people how we see the problem so that, at government level, we can consider together what our policies should be. Meanwhile both Foreign Secretary and I will be able to explain where we now stand to George Ball in the course of this week.

Harold Wilson

48. Message from Wilson to Johnson, 2 October 1965[93]

As you know, we have been keeping in close touch about Rhodesia with your Administration at all levels and we are most appreciative of the support which we have received.

We are now entering a crucial phase and the discussions I am to have with Smith next week are likely to be final and decisive. He seems to have retreated from the basis of negotiation which the Commonwealth Secretary established with him earlier this year, and I do not think it likely that we can now reach any agreement with him. The risk of unilateral declaration of independence must therefore be regarded as serious and I know you share with us the belief that this could escalate with disastrous consequences for the whole area and serious damage to Western interests.

If our negotiations unhappily fail, I shall do everything possible to bring home to Smith the consequences of an illegal step in the hope of deterring him from it. If there is still any chance of deflecting him and his colleagues from such a disastrous course I believe that your influence might be a decisive factor. I wonder therefore if you would be prepared to approach Smith in whatever way you think best calculated to bring home to him the gravity of the step which he is apparently contemplating. Subject to the way things go in the next few days I think that a message from you would be most effective immediately after a break-down in the negotiation. Since the timing of such a message could be crucial we will keep your Ambassador closely informed of the progress of our discussions with Smith. I hope very much that you will feel able to intervene in this way and to do so publicly since your message would then have the maximum effect on the Rhodesian public.

---

[93] LBJ Library, NSF, Head of State Correspondence File, Box 9, United Kingdom: Prime Minister Wilson Correspondence, Volume 2 [2 of 2], no. 149a.

49. Message from Johnson to Wilson, 5 October 1965[94]

We agree that the Southern Rhodesian affair could quickly become a calamity, with potentially serious damage to Western interests. We also agree that deterring Smith from any fateful step is by all odds the best course open to us.

If you see fit, we would be glad if you would tell Smith when you see him that we as well as you would take a very poor view of UDI, and that we would necessarily have to oppose it vigorously.

We would also be prepared, as you suggest, to approach Smith directly along the above lines, either through our Chargé in London or by calling in the Rhodesian minister attached to your embassy here. And if deterrence is our prime objective, it may be better for us to convey our views before your decisive meeting with Smith, rather than after. We will do this promptly if you wish. Should negotiations fail, we would certainly be prepared to make our views public in an appropriate way.

I am glad that our two governments are in close touch, since it is important to coordinate our efforts with yours in dealing with this unhappy problem.

50. Message from Wilson to Johnson, 6 October 1965[95]

Many thanks for your message about Rhodesia.[96] I am most grateful for your support in this, as in so many other matters. So far, we have not done much more than state opening positions, but I expect the crunch to come when Smith comes to see me tomorrow, Thursday.

As you say, deterrence is our main objective and, in these circumstances, it would be very helpful if you were able to make your administration's views known to Smith before my decisive meeting with him. May I leave it to you to judge the best way of doing so. Perhaps you would consider using both techniques. I will keep you in touch with developments.

---

[94] LBJ Library, NSF, Head of State Correspondence File, Box 9, United Kingdom: Prime Minister Wilson Correspondence, Volume 2 [2 of 2], no. 146.
[95] LBJ Library, NSF, Head of State Correspondence File, Box 9, United Kingdom: Prime Minister Wilson Correspondence, Volume 2 [2 of 2], no. 144.
[96] See 49.

51. Message from Wilson to Johnson, 6 October 1965[97]

I am so sorry to hear that you are to go into hospital.[98] You have all my sympathy and my warm good wishes for a speedy restoration to full health. The world has a continuing need of your leadership as president of the United States.

52. Message from Wilson to Johnson, 8 October 1965[99]

I am delighted to hear of the success of your operation and look forward to your rapid return to health.

53. Message from Johnson to Wilson, 14 October 1965[100]

Thank you for kind message.[101] I am most appreciative of your good wishes for my recovery.

54. Message from Wilson to Johnson, 29 October 1965[102]

I was most grateful for the message which Secretary Rusk sent to me with your authority for delivery to Mr. Smith if I thought it helpful.[103]

---

[97] LBJ Library, NSF, Head of State Correspondence File, Box 9, United Kingdom: Prime Minister Wilson Correspondence, Volume 2 [2 of 2], no. 142.

[98] On 8 October 1965, Johnson had his gall bladder removed at Bethesda Naval Hospital (see Robert E. Gilbert, 'The Political Effects of Presidential Illness: The Case of Lyndon B. Johnson', *Political Psychology*, 16, 4 (1995): 766).

[99] LBJ Library, NSF, Head of State Correspondence File, Box 9, United Kingdom: Prime Minister Wilson Correspondence, Volume 2 [2 of 2], no. 139a.

[100] LBJ Library, NSF, Head of State Correspondence File, Box 9, United Kingdom: Prime Minister Wilson Correspondence, Volume 2 [2 of 2], no. 137.

[101] See 52.

[102] LBJ Library, NSF, Head of State Correspondence File, Box 9, United Kingdom: Prime Minister Wilson Correspondence, Volume 2 [2 of 2], no. 135.

[103] Rusk authorised Wilson to convey to Smith the following message from Johnson: '1. The United States is gravely concerned at the possibility of a unilateral declaration of independence by Southern Rhodesia. 2. The United States Government fully supports the efforts that the British Prime Minister and his Government are making to arrive at a solution to the question of the future of Southern Rhodesia satisfactory to that colony's population as a whole. 3. A unilateral declaration of independence unresponsive to the rights and interests of the majority of the population and in violation of the existing constitution would be a tragic mistake. If such a step should be taken, the United States would feel compelled to

2. After three days of intensive discussion here,[104] with the government, with the African Nationalist leaders, Nkomo and Sithole, and with every representative body of opinion including the churches, business, the financial community and the defeated opposition, not to mention ex-Prime Ministers of Rhodesia, I have come to the reluctant conclusion that a message from you delivered through me would not have the necessary impact.[105]

3. The situation is bleak. Although I have tried every method of persuasion the African Nationalists are prepared neither to work together nor to make any move from their extreme position to any extent necessary to win even a breathing space. The government are impervious to argument and are collectively like a suicide on a windowsill waiting to jump. Moderate European opinion is paralyzed by a sense of helplessness before impending doom, and subject to personal intimidation which saps their will to oppose. The government is manipulating the organs of publicity such as radio and television although the press is still free.

4. Although I have the sensation of witnessing the final act of a Greek tragedy, there is just the slightest chance that catastrophe may be avoided. I have today pulled out all the stops in working on Smith and have put to him a reasonable alternative to a U.D.I. which no rational man could refuse, namely a Royal commission. The terms of reference would be to seek the highest common factor of agreement between all shades of opinion in Rhodesia on the terms for independence. In these circumstances, a message direct from you to Mr. Smith delivered through your Consul General here in Salisbury would be of infinitely

---

sever the traditional close and friendly ties that have characterized its relations with Southern Rhodesia through war and peace. 4. The United States Government believes that most people in Africa and in the world at large share the hope that with British help the Rhodesian people will find a peaceful solution to their constitutional problems and eventually take their place in the world community as a united and democratic nation.' (Telegram from the Department of State to the Embassy in the United Kingdom October 22, 1965, *FRUS*: Volume XXIV, *Africa* (Washington, DC: US Government Printing Office, 1999), p. 838.)

[104] On October 24, Prime Minister Wilson travelled to Salisbury in an attempt to break the stalemate in the negotiations.

[105] Johnson did send a message to Smith through the US Consulate General in Southern Rhodesia which stated: 'The United States has consistently supported the efforts of the British Government to arrive at a solution in Rhodesia which will be satisfactory to the population of Southern Rhodesia as a whole. While we recognize that there are grave and difficult issues still to be worked out in pursuit of this objective, we are convinced that a unilateral declaration of independence would be a tragic mistake which would serve the true interests of no one. The United States would have to make known its strong opposition to any such decision, and we do not intend to change our course of firm support for the position of the British Government after any such unilateral declaration.' (Telegram from the Department of State to the Consulate General in Southern Rhodesia, 29 October 1965, *FRUS, 1964–8*: Vol. XXIV, *Africa*, p. 831.)

greater value than a message delivered through me. To make its maximum impact it should preferably be delivered by 9:00 a.m. Salisbury time, tomorrow Friday. Since I have found some doubt here in Salisbury not only in government circles, but also more generally, about the attitude of the United States to a U.D.I., I hope that your message might state your position in unequivocal terms. Even this may not do the trick: but when I think of the consequences of failure to deter this suicidal government, I believe that no means of pressure should be neglected.

55. Message from Wilson to Johnson, 1 November 1965[106]

I am now back in London after a week in Rhodesia and shall be making a statement in Parliament this afternoon. I have asked our Ambassador to let you have the full text of the statement which sets out pretty fully the position we have now reached.

It was an exhausting and in many ways a depressing week, depressing because so many people have their minds in blinkers and they are wrapped up in cocoons of self-delusion which it is terribly difficult to penetrate. To be in Salisbury was to have the sensation of being present at the fifth act of a Greek tragedy. I tried every method to persuade the African Nationalists both to work together and to work the existing constitution: but to no effect. Moderate European opinion, represented by business and finance, is paralyzed by a sense of helplessness before impending doom and, what is worse, subject to the personal intimidation which saps their will. Smith has quite a nice little police state in embryo there. The government have control of television and radio, although the press is still free. Most of Smith's cabinet are impervious to argument and divided only on whether they should commit suicide now or later.

One thing is certain and that is if I had not offered on Thursday, October 21 to go to Rhodesia, U.D.I. would have been with us on Friday, October 22. But I fear that the most I may have achieved is the respite of a little more time before Smith and his cabinet go over the brink. But time is the most precious commodity of all in this problem.

My chief purpose was therefore not to negotiate, although I had many hours of tough discussions with Smith and his colleagues, but to see whether, as a last hope, there was any chance of changing the political climate and finding some last minute formula which would give Smith pause and give the moderates of all races something to support. Hence my talks with every conceivable representative body to whom I gave the carrot and stick treatment: I had to get

---

[106] LBJ Library, NSF, Head of State Correspondence File, Box 9, United Kingdom: Prime Minister Wilson Correspondence, Volume 2 [2 of 2], no. 132.

home to them both the tragic consequences of U.D.I. and the fact that no one was faced with a simple choice of U.D.I. or majority rule tomorrow. There were many alternatives. Hence the proposal for a royal commission, which gives them a way out if they have the will to take it.

Quite frankly, there are so many Gadarene minds in Rhodesia, and that goes for most of Smith's cabinet, if not totally for Smith himself, that I doubt whether good sense has much chance of prevailing. So while I am hoping for the best it is only sensible to prepare for the worst. The worst may come quite quickly but we are quite ready for it.

56. Message from Wilson to Johnson, 2 November 1965[107]

Many thanks for the message which your Consul-General was instructed to deliver to Mr. Smith while I was in Salisbury.[108] Your message came at a crucial moment in our discussions and its clear indications of the consequences of a U.D.I. will, I am sure, have carried great weight with the Rhodesian Cabinet. I am most grateful.

57. Message from Johnson to Wilson, 11 November, 1965[109]

Your letter of August 5, 1965[110] refers to NATO planning involving storage of United States nuclear weapons in the United Kingdom for possible use by Netherlands ASW forces.

You state your willingness to cooperate in carrying out this plan and so to inform SACLANT, on the assumption that the nuclear weapons intended for

---

[107] LBJ Library, NSF, Head of State Correspondence File, Box 9, United Kingdom: Prime Minister Wilson Correspondence, Volume 2 [2 of 2], no. 130a.

[108] See 54, footnote 105.

[109] See TNA, PREM 13/3129.

[110] See 41. Although the State Department insisted that there was 'no sinister motive' behind the delay in Johnson's replies to Wilson's letters of 5 August regarding the use of nuclear weapons stored in the United Kingdom, Roger James of the Foreign Office smarted at the 'extraordinary lack of courtesy' (Letter from James to Oliver Wright, 18 November 1965, TNA, PREM 13/3129). A recently released memorandum by McGeorge Bundy indicates the reasons for the delay. Referring to Wilson's letters, he wrote: 'I think that the questions involved here are sufficiently fundamental to our nuclear arrangements with other countries that the President should not accept the Prime Minister's proposal until we have had an opportunity to consider its implications carefully' (Memorandum by Bundy for the Secretary of State and the Secretary of Defense, 3 Sept. 1965, LBJ Library, NSF, Subject File, '[MLF]—Mr Bundy: For 6 o'clock meeting Monday, 18 October,' Box 25.)

use by Netherlands ASW forces would not be released for use in advance of the joint decision on release for use to United States and British forces of United States ASW nuclear weapons also stored in the United Kingdom under the same NATO plan. I confirm that this assumption is correct.
Sincerely,
   Lyndon B. Johnson

58. Message from Johnson to Wilson, 11 November 1965[111]

Dear Mr. Prime Minister:
Your letter of August 5, 1965[112] proposes three amendments in the Memorandum setting forth the understandings between our Governments on consultation regarding use of nuclear weapons in order to bring the Memorandum into consonance with current NATO planning for use of nuclear weapons stored in the United Kingdom. The amendments would make it clear that all NATO-assigned or earmarked forces in the United Kingdom which are supported with United States nuclear weapons would be covered by the Memorandum instead of only those forces assigned to SACEUR.

I am agreeable to the amendments as proposed and hereby confirm that the Memorandum so amended sets forth accurately my view or our understandings on consultation and on the NATO forces coming within the scope of the consultation.
Sincerely,
   Lyndon B. Johnson

59. Message from Wilson to Johnson, 13 November 1965[113]

I have been much heartened by the message which you have sent to me through Secretary Rusk[114] and by the more than stalwart support which Arthur Goldberg gave to Michael Stewart in the Security Council yesterday.[115] We intend to see

---

[111] LBJ Library, NSF, Head of State Correspondence File, Box 9, United Kingdom: Prime Minister Wilson Correspondence, Volume 2 [2 of 2], no. 124.
[112] See 42.
[113] LBJ Library, NSF, Head of State Correspondence File, Box 9, United Kingdom: Prime Minister Wilson Correspondence, Volume 2 [2 of 2], no. 121.
[114] See 54, footnote 103.
[115] On 11 November 1965, Rhodesia declared UDI. The British government subsequently raised the matter at the UN Security Council, Foreign Secretary Stewart taking charge of presenting the British case.

this through whilst minimising so far as is possible the repercussions on our own and the free world's wider interests.

60. Message from Wilson to Johnson, 29 November 1965[116]

I was very glad to have a talk with Bob McNamara and George Ball last week about the various problems that confront us. I am much looking forward to discussing all these matters with you when we meet on December 17.

George Ball told me that you have now asked Gilpatric to return to your service to take charge of the whole of the Rhodesia operation. This is just to say that we should be very glad to see him just as soon as he has got his eye in.

On that subject, as you may know, Malcolm MacDonald has just spent a few days in Zambia with Kenneth Kaunda and has brought back with him a whole series of requests. Kenneth Kaunda, understandably, is in a very apprehensive and jumpy mood: He desperately wants to be sensible and statesmanlike but he is under great pressure from his own extremists who want him to take energetic but suicidal action against the Smith regime and from the Organization of African Unity who are pressing him to allow Zambia to be used as a base for African inspired operations against Rhodesia.

In these circumstances, he has asked me to provide a British military presence in Zambia. He has two requests: First, a detachment of British troops to take over and guard the Kariba installations on the Rhodesian side of the frontier and secondly an RAF presence in Zambia to deter the Rhodesia Air Force and to pre-empt the O.A.U. He also has made a great number of economic requests.

We considered these requests this morning. We decided to decline to mount the Kariba operation, not least because Smith may well have mined the installations and an operation by us might well accelerate what we want to avoid. We decided to meet the second request by sending a squadron of Javelins to Ndola. The operation, which has been planned on a contingency basis for some time, will start today and should be completed by Tuesday or Wednesday of this week. The Javelins will go into Ndola, the radar environment to Lusaka and men of the RAF regiment will go to both airfields and possibly to Livingstone as well to guard against sabotage etc. We shall thus be in occupation of all the main airfields in Zambia. We have made it a condition of acceding to this request that Zambia will invite no other foreign forces into the country without our agreement. At the same time H.M.S. Eagle, which sailed from Singapore some ten days ago, is off Dar-es-Salaam able to cover this operation, and provide a second strike in the highly unlikely case of its being necessary.

---

[116] LBJ Library, NSF, Head of State Correspondence File, Box 9, United Kingdom: Prime Minister Wilson Correspondence, Volume 2 [2 of 2], no. 118.

Let me make it quite plain that the purpose of this operation is entirely defensive. Its main purpose is to reassure Kaunda and pre-empt a hostile (e.g. Ghanaian or U.A.R.) African presence which might well develop communist overtones. It should also indicate to the Smith regime that we are in earnest and it should enable Kaunda to resist further pressures from the more extremist of his African friends who incidentally, seem to be the more extreme the further they are away from the scene. Kenyatta and Nyerere are both being very reasonable and moderate in this whole business. I do not expect that Smith will react violently, but we are ready for him if he does. Nor do I think that this will make him react on the copper front: This would be a two-edged weapon for him, and one of the rebel ministers on television only last night emphasized Rhodesia's interest in normal relations with Zambia.

But we are well aware that a defensive military presence in Zambia, valuable though it will be, will not of itself quell this rebellion. The economic measures which we and our friends have so far taken may well do the trick, but they will take time and will not start to bite until after Christmas. We have therefore decided to go for the quick economic kill. The Chancellor of the Exchequer will be turning the financial screw more tightly: We shall add all agricultural commodities, minerals and metals to tobacco and sugar on the list of prohibited imports and hope that all other importing countries will do the same. Sir N. Kipping, former Director-General of the F.B.I., has been out to Zambia, and has a plan for replacing Zambia's imports from Rhodesia from other sources. We shall also want to talk to the principal suppliers about cutting out exports to Rhodesia of economically important commodities.

There remains the question of oil sanctions. Here action by Britain alone, even if it were thought desirable, would not be effective without international backing. This is a subject which we want to discuss with your people in the first instance, and discuss very quickly, so I hope you will agree to send Gilpatric to talk to George Brown, who is in charge of the whole economic side of our operations, as soon as possible. Meanwhile we shall take advantage of the presence here of Tom Mann to talk all these measures over with him as well as the contingency plans to keep Zambia going if relations between her and Rhodesia deteriorate.

Overriding everything is my awareness which I know that Kenneth Kaunda shares, that unless we in Britain deal promptly with this rebellion and if possible without force, there is a danger of a racial war in Africa with all that that means for the free world. It is therefore encouraging that not only Kaunda, but Kenyatta, Nyerere and Obote as well, should be taking the view that it is only the presence of British forces in Central Africa which can avert this catastrophe.

You will, of course, realize the relevance of all this to our East of Suez role, on which McNamara will no doubt report to you.

61. Message from Wilson to Johnson, 6 December 1965[117]

Judging by the press reports here you were as surprised as we were at the rise in your discount rate yesterday. If so, I need not to rub in the point that this was a matter of considerable interest to us, just as changes in our rate are of interest to you. We always try to consult your people in advance of changes in our bank rate, especially when the movement is upwards. I should be grateful if you would take account in your general consideration of the change made of the fact that this time we were not consulted.

62. Message from Johnson to Wilson, 8 December 1965[118]

Thank you very much for your thoughtful message on the Rhodesian situation.[119] I cannot express too strongly my admiration for the calm but forceful way you have taken personal responsibility of this complex and difficult problem.

Within the limits imposed on us by Vietnam, we intend to give our utmost support for your efforts to reach an acceptable solution in Rhodesia. As you know, our people are tightening the economic noose. We have established administrative machinery for controls on exports and will put these into effect in tandem with yours. We are asking our importers to restrict the shipment of Rhodesian goods to our shores, though the total value of these imports last year amounted to only $11 million. We will recognise the authority of the newly appointed Board of Governors of the Rhodesian Bank. And we are prepared to talk with our oil companies about the termination of shipments to Rhodesia, depending on the outcome of your analysis of this particular dilemma.

We all hope that these measures will produce the desired objective. At the moment, however, we here feel that it is hard to be certain of favourable results in a short period of time. Because of this, we are convinced that the maintenance of Zambia-Katanga copper exports must take a high place in our planning. Our long-term interests indicate that the only sensible course of action is that which avoids strangling the Zambian economy and dislocating world copper markets for any substantial period of time.

The efforts involved and the possible dangers, both economic and political, are so great that I think we should, as you suggest, arrange to have our people get together before our meeting on December 17. Although Roswell Gilpatric

---

[117] LBJ Library, NSF, Head of State Correspondence File, Box 9, United Kingdom: Prime Minister Wilson Correspondence, Volume 2 [2 of 2], no. 115.

[118] LBJ Library, NSF, Head of State Correspondence File, Box 9, United Kingdom: Prime Minister Wilson Correspondence, Volume 2 [2 of 2], no. 112.

[119] See 60.

will not be available for this, George Ball has himself organized a group within his own office at the State Department which is acting as a focal point for the Rhodesian situation. They are presently discussing with your representative measures in East Africa and at the UN in the coming weeks and going over the Rhodesian items to come up at our meeting—to which I look forward with great pleasure.[120]

63. Message from Johnson to Wilson, 8 December 1965[121]

Thank you for your message on our interest rate change.[122] I agree with you, and express my regret.

64. Message from Wilson to Johnson, 12 December 1965[123]

I have received the message from Ambassador Bruce about President Ayub Khan's discussions with you next week.

I had a long talk with Ayub Khan on Saturday morning before receiving Ambassador Bruce's message, and had in fact without knowing exactly what line you would be taking spoken to him very closely on the lines of your message. I had told him that so far as Britain was concerned, and I felt the U.S. would take the same line, we could not take sides in the sub-continent on the Kashmir issue but would do anything in our power, provided there was good will on both sides, to secure a solution. I had also suggested to him that, while I had not been in touch with you in any way and was only speculating about your views, the U.S. would be very impatient of any long drawn out attack on the Indian position. I also said that I felt that you would be equally impatient when Mr. Shastri comes if he were to subject you to a long attack on Pakistan.

Equally I warned him very strongly that both we and you were very concerned about the Pakistan drift into the Chinese orbit. I felt, and told him this, that the U.S. would be extremely intolerant of any situation in which either India or Pakistan felt that they could waste their substance in riotous armament expenditure and count on American agricultural production to keep their population alive. I pointed out what I have heard that on present trends American food shipments to the sub-continent by 1970 could represent half of

---

[120] Wilson visited Washington between 16 and 18 December 1965.
[121] LBJ Library, NSF, Head of State Correspondence File, Box 9, United Kingdom: Prime Minister Wilson Correspondence, Volume 2 [2 of 2], no. 109.
[122] See 61.
[123] Bodleian Library, Oxford, Wilson Papers, MS. Wilson c. 1581, folios 295–301.

total American food production: in other words, that every ton of food produced by your farmers for American consumption would be matched by another ton produced for consumption in the sub-continent, supplied not on commercial terms but in the words of the immortal Isaiah without money and without price. Clearly no American government could envisage such a development, particularly if India and Pakistan were inhibiting their own economic developments and food production programmes through a concentration on self-destructive armaments. Criticising him for having at India's moment of mortal danger when faced with Chinese attack three years ago,[124] I condemned him for what we all felt that Pakistan was prepared to do—to make mischief at India's expense by linking with China.

I received Ambassador Bruce's message only after he had left me on Saturday morning, but I took the opportunity of a dinner party for Ayub to take him aside and speak to him for over an hour alone. I repeat the word alone because I believe that while he, Ayub, is basically sound he is subject to strong pressures from his advisers, particularly Bhutto, whom I regard as one of the most evil men god ever created. Ayub, and I am glad you take this view, is a man of great integrity but he is basically a simple and deeply patriotic soldier and capable of being pushed around by unscrupulous politicians of the Bhutto variety. I spent the hour rehearsing him in the realities of the discussions he will be undertaking in Washington with you, using of course the material which Ambassador Bruce had given me.

He took all this extremely well. He does not intend to bore you with a long recital of India's sins. He does not, I think, want to argue about alleged inconsistencies in American policy and I think I have satisfied him that United States policy has been consistent, is deeply concerned with Pakistan's well being on the basis of neutrality between India and Pakistan, but has to take account of strong feelings in Congress and American public opinion that it is unrealistic to keep Pakistan afloat by massive aid programmes at the very time when Pakistan appears to be moving into the Chinese orbit and is not above snide criticisms of American policy both in relation to the sub-continent and more widely.

Ayub took these points very much on board. He stressed to me last night, as he had done in the morning, that a Pakistan is a small country with three very large neighbours. First, Russia, who though not immediately contiguous is at one point only 17 miles away. Second, India, which while we may think of little account militarily is regarded by Ayub as a permanent military threat as a country now determined to obliterate Pakistan's independent existence. Third, China. I think Ayub is probably genuine about this but I am not sure that all his closest advisers are.

---

[124] Wilson is referring to the Sino–India conflict of October–November 1962 over a contested Himalayan border.

Ayub stressed more than once he and he alone was responsible for bringing Pakistan into the system of Western alliances,[125] to some extend in the face of critical Pakistani public opinion. I think he wants to continue on this basis but he stressed that public opinion in Pakistan is strongly anti-American and my colleagues received evidence of this from other Pakistan ministers accompanying him during the period while I was speaking to Ayub alone. I expressed to Ayub very frankly my anxieties about Bhutto. He took this very well but said that Bhutto does represent public opinion in Pakistan. I suggested that Bhutto was playing on these feelings rather than representing them and was, to some extent, creating them. I said that we regarded Ayub as the boss in Pakistan. We were convinced of his integrity and loyalty but that our attitude so far as the U.K. was concerned would be very much changed if he were ever replaced by Pakistani politicians of the Bhutto variety. I indicated that this might be the American view also. He spoke somewhat deprecatingly of Bhutto's intrinsic significance but kept on repeating that he represented a powerful strain of pro-Chinese and representative opinion.

There is no doubt that he will enter these talks with you convinced, as I have told him that they are of historic significance believing perhaps for the first time after my talk that they will be conducted with the utmost good will on your side and recognising that they will be productive if they are conducted only in the context of the bilateral U.S./Pakistan relationship and not in the hope of invoking American assistance in the struggle with India on the Kashmir question.

Since he profoundly believes that India, which he regards as an inchoate and disordered political system, is determined to destroy Pakistan, anything you can say on the lines indicated to me by Ambassador Bruce, that you are concerned with their national integrity, will be of the highest value. I think I have pushed him off any idea that what he will be discussing with you is the Kashmir situation and he responded to our views on this by not pressing unduly the Kashmir problem on us. I stressed that we were concerned with the implementation of the Security Council resolution of September 20 and I do not think he will be surprised if you lay your main emphasis so far as Kashmir is concerned on this aspect of the question. I urged him to not to underrate the importance of the fact that India is now moving into a pre-election situation which will not be resolved until after their election in 1967. I emphasized that these elections would be conducted without the presence of the father-figure of Nehru and that Shastri was bound to be responsive to the almost intolerable pressures of visceral, irrational Indian politics, amongst which we must not underrate the importance of anti-British and anti-American lobbies.

Both in the morning and in my evening discussion, he stressed the importance of a coherent Anglo-American approach to these problems. He

---

[125] Pakistan was a member of both SEATO and CENTO.

is going to Tashkent but is no more optimistic about the prospects there than we are. He was a little sore that we, that is Britain and the United States, or alternatively Britain and the Commonwealth, had not taken an earlier initiative. I explained that we were at great pains to ensure that U Thant's and the overriding Security Council initiative should have the right of way. And that when Russia took an initiative we could hardly object, but that we were not going to set up competing mediatory efforts. I think that if Tashkent fails,[126] which is likely since Kosygin will do no more than act as host, we may have to consider whether there should be a new initiative either by the United States with strong British support or possibly within the Commonwealth. This, however, we can leave until after Tashkent and I shall have the chance to discuss these matters with you next week.

Independent mediation is probably not the answer. I still recall the traumatic experience at the Rann of Kutch negotiations, which probably provided the right technique for a solution though in that case we were dealing with a stretch of unoccupied territory under water most of the year, whose only significance related to military patrolling rights and to the element of face involved in these rights. Kashmir on the contrary, apart from its historic significance, involves the rights of many millions of human beings of strong political and indeed religious views. Pakistan cannot relinquish their claims on behalf of the Kashmir people and there are United Nations resolutions which they can quote. Equally India is concerned with Kashmir, partly on military grounds because of their communications with the Chinese border, but equally because they feel that any concession here would mean the beginning of the break-up of the Indian Union.

My private talk with Ayub ended with a strong reiteration on my part of what I said to him earlier that neither Pakistani interests nor world peace could ever be served by a situation in which Pakistan moved into the Chinese sphere of influence and India into the Russian. It ended equally with a strong assertion on his part, and he went so far as to ask me to communicate this to you, that he was uniquely and unpopularly responsible for the identification of Pakistan with our alliances and that he was under the strongest pressure at the present time on these matters.

We have to remember that Ayub, whom I regard as a man of great integrity, but essentially a patriotic man whose horizons are to some extent limited by his military background, is greatly concerned with the question of arms supplies. India is a much more powerful country and has her own internal means of arms manufacture and the prospect of substantial Soviet supplies. It is to our joint interest and indeed in the interest of world peace that Pakistan should

---

[126] An attempt at the beginning of 1966 to create a more permanent settlement of the Indo-Pakistan conflict, especially over Kashmir, was undertaken in the Uzbek capital of Tashkent.

not become dependent on Chinese supplies and I feel that his pressure on you in respect of supplies of military equipment will become a test of the value to Pakistan of the Pakistan/U.S. relationship and equally a test of the value of their continued membership of the alliances in which we are concerned.

I have dictated this message to you in great frankness after saying goodnight to Ayub.

Thinking it over, I believe my description of Bhutto is probably an understatement. I am extremely pleased to hear that the likelihood is that you will be talking to Ayub alone, and the extent to which you can be as frank as I am sure you hope and intend to be depends on the absence from your talks of some of his closet associates. But as I have emphasized to him 20 times tonight, he is the boss and anything you and I can do to bring this home to him, and to emphasize that his relations with you as with us depend on him staying boss, is of fundamental importance.

I look forward to resuming this discussion with you next week after your talks with Ayub have been concluded.

65. Message from Johnson to Wilson, 12 December 1965[127]

I am immensely grateful for your candid message of last night on your sessions with Ayub.[128] The vigorous way you dealt with the matter will certainly make my job much easier.[129] I too will emphasize to Ayub that he is the one leader we can most trust in Pakistan and that we hope he will stay in the saddle. We can discuss this Pak-Indian tangle further when you come here next week.

66. Message from Wilson to Johnson, 17 December 1965[130]

I should just like to confirm the position about the Asian Development Bank. I have spoken on telephone to the Chancellor of the Exchequer and I am, more than happy to say, in the light of our discussion and my talk with Mr. George

---

[127] LBJ Library, NSF, Head of State Correspondence File, Box 9, United Kingdom: Prime Minister Wilson Correspondence, Volume 2 [2 of 2], no. 103.

[128] See 64.

[129] Johnson had discussions in Washington with Ayub on 14 and 15 December 1965. Johnson subsequently told his advisers that he 'felt that good groundwork for the visit had been laid by Prime Minister Wilson' (Record of a meeting, 15 December 1965, *FRUS, 1964–1968*: Volume XXV, *South Asia* (Washington, DC: US Government Printing Office, 2000), p. 513).

[130] LBJ Library, NSF, Head of State Correspondence File, Box 9, United Kingdom: Prime Minister Wilson Correspondence, Volume 2 [2 of 2], no. 101.

Ball, that we shall be providing a total of $30 million to the Asian Development Bank,[131] as our contribution to the work of this most valuable and imaginative venture in economic advance in Asia.

67. Message from Johnson to Wilson, 18 December 1965[132]

Dear Mr. Prime Minister:
It has been a pleasure to talk with you. Our friendship is a source of great comfort to me. And the friendship between our peoples continues to be a source of invaluable strength for the Free World.

I look forward to meeting with you again. In the meantime I wish you well in the difficult task which you and your Government now face.

Mrs. Johnson joins me in sending Mrs. Wilson and you our best wishes for a safe journey home.
Sincerely,
Lyndon B. Johnson

68. Message from Johnson to Wilson, 21 December 1965[133]

Dear Mr. Prime Minister:
I am grateful indeed for your note of December 18 about the Asian Development Bank.[134] Your understanding and support for this undertaking is a great encouragement to me, and I can assure you that I will certainly make best use I can of your decision in my talk with Chancellor Erhard.

Let me say again how much I enjoyed our meeting. I think our talks were good for both our countries and for the great purpose they share.

---

[131] The Asian Development Bank had been an initiative strongly supported by Johnson. The charter for the bank was signed in Manila in 4 December 1965. The bank itself provided loans for development projects and technical assistance (see Lyndon Baines Johnson, *Vantage Point: Perspectives of the Presidency, 1963–1969* (London: Weidenfeld and Nicolson, 1971), pp. 356–7).

[132] LBJ Library, NSF, Head of State Correspondence File, Box 9, United Kingdom: Prime Minister Wilson Correspondence, Volume 2 [2 of 2], no. 97.

[133] LBJ Library, NSF, Head of State Correspondence File, Box 9, United Kingdom: Prime Minister Wilson Correspondence, Volume 2 [2 of 2], no. 95.

[134] See 66. This message was actually dated 17 December.

69. Message from Wilson to Johnson, 22 December 1965[135]

Very many thanks for your letter of 20 December which your Embassy here has delivered to me.[136] The warmth of your message reinforced the tremendous encouragement I received from our meeting. On my return, I found great satisfaction in Britain that we were so close together.

Clearly, we have a lot of hard work ahead. Nevertheless I am sure we shall come out right in the end so long as we work in partnership; if we can persuade our other allies to join us in the great tasks facing the free world, so much the better.

My wife joins me in sending you and Mrs. Johnson our best wishes for 1966. With warm regards,
Harold Wilson

70. Message from Johnson to Wilson, 23 December 1965[137]

Dear Mr. Prime Minister:
I have just completed a day and a half of meetings with Chancellor Erhard in which we have had a good opportunity to talk not merely about the problems presently occupying the German leaders, but also the need for the Federal Republic to play a role in world affairs more nearly commensurate with its resources.

In the course of our discussion the Chancellor presented the case for Germany's participation in some form of collective nuclear defense—a question on which his Government is placing considerable emphasis. In order to make clear the nature of the German interest he gave me a memorandum, a copy of which, with his permission, I am enclosing.[138]

As you will note, the Chancellor has come down squarely on the side of a "hardware solution." I know of your own reservations about this matter and I have taken them into account in my discussions with the Chancellor. I have explained to him that the point of greatest importance was for the three of us to reach an agreement that could form the basis for the possible participation of other powers.

The proposals presented by the Chancellor will give me some problems with Congress, and I am sure they will not be easy for you. But what is essential is a

---

[135] LBJ Library, NSF, Head of State Correspondence File, Box 9, United Kingdom: Prime Minister Wilson Correspondence, Volume 2 [2 of 2], no. 92a.

[136] See 68. The letter is actually dated 21 December.

[137] LBJ Library, NSF, Head of State Correspondence File, Box 9, United Kingdom: Prime Minister Wilson Correspondence, Volume 2 [2 of 2], no. 87.

[138] Not printed.

stable and healthy Germany that can play a constructive role on the side of the West. On balance it seems to me that you and I should make a serious effort to respond to the German proposals as the Chancellor has broadly outlined them in his memorandum.

The nuclear force he describes would appear to fall within the broad framework of your ANF proposal. Unlike the MLF,[139] it would not contemplate the creation of a new weapons system. From our discussion, it would appear that the Chancellor and his Ministers have been generally thinking in terms of an assignment by the United Kingdom of its Polaris submarines and a matching contribution of Polaris submarines by the United States. These submarines would form the basic elements of the force, which might be added to later. It is our impression that the questions of mixed-manning, veto rights, and a "European clause" can be worked out in a manner consistent both with your requirements and ours.

I think it important that we move ahead on this expeditiously since the matter has been so long in limbo. I would hope, therefore, that Ambassador Bruce might have a talk with you when he returns to London about the middle of January. He will bring with him suggestions as to the best way to carry on the necessary discussions among our three Governments in as quiet a manner as possible. Meanwhile, I should greatly appreciate your comments on this development.

Let me say again how good it was to see you and how much pleasure and profit I derived from our conversations. We must keep closely in touch.
Sincerely,
Lyndon B. Johnson

---

[139] The Multilateral Force represented an attempt by the US to divert German ambitions for a national nuclear force by giving Germany a role in the use of nuclear weapons. It also sought to limit the independence of the nuclear weapons already possessed by Europe's nuclear powers, France and Britain. The MLF was to consist of a multinational force with nuclear armed warships manned by multinational crews. It remained unpopular with British policy-makers, the Chief of the Defence Staff, Lord Mountbatten, dismissing it as 'the greatest piece of military nonsense he had come across in fifty years' (Kristan Stoddart, *Losing an Empire and Finding a Role: Britain, the USA, NATO and Nuclear Weapons, 1964–70* (Basingstoke: Palgrave Macmillan, 2012), p. 66). Shortly after achieving office Wilson produced his own variant, named the Atlantic Nuclear Force (ANF) under which Britain would commit its nuclear forces, including Polaris submarines, to the ANF for the duration of NATO. The British also looked to the US to commit an equivalent number of Polaris submarines to the ANF. The Polaris submarines, however, would be nationally, not mixed, manned (Saki Dockrill, *Britain's Retreat from East of Suez: The Choice between Europe and the World?* (Basingstoke: Palgrave, 2002), p. 60).

71. Message from Wilson to Johnson, 24 December 1965[140]

May I congratulate you most warmly on the Christmas truce in Vietnam. I am sure that this will greatly strengthen the realisation by world opinion of your desire to take any opportunity of halting the conflict there. The sad thing is, of course, that the truce is limited strictly to thirty hours, though we must all hope that it will go on longer than that. I am sure that it will have occurred to you that there would be great advantage in the first shot after the truce being fired by the other side.

I much appreciate the messages you have sent me since our talks in Washington last week.[141]
Very best wishes for Christmas and for the New Year.
Yours sincerely
Harold Wilson
P.S. I have just seen your message about your talks with Chancellor Erhard.[142] I am most grateful for this full account and will reply as soon as I have had a chance to reflect on it.

72. Message from Johnson to Wilson, 29 December 1965[143]

As I told you during our visit I have been giving every possible thought to the ways and means by which we might bring peace in Viet-Nam. For sometime the Soviet Union and some Eastern European governments have hinted that the major impediment to any diplomatic initiatives on their part was our bombing of North Vietnam and they implied that if the bombing were suspended for a while they might be prepared to make efforts to bring Hanoi into line. However, none of the governments has given us the slightest assurance of any specific action that might follow a suspension of bombing.

Nevertheless I have concluded that I should test the seriousness of these Communist hints to see if some progress toward peace could be made.

We have stood down bombing of North Viet-Nam since Christmas Eve and I intend to continue the suspension for some days. We are advising the governments of the USSR, Poland and Hungary that, barring a major provocation, the suspension of bombing will continue beyond the New Year. I

---

[140] TNA, PREM 13/621.
[141] See 67 and 68.
[142] See 70.
[143] LBJ Library, NSF, Head of State Correspondence File, Box 9, United Kingdom: Prime Minister Wilson Correspondence, Volume 2 [2 of 2], no. 82.

am taking steps to have the word passed directly to the regime in Hanoi through our Ambassador in Rangoon.

I have no great hope that anything useful will come out of this, but I do not want to leave any stone unturned in the search for peace. Obviously, we can make no commitments publicly or privately that would limit our freedom of action in the event of a major contingency or serious provocation. By the same token, I do not wish to commit myself now to any specific date for resumption.

We shall, of course, continue our air, ground and sea operations in South Viet-Nam and some reconnaissance of North Viet-Nam.

In furtherance of this initiative I am sending Ambassador Goldberg to Rome to see the Pope and am also sending Ambassador Harriman to Warsaw to see what can be developed there. While there will undoubtedly be considerable speculation stemming from our continued stand-down of the bombing we do not propose to make any public announcement at this time.

I did not want to take this action without your being fully informed. The whole story is known to only a handful of my top advisors and I would appreciate it if you would treat this information as a matter to be closely held between the two of us.

Of course, I should greatly appreciate any advice that you might have and steps that you might feel you could usefully take. This is an enterprise that has the greatest importance for the peoples of the Free World.
Sincerely,

73. Message from Wilson to Johnson, 31 December 1965[144]

I was very glad to receive your message of December 29 about your renewed efforts to seek peace in Vietnam.[145] I am sure that you are right to make this attempt, however discouraging the North Vietnamese attitude still appears, and I shall be most interested to hear whether there is any reaction from the other side. Indeed, I have already asked your Embassy in London whether either Goldberg or Harriman could find time to stop in London on their way back and give me a personal account. It is most helpful to us to be kept in such close touch with what you are doing in Vietnam and I am most grateful.

You asked whether I had any suggestions to offer or whether I thought there were any steps the British government could usefully take, so I am letting you have the following comments at once. If anything further occurs to us, I will let you know later.

---

[144] LBJ Library, NSF, Head of State Correspondence File, Box 9, United Kingdom: Prime Minister Wilson Correspondence, Volume 2 [2 of 2], no. 80.

[145] See 72.

First of all, though we know that your Ambassador in Rangoon is bringing the pause in the bombing to the notice of the North Vietnamese, you might think it helpful if our Consul-General in Hanoi were instructed to do the same and take advantage of this to start negotiations. If, as we both fear, the North Vietnamese prove intransigent, it might be as well to have it on record that they were approached through every possible channel.

Secondly Her Majesty's Ambassador at Moscow might simultaneously be instructed to remind the Soviet government that, on numerous occasions in the past, Soviet representatives had described American bombing of North Vietnam as an obstacle to negotiations. Now that this obstacle had been temporarily removed, Her Majesty's Government remained in favour of a Geneva Conference and would like to know whether the Soviet government now saw any scope for any new joint move by the co-chairmen.

Thirdly, there is the question of the forthcoming Shelepin mission to Hanoi. Though we have no evidence about the precise purpose of this mission, we think it may be of special importance, because we have the impression that the Soviet government want to isolate China and eventually to bring North Vietnam to the conference table. Subject to appropriate safeguards about duration and the absence of provocation from the North, we believe it would be in the interests of the U.S. government to extend the present pause in bombing of North Vietnam so as to cover the period of Shelepin's visit. I wonder, too, whether you would consider addressing a special message to Mr. Kosygin, expressing the hope that the Shelepin delegation would use its influence in Hanoi in the interests of peace through negotiations.

Fourthly, though this will doubtless have occurred to you already, we think it would be a mistake to attempt any approach to the Chinese (for instance through your contact in Warsaw) at present, because this would only diminish the impact of anything said to the Russians.

Finally, I have one more general point. This is that we in the West can easily under-estimate the time required by communists, particularly such relatively unsophisticated and suspicious communists as the North Vietnamese, to take stock of a new development, to argue it out among themselves, to consult their allies and to communicate a new decision to their forces in South Vietnam. In so far as the pause in your bombing of the North is a factor that really might induce the North Vietnamese to change their minds, I am sure that this process will take longer to operate than would ever be the case in the free and flexible organisation of Western governments. Always provided, therefore, that there is no major new provocation from the other side, you may think that the wisest course, taking into account the vast costs and risks involved in stepping up the war, would be to prolong the bombing pause at least until January 23, the end of the Vietnamese new year festival for which the Viet Cong have allegedly offered a further truce. I realise how difficult such a decision would be for you, but I do think the slowness and rigidity of communist thinking provides a genuine and practical argument in its favour.

74. Message from Johnson to Wilson, 31 December 1965[146]

Thank you for your helpful message of today about Viet-Nam[147] and your interest in seeing Ambassador Goldberg tomorrow. I am sure that your discussion with him will be useful to us both.

Regarding your suggestions 1 and 2, I see no objection. Indeed, I have no doubt but that a number of governments are now in communication with Hanoi and Moscow. Britain's role as co-chairman would give your views special significance.

As for your third point, it occurs to me that you as co-chairman might be in a better position to explore the significance of the Shelepin visit than we are. The Soviets have not mentioned this mission to us and have not responded to informal inquiries about it. It is our impression that their mission was planned prior to official information from us as to the suspension of bombing and occurred because of an invitation from Hanoi. In addition, we sense that the Soviets want to avoid any appearance whatsoever of "working with us" against their communist brothers in order to keep greater freedom of action in their communist world and to present less of a target to the Chinese communists who already refer to them publicly as U.S. agents.

Your fourth point is well taken and we agree. We have not attempted to engage the Chinese in discussions on this matter since our latest conversations with them in mid-December continued to reflect a very harsh attitude on their part.

On your general questions on the duration of suspension of bombing, it is not our desire to be impatient since we are seriously probing the possibilities of peace. It is not easy to make a flat commitment because of the possibility of major military actions by the other side. Further, we may be faced with a completely categorical, public and negative response in which case we would have to review our position. But I should be glad to keep in touch with you on this matter as the situation develops.

I appreciate your sending me your comments at once and any further views you have would be most welcome.

---

[146] LBJ Library, NSF, Head of State Correspondence File, Box 9, United Kingdom: Prime Minister Wilson Correspondence, Volume 2 [2 of 2], no. 77.

[147] See 73.

75. Message from Wilson to Johnson, 1 January 1966[148]

I have just had a very useful hour discussion with Arthur Goldberg. I was most grateful for his comprehensive survey of the peace initiative in all its forms.

We discussed one or two possible further steps and he will no doubt be reporting to you direct on the suggestions I have made. I have emphasised that in anything we do we want to keep in the closest touch with you direct. For the time being we shall be in more or less hourly contact with your embassy here.

76. Message from Wilson to Johnson, 5 January 1966[149]

Dear Mr. President,

Thank you for sending me in your message of December 23 such a full account of your discussions with Chancellor Erhard on nuclear questions.[150] It was very good of you to send me the text of the memorandum handed to you by the Chancellor in Washington. I have also received a message from Professor Erhard, who is obviously pleased with his talks with you.

I entirely agree with you about the need for a stable and healthy Germany, playing a constructive part in the Western community, and for nuclear arrangements in the alliance which command the support of our three governments and are acceptable to other parties.

As you say, some of the German proposals are likely to give rise to difficulties for both of us. I will not enter into details of these now. But I agreed that we should respond by giving the proposals joint consideration as expeditiously as possible. I shall look forward to discussing all this with Ambassador Bruce on his return.

At the same time I am sure that it is right to press forward with the work of the NATO Special Committee. When the Nuclear Planning Working Group set up by the Committee has its first meeting, I am glad to see that the first item on its agenda is to be a discussion, to which the German Government will contribute a paper, on the questions to which the non-nuclear members of the alliance attach importance. This should give an ideal opportunity for the German Government to describe their problems and for the Group as a whole to discuss how best they can be met consistently with the general interest.

I have been sorry to hear of Herr von Hassel's illness. But I hope that this will not hold up the meeting of the Nuclear Planning Working Group unduly.

---

[148] TNA, PREM 13/1074.

[149] LBJ Library, NSF, Head of State Correspondence File, Box 9, United Kingdom: Prime Minister Wilson Correspondence, Volume 2 [2 of 2], no. 75a.

[150] See 70.

It seems to me vitally important that we should keep up the momentum of the Special Committee and show that we are seriously tackling this nuclear problem and working to strengthen the cohesion of the alliance.

My hope which I believe you share, is that the Special Committee will result in the establishment of a permanent body for reaching collective decisions on the nuclear policies of the alliance. It is only by continuing consultation that we can achieve a common policy and remove such desires as may exist for less desirable solutions. The exact form and functions of such a continuing body can only be settled by discussion within the alliance. But whatever arrangements eventually emerge, it is of the highest importance that they should be seen to be non-discriminatory, and I am glad to hear you say that the creation of a new weapons system is no longer contemplated. Possible ways of reorganising existing weapons systems might be a suitable subject for consideration by the Special Committee or a successor body.

Yours sincerely,
Harold Wilson

77. Message from Wilson to Johnson, 7 January 1966[151]

Before I set off for this rather extraordinary Commonwealth meeting at Lagos,[152] I thought I would let you know how I see things developing in Rhodesia. I need hardly tell you that I have very considerable qualms about going: but I have decided that it would be more harmful to absent myself than to be present. Faced with this choice of evils, I have decided it was right to go: first, because I think it is in all our interests to try and keep the Commonwealth together and secondly because I am sure that we must do all we can to maintain the prestige and standing of moderate African leaders like Abubakar.

When we last met I told you that I thought that the euphoria of independence and of Christmas would carry the Smith regime over into the New Year, and that they would thereafter start to suffer from post-hogmanay gloom. Thanks to your Administration's ready agreement to join with us in an oil embargo and to help us with a consequential airlift to Zambia and to fairly general support throughout the free world for what we are doing, this is precisely what is now happening. With the introduction of petrol rationing, the dolce vita of the European population is starting to come to an end. Responsible business leaders

---

[151] LBJ Library, NSF, Head of State Correspondence File, Box 9, United Kingdom: Prime Minister Wilson Correspondence, Volume 2 [2 of 2], no. 72.
[152] A Commonwealth conference was held in Lagos on 11–12 January 1966 to discuss Rhodesia (see Harold Wilson, *The Labour Government, 1964–1970: A Personal Record* (London: Wiedenfeld and Nicolson, 1971), pp. 193–6).

are forecasting considerable European unemployment before long. Added to that there is severe drought in Matebeleland where the maize harvest has failed (though this throws up further problems) which we are looking into. Two Johannesburg papers, originally pro-Smith, are now saying he cannot win: the South African Government is cautiously neutral and the Portuguese seem to be hedging their bets.

As economic difficulties begin to press upon the regime, I think we shall find that, administratively, they will not have the experience or competence to deal with it. Indeed, the evidence is now starting to accumulate that many thinking people in Rhodesia realize that the Smith regime cannot win. It is only a matter of time before more and more people come to realize that life can only get worse and that the alternative of returning to constitutional rule is better than any prospect that Smith has got to offer. It is tempting but unwise to try and put a date to the turning point, and I will not attempt to do so: but I personally am convinced that it will come and that it could come sooner than we think.

I am therefore totally convinced, privately, that we have Smith on the run, and that it will not be long before this becomes clear publicly. It may soon be wise to start thinking of peace terms. While we want to bring Smith down and bring him down quickly, we must be able to discredit Smith utterly if we are to make sense of the reconstruction period. There can be no question of negotiating with Smith as equals. But this does not mean that we should not be thinking of methods of restoring the rule of law in Rhodesia and we are hard at work on this. As soon as our ideas are clearer I will be in touch with you again. Any public announcement of our peace aims will need very careful timing: I cannot afford to lose my African audience by giving them any reason to think that we are weakening in our resolve to bring Smith down: equally I must make a statement early enough to give the Europeans hope for better things if they reject Smith. The problem of my four constituencies is always with me.

The next immediate hurdle is of course the Lagos meeting. Now that, with your help, and with that of all our allies and friends, sanctions are clearly beginning to bite, I am more hopeful of being able to turn discussion into constructive channels than I was when Abubakar first made his proposal and visited London before Christmas.

I shall have to give our Commonwealth partners a very frank account of what we are doing and try to make them share my own conviction that this rebellion will be brought to heel. There will also be some talk about Zambia's problems. I shall, moreover, have to listen to some fairly severe lectures on the need to introduce one man one vote at the earliest possible moment. But I am resolved not to give way to demands for the use of force at once and I shall at this stage be able to do no more than listen to their advice about how to handle matters in the future. It would be fatal to spell out in detail our ideas for constitutional development. It would be bound to offend one or more of my constituencies. If

I can keep the Africans quiet for a few more weeks and avoid senseless action in the Organization of African Unity and embarrassing initiatives in the United Nations the visit will have been worthwhile.

I will let you know how I get on and keep you in touch with my thinking for the future. My people were in touch with yours about the details of current strategy and tactics. I am much encouraged by your resolute support. We shall win.

78. Message from Wilson to Johnson, 7 January 1966[153]

In my earlier message today,[154] I mentioned that drought in Rhodesia was presenting Smith with problems and might have repercussions on ourselves.

My colleagues and I discussed this further this morning and it is clear that the drought is prevalent throughout Central Africa. We have, therefore, decided that it would be right, on humanitarian grounds, to prevent starvation leading to rioting and bloodshed to see what we can do to help. As we are proposing to press sanctions on Rhodesia on other fields, we might appear to be inconsistent: but I think that opinion generally would draw the necessary distinction.

I have, therefore, this morning been in contact by telephone with Bob Menzies and Mike Pearson and we have agreed to look into the possibilities of a joint Commonwealth initiative to relieve the famine. If wheat is a suitable substitute for the failure of maize, then both Australia and Canada will be able to help from their own stocks: we should of course make a financial contribution. If maize is essential, then we may have to make this a combined operation bringing you in. But you have done so much already that we shall not do so unless it is absolutely necessary. I know that famine in India is in all our minds.

I shall be letting it be known, informally, this afternoon that Menzies, Pearson and I are in touch on this problem.

79. Message from Johnson to Wilson, 7 January 1966[155]

It was most considerate of you to share your thoughts on the Rhodesia crisis again on the eve of your departure for Lagos.[156] We on this side certainly appreciate the delicacy of the situation you face, as well as the problem of supplying Zambia

---

[153] LBJ Library, NSF, Head of State Correspondence File, Box 9, United Kingdom: Prime Minister Wilson Correspondence, Volume 2 [2 of 2], no. 70.

[154] See 77.

[155] LBJ Library, NSF, Head of State Correspondence File, Box 9, United Kingdom: Prime Minister Wilson Correspondence, Volume 2 [2 of 2], no. 68.

[156] See 77.

while applying sanctions to the Smith regime. After your meeting in Lagos, we shall look forward to getting your latest estimates and plans. There may be serious difficulties ahead, particularly as to whether the African states will sit still long enough to permit sanctions to bring Smith down.
My best wishes for every success at Lagos.
Sincerely,
   Lyndon B. Johnson

80. Message from Wilson to Johnson, 11 January 1966[157]

In my last message on the Rhodesian problem I said I would keep you informed about how I get on in Lagos.[158] Now that I am here, I am hopeful that with a modicum of luck we should get through this meeting all right. But having spoken to Malcolm MacDonald, who is here from Lusaka, it appears that the situation in Zambia is far from good. I have therefore decided, at very considerable inconvenience that it would be right for me to pay a brief visit to Kaunda to try to get him on the rails again.

   2. The facts of the situation are these. At the right moment, the closing of the Zambia border with Rhodesia could be of decisive influence in giving Smith a coup de grace but it is essential that this card should be played at the right time. If it is played too early before the Smith regime and Rhodesian opinion are convinced that the game is up and before we have taken all the necessary steps to see that Zambia could survive the few weeks of final collapse in Rhodesia and possible cut off of supplies from the copper belt, this key move in the whole process could ruin Zambia without overthrowing Smith. The timing is therefore of the essence. Kaunda, who is understandably, in a very nervous frame of mind, is threatening to close the border before we are ready for it, before he can survive it and before it will be really effective in terms of bringing Smith down.

   3. My main objective in going to Lusaka will be therefore to try and steady him and to get our strategy better co-ordinated. There are in addition other things to discuss with him. I plan to be in Zambia on Wednesday evening and Thursday morning. It would be an immense help to me if you felt able, before my arrival, to send a personal message to President Kaunda through your Ambassador in Lusaka saying that I have explained our strategy fully to you, expressing your confidence that economic sanctions were working, that the crunch with Smith might be approaching but that it was essential in everybody's interests to get the timing of the final sanction of closing the Rhodesia border with Zambia

---

   [157] LBJ Library, NSF, Head of State Correspondence File, Box 9, United Kingdom: Prime Minister Wilson Correspondence, Volume 2 [1 of 2], no. 64.

   [158] See 77.

right; and that you would hope that he, Kaunda, and I would reach agreement on this in everybody's interest. He simply must be made to realise that the vast efforts which you and we are making at great cost to ourselves need to exert their maximum effect but that given time they should put Zambia in a position where she could safely administer the final blow.

81. Message from Wilson to Johnson, 12 January 1966[159]

This just to let you know that since my last message,[160] Kaunda has agreed to see me in Lusaka. I shall now be definitely be [sic] going there tomorrow.

I am, however, rather disquieted about activities of certain of our maverick M.P.s in Salisbury which would certainly lead if allowed to go unchecked to pressures from parliamentary opinion that we must negotiate with Smith. There are also some indications that the Governor[161] and Beadle may be thinking along these lines too. For reasons which I am sure you will understand, I cannot regard Smith and his regime as people to whom one could possibly entrust the future of Rhodesia, although I do not rule out the possibility that one Rhodesian front might be represented in any advisory or executive council that might be set up after the rebellion is at an end. I have repeatedly made it clear that I regard Smith's future role as limited to discussing with the Governor the mechanics of bringing the rebellion to an end.

Faced with these difficulties in my British and Rhodesia constituencies I have decided to ask the Commonwealth Secretary[162] to go to Salisbury after our meeting with Kaunda in Zambia. His overt mission will be the strictly limited one of holding consultations with the Governor: his private one of keeping the Governor on the rails. He will not ask to see Smith but will not refuse to see him if Smith asks but any meeting would take place at Government House in formal circumstances. I should be grateful if you would keep knowledge of this proposal on a strictly need to know basis until it becomes public.

It remains to be seen whether the regime makes difficulty about the aircraft landing. Either way I have my answer to my parliamentary critics: and if the Commonwealth Secretary gets in we have the added bonus of proper talks with the Governor.[163]

---

[159] LBJ Library, NSF, Head of State Correspondence File, Box 9, United Kingdom: Prime Minister Wilson Correspondence, Volume 2 [1 of 2], no. 62.
[160] See 80.
[161] Sir Humphrey Gibbs.
[162] Arthur Bottomley.
[163] The original sentence read: 'Either way I have my Parliamentary critics ... ' An amendment was subsequently sent (LBJ Library, NSF, Head of State of correspondence

Things might have been worse here although we are not out of the wood yet. Abubakar has been as helpful as he can be, but whatever the outcome, I am sure I was right to come. I shall be dropping in on Kenyatta on my way back.

82. Message from Johnson to Wilson, 12 January 1966[164]

I have read with great interest your latest message[165] and am weighing in at Lusaka in an effort to steady Kaunda. In this message I underlined the importance of close coordination with you, particularly in avoiding premature severance of economic ties with Rhodesia.

83. Message from Wilson to Johnson, 14 January 1966[166]

I am now back in London after my round Africa safari having seen all seven African heads of government with whom we are in relations, the only notable omissions being of course Nkrumah and Nyerere. It has been well worth while and I think my Commonwealth and African constituencies are now quiescent at least for the time being.

The Commonwealth Prime Ministers' Meeting at Lagos went in the end far better than I could reasonably have hoped. The meeting itself was not without its moments, particularly my debate with Field Marshal Margai of Sierra Leone about an opposed landing in Rhodesia on the first day and a very rewarding closed session at the end of the second day when only heads of government were present without their advisers and in the course of which I was able to take them pretty fully into my confidence both about present policies and future objectives. As you will have seen from the communiqué the Commonwealth as a whole have reaffirmed their recognition that Rhodesia is a British responsibility and while in a sense I have had to account to them for that responsibility, they are now content to let me discharge it for the time being in my own way. There were some members—a minority I am glad to say—who still hankered after the use of force: but the Commonwealth collectively has agreed to give sanctions a fair run. Your own decision on asbestos and lithium could not have been better timed to make maximum impact. The meeting was I think a victory for

---

File, Box 11, M.O.D. 8/30/65–12/31/66 [2 of 2], no. 52) and has been incorporated in the version above.

[164] LBJ Library, NSF, Head of State Correspondence File, Box 9, United Kingdom: Prime Minister Wilson Correspondence, Volume 2 [1 of 2], no. 59.

[165] See 81.

[166] LBJ Library, NSF, Head of State Correspondence File, Box 9, United Kingdom: Prime Minister Wilson Correspondence, Volume 2 [1 of 2], no. 55.

moderation. It has strengthened the Commonwealth vis-a-vis the extremists of the Organization of African Unity and it has held at least for the time being, the position in the United Nations on Chapter VII. It has added to the prestige of the sound moderate leaders like Abubakar; above all, I have avoided being pressed any further than my public position in the House of Commons. The price of this has been the very modest one of the establishment of two committees to meet in London and an undertaking to meet the Commonwealth again if, by July, sanctions have still not succeeded in their objective, to that extent time has been gained. All in all commonsense and realism prevailed.

I then went on to Lusaka where I have had very good meetings with Kaunda, both privately and with his ministers. Your own very helpful message had eased my path for me.

I had two main objectives: first, to secure Kaunda's agreement that plans for the quick kill (the closing of the Zambian frontier with Rhodesia) should be carefully coordinated between Zambia and Britain, [sic] Kaunda is no longer suicidal and I managed not only to secure acceptance that we should not proceed to the second front before mid February, but I also have a fair prospect of getting their agreement, that even when the Zambian frontier is closed to Rhodesian industrial goods, coal will be exempt, with all that that means in airlift terms. This date of mid February is the earliest at which, on the best expert advice, it would be prudent to contemplate delivering the death blow to illegality. Even so it may mean that Zambia will be reduced to a care and maintenance basis for a period of indeterminate length.

My second objective was to try and persuade Kaunda to accept British forces in Zambia so that at the right moment, they would be ready to move into Rhodesia either invited or unopposed. On this I think I have got Kaunda away from his insistence on placing troops across the Zambezi and though he has not yet agreed to accept a Commonwealth presence on the Zambian side of the frontier with Rhodesia, he is now, I think, at least more ready to contemplate something along lines I could accept. All in all, he is a bit more relaxed, much more ready to give sanctions a chance, and does at least accept that we really mean to bring Smith down. He does of course feel himself very exposed economically and, politically, he finds it very difficult to accept a position in which Zambia, for purely practical reasons, is forced to take up a less uncompromising attitude than his fellow Africans towards commercial ties with Rhodesia, because of the inevitable interdependence of the two neighbour economies. For the time being, however, I think we have got him on the rails again.

In Nairobi I had an hour meeting with Kenyatta, and found him as usual wise, relaxed and completely sympathetic, both on sanctions and on the inevitability of gradualness towards majority rule in the reconstruction period.

As you will have seen, the Commonwealth Secretary did not in the end manage to get to Salisbury to see the Governor. But as I indicated in my earlier message, I can play at home the difficulties about personal safety and recognition as usefully as if he had gone in. My qualms about the Governor remain, home African and world fronts now in tolerable order—and I realize of course that the most overworked phrase in this message has been for the time being—I can now concentrate on the internal Rhodesian situation.

All in all, the past week has been time well spent. The situation has of course been transformed by the oil sanctions and the working of the Zambia airlift. In consequence the Commonwealth in general and Commonwealth Africans in particular now accept Britain's responsibility and good faith and this means that we can now make the running ourselves. The point of major difficulty which lies ahead is how to translate economic hardship in Rhodesia into a political readiness to capitulate. For this the Europeans in Rhodesia will have to be given some assurances for their future as well as evidence of continuing and growing hardship if they persist in rebellion. The time is approaching therefore when I shall have to make a public statement on our peace aims. This I shall probably have to do before Parliament reassembles during the last week of January. This will have to be accompanied by a further tightening of the sanctions screw in order to demonstrate that we are not peace-making from weakness. You have experience in such strategy. I will be in touch with you again.

84. Message from Johnson to Wilson, 24 January 1966[167]

Now that our suspension of bombing has run for a month, I want to let you know where we stand now. It has been a great help to have your staunch support on Vietnam throughout these last months, and with some hard decisions right ahead of us, I want to be sure that you have a full picture of our thinking.

It seems pretty clear to us that the pause has been successful everywhere except in Hanoi and Peking. The other communists make routine noises, but I think that they know as well as we do that the real obstacle to a peaceful settlement is not here but in Hanoi. We have the impression that Shelepin tried and failed on this matter, although it is not at all clear that he tried as hard as he could have. But we have nothing that is at all helpful from Hanoi. In recent days their chargé in Vientiane has made an approach to Souvanna Phouma, but nothing in what he said indicates any shift whatever in the basic four-point position.[168] Since they have already gossiped about this probe in Paris in wholly distorted terms,

---

[167] LBJ Library, NSF, Head of State Correspondence File, Box 9, United Kingdom: Prime Minister Wilson Correspondence, Volume 2 [1 of 2], no. 53.

[168] On 8 April 1965, DRV Premier Pham Van Dong enunciated his four-point programme of settlement: US withdrawal, no foreign alliances for South Vietnam, the implementation of the programme of the National Liberation Front in South Vietnam, and reunification to be decided upon exclusively by the Vietnamese without outside interference

we are persuaded that is not a serious effort, but a last-minute attempt to pretend a response which has not in fact occurred. I am asking my people to give Patrick Dean the full details on this so that you will be able to judge it for yourself.

All our evidence shows that the infiltration has continued and that there has been an intensification of training and repair and resupply in the North under the cover of the pause. The communists in the South don't seem to honor even their own ceasefires, and there was a total of more than 80 incidents, large and small, in the New Year truce. Throughout the pause, all the allied forces in South Vietnam have been taking causalities, and the New Year truce period has been no exception.

In this situation, it is clear to all of us that we must not let the pause go on indefinitely. If we were to abandon the bombing of the North with nothing whatever to show for it, all our experts agree that we would simply encourage extremists in Hanoi and decrease the long-term prospect that they may be persuaded to move toward a peaceful settlement. They would feel that their kind of 'peace-lovers' were carrying the day in our country and among our friends, and the hard-liners among them would be strengthened. This argument alone is persuasive, but I am sure I do not need to tell you that the American people simply would not sit still for a one-sided action of this sort. The pause has had very strong understanding and support here so far, but this support is matched by a determination that if we get no answer from the communists, we must do what is necessary to back up our men in the field. Our commanders have behaved with great discipline over the last month, and they have been entirely loyal in their execution of my orders. But I have to take account of the feeling which one of them expressed directly to us in Washington—that the pause is making his people fight with one hand tied behind them. Our commanders want peace as much as everyone else, but I cannot explain to them or to anyone else why the pause should be continued after a full and fair trial has produced no response.

I cannot tell you today just when we may have to resume. It could be very soon indeed, but I am determined to keep my own freedom of action on this point as long as possible. We have strong indications that the Viet Cong are planning major attacks for the period immediately after the Vietnamese new year, and my current thinking is that it will be wise to wait for a day or two to see what happens on the ground. Meanwhile, we plan to make it more and more clear to our own people and to the world that that while the pause has been extremely helpful for proving our purpose of peace throughout the world, and increasing general diplomatic pressure on Hanoi, it has not been effective in producing a real response and therefore its days are plainly numbered.

(*FRUS, 1964–1968*: Volume II, *Vietnam, January–June 1965* (Washington DC: US Government Printing Office, 1996), pp. 544–5).

At the same time, I am trying to make it clear as I can that the end of the pause will not mean any slackening whatever in or general effort to find a way toward the peace table. I have instructed all my people to examine every possible means of continuing public and private political efforts, and in this connection I will be most grateful for any suggestions or proposals that you may wish to offer. Some people may say that the failure of the pause means that there is no chance of peace. I take the opposite view. I think we have to keep trying one thing after another on this front just as we do on the military front until finally we get it across to these people that they are not going to have their way by force, and that peace is in their interest just as much as it is in the interest of all the rest of the world.

When we do resume bombing, we shall have to make very difficult decisions on the proper targets and on the proper weight of attack, just as we have had to do ever since we began sustained air attacks almost a year ago. We will take these decisions very carefully and one step at a time, and you can be sure that there will be no helter skelter escalation and no bombing of civilian targets or population centers. The bombing is a way of increasing the costs of the war effort Hanoi has mounted against the South. It is not an end in itself, and never will be while I am making the decisions. The decisive battlefield is still in South Vietnam, and it is there that we will continue to make our main effort.

Finally, let me say that when we do make the decision on the timing of the resumption of the bombing, I will make sure that word gets to you at once. There may not be much time between the decision and the first air operations, for the simple reason that I will not make this decision until it has become plainly necessary. Meanwhile, I think it important that as one of those who have most strongly supported our peace effort, you should have this full account of our thinking in advance.

85. Message from Wilson to Johnson, 26 January 1966[169]

I am grateful for your message[170] and for the very full explanation of why you may have to resume bombing in North Vietnam soon. I believe that if you are forced to this decision history will show that you and your administration have made the most honest and commendable efforts to avoid further conflict. I have just heard of the further contact which you are seeking to make with the North Vietnamese through their ambassador in Moscow, in which I take it you will

---

[169] LBJ Library, NSF, Head of State Correspondence File, Box 9, United Kingdom: Prime Minister Wilson Correspondence, Volume 2 [1 of 2], no. 51.

[170] See 84.

make it clear to them that the bombing pause cannot continue indefinitely in the absence of any reasonable response to the various approaches made to them.

I am impressed by what you say about the military factors. In the final analysis the resumption of bombing turns on politico-military considerations. You must be the only judge of where the balance of advantage lies, but I am sure that in view of the gravity of the decision you will insist that the burden of proof rests with the military. We have every confidence in your judgement and will, of course, support you in your decision.

It is of course of vital importance to the American image in the world, as well as to us and your other friends who will wish to defend your actions, that everything possible should be done to bring home your case to world opinion. It should be informed of how hard you have tried to avoid the resumption of bombing and that you are forced to it only as a military necessity and after going to the limit in trying to get Hanoi to negotiate, or at least to accept a de facto cessation of hostilities. It is with this in mind that I put to you the following suggestion. It is that if your present attempt fails you should then make public not only this last approach, but also all the evidence you are able to release of the use which the North Vietnamese have made of the bombing pause and the two holiday truces to reinforce their own military and to inflict casualties on American and South Vietnamese troops and civilians.

I am all too conscious that the above is of very meagre assistance to you in the decision with which you are faced. But it might help us and other friends of yours in the support which we shall give you.

In any event I agree with you that even if you have to take this action we should continue our efforts to get the North Vietnamese to negotiate.

86. Message from Wilson to Johnson, 26 January 1966[171]

We finished on Sunday the series of meetings in which we have been reviewing our defence expenditure. Tomorrow Michael Stewart and Denis Healey will begin further technical discussions with their opposite numbers in Washington.[172] Of course, we have not reached the stage of firm decisions: it was always intended that this should be delayed until there had been full consultation between our two governments. In any case, I hope that we shall be in touch again personally when the talks at technical level have been concluded. For the fact is that these discussions and the decisions taken in the light of them are going to have

---

[171] LBJ Library, NSF, Head of State Correspondence File, Box 9, United Kingdom: Prime Minister Wilson Correspondence, Volume 2 [1 of 2], no. 47.

[172] See Memorandum of conversation, 27 January 1966, *FRUS, 1964–1968*: Volume XII: *Western Europe* (Washington, DC: US Government Printing Office, 2001), pp. 516–28.

consequences not only over the next few years, but for decades. I see them as confirming a pattern of interdependence not only in Europe but over the whole world. And we should not forget that they will determine our joint posture long after current anxieties over Vietnam, Indonesia and nuclear sharing with Germany have receded into the past.

We know from the talks we had in December how much we see eye to eye on these problems, and I am sure you attach the same importance as I do to our maintaining personal contact on them.

87. Message from Johnson to Wilson, 27 January 1966[173]

I have just learned of the victory of the Labour Party candidate.[174] I know how much this means to you and I send you my warm congratulations.

88. Message from Johnson to Wilson, 30 January 1966[175]

Thank you for your most helpful and understanding message of the 26th,[176] concerning the resumption of bombing of North Vietnam.

As you know, I have waited these last few days on the faint chance that some constructive response would be received through our contacts in Moscow and Rangoon and through the dubious approach made in Vientiane.[177] Moscow and Rangoon have now produced clear negatives, and nothing has been received after 12 days to indicate that the Vientiane matter ever had any real significance.

Meanwhile evidence has become increasingly abundant that infiltration has continued at a high rate, and Viet Cong military activity in the South has throughout been at normal levels, with heavy engagements in recent days both at their initiative and at ours. I should note that in the Moscow approach our representative specifically underscored to Hanoi's man that we were prepared for any confidential indication that there was in fact any conscious change

---

[173] LBJ Library, NSF, Head of State Correspondence File, Box 9, United Kingdom: Prime Minister Wilson Correspondence, Volume 2 [1 of 2], no. 45.

[174] On 27 January, the Labour Party candidate secured victory in the Hull North by-election with an increased majority, thanks to a four and half per cent swing to Labour compared with the 1964 general election. This result was achieved despite apparent interference from sympathizers of Rhodesia who distributed literature urging constituents to vote against Labour (Wilson, *The Labour Government, 1964–1970*, pp. 198–9).

[175] LBJ Library, NSF, Head of State Correspondence File, Box 9, United Kingdom: Prime Minister Wilson Correspondence, Volume 2 [1 of 2], no. 43.

[176] See 85.

[177] See 84.

in the military pace. There has been no response to this suggestion. Our firm conclusion is therefore that Hanoi has decided not to respond in any way by word or deed.

We will therefore be resuming the bombing Monday, Saigon time. I ask you to treat this information in the utmost confidence for obvious reasons of military security.

Since our previous correspondence has covered the factors thoroughly, I do not have to repeat them here. The essence of the matter is that we cannot, in justice to our own forces, and the South Vietnamese, permit the military supply lines and other related targets in North Vietnam to go untouched any longer. I am very grateful for your mention of the importance of making clear just what has been going on during the suspension, and we shall make public full statements in this regard. They will be moderate in tone however, because we do not want to give ammunition to advocates of extreme measures.

I am also planning to have Arthur Goldberg make a full statement at the UN, and our further tactics there may be modelled on your handling of Rhodesia, but there is no decision on that tonight and we will be in touch with your people on it tomorrow.

I want you to know above all how grateful I am for the firm support that you and your government have shown throughout the Vietnam conflict as well as during this suspension. Your assurance that you will support us firmly in the present hard decision to resume is another encouraging proof of the depth of our understanding.

89. Message from Wilson to Johnson, 9 February 1966[178]

As I think you know, the Foreign Secretary and I have had over the past ten days to face the most dangerous attack from within the Parliamentary Labour Party on the question of Vietnam. It centred round the decision to resume bombing and was activated by the very clear statement put out by the Foreign Secretary that the bombing decision had not only our understanding but our support. This led to the despatch on the same Monday evening to Fulbright a telegram signed by 90 Labour M.P.s, covering not only the usual Vietnam names but a wide consensus right across the Party, including some who had previously supported our action.

Two days later, I addressed a full meeting our Parliamentary Party when I repeated my full support of the Foreign Secretary's statement and took full responsibility for it. At the same time, I felt it right to make a very strong attack

---

[178] LBJ Library, NSF, Head of State Correspondence File, Box 9, United Kingdom: Prime Minister Wilson Correspondence, Volume 2 [1 of 2], no. 41.

on those concerned and got considerable mileage out of pointing out that during the 40 days bombing pause there was not a sound out of them commending the United States Administration for the opportunities they had opened up for a peaceful settlement, and this in the face of not only strong political pressures at home but very real military risks. What I think was really damaging to the critics was my repeated jibe that none of them during this period had thought it fit to send a telegram to Ho Chi Minh demanding now that he should respond in kind, or to demonstrate with peace-in-Vietnam banners outside the Chinese Embassy. This had the effect of detaching from the lobby all but the irreconcilables, but their attack continues and gets a great deal of support from Party supporters in the country.

Next, the Opposition who on the whole have supported the United States position on Vietnam and have given in the main general but not enthusiastic support to Her Majesty's Government, had yesterday a Parliamentary Day on which they had the right to choose the subject for debate and no doubt hoping to profit from the disagreement on our own side chose Vietnam in the hope of exploiting what they called the split.

The Foreign Secretary and I decided to meet the challenge head on whatever the risk. At the same time I decided to pitch into the Opposition leadership as well for their opportunism.

I am glad to say that the operation was a total success. I was able to make good use of some of your statements from Hawaii particularly on the more positive questions of economic development, the social structure, etc. There was strong criticism of the South Vietnamese Government and of their apparent resistance to negotiations. On this I am bound to say I rode the punch a little and said fairly frankly all I suspect you really think but can hardly say. A major difficulty for us here, as for you, is the image of the South Vietnamese Government.

One result of the rout was a telegram to Ho Chi Minh sent by senior members of the Party including the Chairman and Vice Chairman of the Backbench Parliamentary Committee and signed by four privy counsellors, including the Nobel prize winner, Noel-Baker, who a week before had been at the centre of the Fulbright telegram episode.

All in all I am well satisfied with the outcome but I thought you would like to have this appraisal of the situation as seen from here. We have got over a very awkward moment though it shows once again the difficulties I am bound to have from time to time when subject to group pressures with a parliamentary majority so much less than my real present majority in the country.

You certainly have my sympathy and good wishes as you grapple with this intolerable problem.

90. Message from Johnson to Wilson, 11 February 1966[179]

I thought you might share some of my impressions of the recent conference at Honolulu with leaders of South Vietnam.[180]

We talked almost exclusively about the economic, social, and political problems of the country. I found the young Vietnamese leaders lucid and apparently determined to carry forward a policy of quite radical and constructive change. Moreover, they talked in terms of specific and realistic targets. They seemed to have learned something from past mistakes. They do not pretend that they can do all the constructive things they want to do in a year. They intend to concentrate during 1966 on four critical areas.

I enclose copies of the Declaration of Honolulu, our joint communiqué, the statement I made in Los Angeles on my return, and the statement by Prime Minister Ky on the first morning of the conference.[181] It may interest you to note that their statement of 'The Purposes of the Government of Vietnam,' in the Declaration of Honolulu, flows directly from Ky's own rather impressive statement to all of us.

There is now no question in my mind that what they say is what they think and they intend.

We cannot, of course, be sure that this particular government will prove stable.

We are also conscious that it is one thing to articulate good purposes and programs with sincerity; it is something different actually to put them into practice. The administrative capacity of any government in a developing country is limited; and in Vietnam that capacity is tied up substantially in fighting a difficult war.

As you may have gathered, an agricultural mission, headed by Secretary Freeman is now in South Vietnam. It will be followed in a few weeks by an education mission headed by Mr. Francis Keppel, Assistant Secretary of Health, Education, and Welfare. Further along, a medical mission headed by our Surgeon General, William H. Stewart, will also go and seek to energise the programs on the spot.

We plan economic assistance to South Vietnam this year on the order of $650 million, designed not merely to meet the basic needs of the country but also to carry forward these programs in rural construction, education, health, and assistance to refugees.

---

[179] LBJ Library, NSF, Head of State Correspondence File, Box 9, United Kingdom: Prime Minister Wilson Correspondence, Volume 2 [1 of 2], no. 37. This was a circular message sent to a number of chiefs of state or government. Only the final paragraph was particular to the message sent to Wilson.

[180] This took place between 6 and 8 February.

[181] Not printed.

I plan to meet again with the South Vietnamese leaders and our own people from Saigon some months hence to measure the extent to which progress has actually been made in these dimensions of our common policy.

I did wish you know that, on balance, I was heartened by meeting these young nationalist, revolutionary leaders. I saw a good deal of them in private as well as in larger meetings. They were poised, with a good sense of direction.

Knowing your understanding of our broad objectives in Vietnam, I wished you to share something of this encouraging experience.

In closing, let me thank you for your recent personal message about your political situation.[182] I continue to admire enormously your fortitude and skill in dealing with your opposition. We seem to have some of the same problem here, but I have no doubt that we shall be able to keep it under control.

Sincerely,

Lyndon B. Johnson

91. Message from Wilson to Johnson, 14 February 1966[183]

I have been giving much thought lately to what I might say about Vietnam during my visit to Moscow from February 21–24. As you know, we have already been in full agreement with your view that the Geneva Conference should be reconvened and have made repeated efforts to persuade the Russians to this. They have always replied that they can do nothing and that the North Vietnamese should be approached direct. Both you and we have done this with no more success, but it seems to me that I ought to make another attempt while I am in Moscow.

2. What I had in mind is to try to arrange a personal meeting with a North Vietnamese representative there, preferably with some fairly senior man who might come from Hanoi for the purpose, but, failing that, with their representative in Moscow.

3. If such a meeting can be arranged, I would propose to explain that the United States cannot be expected to accept the Four Points[184] as they stand and that is useless to suppose that your Government will be worn down by any military pressure North Vietnam can exert. I would then try to probe the North Vietnamese about possible ambiguities or loopholes (not that we have seen much sign of this so far) in their own proposals and would again offer to transmit any messages or proposals they may have.

---

[182] See 89.

[183] LBJ Library, NSF, Head of State Correspondence File, Box 9, United Kingdom: Prime Minister Wilson Correspondence, Volume 2 [1 of 2], no. 34.

[184] See 84, footnote 168.

4. I have little hope that such a meeting, if the North Vietnamese agree to it, would produce early or visible results.[185] But it might help to get some of the realities of the situation through the barrier Hanoi has erected against the outside world. It would also be a further demonstration of our will to peace and determination to try every means of obtaining it.

5. If the North Vietnamese representative refuses to see me (as may well happen) I should then at least be able to tell the Russians, with added force and emphasis, that their cooperation in joint action by the co-chairmen is indispensable if there is to be any progress towards a peaceful settlement.

6. If a meeting between myself and a North Vietnamese representative is to stand any chance at all of being useful, it would naturally be necessary for me to propose this to the North Vietnamese in advance. There must be time for Hanoi to be consulted and to send a special representative, or, at the very least, full instructions. So I would like, within the next 24 hours, to tell our Ambassador in Moscow to get in touch with the North Vietnamese representative there and make this proposal. I hope this idea will be acceptable to you, but, if you see any strong objection to it, I should be most grateful if you could let me know at once.

92. Letter from Johnson to Wilson, 14 February 1966[186]

I hasten to let tell you how appreciative I am of your message of this morning about the Vietnam part of your visit to Moscow.[187]

I am glad that you agree that another hard attempt should be made to persuade the Russians to join as co-chairman in convening the Geneva Conference. My attitude on such a conference has been made clear repeatedly since last February, but if you plan to make public your efforts in this direction, and if you think it would be helpful, I am prepared prior to your arrival in Moscow to state again publicly our sympathetic support.

I agree that it would be a good idea for you to try to talk to the North Vietnamese representative in Moscow. I know of nothing that would indicate we could have much hope that such a meeting would produce a useful response, but I completely agree that it is wise to take every opportunity to impress the realities of the situation on the Government of North Vietnam. You would

---

[185] In his memoirs, Wilson recalled that 'we did manage to get a line through to Hanoi. With Mr Kosygin's agreement Lord Chalfont [Minister of State for Foreign Affairs] had a six-hour talk at the North Vietnamese Embassy with a high-powered delegation then in Moscow, but without any concrete result' (Wilson, *The Labour Government, 1964–1970*, p. 214).

[186] LBJ Library, NSF, Head of State Correspondence File, Box 9, United Kingdom: Prime Minister Wilson Correspondence, Volume 2 [1 of 2], no. 31.

[187] See 91.

be in a strong position to do this, and I think the approach suggested in your paragraph 3 is a reasonable one.

Since the end of the bombing suspension, we have received one communication from Hanoi to which we are about to reply. We do not see much light in their communication, but we will supply the text of Hanoi's message, as well as our reply, through your Ambassador here for your background information. I am sure you will appreciate the great sensitivity of this contact, which we are taking unusual steps to maintain. I would thus hope you would make no mention of this contact, or the specific contents of the messages, to either the Soviets or DRV representative if you see him. Your continuous and constant interest gives me strength and I send my thanks and the gratitude of my countrymen.

93. Message from Wilson to Johnson, 16 February 1966[188]

In my message of January 26,[189] I said that I would get in touch with you again when we had taken our decisions on the defence review.

The Cabinet have now taken their decisions and these will become public knowledge when the White Paper on Defence is published on February 22.[190] I think you will find that our decisions follow very closely the outlines I gave you of our provisional thinking when we met last December. Denis Healey will give Bob McNamara fuller details when he is in Washington later this week.

These decisions have naturally been the subject of a great deal of discussion and will doubtless stimulate some controversy, but this is inevitable. I am quite sure that they are the right decisions, for Britain and for the general interests of the Free World. I am sure that they provide a sound basis for our continued cooperation which, as you know, is at the heart of all our overseas policies.

Incidentally, Denis Healey will be able to tell Bob McNamara how he got on in Australia and Southeast Asia. I think he succeeded in getting the minds of our friends in the antipodes moving in the right direction.

---

[188] LBJ Library, NSF, Head of State Correspondence File, Box 9, United Kingdom: Prime Minister Wilson Correspondence, Volume 2 [1 of 2], no. 26.

[189] See 86.

[190] Starting from the premise that 'military strength is of little value if it is achieved at the expense of economic health', the White Paper announced the phasing out of Britain's aircraft carriers, the limited purchase of American F111A strike aircraft, and the abandonment of the military base in Aden by 1968 (*Statement on the Defence Estimates 1966: Part I: The Defence Review* (London: HMSO, 1966), Cmnd. 2901).

94. Message from Wilson to Johnson, 16 February 1966[191]

I should, I think, let you know that we have just had to take a most difficult decision on whether or not to allow the sale of a number of Trident aircraft to China. These are medium range civil aircraft with three jet engines which compare closely with the Boeing 727. The Chinese government have shown great interest in this aircraft and had invited Hawker Siddeley Aviation Limited to send a delegation to Peking. We have decided not to permit the sale.

This decision was however difficult for us. China is in urgent need of modern civil aircraft and represents a large potential market we cannot afford to deny ourselves. Our aircraft industry is badly in need of export orders and the frustration of this sale on political grounds will, when it becomes known, be unpopular in this country. Also, our refusal to sell these aircraft, which are not subject to the COCOM embargo,[192] might well have an adverse effect on other aspects of our trade with China. Furthermore, we have had to bear in mind that the Chinese will have little difficulty in finding an alternative source of supply either in the Soviet Union or possibly in another Western country.

Nevertheless, I decided that we must be prepared to sacrifice these clear commercial advantages mainly because of the present situation in Viet Nam and the inevitable reactions in India to such a sale.

I am bound, however, to mention that a great deal of public attention is being given here to our aircraft industry. As I say, this decision is going to be unpopular. It would be a considerable help to me if your authorities were to look sympathetically on our efforts to secure sales of British aircraft in the United States. I have particularly in mind the HS.125 executive jet, an aircraft type for which I understand a requirement exists in the U.S.A.F. I should like to be able to say that you are giving this aircraft favourable consideration in that context.

---

[191] LBJ Library, NSF, Head of State Correspondence File, Box 9, United Kingdom: Prime Minister Wilson Correspondence, Volume 2 [1 of 2], no. 22a.

[192] The Coordinating Committee for Multilateral Export Controls (COCOM) was set up by Western powers during the Cold War to place an arms embargo on the Council for Mutual Economic Assistance (COMECON), an economic organization of Eastern bloc countries under Soviet leadership.

95. Message from Wilson to Johnson, 17 February 1966[193]

Thank you for your two messages about Vietnam: one with your encouraging impressions of the Honolulu meeting and the other about my forthcoming visit to Moscow.[194]

I was particularly grateful to have such a prompt and encouraging response to my idea of making contact with the North Vietnamese. The necessary instructions have gone to our Ambassador in Moscow and I will keep you in touch with future developments as they occur.

I was also most grateful for your offer of a further public statement of your readiness to attend another Geneva Conference. But I think American willingness to negotiate has already been made crystal clear to every reasonable human being. A further statement on the eve of the Moscow visit—and while the North Vietnamese may still be considering my proposal of an exploratory talk—might thus seem to add nothing to your known position, but be interpreted by suspicious men in Hanoi as suggesting that you have sponsored my proposal. To anyone of their tortuous cast of mind this suggestion could be enough to tip the scales against an acceptance. I should prefer, though with renewed gratitude, to decline this offer for the present. We might perhaps think of it again when considering the outcome of my proposal and of my discussions with the Russian leaders.

I look forward to hearing the details of your own contacts with the North Vietnamese and will keep my knowledge of them strictly to myself and my immediate advisers.

Finally I want to thank you for the kind words with which you ended your latest message. It is not difficult for me to go on trying, but I do deeply admire your own patient determination to explore every chance of peace in spite of all the sacrifices your forces are making in Vietnam and of the stubborn intransigence of the other side.

96. Message from Johnson to Wilson, 20 February 1966[195]

As you leave for Moscow, I want to share my thoughts with you on one further problem that you may have occasion to discuss with the Russians. This is the problem of relations between the negotiations on non-proliferation and our

---

[193] LBJ Library, NSF, Head of State Correspondence File, Box 9, United Kingdom: Prime Minister Wilson Correspondence, Volume 2 [1 of 2], no. 20.
[194] See 90 and 92.
[195] LBJ Library, NSF, Head of State Correspondence File, Box 9, United Kingdom: Prime Minister Wilson Correspondence, Volume 2 [1 of 2], no. 16.

efforts to get an agreed Atlantic nuclear policy. I think we have to walk a careful line between contending groups which would give one or the other of these related problems an overriding priority.

The Soviet Government continues to assert that any form of cooperation with Bonn in the nuclear field is dangerous. While this position may in part reflect a genuine concern about the Germans getting control over nuclear weapons, it is also plain that the Soviets are seeking to use the issue as a means of causing trouble in the NATO Alliance.

The main point of Soviet tactical pressure in the coming weeks is likely to be the language of the non-proliferation treaty. They will be pressing for language which would bar what they call "access" to nuclear weapons by non-nuclear powers. Their evident purpose is to foreclose the possibility of nuclear arrangements in NATO which would involve the Germans more intimately in the business of nuclear defense.

We are inclined to think that the best way to counter the Soviets on this—and to get on with a constructive treaty—is to focus discussion on the true meaning of proliferation, and, at the same time, to convince Moscow that we will not sign a treaty which would rule out NATO nuclear arrangements which would not, in fact, involve proliferation.

In our new draft treaty, we have suggested that proliferation results when a non-nuclear nation acquires its own national control, or the right or ability to fire nuclear weapons without the concurrent decision of an existing nuclear nation. In addition, there should be no increase in the number of states and organizations which have control of nuclear weapons. In general, the draft represents an attempt to come to grips with the real problem of proliferation without sacrificing the legitimate interests of the non-nuclear members of the Alliance.

In any case, I think it most important that we not let the Soviets maneuver us into a position which would arouse strong and honest resentment in Germany. To let them do this would be no service to the cause of non-proliferation, since it would increase the very dangers that the Soviets constantly stress.

The Soviet Government is surely not blind to one further aspect of this matter—namely, that there is on this issue, a pronounced difference of emphasis between your public opinion and ours. They are bound to see advantage in trying to exploit that difference to set us against one another. We must be careful not to fall into that trap.

My own view is that we should keep an absolutely even handed view of these twin problems. A sound non-proliferation agreement and a sound Atlantic nuclear policy are in truth mutually consistent and reinforcing. I do not accept the argument that we must finally solve the Alliance nuclear problem before there can be a treaty. But I think we should equally reject the notion that we can push aside the Alliance problem now, and go along with a treaty which would rule out, or drastically narrow, possibilities for a NATO nuclear arrangement which would not result in proliferation.

On non-proliferation, we can meet the legitimate interests of the Soviet Government because they are the same as our own. But we must not let the Soviets use this most important issue to undermine German confidence in our willingness to treat their nuclear problem seriously and constructively. This course naturally tempts some in Moscow, but it is no more in the Soviet interest than in ours.

I thought it would be useful for me to give you this indication of my own thinking, because of the great advantage which comes to us both when we stand together.

I hope you will have a good trip and I send you once again my best wishes for success in your effort to get Soviet help in reconvening a Geneva Conference. I am doing what I can to keep the public discussion here from complicating your task, but it is an understatement to say that I do not control it completely.

97. Message from Wilson to Johnson, 23 February 1966[196]

There has been some mutual plain speaking in my talks in Moscow, including useful sessions in private with Kosygin in the Kremlin and during intervals at the ballet. It is disappointing that fears that there would be no give in the Russian attitude to Vietnam have been confirmed. Even so I think I may have been able to get across to Kosygin some sense of the anxieties you personally feel about Vietnam and of the sincerity behind the peace overtures which were made during the bombing pause.

You should know that the communiqué which will be issued tomorrow will refer to discussions on the urgent need for arrangements to prevent the spread of nuclear weapons and to extend the 1963 Test Ban Treaty to include underground tests. I have put to the Russians, and it may survive in the communiqué, the idea that as a stimulus to the Geneva Conference there should be a high level political meeting of the nuclear powers concerned during the spring to ascertain whether the conditions for definitive agreements have been established. I have in mind a meeting between, for example, Dean Rusk, Gromyko and Michael Stewart, rather on the lines of the one that Averil [sic][197] will remember attending with Quintin Hogg.[198]

---

[196] LBJ Library, NSF, Head of State Correspondence File, Box 9, United Kingdom: Prime Minister Wilson Correspondence, Volume 2 [1 of 2], no. 14.

[197] Wilson is evidently referring to Averell Harriman.

[198] In 1963, President Kennedy and British Prime Minister, Harold Macmillan, had written to the Soviet leader, Nikita Khrushchev, conveying their willingness to send senior negotiators to Moscow to discuss a test ban. The United States was represented by Averell

98. Message from Johnson to Wilson, 25 February 1966[199]

I am slow in sending you a line of thanks in acknowledgement for your messages of last week about aircraft sales and about your defense review decisions.[200] It has been very helpful to us to have the benefit of full and private discussion with you ahead of time, and our people will be looking to your final conclusions with the greatest interest. I have heard from Bob McNamara of the very important agreements which he and Denis Healey have worked out on some parts of this field, and have asked my people to think very carefully about the subject of aircraft procurement. I can tell you, without any staff study, that we are very glad of your decision not to sell that particular airplane to China right now.

While I am at it, let me thank you too for your personal account of the beginnings of your Moscow visit.[201] Our good work together in recent months shows how helpful it is to keep in touch with each other on all these matters.

99. Message from Wilson to Johnson, 26 February 1966[202]

I thought you might like to know how I got on during my three days in Moscow.

It was, to quote the Iron duke, hard pounding.

On Vietnam, we made, as expected, absolutely no progress at all and this was accurately reflected in the communiqué. This was not because the Soviet Union would not like to use their influence to bring Hanoi to the conference table but principally because they are boxed in at present by the imminence of the 23rd party conference and with this key event only a month away they simply do not dare take any action which would leave them open to criticism in the Soviet Bloc that they might be wavering in the slightest degree in their support for their Communist allies. In one of the intervals at the ballet, which were fortunately fairly long I had a very frank private talk with Kosygin. I said is it possible to add anything on Vietnam. He said it really is very difficult. I was in no doubt at all that he was trying to tell me that it was impossible for him to move at present because the Chinese would take advantage of any such movement on his part. These people, like us, are politicians and he and Brezhnev, with whom I also had a very long frank talk, are as nervous about their forthcoming Congress which

---

Harriman, the British by Quintin Hogg. The treaty was initialled on 25 July and signed on 5 August 1963.

[199] LBJ Library, NSF, Head of State Correspondence File, Box 9, United Kingdom: Prime Minister Wilson Correspondence, Volume 2 [1 of 2], no. 10a.

[200] See 93 and 94.

[201] See 97.

[202] LBJ Library, NSF, Head of State Correspondence File, Box 9, United Kingdom: Prime Minister Wilson Correspondence, Volume 2 [1 of 2], no. 6.

they are performing for the first time, as any western politician I met facing a similar confrontation.

As you well know the Minister of State at the Foreign Office, Lord Chalfont, whom I took with me to Moscow, had a four hour discussion with the North Vietnamese charge d'affaires. Again he made no progress but there may be some advantage in the future of having opened up a fresh channel of communication against the time, which obviously must come, when the Communists are prepared to talk.

The other main topic of discussion revolved around the complex questions of European security, disarmament, the non-proliferation of nuclear weapons and nuclear sharing in the Atlantic Alliance. Not for the first time I came up against the Soviets [sic] obsession with the prospect of Germany obtaining access to nuclear weapons, an obsession, based on past experiences, which has now achieved the status of folklore. The fact that this obsession goes hand in hand with very considerable confidence in their own immense strength does not lessen its force or reality. In this general field I had the impression that the Soviets would like to make progress and were genuinely concerned at the continued existence of the well known stumbling blocks: the question of Germany in relation to non-proliferation and the question of inspection to a comprehensive nuclear test ban treaty. I told them I was equally concerned about non-proliferation and asked them to turn their eyes away from a sole fixation on Germany to the no less pressing dangers in the Middle East and Far East: I referred to the Arab-Israeli dispute and India's fears of China. It was in this connection that I put forward my proposal that since the experts at Geneva[203] had really taken their discussion as far as they could what was now needed was a political initiative. I suggested we adopt the procedure tried with success before the partial Test Ban Treaty was signed for a political meeting at, say, Foreign Minister level of the three nuclear powers and which I mentioned to you in my earlier message. In the event this proposal did not survive in the communiqué: but the Russians have undertaken to consider it and let me have a reply in the next few weeks. They have also asked Lord Chalfont to go back to Moscow to continue talks in this field although no date has yet been fixed.

While we neither got nor expected to get very far on questions of substance I was more than content with the general atmosphere surrounding the visit and with the fact that blunt talking did not mean an atmosphere of hostility. The Russians were very rough on Britain, the United States and Germany, and plugged the line that alliances such as NATO were now out of date: but I made it very clear throughout if they had the allies and loyalties, so did we, and that I spoke from a position four-square within the Western Alliance. I had about

---

[203] The Eighteen-Nation Disarmament Committee, established under the auspices of the United Nations at the end of 1961, met regularly in Geneva between 1962–69.

six hours with Kosygin, an hour with Podgorny, a two and half hour meeting with Brezhnev which was laid on at very short notice and an hour's chat with Mikoyan. Another interesting point was that after my first four meetings with the Soviet leadership, the final—communiqué—meeting was postponed while they had a meeting of the Presidium, obviously called to discuss collectively the result of the previous talks. Although the resultant communiqué was fairly thin, except on bilateral matters, I am sure the Soviet leadership regarded the visit as well worth while: my experts tell me that the word constructive is an official way of saying that they were glad the talks had taken place. At all events, word must have gone out to put out the bunting: on my drive to the airport, the Soviet and British flags were on very flag post and there were banners everywhere about Anglo-Soviet friendship.

For my part I have now a much clearer personal knowledge of the men we are dealing with and that, in this modern world, is a very good thing in itself. Kosygin I should judge to be a very tough, not very humorous administrator type: Brezhnev I found a very impressive more extrovert figure. They really seem to run, at any rate at present, a collective show and when I discussed this privately with Kosygin, he waxed passionate for the first time in expressing the determination of himself and his colleagues never again to allow a one man dictatorship to grow up of either the Stalin or Khrushchev variety. Kosygin has accepted my invitation to pay a return visit and although no date has been fixed I would judge that we shall see him some time during the summer.

I spent a lot of time in my private talks with them always before a witness of course trying to educate them. I told Mr. Kosygin that his repeated reference to the Americanski was based on ignorance. I said they were wrong to think all Americans or any other Western nation as given to uniform and monolithic thinking, no doubt an error based on their Marxist interpretation of what a county or a people would be doing at a particular stage of historical development. I said that there were lots of Americans and to my knowledge they had many different ideas and views but when it came to the decision making process there was one American, the President. This might be difficult for him to understand with their well-known collective decision making machinery, etc., but the United States elected their President by democratic means for four years and once elected executive responsibility was his and his alone, subject to such advice he might take and subject to the need to carry Congees with him.

Equally I lectured him at great length on the Germans. I told him that no German statesman I knew had any intention of securing nuclear power for Germany. I agreed that there was a new generation which might harbour nuclear ambitions. I asked him to believe his anxieties about this were not exclusive to him, and that we and indeed no less leading Americans naturally were guarding against this possibility. The only argument lay as to the best method of ensuring our common objective. The argument about MLF or ANF or any other method of nuclear sharing was an argument which, while partly related to the greater effectiveness of NATO which was under examination, was also an argument as to the best means of meeting Germany's legitimate demands on a basis which could not lead to more dangerous ambitions. I also indicated to him our, that is British, opposition to the development of an independent European nuclear deterrent and hence our opposition to the so called European clause in the various drafts tabled at Geneva last August. I do not delude myself that my seminar was wholly productive but I do believe I was giving them some problems to chew over. I am convinced that they want to maintain an active dialogue with the West: that they find some difficulties in pressing this too publicly, particularly before their Congress which of course has an international as well as a national character. I think that mainly because of Vietnam they see difficulties in the immediate future in having too public a dialogue with you, but they may be ready to keep it going through us. But they are in no doubt as I have said earlier that they will be negotiating with us as your loyal allies. When I said to them that it must be clear that they were in the Eastern camp and we were unequivocably in the Western camp, they understood this.

100. Message from Wilson to Johnson, 27 February 1966[204]

I think I ought to tell you that I have decided to advise the Queen to dissolve Parliament and to hold an immediate general election. This is being announced tomorrow (Monday) just after mid day your time, and will take place on 31 March.

I do not need to worry you with all the reasons why I have reached this conclusion. As a more accomplished politician you may possibly have reached the same conclusion before I did. But although we have managed to do everything that we tried to do with our majority—the smallest majority in British parliamentary history—I think we are moving into a period where things we are going to want to do may be more difficult. We want to toughen up and speed the measures needed to strengthen our economy and this will mean some pretty tough confrontations with various vested interests.

These confrontations will be easier if we can get a more substantial mandate and if there is not expectation of an early election. I don't know whether you are fortunate or unfortunate in having a fixed election date. In our case the so-called freedom a prime minister has is somewhat limited. If I do not do it now, the whole of the spring and late summer, because of holidays and other reasons, will be closed to me and I might become a prisoner of a very constricted

---

[204] LBJ Library, NSF, Head of State Correspondence File, Box 9, United Kingdom: Prime Minister Wilson Correspondence, Volume 2 [1 of 2], no. 3.

parliamentary situation just at the moment of time when we want to put on the legislative heat. Moreover, I am, of course, at the mercy of the almighty in respect of the deaths of sick M.P.s. So far he has been extremely merciful but should he become more unselective in his choice of legislative advisers, I might be left with a long period with no majority at all when I want it most.

I am not proposing to ask you to come and help us during the election. There are, of course, abundant precedents. Eisenhower in 1955 agreed to Eden's request for an early summit meeting to which in fact Eisenhower was strongly opposed. In 1959 he conferred the same electoral benefit on Macmillan and indeed allowed himself to be toted through 14 London marginal constituencies in an open car with Macmillan beside him. I have no such requests except that if you were thinking of doing anything which might be positively unhelpful, I hope that you would at any rate give me a little notice.

Heath is now attacking our defence review on the grounds that it drives us too closely into relations with you. Douglas-Home in a presumably ghosted article in today's Sunday Express listing the election issues, calls on the electors to vote Conservative so that we do not accept satellite status to the United States. I have no doubt that this will be one of their themes and that they will make an appeal to the latent anti-Americanism amongst some of our electorate which they called into being with some success at the time of Suez. If I took this particular threat seriously, I might suggest to you that we should have a row in order to help me, but quite honestly I cannot think of anything to have a row about. Should you think of a suitable subject you will no doubt let me know.

It may be that during the next four weeks difficulties may arise and as I am very anxious to safeguard our future relations not only bilaterally but within the Alliance generally, you may find me getting in touch with you. If I get too hysterical you will no doubt dismiss it as the election fever. Quite honestly you may find me, if driven, taking a slightly anti-German line. If I have to deploy xenophobia, which I hope will not be necessary, I would rather it be of that variety than the Tory anti-Americanism, and the Germans have been warned that this is possible since they quite unscrupulously attacked me in their last election as a means of discrediting the S.P.D. I did not react at the time because I know what politicians are like during elections, though I made it clear to them that I reserved the same right when the time came. But I would hope it would not go too far.

The other big issue relates to sterling. Election speculation has led to a little weakness in the last week or two because elections mean instability and also because there has been some fear that if the Conservatives got in they would do what we did not do and devalue sterling on the day they took office blaming it on their predecessors. But now the expectation of a Conservative victory is quite small. The polls give us an all-time high in our lead and the betting odds are 6–1 on Labour, 7–2 against the Tories. I am not, however, as complacent as this since an expectation of easy victory leads some times to people not bothering to vote. After all there is 1948 in your country as a warning to me.[205]

So far as sterling is concerned I am convinced an early election is essential. If we do not go now we shall have a continual period of electioneering through the spring, summer and autumn which could have a more serious effect on sterling. Moreover my colleagues and I feel that we may need tougher measures and these would be easier in a post-election rather than pre-election situation, though we do not intend during the election to disguise from the electors the seriousness of the situation and what measures we may have to take.

I am sorry to trouble you with all these arguments about our internal situation and I am addressing them to you less in your capacity as head of government than in your other capacity as a full-time student of political affairs. But during the next month we may need to be in touch with you should the election situation create difficulties which may have more prolonged effects either bilaterally or in the wider field of international affairs.

101. Message from Johnson to Wilson, 28 February 1966[206]

I am most grateful for your good message of last evening.[207] I will not break the rules by wishing you good luck but entirely understand your problem. Let's by all means stay in touch.

102. Message from Johnson to Wilson, 3 March 1966[208]

I am most grateful for the splendid account of your talks in Moscow.[209] They are a frustrating lot, but we must keep hammering away. And right now, you are in a better position to do so than I.

I am glad Lord Chalfont made contact with the North Vietnamese chargé. The more channels we have open the better.

---

[205] Wilson is referring to Republican Thomas Dewey's unexpected defeat by sitting President, Harry S. Truman, in the 1948 presidential election.

[206] LBJ Library, NSF, Head of State Correspondence File, Box 9, United Kingdom: Prime Minister Wilson Correspondence, Volume 3, no. 29.

[207] See 100. Bromley Smith, Executive Secretary of the National Security Council, had advised a 'short warm, non-substantive reply' (Smith to Read, 28 February 1966, LBJ Library, NSF, Head of State Correspondence File, Box 9, Volume 2 [1 of 2], no. 4).

[208] LBJ Library, NSF File, Head of State Correspondence File, Box 9, United Kingdom: Prime Minister Wilson Correspondence, Volume 3, no. 26.

[209] See 99.

I am also glad you lectured them about the Germans. I wish the Russians would get it through their heads that we are just as interested as they are in keeping Germany from going off the deep end.

On a possible meeting of foreign ministers on non-proliferation, I am open-minded. If the Geneva talks develop to the point where a meeting would be useful, I would hope that you and I could discuss it directly.

On a different matter, I have now talked to Bob McNamara about the HS. 125.[210] He tells me that other pressing priorities make it questionable whether he will spend any money on aircraft of that type. If he should decide to buy any, he will, of course, give careful consideration to the HS. 125. Bob points out, however, that the cost of your plane would pose serious difficulties. His people calculate that it is 50–100 percent more expensive than similar U.S. aircraft. Nevertheless, if he decides to go ahead, he will be in touch with your people.

In any case, I hope the F-111 arrangement[211] worked out between Bob and Denis Healey will be of help. I have in mind both our $325 million procurement commitment, and the $400 million target for British sales to third countries. Most of these third country sales should result in orders for your aircraft industry.

Incidentally, Bob tells me that the Nuclear Planning Working Group[212] meeting came off very well. He is hopeful that this enterprise will become increasingly productive and looks forward to the next meeting in London.

Let me say once more how much I appreciate your readiness to keep in close touch on the many problems which confront us. It is of great comfort to me, and a good thing for our countries, the Alliance, and the world.

---

[210] See 94.

[211] See 93, footnote 190.

[212] The Nuclear Planning Group represented a 'software' solution to the vexed problem of nuclear sharing within NATO.

Chapter 2
Dissociation, NATO, and the Continuing Crisis in Rhodesia, March 1966–January 1967

103. Message from Johnson to Wilson, 7 March 1966[1]

I have asked David Bruce to give you a copy of the letter I have received from General de Gaulle.[2]

I am responding to the General that his proposed actions raise the most serious questions for the Alliance and that I am consulting with the other governments affected.

I know that this comes at a difficult time for you. Germany lies at the heart of the problem of maintaining a safe and healthy Europe. You and I know how delicate questions of international affairs can intrude themselves into the course of a political campaign, as they did into the last German election. I feel that the crisis precipitated by the General should lead both sides in Britain to refrain from any comments in the campaign that might give aid and comfort to the General in his attack upon the great post-war structure of defense which we have all built together.

I understand that you also will be receiving a letter from General de Gaulle.[3] Just as soon as that it is received, it is essential that we be in touch so that the key allies can speak with a single voice.

---

[1] LBJ Library, NSF, Head of State Correspondence File, Box 9, United Kingdom: Prime Minister Wilson Correspondence, Volume 3, no. 23. This message superseded an earlier one of the same date which was evidently never sent. Referring to Wilson's message of 27 February (100), Johnson remarked: 'I fear that anti-German sentiments expressed in the course of your political campaign might simply serve to give aid and comfort to the General and complicate the problem of dealing effectively with his tactical maneuvers.'

[2] In his letter of the same date, de Gaulle declared: 'France proposes to recover the entire exercise of her sovereignty over her territory, presently impaired by the permanent presence of allied military elements or by constant utilization which is made of her space, to terminate her participation in "integrated" commands and no longer place her forces at the disposal of NATO.'

[3] The letter, dated 9 March, was relayed to Johnson by Ambassador Dean the following day (Letter from Dean to Johnson, 10 March 1966, LBJ Library, NSF, Head of State Correspondence File, Box 9, Volume 3, no. 21).

104. Message from Wilson to Johnson, 10 March 1966[4]

You may have noticed that we have been having a little difficulty with sterling in the last day or two. It is clear that this is basically a matter of electionitis—those who operate in the foreign exchange markets dislike the instability that comes from normal democratic processes.

A particular group of them operating in such comfortable places as Hamburg are devoting themselves to turning an honest penny by speculating on the expected fall in the rate. The speculators will no doubt run for cover as soon as the election is over - and the way our opinion polls are going I may be able to offer them a considerable period of stability.

In the meantime, however, if we just let the rate go, speculation could snowball to serious proportions. In any case attack is the best form of defence and we have a good chance of effective action over the next few days, particularly as we are publishing some good trade figures tomorrow. So the Bank of England will be moving in right away with the Fed., with all guns blazing, to try to hold rate at around its present level. The Fed. turned the New York market yesterday at no great cost. They are experts at the technique and I know that we can rely on them to go on applying it.

However, it is possible that the situation will call for rather more massive intervention than we had expected and my purpose in sending this message is to ask you to keep a benevolent eye on the situation in case further encouragement or greater resources are needed on your side. This is precisely the kind of situation which was envisaged when the support operation was mounted last September and just as the opposing forces turned tail when they realized what they were up against (at negligible cost to the home side) so I am sure that this time the mere knowledge that the Dollar and Sterling have linked arms should do the trick.

I have heard suggestions that your prime rate may be raised in the near future. Whatever the technical reasons for this, and I do not doubt that they are strong, this could well increase our difficulties. I do not know whether this has come your way but in any case I am sure you would see that wider considerations are not overlooked.

---

[4] LBJ Library, NSF, Head of State Correspondence File, Box 9, United Kingdom: Prime Minister Wilson Correspondence, Volume 3, no. 19.

105. Message from Johnson to Wilson, 10 March 1966[5]

Thank you for your message on sterling.[6] I will, of course, keep an eye on the situation. However, my people tell me that they are confident that the resources available to you will suffice to hold the line. As I understand it, the September arrangement is still in place, and you also have available from us the regular Federal Reserve swap.

In any case, let's by all means stay in touch.

On the prime rate,[7] I frankly don't know how long we can hold out. You will understand that for external as well as internal reasons, it is essential that we not allow demand to get out of hand. I do not believe that a rise in the prime rate would be helpful. But the banks are under great pressure and I don't and can't control them. In any case, my experts do not believe that a rise in the prime rate would cause you appreciable difficulty although I think it would be ill advised from our standpoint. For the time being at least I think we will be able to avoid any rise in the discount rate,[8] which might be unsettling for you.

106. Message from Johnson to Wilson, 10 March 1966[9]

I want you to know that we got the news about the Morgan Guaranty increasing its prime rate an hour after I approved my earlier message.[10] As you see, I really don't control them. At the moment, they are not exactly my favorite people.

107. Message from Johnson to Wilson, 11 March 1966[11]

Dear Mr. Prime Minister:
On behalf of the American people, I extend warmest greetings and best wishes on the occasion of your fiftieth birthday. Mrs Johnson joins me in the hope that this day finds you in the best of health and spirits.

---

[5] LBJ Library, NSF, Head of State Correspondence File, Box 9, United Kingdom: Prime Minister Wilson Correspondence, Volume 3, no. 13.
[6] See 104.
[7] The interest rate that commercial banks charged their most credit-worthy customers.
[8] The rate that eligible depository institutions were charged to borrow short-term funds directly from the Federal Reserve.
[9] LBJ Library, NSF, Head of State Correspondence File, Box 9, United Kingdom: Prime Minister Wilson Correspondence, Volume 3, no. 17.
[10] See 105.
[11] LBJ Library, NSF, Head of State Correspondence File, Box 9, United Kingdom: Prime Minister Wilson Correspondence, Volume 3, no. 9.

Lyndon B. Johnson

108. Message from Johnson to Wilson, 11 March 1966[12]

Dear Harold:
The ceremonial quality of my official birthday greeting reflects your current problem. Let me add on a personal basis that Mrs. Johnson and I wish you the best and happiest of birthdays—and many happy returns.
Lyndon B. Johnson

109. Message from Wilson to Johnson, 11 March 1966[13]

Both your birthday messages received and points taken.[14] Very many thanks.

110. Message from Wilson to Johnson, 21 March 1966[15]

The General's rogue elephant tactics[16] within the Alliance are going to present you, me and other Allies with major decisions before too long. Before we come to the point of decision making, I think that you and I should exchange views personally, and I will be sending you another message very soon. Meanwhile, I am most anxious that ideas on your side of the Atlantic should not harden too much while we are evolving ours.
Broadly speaking, my present conclusions are:

1. The General's action both poses a threat and offers an opportunity.
2. The continuation of the Alliance is vital but the present provides an excellent opportunity for a radical examination of its structure, force levels and financial arrangements.
3. Germany should be encouraged to look for the ultimate satisfaction of her own interests in peaceful reunification and adapt her short-term policies on NATO nuclear matters.

---

[12] LBJ Library, NSF, Head of State Correspondence File, Box 9, United Kingdom: Prime Minister Wilson Correspondence, Volume 3, no. 8.

[13] LBJ Library, NSF, Head of State Correspondence File, Box 9, United Kingdom: Prime Minister Wilson Correspondence, Volume 3, no. 6.

[14] See 107 and 108.

[15] LBJ Library, NSF, Head of State Correspondence File, Box 9, United Kingdom: Prime Minister Wilson Correspondence, Volume 3, no. 3.

[16] See 103.

4. In bringing our Alliance structure up to date, we should also look to détente with the East and take care not to overcompensate for France's defection in a way which would make progress with the East more difficult of accomplishment.

This is only a summary of my present thoughts, and I will be sending you a further message when I have more time to elaborate what is in my mind. Long term decisions will of course be difficult for Britain to take for the next ten days, but I hope you agree that these important issues need not be rushed, and that there is time for you and me to work them out between ourselves.

111. Message from Wilson to Johnson, 23 March 1966[17]

As you know, Lord Chalfont is going off to Moscow tomorrow for further discussions on disarmament. The subject of a possible meeting of Foreign Ministers to give impetus to the Geneva discussions is bound to come up. Our Ambassador in Moscow has reported that Gromyko raised this subject with him yesterday and told him that the Soviet Government had heard through their Ambassador in Washington that the United States view was that such a meeting would not be timely or expedient. I should of course very much like to know in advance of Lord Chalfont's further talks with the Russians whether this report is true. I had understood from your message of 3 March that you have an open mind on this possibility and that you would hope to discuss the proposal with me if we got to the point where such a meeting might be useful. I hope this still represents your view.

Mr. Gromyko also raised the question whether the proposed meeting, if it takes place, should be of all five nuclear powers, or only of those three represented at the Geneva conference.[18] On this too I should be grateful to know what you think.

112. Message from Johnson to Wilson, 23 March 1966[19]

On the NATO problem, I agree we must think out the position carefully and I look forward to a fuller account of your thinking.[20] For the moment let me only

---

[17] LBJ Library, NSF, Head of State Correspondence File, Box 9, United Kingdom: Prime Minister Wilson Correspondence, Volume 4, no. 75a.

[18] Britain, the United States, and the Soviet Union.

[19] LBJ Library, NSF, Head of State Correspondence File, Box 9, United Kingdom: Prime Minister Wilson Correspondence, Volume 4, no. 73.

[20] See 116.

say that our best hope of security in the future is for our two countries to work with the Germans in a meaningful partnership. We must avoid the rankling discrimination that has caused so much grief in the past.

Meanwhile, if our other allies will stand with us, we should be able over time to settle the great unfinished business of Europe. But, as I said in a speech I made this morning, to surrender the strength we have built through NATO "by isolation from one another would be to dim the promise of that day when the men and women of all Europe shall again move freely among each other."

113. Message from Johnson to Wilson, 23 March 1966[21]

Have heard reports of unidentified flying object in your vicinity.[22]
Can you verify?

114. Message from Johnson to Wilson, 24 March 1966[23]

I will be most grateful in hearing what progress Lord Chalfont makes in Moscow.[24] I would have thought from the way the discussions have been going in Geneva that the prospect is not very promising.

I should think we could better judge the advisability of a Foreign Ministers meeting after we know what Gromyko has to say. A meeting which makes no progress would surely be worse than no meeting at all.

Unless Gromyko gives some definite indication of a change in the Soviet position, I would be inclined to wait and see what transpires at the Soviet Congress before making any approaches to the Russians on a meeting. It seems to me unlikely that the Soviets would now want an announcement of a Foreign Ministers meeting in view of the communication which they have just received from Peking. This would also affect the question of whether the Chinese Communists should be included. It would seem almost certain that they would not attend and inviting them would cause complications with other countries, such as India.

In general, therefore, I would await further developments before we make another move.

---

[21] LBJ Library, NSF, Head of State Correspondence File, Box 9, United Kingdom: Prime Minister Wilson Correspondence, Volume 4, no. 71.

[22] Wilson was hit by a glass vial as he addressed a rally in Slough.

[23] LBJ Library, NSF, Head of State Correspondence File, Box 9, United Kingdom: Prime Minister Wilson Correspondence, Volume 4, no. 67.

[24] See 111.

115. Message from Wilson to Johnson, 25 March 1966[25]

Many thanks for your telegram about the unidentified object.[26] Object has now been identified. You will rejoice to hear that it was not of U.S. origin. The warhead was, in fact, German, and the fissionable contents were ferrous sulphide and mild hydrochloric acid.
The result of the fission being a somewhat dirty bomb. However, no permanent damage, and all is now well.
Thank you for your enquiry.

116. Message from Wilson to Johnson, 29 March 1966[27]

I promised to send you some further thoughts on the problems which General de Gaulle's latest moves present for us all.[28]

I see that you have been giving a great deal of personal consideration to these problems with your top advisers and I very much hope that they will continue to take Patrick Dean fully into their confidence. But none of this is a substitute for the sort of plain speaking between you and me which friendship and common interest permits. I know you will reciprocate.

I start from the proposition that NATO is vital to the safety of Britain and that it must therefore continue. I believe this is to be so for a number of reasons:

First, because it commits the United States to the defence of Europe;

Secondly, because it provides a tolerable context in which not only Britain, but most of Europe as well, have been able to accept Western German rearmament;

And thirdly, because it is only an [sic] integrated and interdependent alliance which can provide a credible deterrent against attack from the East and effective resistance if attack should come.

I also start from the proposition that the General's 19th century nationalism, his anti-American motivation and above all his bull in a china shop tactics are certainly dangerous to the alliance and possibly malevolently so. But I think it would be wrong to conclude from all this that all the General's thoughts are wrong-headed, his assessments of the way the world is moving completely wide of the mark and that everything he is trying to do is totally unacceptable to us all.

To begin with, the General seems to be acting on the basis that he regards Europe twenty years after the end of the war as being tolerably safe from military

---

[25] LBJ Library, NSF, Head of State Correspondence File, Box 9, United Kingdom: Prime Minister Wilson Correspondence, Volume 4, no. 65.

[26] See 113.

[27] LBJ Library, NSF, Head of State Correspondence File, Box 9, United Kingdom: Prime Minister Wilson Correspondence, Volume 4, no. 62a.

[28] See 110.

attack from the Soviet Union. This is partly because NATO exists to repel such an attack and he can operate with relative impunity under the American nuclear umbrella which is presumably why he denounces the organisation rather than the alliance as such. It is also because in his view the Soviet Union has changed and is still changing in character and because therefore the very nature of the threat from Russia has altered and the intensity of the military threat diminished. For example, he would say that the main centre of conflict has shifted to Asia, although he is unwilling to draw the natural conclusion that NATO cannot confine its attention to the Atlantic area alone and he remains determined not to become embroiled in the containment of communism in Southeast Asia. The General goes on from his premises to argue that since the dangers have lessened we should go over to what one might call peaceful attack and seek to promote a detente with the Soviet Union at the expense of the United States presence in Europe. Although we cannot be sure that the threat would remain dormant if NATO no longer existed to contain it, there is some attraction in both these propositions. We have armed, not merely to be able to resist attack if it should come, but so that we can parley with confidence. Where I disagree with him, and this is fundamental, is in his apparent belief that you can talk with the Russians from a position of weakness and disarray.

I regard the General's action therefore both as a threat and as an opportunity. Of course we must maintain the cohesion of the alliance, but we must guard against over compensating for the French defection to an extent which would make any further progress with the Soviet Union more difficult of accomplishment or in a way which puts France beyond the pale. I see no reason why the fact that we have, and are likely to continue to have, difficulty with the Communists in the third world should prevent us from recognising that things are reasonably stable in Europe and the Atlantic area at present and that we may be able to profit from this to do some of the things that we all want to do: For example, to slim the vast military headquarters apparatus in Europe and possibly streamline the actual level of our forces deployed on the continent, and above all to reach fairer arrangements about the problem of foreign exchange costs which plague us both: to turn our allies' attention to some of the problems which you and I face in the Indo-Pacific area, as Bob McNamara tried to do last December: and from this base of a reconstituted alliance to see whether we can carry the present state of détente further, perhaps by pressing the Russians to accept something like an up to date version of the 1959 Western Peace Plan[29] or in other ways. It remains to be seen whether the Russians would be ready to respond. Indeed, their present mood may be that de Gaulle's action has given them something of

---

[29] Presented to the Soviet Union by US Secretary of State, Christian Herter, at the East-West Foreign Ministers' conference held in Geneva in May 1959, the 'Western peace plan' aimed to settle the problem of Germany's future and cut the armed forces of both sides.

a breakthrough and his visit to Moscow may give them further encouragement. But all this is something which I believe we should consider carefully together, to see whether despite the French attitude progress can be made.

I recognise, as you do, that the position of Federal Germany is crucial in all this. My view is that, while it remains as essential as ever to keep Germany integrated in the Western Community in the framework of the 1954 Agreements,[30] the opportunity which now exists for us all to re-examine the structure and purpose of NATO also provides an opportunity for Germany to re-assess her legitimate national objectives. All of us, as loyal allies, recognise the Federal Republic as the sole authority to speak for Germany as a whole: we refuse to recognise the Soviet Zone as an independent state and we support Germany's claim for reunification in peace and freedom. This is indeed an essential element in any lasting settlement with Russia. But the Germans themselves will be the first to recognise that they should shape their present policies always with a view to the ultimate achievement of reunification. This is why it seems to me that we should work now for a solution of the NATO nuclear problem which will meet the German need for a share in the consultative and decision-making process without prejudicing her other ambitions. As I see it, this rules out what is normally called the hardware solution. It would seem to point to something like the establishment of a permanent body of restricted membership within NATO, with consultative functions over the whole Western strategic deterrent and some executive functions over the American and British strategic nuclear forces assigned to NATO. This would in fact contain many of the elements of our ANF proposals, including the assignment to NATO for as long as NATO lasts of our strategic forces and an equivalent number of yours, together with the association of non-nuclear powers in the deployment, targeting and management of these forces, subject always of course to your and our veto, and in consultation on the world-wide policy for the deterrent. Whether we can persuade the Germans of this is, of course, another matter. I shall certainly have a go at Erhard over it when he comes here at the end of May and cultivate the idea that it is only by working for a gradual process of detente with the East that we shall come to reunification in the end. I am encouraged to some extent by the latest German peace initiative in the context of the 23rd Party Congress[31]: I thought when I saw it that here was a helpful statement by Germany of Germany's problems.

These are the considerations which have led me to the broad conclusions which I have already conveyed to you, namely:

---

[30] On 23 October 1954, West Germany was invited to join NATO.
[31] The 23rd Congress of the Soviet Communist Party met between 29 March and 8 April 1966.

1. The General's action both poses a threat and offers an opportunity.
2. The continuation of the alliance is vital but the present provides an excellent opportunity for a radical examination of its structure, force level and financial arrangements.
3. Germany should be encouraged to look for the ultimate satisfaction of her own interests in peaceful reunification and to adapt her short-term policies in NATO accordingly.
4. In bringing the structure and institutions of our alliance up to date, we should always keep our eyes on the importance of an eventual detente with the East.

This, as I said at the start, is only my background thinking. In working out our specific policies, I am sure that we must work, as I said on my return from Moscow, from a position four square within the Western alliance, and especially on the basis of full agreement between the two of us and also with Germany.

117. Message from Johnson to Wilson, 1 April 1966[32]

There is nothing more warming to a politician's heart than the soothing sound of voter approval. But I hope you have less trouble with your big majority[33] than I have with mine. All of us in the White House were rejoicing over your sensational victory until I realized the problems my increased majority in 1964 brought me. Tread carefully. Don't forget, mandates are very temporary affairs.

But this is prickly of me. I ought to let you enjoy the sweetness of victory one night without someone rising to testify about problems.

Sleep well, my dear friend. You've earned it. It's comforting to me to know you are still at the British helm. I feel better about the future.

118. Message from Johnson to Wilson, 1 April 1966[34]

I understand you will be seeing Prime Minister Gandhi Saturday and want you to have my initial reaction to her talks here.[35]

We made no hard and fast decisions, and it will probably take several weeks to know exactly where we go from here. However, I am confident that she

---

[32] LBJ Library, NSF, Head of State Correspondence File, Box 9, United Kingdom: Prime Minister Wilson Correspondence, Volume 4, no. 59.

[33] Wilson's Labour Party secured an overall majority of 97.

[34] LBJ Library, NSF, Head of State Correspondence File, Box 9, United Kingdom: Prime Minister Wilson Correspondence, Volume 4, no. 56.

[35] Mrs Gandhi had talks in Washington, including two meetings with Johnson, on 28 and 29 March 1966.

understands the nature of the economic changes we would like her government to work out with the World Bank—liberalization of India's import control policies as a well as internal price, marketing and other business controls which have been inhibiting economic growth and adjustment of exchange rates and tax policies to support such liberalization. I believe she also understands the need to move rapidly toward self-sufficiency in food, making adequate fertilizer available to the farmers and vigorously seeking to attract foreign private investment in fertilizer production. She also understands the importance of a vigorous family planning program.

For my part, I made it clear I understand that such a program would require assurances of substantial financial support. I told her that, if India actually takes the necessary steps to the satisfaction of the World Bank and the consortium donors, we are prepared to help, subject of course to Congressional appropriations.

The next move in my view is up to her. I understand confidentially that George Woods urged Mrs. Gandhi to send her Finance and Planning Ministers to Washington promptly to work out economic details. We do not know whether she will do this, but I regard this as crucial to our next steps.

I have also sent to the Congress a special message on the Indian food crisis in hopes of stimulating a bigger international effort to help India and to gain Congressional support for our general efforts to put India on its feet. Response here so far has been good.

You should feel free, if you wish, to tell Mrs. Gandhi that you are sure the United States will help her economic efforts provided she is determined to work out a program acceptable to the World Bank. You may want to argue that the time for her to move is right now, before she gets bogged down later this year in her election campaign. At the very least, I hope you can urge her to send some of her key people back right away to talk with the Bank.

119. Message from Johnson to Wilson, 1 April 1964[36]

In the great democratic tradition, the British people have made their choice. On behalf of all Americans, I extend warm congratulations to you and your countrymen.

In company with our friends and allies around the world, our two nations have great tasks to perform. I very much look forward to continuing our work together in the cause of peace and freedom everywhere.

With warmest personal regards.
Sincerely,
    Lyndon B. Johnson

---

[36] LBJ Library, NSF, Head of State Correspondence File, Box 9, United Kingdom: Prime Minister Wilson Correspondence, Volume 4, no. 54.

120. Message from Wilson to Johnson, 1 April 1966[37]

Your message[38] was the first thing I saw on my return from Huyton[39] to Downing Street. My constituents could not have given me a better send off nor your kind message a warmer welcome.

At last I have elbow room and time for tackling our big problems. The knowledge of your steadfast support in the past gives me confidence for the tasks ahead. But first, as you say, to sleep. No, first I must mend my fences with our charming friend, Indira Gandhi,[40] whom I meet at the airport tomorrow: then to sleep.

121. Message from Wilson to Johnson, 22 April 1966[41]

I want you to know of a new and potentially important development.

I received on the afternoon of April 19 a message from the Governor saying that Smith had been to see him and Beadle the night before to say that he would like to start talks to settle the present situation. He would attach no preconditions whatsoever to the commencement of talks and recognised that they must be canalised through the Governor. He was prepared for talks to start at any level that I might suggest.

As luck would have it, my private secretary, Oliver Wright, had just taken off for South Africa to be on hand for the exchanges our ambassador has been having with Verwoerd. We managed to haul him off the plane when it transited Salisbury and he and Hennings (our man there) were instructed to talk to the Governor and Beadle and to try to discover whether the initiative had indeed been taken by Smith himself: whether no preconditions meant what it said, and particularly that we were not expected to recognise the fact of independence:

---

[37] LBJ Library, NSF, Head of State Correspondence File, Box 9, United Kingdom: Prime Minister Wilson Correspondence, Volume 4, no. 52.

[38] See 119.

[39] Wilson's constituency.

[40] This is an oblique reference to the Indo-Pakistan war of 1965. India's counter-attack on the Punjab, the heartland of Pakistan, following Pakistani infiltration into Kashmir, had been criticised by Wilson. The British High Commissioner in New Delhi, John Freeman, subsequently reported that Indian hostility towards Britain was 'more serious than at any time since independence,' adding that its basic cause 'lay rooted in the Indian conviction that our failure to condemn the August Pakistan infiltration and the September Pakistan attacks revealed their long suspected fear that we supported Pakistan on the Kashmir issue' (Letter from C. C. W. Adams to J. O. Wright reporting Freeman's views, 22 Oct. 1965, TNA, PREM 13/396.).

[41] LBJ Library, NSF, Head of State Correspondence File, Box 11, M.O.D. 8/30/65–12/31/66 [1 of 2], no. 34.

whether Smith could accept the six principles: to what extent the regime as a whole supported the suggestion of talks: and how the governor thought any talks should proceed.

From what Wright has reported, it seems reasonably fair to say that the initiative was Smith's own and that no preconditions meant what it said. It is much more difficult to establish to what extent Smith carries the support of his colleagues.

Both Beadle and the Governor are convinced that he has support in the country for what he is doing and could carry it with him. The problem is clearly the wild men in the Rhodesian Front.[42] My personal hunch is that Smith is under increasing pressure within the Party and there are growing signs of a possible split. Against this background, it is difficult to interpret exactly what he is trying to do through his present initiative.

On the other hand, it is clear, from what Wright was able to learn, that the effect of our economic sanctions is at last beginning to make an impact on the Rhodesian leaders, as well as on the rank and file. Moreover, the Governor told him that about 3,000 unemployed Europeans had already packed up and gone to South Africa and that 4,000 more are either unemployed or underemployed: and our passport office has increased its business this week about five fold over the normal. Here again precise conclusions are clearly impossible but, as Wright puts it, a superficial judgment is that whereas the wallpaper is still intact, the walls behind it may be beginning to crack and the Governor believes that the regime and business community know this.

It is for reasons such as these that the Governor and Beadle think that Smith's approach may mark a break-through and want to get talks going. But of course it is not as simple as that. I myself am not more than cautiously optimistic. It is clear that, both economically and politically, the regime is in great difficulties. But before we can get into any substantive talks we must be as sure as we can that this is a genuine initiative and not simply a trap designed to restore Smith's hold over the Front. We must also have some estimate of the extent to which he is a free agent: he may be trying to break away from his wild men, or alternatively, he could be speaking for a relatively united cabinet which he can still control. Moreover, even if he is sincere in his purpose and we managed too [sic] have some reasonably serious discussion, there is clearly no guarantee of this resulting in his agreement to an acceptable solution. In short, we have to be satisfied that the situation as a whole offers at least a prospect of getting an ultimate settlement of a kind that you and I would regard as right and defensible before our own and world opinion.

---

[42] Formed in 1962 and led by Ian Smith from 1964, the Rhodesian Front opposed black majority rule.

Accordingly I am sending Wright back this weekend from South Africa to Salisbury and have told him to try, in a confidential talk with Smith himself, if Smith will agree to this, to get a direct and first hand impression of Smith's state of mind and real motives. Wright will say that I am willing to consider the possibility of opening informal talks (but not, at least at this stage, anything that could be qualified as negotiations): and I have asked him to ascertain from Smith personally on what basis he envisages such talks taking place. He is to try to obtain direct confirmation that no preconditions means just that: and to sound Smith out on the likely attitudes of his colleagues. Wright will then report back to us, return to South Africa, and lie low there in case I need to use him again. If he manages to have this kind of confidential talk with Smith, we should see our way ahead a little more clearly next week. Meanwhile it is of vital importance that news of this should not get out. Obviously Smith can leak it any time he wants. If he does at least we shall know where we stand. But the fact that Wright's visit this week has so far not become known, and that the regime authorised our mission to use their diplomatic cyphers [sic] for the Governor's message and our replies, are mildly encouraging straws in the wind. I wish we had rather more substantial evidence of Smith's bone fides. But, just as we can clearly given [sic] no outward sign of let-up on sanctions even while secret talks may be going on, so I suppose we cannot expect any public let-up on the Rhodesian side. An example of this kind of public difficulty arose for me in the House of Commons yesterday. I have told Wright to explain to Smith personally how concerned I was that from now on we should avoid in any public pronouncements anything that might prejudice the possibilities which may now be opening: but in the circumstances I could not have taken any other line in the House without risking premature disclosure. In fact what I said yesterday was said in Smith's own interests.

We are holding this exceptionally tight here and I know you will do the same. But I wanted you to know of it. It is a glimmer of light which may well go out. But, despite all the risks, I believe we are doing the right thing in following it up.

122. Message from Johnson to Wilson, 23 April 1966[43]

Your report to me on the Rhodesian feeler[44] was another manifestation of your constant thoughtfulness.

I find it most heartening.

---

[43] LBJ Library, NSF, Head of State Correspondence File, Box 9, United Kingdom: Prime Minister Wilson Correspondence, Volume 4, no. 45.

[44] See 121.

We feel with you and for you in your efforts to surmount peacefully this critical problem.

I am sure you have seen the Rhodesian negotiating document attributed to Evan Campbell, which our intelligence services have acquired. It has given me some encouragement.

I will greatly welcome your further thoughts as this contact unfolds.

123. Message from Johnson to Wilson, 26 April 1966[45]

I want you to know that I continue to appreciate your efforts to stop British flag vessels from calling at North Vietnamese ports. I know how difficult the problem is, and the fact that there has been improvement in the situation is most helpful to me. Unfortunately, however, Congress and public opinion are still unhappy that this trade has not been halted altogether.

The names and the registry of free world ships in the North Viet-Nam trade are now published regularly by the Maritime Administration as is the case with ships in the Cuba trade. The latest list shows six calls by British flag ships and only three calls by ships flying the flags of other free world nations since January 25. This is giving rise to questions as to how my Administration can go on supporting Great Britain in economic sanctions against Rhodesia when British flag vessels are permitted to continue in the North Viet-Nam trade. Our officials explain the difficulties that your Government faces in dealing with the problem, but emotions are, unfortunately, more powerful than logic. So long as the trade persists there is danger that the Congress may try to tie the Administration's hands in helping out on Rhodesia.

I appreciate the vulnerability of Hong Kong with respect to the Chinese Communists and our own interest in your ability to maintain your position there. I would accordingly not presume to suggest how you might pursue the matter. I can only tell you how deeply I feel that an early solution is necessary in the interests of both our countries.

---

[45] LBJ Library, NSF, Head of State Correspondence File, Box 9, United Kingdom: Prime Minister Wilson Correspondence, Volume 4, no. 38.

124. Message from Wilson to Johnson, 27 April 1966[46]

I was very grateful for your kind reaction to my message about the Rhodesian feeler.[47]

As you can imagine, things have moved fast since then. Wright's report of the businesslike talk he had with Smith and his general impressions of the situation derived from this talk and from what the Governor and Beaddle [sic][48] said to him was sufficiently forthcoming, in our view, to justify continuing the dialogue. Briefly, Wright recognized that only the next round of talks could establish whether a basis for negotiation existed. But he thought that the omens were pretty good and firmly recommended that we should at least go on to the next round.

Accordingly, I sent him back to reach agreement with Smith on the holding of strictly informal talks with no pre-conditions to establish whether a basis existed for the subsequent negotiation of an acceptable settlement. We are appointing Duncan Watson, with Oliver Wright, to represent us at these talks and have proposed that the first round at least should be in London, though it may be desirable for the subsequent rounds to take place in Salisbury.

Before Wright had been able to put this to Smith, the news had begun to break in the South African press, though it is not absolutely clear whether the leak was in South Africa or in Salisbury. At all events, I had been convinced that we should not be able to keep this secret and had told Wright to warn Smith that if the news broke, a statement would have to be made. He managed to agree to a short text with Smith and this is contained in the first paragraph of the statement I shall now make in the House this afternoon. The text of this is attached.[49] To protect Smith, we have agreed not to say specifically that he first approached the Governor. But the text clearly implies that the initiation was made in Salisbury.

With luck, this publicity should not make it too difficult for us to pursue these exploratory talks. But you will realize that it is still an entirely open question whether the talks will reveal that any solid basis exists for an eventual solution. I know that you share our hopes. I am sure that you also share our recognition of the pitfalls.

I will, of course, continue to keep you posted.

---

[46] LBJ Library, NSF, Head of State Correspondence File, Box 9, United Kingdom: Prime Minister Wilson Correspondence, Volume 4, no. 41.
[47] See 122.
[48] Wilson is evidently referring to Sir Hugh Beadle.
[49] Not printed. See *Parliamentary Debates (Hansard): Commons, 1966–67*, Volume 727, cols. 708–9.

125. Message from Johnson to Wilson, 27 April 1966[50]

I thank you for the interim report.[51] You appear to be playing this nibble just right: although I agree the fish isn't hooked or landed.

126. Message from Wilson to Johnson, 3 May 1966[52]

I thought you would like to have advance notice that in his budget statement on Tuesday, the Chancellor is going to announce that our import surcharge of 10 percent will be removed when the powers to levy it lapse in November of this year.

This is something of a bold step since we have not got rid of our payments deficit yet, but we are making progress and I think this gesture of confidence may help. It will certainly help us in our dealings with the EFTA countries who were particularly resentful of the surcharge when we first introduced it.

You, and indeed all your people, have always been very understanding of our difficulty and I should like to take this opportunity of thanking you once again for your forbearance over it.

127. Message from Wilson to Johnson, 9 May 1966[53]

Thank you for your message about the British flag vessels going to North Vietnamese ports, which I received on April 27.[54] I fully understand why you would like to see this traffic reduced still further and, if possible, eliminated altogether. So would I. While it continues it will be an embarrassment for both our governments because of the political and emotional feeling it engenders. I can also understand the disposition of Congress and public opinion to link the questions of Vietnam and Rhodesia, though I would hope that Congress would understand both our own difficulties and also the strength, indeed virtual unanimity, of world opinion, within the United Nations and elsewhere that is behind us on Rhodesia.

---

[50] LBJ Library, NSF, Head of State Correspondence File, Box 9, United Kingdom: Prime Minister Wilson Correspondence, Volume 4, no. 36.
[51] See 124.
[52] LBJ Library, NSF, Head of State Correspondence File, Box 9, United Kingdom: Prime Minister Wilson Correspondence, Volume 4, no. 34.
[53] LBJ Library, NSF, Head of State Correspondence File, Box 9, United Kingdom: Prime Minister Wilson Correspondence, Volume 4, no. 28b.
[54] See 123.

I am satisfied that the participation by United Kingdom ships in the North Vietnamese trade has now been virtually eliminated, thanks to the influence exerted by our people on the British Chamber of Shipping, and through it, on United Kingdom shipping companies. This leaves us with the problem of Hong Kong ships, though even with these the Governor of Hong Kong has had some success by means of influence and persuasion, so that the number of ships engaged in the traffic has gone down. I think that the figures in your possession do not yet perhaps reflect this reduction.

We are thus approaching the limit of what we can do either in Hong Kong or in the United Kingdom without legislation. I feel I must tell you quite frankly that political and public opinion in this country would be strongly opposed to our enacting restrictive legislation: in any case we have persuaded all the ships without commitments to leave the trade and there is no longer a problem here. The danger is that the debates on such legislation would provide a custom-built and continuing platform for all those who are at all times bursting to make a speech on Vietnam, and this might endanger the ever-vulnerable control we have been able to retain in the House on the Vietnam issue.

As regards Hong Kong it would be difficult to legislate on such a matter except on the basis of some corresponding United Kingdom legislation. I am convinced that if we tried this it would only provoke reactions which would jeopardise the usefulness of Hong Kong to the United States effort in Vietnam.

In so far as two or three Hong Kong ships are still on charter to Japan, which has a comparatively big trade with North Vietnam, and these ships are liable to be sent to North Vietnamese ports, I wonder if you can help us by suggesting to the Japanese that they should reduce their trade. If the figures, and the reports we have from Hong Kong, then show that the problem is down to the irreducible minimum of Communist-owned Hong Kong ships, I think this is as much as we can realistically expect.[55]

---

[55] The Executive Secretary of the State Department, Benjamin Read, remarked: 'The Department does not consider it advisable to send a reply to Prime Minister Wilson's message of May 9 to the President on North Vietnam shipping. We do not feel there are any additional persuasive considerations which can be advanced to Wilson at this time. We would propose to maintain the pressure on the British on this issue at other levels, keeping under review the desirability of another Presidential message to Wilson depending on developments' (Memorandum from Read to Walt W. Rostow, 16 May 1966, LBJ Library, NSF, Head of State Correspondence File, Box 9, Volume 4, No. 29).

128. Message from Wilson to Johnson, 20 May 1966[56]

I should like you to know that we shall be making an announcement at 5:00 P.M. London time today (1:00 P.M. Washington) that the talks between the British and Rhodesian officials will be adjourned to enable both sides to report back to their principals. We shall also announce that the talks will resume shortly but shall not at this stage announce the date or place of resumption. For your own private information the date is likely to be about Whitsun (May 29) and the place Salisbury. If possible at Government House, if not at some neutral place like the University.

The officials have had some nine meetings all told and the general impression we have received is that although the Rhodesians have certainly not come to Canossa and have not abandoned rebellion as a fall back position, they are genuinely looking for a way out and would now like to negotiate the independence they so foolishly seized last November. They have told us that they accept that independence, if granted, must come within the ambit of our six principles. Indeed, they have shown particular interest in our sixth principle, which envisages protection for the European minority after majority rule. This suggests that Smith, at any rate, has accepted the inevitability of African assumption of power and is now looking for adequate safeguards to guarantee the security of Europeans when that day arrives. Another promising line of thought to emerge was the idea that the Westminster type of constitution, with its all or nothing characteristics, may not really be the answer to Rhodesia's practical problems. There might be scope for useful discussion on these lines, for one of the advantages of an alternative system would be to give the Africans some power now, immediately, and to enable the Europeans to retain some power after majority rule.

There are still a lot of hurdles ahead, in particular the question of the return to the rule of law. But I am not unhopeful. We have not abandoned our stand of principle of last November. But our ideas, which then fell on deaf ears, are now finding better receptivity. Sanctions are clearly working, inexorably, if slowly, and Smith will be negotiating against a deteriorating economy.

But our basic aim is reconciliation, not punishment. To secure a just and decent future for all races in Rhodesia must be a major British interest and, I would have thought, a major free world interest too. I am beginning to allow myself to hope that we may be able to bring it off.

---

[56] LBJ Library, NSF, Head of State Correspondence, Box 9, United Kingdom: Prime Minister Wilson Correspondence, Volume 4, no. 26a.

129. Message from Johnson to Wilson, 21 May 1966[57]

I have given further thought and study to the problems posed for us by General De Gaulle's decisions and I hope to send you my thoughts on these matters in the near future. Meanwhile, Dean Rusk and George Ball have had a good visit with George Thomson, and I think we are in basic agreement as to how to proceed.

As you may have noted in my talk on the occasion of the Polish millennium, I share your view that we should actively explore possibilities for the east from our Atlantic base.

I know Chancellor Erhard will be visiting you next week, and your talks can be very important: taking account of the comments in your letter of March 29,[58] I would like to make several points that may be relevant to those talks.

The heart of the matter is this: so long as France and Germany were working closely together to build an integrated Europe there was some assurance of stability in German policy and attitudes. Now that France is no longer taking part in this joint effort—and, indeed, placing heavy pressure on German political life—there is grave danger that the Germans will over time feel that they have been cast adrift. A growing sense of uncertainty and insecurity on their part could lead to a fragmentation of European and Atlantic relations which would be tragic for all of us.

On our part, we cannot risk the danger of a rudderless Germany in the heart of Europe.

On the other hand, any exaggerated bilateral relationship between the United States and Germany offers many disadvantages.

I believe, therefore, that it is imperative for our three countries to stay as close as possible to each other. On that basis Europe and the Atlantic world can be rallied.

Such a relationship will be healthy and lasting only if it is based on the concept of German equality with the other major European countries. We have seen before an attempt to keep Germany in second class status. It failed then and it would fail again.

In this circumstance, we should make a special effort to maintain the closest unity of action with the Germans during the coming months of tension.

I am sure, therefore, that it would not serve our common interests now to try to press the Chancellor to accept a nuclear solution that he might consider at variance with the concept of equality.

As you know, the United States did not invent the nuclear issue. We have simply tried to respond to concerns expressed by others.

---

[57] LBJ Library, NSF, Head of State Correspondence, Box 9, United Kingdom: Prime Minister Wilson Correspondence, Volume 4, no. 19.

[58] See 116.

These concerns first became evident when, in December 1957 the NATO heads of government agreed that missiles of strategic range should be placed at the disposal of SACEUR.

Both your government and mine saw serious disadvantages in national land-based deployment of these missiles. That is why the proposal for a joint sea-based force was first developed. The British Government stated in December 1962 that they would "use their best endeavours" in closest consultation with our NATO allies to develop a multilateral sea-based force.

In December 1964 you put forward the alternative proposal for an Atlantic nuclear force. I agreed that this should be fairly and fully discussed among the interested countries. We used our best efforts to guide German thinking along this line. A year later Chancellor Erhard gave a memorandum reflecting German views which went a long way to meet your proposals.

Against this background, it seems important that we not leave the Germans under the impression that we have shifted our views just when they were moving towards us or that we do not take the Chancellor's proposal seriously.

I do not mean at all that I am wedded to any particular solution to this problem. We are doing staff work over the whole range of options. We should not foreclose any of them. I hope this will also be your view and that none of our three governments will freeze its position until we all discuss this question more fully.

It seems to me that what is at stake in all of this is a political question of the deepest moment: Germany's relations with the West. In the context of the present crisis, the pressures on the Germans it has already generated, and the likelihood that those pressures will increase as French diplomatic maneuvers add further confusion, we must all keep together.

In the long pull, I am sure that the one best hope of stability and peace lies in the inclusion of Germany in a larger European unity, in which any latent nationalistic drives can be submerged. I am sure, also, that you and your country hold the key to this possibility and that you can play a role of great leadership in Europe. When all is said and done, no one has come up with a better formula than that of European unity and Atlantic partnership, and I doubt that anyone will. Sincerely,

130. Message from Wilson to Johnson, 25 May 1966[59]

I shall be sending you tomorrow a full account of my discussions with Erhard,[60] which went extremely well. We are in complete agreement on the whole NATO situation. With reference to your message of last Saturday,[61] nuclear sharing was not mentioned by either of us though it was raised in the discussion between the Foreign Secretaries.

My immediate purpose, however, in sending this message relates to the visit I had from David Bruce yesterday, that is to say Monday. He told me of your present intentions in connection with oil installations at Hanoi and Haiphong, while explaining that no final decision had been taken.

As I am sure you know, we have always made clear that any bombing of either of these cities would create a situation where we would have to dissociate ourselves from the action taken. This was, you will remember, fully explained at our meeting in December and, as I think your embassy has reported to you, I have said this more than once when under pressure in the House of Commons. You will therefore understand that I shall have to make a statement of this kind if this action takes place, though you will realise equally that this will not affect my general support of American policy in Vietnam, except in this particular aspect of its execution.

Knowing as I well do the tremendous problems with which you are faced and recognising the tremendous pressures in which you are situated, I would nevertheless ask you to reconsider whether this action, whatever its results in terms of immediate military advantage, is worth the candle. The decision will be yours, and I know you understand our difficulties and the nature of the statement we would have to make. It will make no difference to our basic position, but I would not want there to be any possible danger that you would take this action in possible ignorance of what our reaction would have to be.

131. Message from Wilson to Johnson, 26 May 1966[62]

Before giving you the promised account of my talks with Erhard, I should just like to say, without going into the question of nuclear hardware how much I

---

[59] LBJ Library, NSF, Head of State Correspondence File, Box 9, United Kingdom: Prime Minister Wilson Correspondence, Volume 4, no. 17a.

[60] See 131.

[61] See 129.

[62] LBJ Library, NSF, Head of State Correspondence File, Box 9, United Kingdom: Prime Minister Wilson Correspondence, Volume 4, no. 15.

agree with what you said in your message of the 21st on the need to maintain the closest unity of action with the Germans during the difficult period ahead.[63]

As I said in my message yesterday,[64] our talks with the Chancellor went very well indeed, as I think the communiqué (which you will have seen) brings out pretty clearly. Indeed, I believe it is not an exaggeration to say that they represent something of a high-point in our relations with Germany. I had two private talks with Erhard, when we spoke to each other with complete frankness and found a most encouraging community of approach to the essential problems. The same spirit characterized our more formal meetings. Although I had to take a pretty tough line with him about the foreign exchange costs of our troops in Germany, the atmosphere remained entirely cordial, and I think the Chancellor has gone home sincerely concerned to help find a solution to this problem. I left him in no doubt that, for us, it is a crucial one and that we meant what we said in the Defence Review White Paper.[65] As you will have seen, we have agreed that our Ministers will get together soon to study this again.

We have also agreed that the Chancellor of the Exchequer should go to Bonn to talk about liquidity problems. Here again, I felt a heartening degree of mutual understanding with the Chancellor.

What he and I spoke of most to each other, and what dominated the whole of our talks, was, of course, the series of problems that concern us in the Alliance. It seemed to me that there was virtually total agreement between us, both that the first priority is to resolve the crisis imposed on us by General de Gaulle: and on the way in which this should be tackled. I also detected a growing awareness on the Chancellor's part that the Alliance should be organised for political progress, as well as for military defence, and that we cannot afford to allow de Gaulle to pose successfully as the only champion in the West of detente and peaceful settlement of East–West problems—including, most vital of all, the German problem. I was greatly impressed by Erhard's robust attitude on the whole French problem. His attitude, despite the strong political pressures he faces from those German politicians who put the French Alliance above their NATO loyalties, is just as firm as that of your own Government and ours. As you will know, he agreed the paper which had emerged from George Thomson's talks in Washington with only the most minor drafting amendments and will cooperate in the proposed meeting in Paris next week.

---

[63] See 129.
[64] See 130.
[65] 'As things now stand, we think it right to maintain our ground forces in Germany at about their existing level until satisfactory arms control arrangements have been agreed in Europe provided, however, that some means is found for meeting the foreign exchange costs of these forces' (*Statement on the Defence Estimates 1966: Part I: The Defence Review* (London: HMSO, 1966), Cmnd. 2901, p. 6).

As I told you, nuclear sharing was not mentioned between Erhard and myself. This was not for lack of any opportunity on his part. But frankly, I think we both felt that, at the present juncture in the Alliance's relations with France, this was really a secondary issue. Schröder, of course, raised it with Michael Stewart, but in an entirely sensible and sober way. He spoke of it as a long-term problem which would have to be settled, in his view, through some integrated collective weapons system in addition to consultation; and he asked us at least to keep the options open. Michael Stewart agreed that we should keep an open mind about a solution of the problem. But he reminded Schröder of the continuing link between the nuclear question and disarmament and non-proliferation; while we could certainly not give the Russians a veto on our arrangements in NATO, we had to bear likely reactions in mind in making our own decision.

In the communiqué we have confined ourselves to agreeing on the importance of continuing the studies of the nuclear organization of the Alliance.

I am sure you will agree that it is wise to leave it there for the time being. I know the importance which you attach to an understanding on this matter between the Germans and ourselves and this has been much in my mind. I trust that when the time comes for further discussion, we shall have found that the differences between us all are less than has sometimes been imagined.

We also had a useful short exchange about our own future relations with EEC. The Chancellor made it clear that he did not think there was any real likelihood of an effective negotiation for British entry at present, even supposing that this could be done with due regard to our essential interests. But we were able to make clear our continued willingness to enter into such a negotiation if the opportunity presented itself, and I was encouraged by the evident anxiety of the Chancellor to see us and other EFTA countries in an expanded Common Market on satisfactory terms. I felt that we were thinking along very similar lines.

To sum up, I genuinely believe that the unity of purpose and the unity in action of the Alliance will have been strengthened by this meeting, and I am encouraged by the virtual identity of approach which our three Governments, which are after all key members of NATO, are taking to the present crisis in the Alliance: and to the wider problems of Britain's relationship with Continental Europe and to the continuation of the vital link across the Atlantic, between yourselves and all of us in Western Europe. As I see it, our purpose now must be not only to re-adjust at the particular points where General de Gaulle has made his thrusts, but also, as we have agreed between us, to make a comprehensive reorganization across the board. Our purpose here (and I believe that you, the Chancellor and I are all agreed on this) must surely be to maximise our military efficiency and to do so as economically as possible; but also, and just as important, to put us in the best political posture for improving East-West relations.

I have indeed read with attention your speech on the occasion of the Polish Millennium,[66] and should like to say, if I may, how admirably I think you expressed our common purpose.

I much look forward to the further thoughts on these matters which you promised in your message.

132. Message from Johnson to Wilson, 27 May 1966[67]

It was really good and strengthening to know that your meeting with Erhard went well.

I understand the political strains on your side in making this relationship solid, as well as the financial issues which you as well as we have to face with the Germans. On the other hand, as you clearly perceive and express, right now—and far into the future—the three of us must lean in and stay together.

Our next test—and it is certainly critical—is Brussels.[68] But we have every reason to go into it in reasonably good heart.

On some of the longer range issues in your letter,[69] I am awaiting the completion of staff work before putting to you some constructive possibilities. I am determined that, if at all possible, we shall accompany the difficult defensive moves we have to make with evidence that the fourteen, at least, can move forward on many fronts.

Let me say that I was very pleased to hear you and Erhard had a good talk about your EEC situation.

At my instruction Bob McNamara will be sending over an officer[70] to brief you fully about the two oil targets near Hanoi and Haiphong.

I am coming to believe it is essential that we reduce their oil supply in the light of radical increase in the flow of men and material by truck to South Vietnam.

But I am determined that their civilian casualties be low and minimal.

As you may have noticed, I spoke yesterday about Africa. I sense in my bones that a powerful tide of moderation is running through Africa, despite Rhodesia and all the rest. I feel we have a responsibility to help these people prove to themselves that they can make progress, otherwise out of frustration we may face extremism down the road. I hope your experts will be collecting their best ideas about sensible next steps in African economic development and

---

[66] See *Public Papers of the Presidents of the United States: Lyndon B. Johnson, 1966: I* (Washington, DC: US Government Printing Office, 1967), pp. 475–8.

[67] LBJ Library, NSF, Head of State Correspondence File, Box 9, United Kingdom: Prime Minister Wilson Correspondence, Volume 4, no. 9.

[68] The North Atlantic Council met in Ministerial Session in Brussels on 7 and 8 June 1966.

[69] See 131.

[70] Colonel Bernard Rogers.

exchanging views with mine. I greatly respect Britain's experience and good sense in that continent.

133. Message from Johnson to Wilson, 2 June 1966[71]

On behalf of Her Majesty's Government I send you our warmest congratulations on the news of the outstanding success of Surveyor 1's soft landing on the moon. I should be grateful if you would also convey your congratulations and good wishes to all those responsible for this magnificent further achievement in the conquest of space.

134. Message from Wilson to Johnson, 3 June 1966[72]

I was most grateful to you for asking Bob McNamara to arrange the very full briefing about the two oil targets near Hanoi and Haiphong that Colonel Rogers gave me yesterday.[73] If I may say so, Colonel Rogers did this with the greatest skill, courtesy and good sense. Michael Stewart and I found it very interesting and valuable.

I know you will not feel that I am either unsympathetic or uncomprehending of the dilemma that this problem presents for you. In particular, I wholly understand the deep concern you must feel at the need to do anything possible to reduce the losses of young Americans in and over Vietnam: and Colonel Rogers made it clear to us what care had been taken to plan this operation so as to keep civilian casualties to the minimum.

However, as David Bruce will have told you, I am bound to say that, as seen from here, the possible military benefits that may result from this bombing do not appear to outweigh the political disadvantages that would seem the inevitable consequence. If you and the South Vietnamese Government were conducting a declared war on a conventional pattern (as in the case of World War II which Colonel Rogers mentioned at one point in a form of analogy) this operation would clearly be necessary and right. But since you have made it so abundantly clear—and you know how much we have welcomed and supported this—that your purpose is to achieve a negotiated settlement, and that you are not striving for total military victory in the field, I remain convinced that the bombing of

---

[71] LBJ Library, NSF, Head of State Correspondence File, Box 9, United Kingdom: Prime Minister Wilson Correspondence, Volume 4, no. 6.

[72] LBJ Library, NSF, Head of State Correspondence File, Box 9, United Kingdom: Prime Minister Wilson Correspondence, Volume 4, no. 4.

[73] See 132.

these targets without producing decisive military advantage, may only increase the difficulty of reaching an eventual settlement. In particular it seems likely to make it a good deal more difficult to bring the Russians to a more realistic assessment of their responsibilities here—something which must be in all our interests.

The last thing I wish is to add to your difficulties. But, as I warned you in my previous message,[74] if this action is taken we shall have to dissociate ourselves from it, and in doing so I should have to say that you had given me advance warning and that I had made my position clear to you. For this reason I have felt it my duty to set these arguments out again before you as fully as possible.

Nevertheless, I want to repeat what I have asked David to make clear to you, that our reservations about this operation will not affect our continuing support for your policy over Vietnam, as you and your people have made it clear from your Baltimore speech onwards.[75] But, while this will remain the Government's position, I know that the effect on public opinion in this country—and I believe throughout Western Europe—is likely to be such as to reinforce the existing disquiet and criticism that we have to deal with.

You have been good enough to explain your problems. I felt I owed it to you to set out our views again at some length. But perhaps the best thing might be for us to meet again briefly before too long. David Bruce will have told you what is in my mind, and in particular how much I realize that a visit immediately before or after the bombing, if it takes place, would no doubt be too difficult for you and lead to wrong interpretations being put on our joint purposes. But I hope, nevertheless, that we may be able to see each other reasonably soon. There will be a lot of talk about, especially after the NATO meeting.[76]

135. Message from Wilson to Johnson, 10 June 1966[77]

Dean [Rusk] will have told you of the useful talk we had today. I wish we could help you with a few helicopters in Thailand and we shall of course, as I promised to him, look carefully at this. But I honestly believe that to act as you suggest would involve us in very serious political difficulties here over our Vietnam policy. I don't think that it would really be worth risking this for the sake of the relatively marginal support for the Thais that Dean's proposal would represent.

On the other hand I think both Dean and I were equally taken with the idea I mentioned to him of my trying soon to have a further talk with Kosygin and

---

[74] See 130.
[75] See 34, footnote 65.
[76] See 132, footnote 68.
[77] LBJ Library, NSF, Head of State Correspondence File, Box 10, United Kingdom: Prime Minister Wilson Correspondence, Volume 5 [2 of 2], no. 165.

Brezhnev. This is not of course designed to take the wind out of de Gaulle's sails[78] (though if it were a by-product so much the better) but because I believe we have a common interest in doing what we can to keep the Russians in play. The time will come when they feel the need to talk turkey: and it is only by regular probing that we may well hope to exploit that moment when it comes. In any case, there may well be some ideas (whether those that Dean mentioned to me or any others we can jointly think up) which it would be useful to try on them.

Dean tells me that you share my feeling that we should now aim to have another talk (which need take very little of our time and could be simply over lunch). On the whole, I should much prefer this to be before I go to Moscow so that I am fully up to date on your thinking when I talk to the Russians. But, of course, I shall fully understand if the timing makes this difficult for you. In that case, I could come over after my return from Moscow and would at least be able to give you a first hand account of their views.

I am sure it is right for us not to meet too near the bombing. I should not wish to come before it. It would be a political mistake for both of us if people could say that I was making a trans-Atlantic dash, with my shirt-tails flying, to put pressure on you. Against this background I wonder if I might aim to fly over for not more than a day right at the end of the month or at the beginning of next. The British Trade Fair in Moscow, which will provide the cover for seeing Brezhnev and Kosygin, opens on July 8 and I could get there over the weekend of July 9/10. But if this timing does not suit, then I think we should aim at a post-Moscow exchange, in which case I could come over, say, on July 15. Any of these dates would satisfactorily avoid any clash with de Gaulle's Soviet trip (June 20–July 2) and Pompidou's visit to me (July 6–8).

If these ideas make sense to you, I think we should not delay in saying something publicly. As Dean will have told you, I have a tricky Parliamentary Party meeting on June 15 (though it is causing me no loss of sleep) and I think there is some slight advantage in letting it be known that we are to meet before rather than after this, simply because an announcement after may get a bit close to your own D-Day. What I should like, if you agree, is for us to announce simultaneously on June 13 or 14 that we have agreed, in the light of my useful talk with Dean Rusk, to have a further brief meeting, as we like to do at fairly regular intervals: and that this will probably take place at the end of June or early July.

Meanwhile I am checking on what is known of the Russian leaders' likely movements around July 8–10. If they look like being in Moscow, I will probably announce towards the end of next week my intention to pay a short visit to the British Trade Fair.

---

[78] Wilson is evidently referring to de Gaulle's forthcoming visit to the Soviet Union.

I enormously look forward to another talk with you. I was glad to learn from Dean that you find our exchanges and messages useful. I most certainly do. But, as we both know, the spoken word and the probe still have the edge over the written word. So I hope we can manage to meet soon.

136. Message from Wilson to Johnson, 10 June 1966[79]

Dean [Rusk] spoke to me today about the Hanoi/Haiphong operation. I gather that, though you have still taken no final decision to bomb the oil targets, the balance of probability is that you will do so within the next ten days. Dean tells me that you understand why we must publicly disassociate ourselves and you know that the bombing will not affect our general support. But if you decide on the bombing, I don't see how this can fail to affect the prospects for reconvening a Cambodia Conference or of suggesting a meeting at Geneva for those who wish to come—two ideas that Dean mentioned to me yesterday. But I will say no more on this, beyond saying how much you have my personal sympathy in finding yourself confronted with such a choice.

137. Message from Johnson to Wilson, 11 June 1966[80]

Dear Harold:
I deeply appreciate your message of congratulations on behalf of Her Majesty's Government on the successful flight of the Surveyor I spacecraft and its soft landing on the moon.[81] I thought you might want these copies of photographs of the surface of the moon taken by the Surveyor I spacecraft.

These and other photographs will be distributed to the scientific community of the world in the hope that they will contribute to our combined understanding of the lunar surface.

We are hopeful that knowledge obtained from this mission will serve mankind and contribute to the success of future efforts to continue the peaceful exploration of outer space.

I have the strong feeling that if we are wise and earnest, what is happening in outer space can help us live better together on earth.
Sincerely,
LBJ

---

[79] LBJ Library, NSF, Head of State Correspondence File, Box 10, United Kingdom: Prime Minister Wilson Correspondence, Volume 5 [2 of 2], no. 162.

[80] LBJ Library, NSF, Head of State Correspondence File, Box 10, United Kingdom: Prime Minister Wilson Correspondence, Volume 5 [2 of 2], no. 152.

[81] See 133.

138. Message from Johnson to Wilson, 14 June 1966[82]

Dean Rusk has told me of his private talk with you about the problem of POL in Haiphong and Hanoi.[83] Specific orders have not yet been issued but I see no way of avoiding such action, given the expansion of the illegal corridor through Laos, the continuing buildup of North Vietnamese forces in South Viet Nam, the growing abuse of Cambodian neutrality, and the absence of any indication in Hanoi of a serious interest in peace.

We expect costly fighting during the Monsoon season, the first engagements of which have undoubtedly come to your attention. I must do what I can to reduce our casualties at the hands of those who are moving in from the north.

I deeply hope that you will find a way to maintain solidarity with us on Viet-Nam despite what you have said in the House of Commons about Haiphong and Hanoi.[84] We are not talking about an air assault on civilian centers but a specific attack on POL installations with a direct relevance to the fighting in the south. I hope that you can give further thought to your own interests and commitments in Southeast Asia under the SEATO Treaty. Dean tells me that, in his talk with you and your colleagues, several references were made to the "revival of SEATO." South Viet Nam and five signatories of SEATO are not talking about a revival but are committing troops to repel an armed attack from the north. Nor do I believe that your role as co-chairman means that Britain should stand aside; the other co-chairman is furnishing large quantities of sophisticated arms and other assistance to North Viet Nam and is, therefore, an active partner in the effort to take over South Viet Nam by force.

I know that you have some problems about Viet Nam, as do I. But I believe that it is sound for us to base our policy on the simple principles of the Geneva Accords and the SEATO Treaty, and on the assumption that North Viet Nam will not be permitted to seize South Viet Nam. Since we are determined about the latter point, much of the present criticism will come right at the end of the day.

I gather Dean spoke to you of the possible combination of points which would put a different cast upon disassociation by you from a decision to strike the POL. Quite frankly, I earnestly hope that you will not find it necessary to speak in terms of disassociation. But it would be important to us if you could include the following elements:

---

[82] LBJ Library, NSF, Head of State Correspondence File, Box 10, United Kingdom: Prime Minister Wilson Correspondence, Volume 5 [2 of 2], no. 158.

[83] See 136.

[84] On 8 February, Wilson had told the Commons that 'We have made it clear in Washington that we could not support any extension of the bombing against North Vietnam by stages to Hanoi and Haiphong' (*Parliamentary Debates (Hansard): Commons, 1965–66*, Volume 724, col. 229).

1. You were informed of the possibility that such an action would, in our minds, become necessary.
2. You expressed your own views to us in accordance with statements which you have already made in the House of Commons.
3. The particular step taken by U.S. forces was directed specifically to POL storage and not against civilian centers or installations.
4. Since Britain does not have troops engaged in the fighting, it is not easy or appropriate for Britain to determine the particular military action which may be necessary under different circumstances.
5. It is a great pity that Hanoi and Peiping have been so unresponsive to unprecedented efforts by the U.S. and others to bring this problem from the battlefield to the conference table.
6. Britain is satisfied that U.S. forces have no designs against civilian populations and are taking every possible precaution to avoid civilian casualties.
7. Britain as a member of SEATO fully understands and supports the determination of its fellow SEATO members to insure the safety and the self-determination of South Viet Nam.

I would hope that you could in this context affirm your support for the effort in Viet Nam and your understanding that it is Hanoi which is blocking the path to peace.

The timing of a visit to Washington is somewhat complicated.[85] You and I agree that there should be a good deal of blue sky between your visit and possible action in Viet Nam. That alone would suggest that the month of June is out, as we now look at the calendar of events. When we get into July, I shall expect to be away for almost a full week surrounding July 4th. You have Pompidou's visit on July 6–8 and your possible visit to Moscow on July 9–10. I have just suggested to President Senghor that he come here July 11–13.

It appears, therefore, anything before mid-July is blocked by our respective calendars.

If you feel a talk at that time is essential, we can say now that we expect it to be held in mid- or late July, leaving the precise dates open for further determination. In response to questions as to why you are coming, perhaps we both should simply say that we have felt occasional talks to be worthwhile and that a number of matters of mutual interest could be usefully discussed, and that mid-July appears to be a mutually convenient time.

I was much interested in what Dean told me of your talks about Rhodesia and the maritime strike. You have my best wishes in bringing both of these troublesome matters to an early conclusion.

---

[85] See 135.

139. Message from Wilson to Johnson, 15 June 1966[86]

Many thanks for your message of June 14.[87] I am grateful for your frankness and I think that each of us now fully understands the others [sic] position about the bombing of the oil installations.

This exchange however reinforces my view that we should try to have a short meeting. The SEATO problem will of course be central to the talks which Dean Rusk and Michael Stewart will be having later this month in Canberra. But there are a number of things, including whatever may emerge from those talks, which you and I should usefully discuss soon.

I shall not now be going to Moscow on July 9–10. I could, if you thought fit, aim to see you after a later trip to Moscow, but I think that from the point of view of both our interests it would be better for us to have had a good talk before I decide on a Moscow visit.

I should, therefore, like to accept your suggestion that we should meet in mid or late July.

This leaves the timing of the announcement. I think you agree that for both of us it is politically desirable not only that there should be plenty of blue sky between the bombing and my visit, but that the announcement of the visit should be made as far in advance of the bombing as possible. This being so, can we agree now to announce, preferably before this weekend, that we have decided to meet in mid or late July, taking the line in response to questions which you suggested in your message.

140. Message from Johnson to Wilson, 23 June 1966[88]

Dear Mr. Prime Minister:

I am writing to let you know that we now feel it necessary to go ahead with the operation against POL installations which Dean Rusk discussed with you and Michael Stewart during his London visit.[89]

I have taken this decision only after carefully reviewing the whole matter again, and particularly after receiving a full and complete report of the mission carried out by Ambassador Ronning in Hanoi last week. The State Department is prepared to give you fuller details on the Ronning findings. In essence, Ronning found Hanoi unwilling to discuss any conditions even for preliminary

---

[86] LBJ Library, NSF, Head of State Correspondence File, Box 10, United Kingdom: Prime Minister Wilson Correspondence, Volume 5 [2 of 2], no. 148.

[87] See 138.

[88] LBJ Library, NSF, Head of State Correspondence File, Box 10, United Kingdom: Prime Minister Wilson Correspondence, Volume 5 [2 of 2], no. 143.

[89] See 136.

talks that could remotely be acceptable. While there were some slight changes in Hanoi's treatment of particular matters, the sum total of their position appeared to be that they were unwilling to engage even in the kind of preliminary talks we had with them in Rangoon unless we were prepared to cease bombing and permanently, without any reciprocal action whatever on their part.

In the face of this discouraging reading, and in the light of accumulating evidence both of the importance of the POL installations and a program to disperse them beyond our reach, I have concluded that there is simply no choice but to go ahead. The operations depend on the weather, and I ask that you hold this information in the fullest personal confidence. When they are carried out, we expect to announce them in Saigon, and will do our best to give you advance notice.

We shall of course be depicting the operation solely as an extension to a limited extent of existing policy. I can assure you that I shall continue to guide our operations personally and that they will be directed solely against valid military targets and not against population centers. Our military commanders have accepted the most stringent operating orders in order to prevent any significant civilian casualties, or any other damage unrelated to the precise objectives.

With warm regards,
Lyndon B. Johnson

141. Message from Wilson to Johnson, 23 June 1966[90]

Dear Mr. President,

David Bruce has just given me your message of today saying that you now feel it necessary to go ahead with the operation against the POL installations near Hanoi and Haiphong.[91] I shall of course hold this in complete confidence until the announcement is made in Saigon.

I am grateful to you for this advance warning and also for the helpful background given in your message. I was sorry to learn that Ambassador Ronning obtained such a totally negative response from Hanoi.

As you know, I understand and have great sympathy for your problem here. But you also know my reservations about this particular action. I need not repeat them here but I feel I should record again that, when this action is taken, I cannot do otherwise than make it publicly clear that the British Government must dissociate themselves from it. But I wish to assure you that, in this statement, we shall make it equally clear that we remain convinced that the United States

---

[90] LBJ Library, NSF, Head of State Correspondence File, Box 10, United Kingdom: Prime Minister Wilson Correspondence, Volume 5 [2 of 2], no. 141b.

[91] See 140.

Government are right to continue to assist the South Vietnamese and that the onus for continuing the fighting and refusing a negotiation rests with Hanoi. I shall also do my best to include in the statement as many as possible of the points made in your personal message to me of June 14.[92]

With warm personal regards and best wishes,
  Harold Wilson

142. Message from Wilson to Johnson, 1 July 1966[93]

Naturally my thoughts have been very much with you during these past two exceptionally difficult days and even at this distance I am able to have some view of all that you have been going through. Indeed, in the somewhat rough exchanges in the House of Commons which followed my statement yesterday, Wednesday, to Parliament,[94] I made a point of saying something of what you had gone through and the agonies of decision you had had to face over these many months.

I know things will be made no easier for you, any more than they are for me with my infinitely smaller burden in these matters, by the knowledge that many of your critics, whether in Congress, the press or the public, like mine, are and have been more vociferous in their criticism than fertile in providing any constructive alternative. In another context in Parliament this week, when I was being attacked over my decision to rough it up with the Communists on the seamen's strike, I had to tell some of my own leftwing that I did not resent their indulging in the luxury of negative criticism, but that some of us have the responsibility of government and have to govern. This is I am sure what above all other things you must be feeling.

I know it is the more difficult for you that, as I understand it, today the situation remains as you explained it to me last December that your critics are almost equally divided into those who want you to do a great deal more and those who want you to do a great deal less. On both sides there are those who go to impossible extremes of demanding either out and out war or out and out surrender. In fact, many of our more moderate British critics are gradually being manoeuvred into taking their stand with extremists whose views as put forward they would probably, if challenged, repudiate. The fact that the British people are physically remote from the problem and, in particular, are not suffering the

---

[92] See 138.
[93] LBJ Library, NSF, Head of State Correspondence File, Box 10, United Kingdom: Prime Minister Wilson Correspondence, Volume 5 [2 of 2], no. 137.
[94] See *Parliamentary Debates (Hansard): Commons, 1966–67*, Volume 730, 29 June 1966, cols. 1796–1810.

tragedy of losses which your people are suffering serves to increase the lack of understanding of my full support for your basic policy.

I know that you must feel that some actions and statements of ours in the past few days have not been helpful. And there are no doubt in both countries those ready to exploit those actions for the sake of sowing discord between the governments or of pushing the two of us further apart, you in one direction me in another, from the position we have jointly held and still hold. I am being pressed to acknowledge that the logic of disagreeing with this particular operation would be a total denunciation of the whole of your Vietnam policy. This I have firmly rejected, not only because I distrust the motives of those who put this argument forward, but because their argument itself is balls. I know only too well the different motives among my own critics, varying from disappointment at not having been given office to confused international loyalties, which generate the usual double-standard myopia towards any action taken by the United States, as compared with those to whom they are always more tolerant. These motives may also operate with your critics, but you will know better than I can.

But also among the critics of both of us are very many really decent people, most of them incapable of formulating an alternative policy but bewildered as to where we are going, and what the outcome will be. Some but not all believe that the only possible result will be escalation and a third world war. What disturbs both of us I know, is that among these people are some of the best and most progressive members of the liberal establishment of our two countries. And indeed among that establishment there is a wider malaise about the whole situation, even if this is not expressed in critical or vocal terms. And those who think or say these things will never understand either of us unless they realise that you and I also belong to this same group and share their malaise and anxiety. The difference, of course, is that, whereas they can go away and return to their own day to day pursuits, those of us who have the responsibilities of government cannot, whatever our feelings, escape from the necessities of decision. This is what government means. Whatever the differences we may have had on one or two of these recent problems, I am bound to tell you, after the deepest heart searching, that I cannot see that there is any change in your basic position that I could urge on you. That position I sought to define on Wednesday in the House of Commons in the following words:

> The United States are right to continue the assist the millions of South Vietnamese, who have no wish to live under communist domination, until such time as the North Vietnamese government abandon their attempt to gain control of South Vietnam by force and accept the proposal for unconditional negotiations which have repeatedly been put forward by the United States.

Indeed, if there were a viable alternative policy, I know that you, with all the agonized consideration that you have given to this problem, would have reached it more quickly than I. And I want you to realise that where we have differed in detail—but never in basic policy—and have had to express a different point of view, while we recognise that this can only add to your difficulties (and especially this time be more than a little hurtful), we believe that what we have done is right and necessary. I must be quite frank in saying that this is the price I have to pay for being able to hold the line in our country where the public reaction is very widespread even if, as I have said, it stems from widely differing motives.

But I intend to go on holding the position. Today, Thursday, we had by far the roughest outburst from a large section of my own party in the House. Since it arose on a discussion with the leader of the House on the immediate procedure and timetable, I could not myself intervene directly in the exchanges. But in addition to our own people, and of course the twelve strong Liberal Party, the Conservatives were to my mind in the most cynical manner trying to exploit the difficulties and trying to create a situation which would make it harder for us, in the light of the attitude of our backbenchers, to maintain the line of our own support. As a politician I can of course understand their motives, even if, on so grave an issue, I equally despise them. Again there may be some in your country about whom you feel the same, for ambition does not always express itself in constructive statesmanship.

In all these circumstances I am extremely pleased that we were able to announce before this week's events that we shall be meeting next month and I also think that we were wise in agreeing that there must be some clear blue sky between this week's events and our projected meeting.

I lose no opportunity—I must have said it a hundred times in the House, and at least a dozen times this week—of saying that the responsibility for every action in this war lies with those who refuse to come to the conference table. The enemies of negotiation are the enemies of peace. And time and time again I have pinpointed them. This is why I so warmly welcomed the phrase which Dean Rusk used to me and which I got his permission to quote when he proclaimed his willingness to go to Geneva at a drop of the hat, if there were anyone there to meet him, and equally I welcomed the reaffirmation yesterday of this attitude by Secretary McNamara.

Equally I know these most recent actions were taken only after a final effort to see whether the latest line into Hanoi, the Ronning Mission,[95] produced any greater willingness to talk, which it manifestly did not.

Naturally I have been wondering whether there was any further initiative I could take. There is one, as you know, which I discussed with Dean Rusk. But I wanted to make it abundantly clear that I would not contemplate taking

---

[95] See 140.

any steps towards it unless I thought it had your agreement, not grudging or reluctant agreement, but wholehearted feeling that it was right and that it would not add to your difficulties. This is the possibility at this moment of trying to see whether there is anything I can do personally with Kosygin whose position on Vietnam I described to you on my return from Moscow in February.[96]

It was inevitable that Wednesday's events would produce explosive statements from the Russia and from their satellites, East and West. I would be doubtful whether it would produce more than that. As always, the Russians who I am convinced desperately want to see the end to this Vietnamese war, have to act in a competitive situation within the communist world. My hope, and I trust I am not too optimistic, is that the events of last Wednesday may yet have an opposite and more positive effect in underlying the urgency of the Vietnamese situation and in emphasising the fact that action might be taken, by for example the Chinese, which would lead to the situation getting out of hand. I am counting here less on the public position the Russians have to take than on what I believe to be their innate realism and their desire to keep some control over the situation and not be carried into escalation by other less realistic and responsible forces within the communist camp.

As you know, if I wanted reasonable cover for a quick visit to Moscow, it lies to hand with the opening next week of the British trade fair in Moscow. I have been associated with Anglo-Soviet trade for the last twenty years from my earlier ministerial days and indeed as an opposition leader visited the last British trade fair in Moscow five years ago. Naturally I would only think of going and spending several hours touring those fetid marquees in sizzling heat if I were certain of meeting Kosygin for an hour or two to discuss other matters. As I said to you in an earlier message, I would have preferred to have visited Washington before contemplating such a visit, but the trade fair ends on 25 July and I may have been to Washington by that time. In any case, the wrong impression might be gained if, immediately after leaving Washington, my shirt tails were seen flying not only over the Atlantic but over the Pripet Marshes[97] as well.

What I have in mind, if I felt it was acceptable to you, was that I should go before my Washington visit, ostensibly for the trade fair but in fact to discuss with Kosygin all aspects of South East Asian affairs, not only Vietnam but the new initiative suggested by Sihanouk in his letter to the two co-chairman,[98] action on which I know to be very much in the minds of your government as the next step. It would be a tragedy, if we failed at least to try to winkle the Russians out of their shell. So far as Vietnam is concerned I want to discuss very

---

[96] See 99.
[97] Wetlands in Eastern Europe.
[98] In June 1966, Sihanouk had called for a reinforced International Control Commission which since 1954 had overseen the Geneva Accords.

frankly with Kosygin whether there is any point in moving towards an initiative to recall the Geneva Conference and in any case to stiffen him in what I am sure is his desire, namely to exert the maximum pressure in Hanoi for a more constructive attitude.

I think this might be useful. In my view it is a gamble where the odds are pretty long against immediate success. But, so far as I can see, it is a gamble which, if it fails, will cost nothing to the Western position. Indeed failure, as in the case of the failure of previous peace initiatives, will strengthen our position in other countries and with our own public opinion I cannot believe that failure could possibly do any harm to the Western cause or to you personally. Indeed, it might give useful further proof, if that were needed, of where the responsibility for the continued fighting lies. It might involve some risks for me in the House of Commons and I can already hear in advance the gibes from the Opposition. But I have handled them before and can do so again.

However, whatever the assessment of the odds and the stakes in the gamble I have suggested, there is one price I am not prepared to pay and that is to go forward with such an initiative unless I feel that you were agreeable and that it was not going to make your already agonising task more difficult.

On other issues, domestic and overseas, especially in the Rhodesian and the Vietnam context, I have quoted what was, I think, the last word, as said by one of your presidential predecessors. I have no doubt you have used it, as I have, and that you feel with me that Lincoln was right when he said (and I have his words in a framed plaque on my wall)

'If I were trying to read, much less answer all the attacks made on me, this shop might as well be closed for any other business. I do the best I know how, the very best I can: and I mean to keep on doing it to the end. If the end brings me out all right, what is said against me will not amount to anything. If the end brings me out all wrong, ten angels swearing I was right would make no difference.'

143. Message from Johnson to Wilson, 2 July 1966[99]

Your message[100] gave me the picture of your political problem and how you intend to deal with it. My problem is not merely political. I must also convince Hanoi that the will of the United States cannot be broken by debate or pressures—at home or from abroad.

We must and will continue to apply hard military pressure. There should be no ambiguity about this. It would be useful for the Soviets to be clear on

---

[99] LBJ Library, NSF, Head of State Correspondence File, Box 10, United Kingdom: Prime Minister Wilson Correspondence, Volume 5 [2 of 2], no. 132.

[100] See 142.

this point. Yet it may give you some problems in connections with your trip to Moscow.

If you do go to Moscow, I would hope you could canvass all useful possibilities with Kosygin and his colleagues and that your joint responsibilities as co-chairman might lead to some constructive initiative. In any event, Sianouk's [sic] communication to the co-chairman might enable you to get something started about Cambodia.

Assuming that you go to Moscow during the trade fair, an acceptable date for your visit here would be July 29.
Best wishes,
Lyndon B. Johnson

144. Message from Wilson to Johnson, 15 July 1966[101]

Before I leave for Moscow, I wanted you to know how I expect to handle my talks with Kosygin on two of the major topics that seem bound to come up.

First Vietnam. As I have told David Bruce, I believe that my purpose must be to make absolutely clear to the Russians my firm belief that you mean business and intend to continue applying hard military pressure, however long it takes.

As David knows, I have very little hope that the Russians can be brought to take more positive action because of the diplomatic strait-jacket in which their rivalry with the Chinese within the Communist world compresses them. But I am likewise convinced that they are thoroughly worried at the limitations this imposes on the conduct of their foreign policy: and even more at what must seem to them the real danger that excessive Chinese intransigence could drag them into a confrontation with yourselves. They cannot want to find themselves in a Cuban situation, at one remove, so to speak. The more convinced they are of your determination, the more I believe we can hope to exploit their apprehensions.

It is against this general background that I propose, as I have told David Bruce, to raise with them the question of the treatment by Hanoi of your prisoners of war, pointing out that, quite apart from the ethics of this matter, maltreatment of your prisoners is bound to increase the legitimate indignation and resolution of the American people: it is therefore much in their own interest to ensure that Hanoi does not depart from the principles of the Geneva Convention.

Secondly, disarmament. David has communicated to me the strong feeling within your Administration that it would be premature and even harmful for me to raise in Moscow the questions of a comprehensive test ban treaty or of non-proliferation. It would be unrealistic, I believe, to think that when disarmament

---

[101] LBJ Library, NSF, Head of State Correspondence File, Box 10, United Kingdom: Prime Minister Wilson Correspondence, Volume 5 [2 of 2], no. 130.

comes up (as seems inevitable) the Russians will not themselves raise these topics in one form or another. And if I detect any indication on their part of an advance towards constructive negotiation, it would equally clearly be wrong for me not to probe this cautiously to see whether it is purely tactical or has some real substance to it. But you can rest assured that my purpose will not be to enter into a negotiation and even less to compromise in any way our existing positions on either of these aspects of the problem. I was encouraged to learn from what Bruce has told me that you are actively considering possible courses of action in these fields. I shall look forward to discussing them with you when we meet and to giving you an account then of whatever may be said by the Russians.

As I see it, I have two essential purposes in this trip. First, to persuade the Russians that neither they nor anyone else should base their calculations on a misconception of your own courage and convictions; and that it is therefore profoundly to their interest to work more vigorously for a negotiated settlement in Vietnam. Secondly, that if they think they can drive a wedge between you and me, they are sadly mistaken. The value to them of the British connection with the Vietnam situation lies essentially in our firm belief in the inviolability of the Atlantic relationship.

145. Message from Wilson to Johnson, 19 July 1966[102]

Before I went to Moscow I told the House of Commons that I could already hear the gibes that would greet my return: and that this in no way affected my belief in the value of meeting the Soviet leaders face to face and trying to bring them a sense of their responsibilities. As the editorialists lick their pens to describe the failure of the mission, I am returning more convinced than ever that the sort of unsensational relationship that is growing up between Kosygin and myself has real—if still largely potential—value.

There is at present no give whatever in the Soviet position (public or private) over Vietnam. Kosygin was quiet (and at all times courteous and friendly) but bitter and tough. He casts you as the bloodthirsty villain of the piece and his purpose is clearly to work for your increasing isolation and friendlessness with world opinion. In a sense, this personalized attack gave me the perfect opportunity to hit back at the outset, and to say in the clearest possible terms how dangerously I thought he was misjudging both yourself personally and the temper and resolution of the American people. I returned to this theme throughout our talks and it was practically the last thing I said to him as he drove me to the airport this morning.

---

[102] LBJ Library, NSF, Head of State Correspondence File, Box 10, United Kingdom: Prime Minister Wilson Correspondence, Volume 5 [2 of 2], no. 127.

We had a three-hour formal meeting in the Kremlin yesterday morning and over two hours privately together in the late afternoon. On at least three separate occasions his attitude gave me the opening I needed to press him to intervene with Hanoi over your captured airmen, which I did with vigour. I wish I could report any sign of success. But I am afraid he took a totally unhelpful and indeed contemptuous line about them. It was disheartening to listen to.

If that were all, it might seem fair to accept the superficial judgments in the press. But our long talk alone, while totally unproductive of change in the Soviet attitude, was, I believe one of the frankest exchanges Kosygin has yet had with any Western leader. He told me that I could as he put it give you my impressions of his views (while insisting that I must not appear in any way to be involving him in some kind of negotiation with you over Vietnam); and I look forward to doing so on the 29th.[103] In particular he had some interesting and revealing things to say about China. Indeed here, quite clearly, lies the root cause of his problems, coupled with his continuing misconception about your own position. I may have done something to shake him on that. But his obvious sense of frustration stems, I am sure, from the fear that, on the one hand, any Soviet pressure on Hanoi might only drive the North Vietnamese further into the arms of Peking; but, on the other hand, that if Russia is forced, as he said, to remain on the sidelines, the Chinese may do something foolish which could get him into a confrontation with you. In short, he is at present a reluctant micawber. I have left him in no doubt that nothing is going to turn up from me, in terms of a withdrawal of British support from your policies; but that if, at any time, he needs my help or cooperation in getting a negotiation under way, I too, like Dean, will fly anywhere to meet him, at the drop of a hat.

Disarmament was barely mentioned. And on European security, after the standard rigmarole about Germany, he admitted privately that there would have to be careful preparation before any conference, for which he saw no immediate urgency.

On the whole, therefore, a pretty negative balance sheet at present with no practical dividend to declare. But the time will come, and I feel even surer of this after my visit that I did before, when he will want to make an opening; and when it does, we may both be glad that some of the way has been paved in this fashion.

---

[103] Wilson is referring to his forthcoming visit to Washington.

146. Message from Wilson to Johnson, 20 July 1966[104]

In my message to you last night,[105] I purposely said nothing about our current economic problems because I was going straight into a full discussion with the Cabinet, on the basis of the very drastic studies made to give effect to my statement of last Thursday.

My colleagues and I have now examined these in detail and I shall be making a further statement in the House this afternoon. So I now write to let you know how I see the basic issues and how we propose to tackle them. I need not trouble you with the details. John Stevens will go over these with Francis Bator.

We all realize the basic problem that confronts us, namely that our spending and our costs must be brought under control: and that this will mean some real suffering for both the public and the private sectors. To do the trick, the package of measures which I am announcing must have—and will have—a very hard disinflationary impact. In particular, we have decided on a total standstill for the next six months on prices and incomes and on a further six months period of very severe restraint in that field. Of course, no one in Britain will like these measures, especially the wage freeze. But I am convinced that public opinion here now accepts the need for drastic sacrifice and that, in this mood, it will rise to the challenge.

But if we are to ask the British public to cooperate willingly over the sacrifices essential to put our economy to rights, they must equally be satisfied that they are not being asked to carry a disproportionate share of the general cost of Western defence. We cannot, in imposing these measures at home, avoid also reducing our Government expenditure overseas, civil and military and including defence expenditure in Germany as well as elsewhere. But I am telling Parliament that any cut of this nature should not affect the basic lines of foreign policy on which the defence review was founded. This means that they must be consistent with our international commitments and with our common policy in defence of Western interests throughout the world. I hope we can discuss the problem together in this spirit when we meet next week.

---

[104] LBJ Library, NSF, Head of State Correspondence File, Box 10, United Kingdom: Prime Minister Wilson Correspondence, Volume 5 [2 of 2], no. 124a.

[105] See 145.

147. Message from Johnson to Wilson, 29 July 1966[106]

Dear Mr, Prime Minister:
Thank you for coming, my friend. We had a good talk. As you know, our friendship is a source of comfort and strength to me.

I very much enjoyed your toast—and I meant what I said in mine. And I look forward to meeting with you again.

Best wishes to you and your colleagues for a safe journey home. I wish you well in the difficult task which you and your Government now face.

Lyndon B. Johnson

148. Message from Wilson to Johnson, 30 July 1966[107]

I find it difficult to say how much our talks together have heartened me at a time when life has not been altogether easy. There may still be rough water ahead for both of us, but I have no doubt that, so long as we go on pulling together, it will work out all right in the end. Thank you so much for everything—and especially for your very kind message which Phil Kaiser has just given me.[108]

149. Message from Wilson to Johnson, 11 August 1966[109]

I am just off to the Scillies for a two to three week holiday but I could not go without sending you a short report on where we stand with our recent measures to deal with the economic situation.

First, I am glad to say that we have now driven the process and incomes bill through the House of Commons. We have had to face fierce opposition not only from our official opponents who put down what amounted to a censure motion, but also from with the ranks of my own party. An outstanding and encouraging feature of the last two weeks is, however, the fact that both the Confederation of British Industry and the Trade Union Council have approved and supported us in this prices and incomes standstill which is unprecedented in peace time.

We shall have a bit of rough water for the next day or two because the trade figures published today appear to be disappointing. This is mainly because of a

---

[106] LBJ Library, NSF, Head of State Correspondence File, Box 10, United Kingdom: Prime Minister Wilson Correspondence, Volume 5 [2 of 2], no. 121.

[107] LBJ Library, NSF, Head of State Correspondence File, Box 10, United Kingdom: Prime Minister Wilson Correspondence, Volume 5 [2 of 2], no. 119.

[108] See 147.

[109] LBJ Library, NSF, Head of State Correspondence File, Box 10, United Kingdom: Prime Minister Wilson Correspondence, Volume 5 [2 of 2], no. 117.

statistical distortion, the export figures (unlike the import figures) still include about 10 days of the seaman's strike. But there are some silver linings: the price of copper has fallen and if it stays down, it could at this rate improve our balance of payments by up to 75 million pounds in a full year.

You will see that I have reorganized my team to give the boys a fresh stimulus to start the new term in September. Not, this time, a surgical operation. You know George Brown, he will bring a new kind of robustness to the Foreign Office and you can count on him as a staunch supporter of the Atlantic Alliance. Michael Stewart had done very well as Foreign Secretary, and now we are moving into a new phase on the home front, his attributes will find much scope in this field.

Mary and I, of course, followed the accounts of Luci's wedding.[110] It went well, but I know only too well what you suffered with morning dress.

And now for some relaxation: You I hope to Texas, me to the Scillies.

150. Message from Johnson to Wilson, 16 August 1966[111]

Your encouraging short report reached me at the Ranch.[112] I hope the horizon remains clear so that your holiday to the Scillies is not interrupted.
Sincerely

151. Message from Johnson to Wilson, 17 August 1966[113]

I am very glad to extend to you felicitations on the occasion of the fiftieth anniversary of the signature by our two countries of the Convention for the Protection of Migratory Birds.

This Convention is a landmark in international cooperation for the conservation of wildlife. It is an outstanding example of the friendly and successful application for half a century of a convention between our two countries and between the United States and Canada.
Sincerely,
Lyndon B. Johnson

---

[110] LBJ's younger daughter, Luci Johnson, married on 6 August.

[111] LBJ Library, NSF, Head of State Correspondence File, Box 10, United Kingdom: Prime Minister Wilson Correspondence, Volume 5 [2 of 2], no. 109.

[112] See 149.

[113] LBJ Library, NSF, Head of State Correspondence File, Box 10, United Kingdom: Prime Minister Wilson Correspondence, Volume 5 [2 of 2], no. 101.

152. Message from Johnson to Wilson, 26 August 1966[114]

I have become increasingly concerned during the past few weeks about the dangers of an unravelling in NATO which could easily get out of hand. With your urgent need to save foreign exchange in Germany, Erhard's budgetary and political difficulties (not to speak of his problems with his brass), my problems with our German offset and with the Congress on troops in Europe—all against the background of the General's antics—there is danger of serious damage to the security arrangements we have worked so hard to construct during the last 20 years. To you, I don't have to spell out the possible political consequences, especially in Germany. And while I would not think it likely that our Russian friends will develop itchy fingers, one cannot rule it out. In any case, it would be foolish to run down our assets vis-a-vis Moscow without some quid-pro-quo.

It seems to me that the essential step, if we are to hold things together, would be for you, the Germans, and ourselves to get to work immediately to find a solution that would be equitable, meet our respective political requirements, and fully cover the defense needs of the Alliance. I propose to write to Erhard this afternoon—before his budget meeting tomorrow—to suggest that the U.S. join the FRG and the UK in an initial exploration of this entire range of issues: force levels, deployments and the sharing of the foreign exchange burden. I would think that such an exploration should involve our Ministers of Finance, as well as of Foreign Affairs and Defense. And, of course, it would have to be followed by thorough consultation with all our Allies in NATO.

I know that not all of your decisions can await the outcome of such a tripartite exercise. But I very much hope—and I will put this hard to Erhard in connection with his budget—that we will all try to avoid any decisions during the next several weeks which would unduly narrow our choices.

David Bruce will be in touch with you about this proposal in the near future. In the meanwhile, I hope, my good friend, you are having a good rest on your island. After some strictly nonpolitical speech making in the West, I hope to spend Saturday and Sunday at home in Texas observing, as I told the press yesterday, the results of 58 years of very pleasant existence.

With warm regards,
Lyndon B. Johnson

---

[114] LBJ Library, NSF, Head of State Correspondence File, Box 10, United Kingdom: Prime Minister Wilson Correspondence, Volume 5 [2 of 2], no. 96.

153. Message from Wilson to Johnson, 26 August 1966[115]

Thank you for your message of August 26.[116]
   In this cable I am replying only to your last paragraph.
   I send you my very best wishes for a happy birthday and many happy returns.

154. Message from Wilson to Johnson, 29 August 1966[117]

Like you, I am sure we must keep in being the essential arrangements which have deterred aggression in the Atlantic area. I should be the last to want to break down the framework within which the United States has sustained the defence of Europe and a German contribution has been made possible under satisfactory safeguards. Whether the balance of deterrence in Europe need be maintained at its present level is something which we must study urgently together. Indeed, we already have studies in hand: a prime concern must certainly be to work for matching reductions on the Soviet side. You may recall that I told you when we met that Kosygin showed considerable interest in matched reductions.

Against this background I am very ready to agree to the tripartite talks which you propose.[118] On my return to London I shall give urgent consideration to these with my colleagues. I feel bound to say, however, that we should be most reluctant to enter into such talks without bilateral discussions with you first. Obviously the well-being of NATO depends very largely on agreement between its three leading countries, and I realise that you do not want to give any impression of ganging-up with us against the Germans. But since we both keep troops in Germany at a heavy cost in foreign exchange, we share a special interest in these talks: and it seems to me essential that we should first consider our position together. I will arrange for a minister or ministers to be ready to go to Washington this week. Unless we concert our position, there is the risk of the Germans playing us off against each other.

As I emphasised to you when we met at the end of July, my major concern at present is to take effective action to safeguard sterling, both in its own right and as the first line of defence for the dollar. We have taken drastic measures to cut down spending power at home. We are also determined to deal directly with the drain of foreign exchange abroad. A major and urgent part of this is the need to stop the haemorrhage of foreign exchange flowing from the stationing of our

---

[115] LBJ Library, NSF, Head of State Correspondence File, Box 10, United Kingdom: Prime Minister Wilson Correspondence, Volume 5 [2 of 2], no. 94.

[116] See 152.

[117] LBJ Library, NSF, Head of State Correspondence File, Box 10, United Kingdom: Prime Minister Wilson Correspondence, Volume 5 [2 of 2], no. 91.

[118] See 152.

forces in Germany, and what is at stake for us is the success of our programme of economic measures in defence of the currency. If what we are doing is going to result in a lasting cure, we must move fast and I am glad to see that you accept that some of the decisions with which we are now faced cannot await the outcome of tripartite talks.

For this reason I am sure you will understand that we cannot afford to hold up the talks in NATO, on which we have already embarked and of which the next round indeed begins on Monday. I hope that your representatives will be authorised to make a substantive contribution to these talks.

Similarly, the Anglo-German mixed commission already has an agreed timetable and programme of work and in view of the need to secure the highest possible German financial contribution we could not contemplate any interruption of the commission's work.

Let us then advance on all these fronts at once. When you have heard from Erhard, we must consult again about a time and place for our talks. We shall be ready at any time.

155. Message from Johnson to Wilson, 1 September 1966[119]

I fully understand your anxiety to complete the steps necessary to deal with your balance of payments problem. We put the safeguarding of Sterling high on our list of priorities and, as you know, I admire the sturdy measures you have taken so far to put your house in good order.

Yet, as we have found out in this country, steps to stop the outflow of foreign exchange must always be measured against the cost in terms of defense and foreign policy. Thus, I am concerned that the proposals you are considering with respect to the BAOR be carefully handled or they may start the unravelling of our Western defenses. De Gaulle's abrupt action in pulling his own forces out of NATO was a brutal blow at the solidarity of the Alliance, and there could be great danger from further withdrawals that are not related to a common plan.

Above all, we must avoid any actions that might tend to make the Germans feel they were not full partners on the team. Erhard is in deep trouble and the political situation in Germany today is anything but healthy. It is essential to both our countries that we show sensitivity to German opinion which seems more and more confused and apprehensive. For that reason I would think it unwise for us to hold bilateral talks in advance that might lead the Germans to believe that we were preparing a fait accompli. Of course, during the tripartite

---

[119] LBJ Library, NSF, Head of State Correspondence File, Box 10, United Kingdom: Prime Minister Wilson Correspondence, Volume 5 [2 of 2], no. 86b.

talks there will naturally be bilateral exchanges among those taking part, and we will be ready for such talks at the earliest feasible time.

Meanwhile, I hope very much that you will not press the NATO discussions too vigorously. It could greatly complicate the problem if plans were rigidly worked out within the NATO Council before we had a chance for quiet talks among our three Governments.

156. Message from Wilson to Johnson, 2 September 1966[120]

I am pleased to reciprocate your felicitations on the occasion of the Fiftieth Anniversary of the signature by our two countries of the Convention for the Protection of Migratory Birds.[121]

I hope that the friendly cooperation in wild life conservation successfully established over the past fifty years will continue in the future.

157. Message from Johnson to Wilson, 3 September 1966[122]

I thank you for your kind wishes on my birthday.[123] I deeply appreciated your thoughtfulness and would like to extend to you my own warm regards.
Sincerely,
   Lyndon B. Johnson

158. Message from Wilson to Johnson, 23 September 1966[124]

1. I have purposely not troubled you so far with messages about Rhodesia. I know that David Bruce and Pat Dean between them will have kept both you yourself and Dean Rusk well in the picture of recent events and particularly of the exceptionally difficult discussion we had at the Commonwealth Prime Ministers Meeting, as well as the background and reasons for the Commonwealth Secretary's present visit to Rhodesia.

---

[120] LBJ Library, NSF, Head of State Correspondence File, Box 10, United Kingdom: Prime Minister Wilson Correspondence, Volume 5 [2 of 2], no. 84a.

[121] See 151.

[122] LBJ Library, NSF, Head of State Correspondence File, Box 10, United Kingdom: Prime Minister Wilson Correspondence, Volume 5 [2 of 2], no. 81.

[123] See 153.

[124] LBJ Library, NSF, Head of State Correspondence File, Box 10, United Kingdom: Prime Minister Wilson Correspondence, Volume 5 [2 of 2], no. 77.

2. But I believe we shall shortly reach a moment of decision in this Rhodesian crisis. As you will have heard, I came under the strongest pressure during the Commonwealth Conference to use force against the Smith regime, to declare categorically and unconditionally that there would be no independence before majority rule and also to move a resolution of comprehensive mandatory sanctions in the Security Council. None of these propositions was acceptable to us, but I had to fight an excessively difficult and at times bitter action against them. In the end, I believe we came out reasonably well. The majority of the Commonwealth tacitly accepted that we could not be expected to use military force; and that it was reasonable that we should have a little more time to give the regime one last chance of coming to its senses. But in return, I had to agree that, if that last chance were not accepted by the regime, we would support limited mandatory sanctions against Rhodesian exports of raw materials and perhaps at a latter stage an extension of the oil embargo to cover all imports via Mozambique. Provided that the Commonwealth supported us at the United Nations in limiting the impact of the sanctions in this way (i.e., so as to avoid, if possible, an overt clash with South Africa), I also agreed that we would then withdraw all previous offers made to Rhodesia and declare that there would be no independence before majority rule.

3. This was the price we had to pay to buy this additional time for a last showdown with Smith. But it was also necessary if we were to hold the Commonwealth together. And I know that this was an objective that you also strongly desired, given the immense racial tensions in the world and the value of the Commonwealth as a truly multi-racial association in helping to mitigate those tensions. I had broadly two main objectives throughout our Rhodesian discussions: to hold the Commonwealth together and to keep the Rhodesian situation under our own control, so far as possible. There were times when I doubted whether either objective could be attained. As it turned out, we managed to secure both, at least for a limited period of time; and I truly believe that the Commonwealth has emerged stronger rather than weaker from this great test.

4. But time really is now of the essence. The Commonwealth Secretary, whose reports this week show that he is playing a difficult hand with shrewdness and skill, is doing his best to make Smith realize that we and the rest of the Commonwealth mean business and that there really is a limit to our willingness and ability to carry the can internationally for Rhodesia. We believe that the terms we are offering as set out in the Commonwealth communiqué genuinely represent an honourable way out for Smith. But if he is to accept them, he will almost certainly have to bring himself to ditch his own extremists. And I am bound to say that his talks so far with the Commonwealth Secretary do not encourage us to hope that he will have the guts to do this.

5. But if this rather pessimistic forecast proves right, then we are going to be faced with the need for the measures agreed at the Commonwealth Prime Ministers Conference. I hope that initially we can agree in the Security Council on limited sanctions and that this will not therefore involve us immediately in a clash with South Africa. But we can certainly not be sure of this: and in any case a decision to move to further mandatory sanctions of this type may well hasten the day when a clash with South Africa becomes inevitable. This is something which is, I believe, equally repugnant to you and to us. The consequences (as I explained to the Africans at the Commonwealth Conference and as many of them in their heart of hearts fully recognize) are incalculable. They could in the longer run lead to armed conflict with the South Africans and would certainly produce economic warfare, the effect of which, for both our countries in particular but also I believe for Western economic interests generally, would be excessively damaging. But equally I feel bound to repeat the warning that George Brown gave George Ball during the latter's recent visit here to the effect that we must not be counted on to incur the immense international odium that would result from a British veto in the Security Council on any measures bound to result in conflict with South Africa. This is a case where I think you and we would have to stand or fall together; which is why I am addressing you now in the hope that, by judicious action before the moment of decision arrives, you may be able to help us avert the dangers I have just outlined.

6. It is difficult, and indeed inappropriate, for me to suggest what it might be possible for you to do to help us at this juncture. If you felt that it would be productive, I should welcome any action by the U.S. Government that you might think appropriate, designed to bring Smith to his senses and get him to accept that we all of us mean business, and that there is nothing but isolation and disaster at the end of the road for Rhodesia unless he is now prepared to reach an agreement on the basis of this last offer of ours, even if this has to be at the price of breaking with some of his associates.

7. I also believe that South Africa's influence on Smith is potentially of the greatest importance. If you saw any prospect of being able to induce the South African Government to bring pressure on Smith for a settlement, in their own best interests, this might well be the most useful of all. In addition, of course we hope that, if we are forced before the end of the year to work for limited mandatory sanctions at the United Nations, we shall be able to count on your help with other countries designed to keep the sanctions limited. We have made it clear that we shall only work for these sanctions provided we have full support from the Commonwealth for keeping them limited. We mean to stick to this. But equally we must expect that at least the Zambians and a number of other Afro-Asians will press for a great deal more. However, what we really want, if at all possible, is to induce Smith to come to terms.

8. I am sorry to worry you with our troubles when you have quite enough of your own. But I feel justified in doing this because, as I say, I think these are really our joint troubles; and if there is anything you feel you can usefully do now, we may be able to avoid finding ourselves jointly in a much more difficult situation which may confront us within the coming months, particularly at the United Nations and in what may follow from the debates there.

159. Message from Johnson to Wilson, 1 October 1966[125]

I had a strenuous but useful meeting with the Chancellor. As you know, he has now agreed to join with you and ourselves in a tripartite review—to begin promptly—of the entire range of relevant questions: the nature of the threat; strategy, force levels and deployments; burden-sharing; and foreign exchange neutralization. I have in mind asking John McCloy to represent me in these talks. I would very much hope that you could name some public figure of comparable stature and objectivity.

In connection with the points you made to me in your note of August 29,[126] let me say that I can certainly understand why it may be necessary for you to announce in mid-October your determination to reduce by some 33 million pounds sterling the foreign exchange drain associated with the BAOR. However, I am sure you will understand why I must emphasize again the importance of avoiding public commitment to troop cuts and drawdown of stocks until we have completed our tripartite talks. Otherwise, these talks will lose credibility and political usefulness in all three countries and throughout the Alliance. (None of this, of course, arises in connection with the 8 million pounds sterling of the 33 million pounds sterling which would not involve reductions in either troops or stocks.)

In your shoes, I would certainly not back away from the savings target. The question is only whether it would be possible for you to say that the steps by which HMG will realize these savings cannot be decided until the completion of the tripartite discussions. I myself have every intention of insisting that we complete these discussions by mid-January. This should give you time to make whatever moves will be necessary to achieve your savings target in your fiscal year beginning April 1, 1967.

You will not be surprised, incidentally, that the newspaper reports on what was agreed between myself and Erhard are, as usual, thoroughly mixed up. Specifically, we in no sense agreed, either explicitly or tacitly, to the German proposition that there would have to be some fixed upper limit to the amount

---

[125] LBJ Library, NSF, Head of State Correspondence File, Box 10, United Kingdom: Prime Minister Wilson Correspondence, Volume 5 [2 of 2], no. 73.

[126] See 154.

of foreign exchange neutralization after June 30, 1967. Our position was—and is—that the question of future offset will have to be thrashed out thoroughly in the tripartite discussions. (Your people will of course have made available to you the communiqué.)

If we make the tripartite procedure work, it can help us hold off the pressures on each of us, including Erhard, to do things which would badly damage NATO and the Western position in Europe. Indeed, it can give us a start in reconsolidating the Alliance for the longer pull—and on a more sustainable basis—until the day when the French will be ready to rejoin the fold. And, if we fail to make it work, I am afraid we are in for serious trouble.

Thank you for your letter on Rhodesia.[127] I will give you my views in detail within a few days.

160. Message from Wilson to Johnson, 7 October 1966[128]

Thank you for your message of October 1 about your talks with the German Chancellor.[129] I was most interested to have your personal assessment. This was obviously none too easy a meeting.

I am glad that Erhard agrees to a tripartite review of the whole range of questions relating to NATO force levels, strategy and foreign exchange costs. I shall be nominating George Thomson to represent us. As you know, he enjoys my full confidence and has all the required knowledge and judgment. He will I think cooperate well with John McCloy, or whoever else you may ask to represent you at the talks.

The main point which concerns me is timing. From the beginning my agreement to these tripartite talks was conditional upon there being no delay in our own timetable for effecting economies in 1967/68. I fear that, if the tripartite discussions are not to be completed until mid-January, there is no prospect of our achieving the full saving which we plan for 1967/68.

The effective decisions must be taken much sooner than that. Moreover, I fear that for the three of us to be discussing together fundamental questions of concern to all our allies for nearly four months would put an intolerable strain on the alliance. I think we should plan for the tripartite talks to be completed in time for the necessary decisions to be taken at the NATO Ministerial Meeting in December. This suggests that we should instruct those taking part in these talks to concentrate on finding practical solutions and not to get lost in doctrinal

---

[127] See 158.

[128] LBJ Library, NSF, Head of State Correspondence File, Box 10, United Kingdom: Prime Minister Wilson Correspondence, Volume 5 [2 of 2], no. 66a.

[129] See 159.

discussions, and accordingly to complete these talks as soon as possible, and in any case not later than the end of November. I am sure this is humanely [sic] practicable provided of course that the people whom we nominate for these are free, so far as is necessary, from all other responsibilities. Only a timetable of this kind will give the impression, which I am sure we want to convey to everybody, that this is an urgent and pressing problem.

Meanwhile, we shall be having our meeting with the Germans on October 13 at which we shall hear from them what they offer by way of offset next year. I am not very optimistic. Immediately following this George Brown will be talking to Dean Rusk in Washington and on his return to London we shall have a good look at the whole situation once more. I can, of course, assure you that we are determined as you are to play our part in holding NATO together and, as you put it, reconsolidating the alliance for the longer pull.

Warmest regards.

161. Message from Wilson to Johnson, 10 October 1966[130]

I want you to know how impressed we all were by your great and imaginative speech about European reconciliation[131] and the new efforts you are making in that cause. No doubt this will come up if you are able to see George Brown later this week and I shall be very interested in anything further you can tell him of your plans and of your estimate of Soviet and East European attitudes. It is my own strong impression that, despite Vietnam, they want to push ahead with relations in Europe and with you and that this desire has recently grown. This is what makes your initiative so timely.

I was encouraged by what you said about the need to remove territorial and border disputes: and also by your mention of a possible revision in force levels on both sides. As I told you in July, when I suggested this revision to Kosygin he showed some interest in the idea. I am sure that it is worth our pursuing it.

I share your belief in the need for balance between strength and conciliation, between firmness and flexibility. This is not only what we want in the context of the Alliance: I believe that it is at the same time—linked with the possibility of co-operation in the economic field, which is fundamental to their interests—exactly the right way to approach the East Europeans.

---

[130] LBJ Library, NSF, Head of State Correspondence File, Box 10, United Kingdom: Prime Minister Wilson Correspondence, Volume 5 [1 of 2], no. 64.

[131] See Johnson's remarks in New York before the National Conference of Editorial Writers, 7 October 1966 (*Public Papers of the Presidents of the United States: Lyndon B. Johnson, 1966: II* (Washington, DC: US Government Printing Office, 1967), pp. 1125–30).

162. Message from Johnson to Wilson, 18 October 1966[132]

In reply to your good message on Rhodesia,[133] let me begin by saying that I greatly admired the way you handled the Commonwealth Conference. You were certainly right to concentrate on holding the group together and retaining control of the Rhodesian situation. As you say, the Commonwealth is very important to all of us—the more so as racial problems multiply.

If Smith throws away his last chance, you may depend on our full support for the moves spelled out in your letter. Specifically, we will support your withdrawal of all previous offers to Smith, your adoption of a position of no independence before majority rule, and your proposal of limited mandatory economic sanctions in the Security Council.

I know you are aware that there will be strong pressures to broaden the sanctions and to apply them to South Africa. My people—both at the State Department and in New York—seriously doubt that there will be support in the Council for limiting the scope of export sanctions or for restricting to Mozambique any subsequent oil embargo. They believe that the drive to enlarge the target to include South Africa is likely to be overwhelming. Nevertheless, I fully appreciate your problems with a UK veto of such an enlargement.

I do not think that we can help through direct contact with Smith. If you believe it would be useful to have a go at Vorster, I am willing to have my Ambassador reiterate our firm support for your policy and for UN resolutions designed to end the Smith regime. He would try to persuade them that their own interests dictate that they comply with the present voluntary sanctions. He would also point out that the Security Council is likely to impose mandatory sanctions against Rhodesia, and that South African refusal to comply would lead to pressures to extend them to South Africa which would be difficult for us to resist. Perhaps your people in Pretoria could make a similar approach.

In any event, I would suggest that we use the time you have gained to discuss the problems presented if you are forced to give effect to your conference commitments, as well as the contingencies which could arise if things go badly in New York. If you agree, I will get my people in touch with yours.

I want you to know that I think you have been a great force for good in this matter. I know it is a heavy cross, but you are doing Africa and the world a great service.

---

[132] LBJ Library, NSF, Head of State Correspondence File, Box 10, United Kingdom: Prime Minister Wilson Correspondence, Volume 5 [1 of 2], no. 56a.

[133] See 158.

163. Message from Wilson to Johnson, 20 October 1966[134]

Many thanks indeed for your very helpful message on Rhodesia.[135] We are truly grateful for your promise of support if Smith throws away his last chance.

We of course share to some extent the apprehensions of your people, both in Washington and in New York, about the likely difficulties of trying to limit the scope of export sanctions or restricting any oil embargo to Mozambique. But such indications as we have had from Commonwealth Heads of Government are that they will do their best to honour their part of the conference bargain. We shall just have to work hard to achieve the desired result: and this is why your promise of support is of such real practical value to us.

I fully accept what you say about the difficulty of your helping through direct contact with Smith. But I warmly welcome your offer to have a go at Vorster. I believe this could be very helpful, especially if it can be done soon. Without being too sanguine about the likelihood of the South Africans pressing Smith really hard to accept this last chance, I think there is at least a worthwhile prospect of their doing so. George Brown worked on the South African Ambassador here as a preliminary to meeting Muller in New York: and, at that meeting, Muller undertook to think over very carefully what George had said and, for the first time in our dealings with him, he appeared seriously to contemplate the possibility of using South African influence. Accordingly, when he got back here, George sent a further message to Muller, confirming what he had told him of the terms we have now put to Smith and warning him that, as Smith was on the brink of a decision, any South African action would have to be immediate to affect it. We do not, of course, know whether the South Africans have yet taken any action but I shall be very grateful if you will, as you suggest, now instruct your Ambassador in Pretoria to act on the lines you propose. This will most usefully reinforce our own approach to Muller. Moreover, the timing should be just right. Smith yesterday gave our emissary in Salisbury his oral reply. As we expected, it temporises. Smith promises us a written reply within the next week or so. His oral reaction has been essentially negative: But I still think there may be an outside chance of getting somewhere with him before our end-November deadline: and, perhaps more important, before the November 11th Anniversary of I.D.I.[136] If the South Africans can be induced to weigh in constructively while he and his colleagues are still deliberating, this might yet tip the scales.

---

[134] LBJ Library, NSF, Head of State Correspondence File, Box 10, United Kingdom: Prime Minister Wilson Correspondence, Volume 5 [1 of 2], no. 54.

[135] See 162.

[136] Wilson means UDI, which was declared on 11 November 1965.

Meanwhile, however, we clearly have to prepare for the worst: and I am sure it is right, as you suggest, that our people should get together to consider the contingencies.

I am not quite sure at what point this will reach you in your present travels. But it brings you my warmest wishes for a profitable outcome. George has given me a heart-warming account of his reception in Washington and especially from yourself. Clearly there can be no room for excessive optimism about current trends in Soviet attitudes. But it seems as though there may be at least a chink of light at the end of the tunnel.

164. Message from Johnson to Wilson, 22 October 1966[137]

We were grieved to learn of the tragedy which has struck the British nation at Aberfan, Wales.[138] The people of the United States join Mrs. Johnson and me in extending through you our heartfelt sympathy to the British people and, particularly, to the families of the victims.

165. Message from Wilson to Johnson, 22 October 1966[139]

I am deeply grateful for your message of sympathy at the Aberfan tragedy.[140] This will be greatly appreciated throughout Britain and particularly by the people of Wales: and on their behalf I send to Mrs. Johnson and yourself my warm thanks. I visited Aberfan myself last night. It was a nightmare visit. All our hearts must go out to the families and especially to the parents of the children who lost their lives.

166. Message from Wilson to Johnson, 4 November 1966[141]

I was so sorry to hear of your operation,[142] and was glad to read that it is only a minor affair. But I can imagine how frustrating it must be for you, at this

---

[137] LBJ Library, NSF, Head of State Correspondence File, Box 10, United Kingdom: Prime Minister Wilson Correspondence, Volume 5 [1 of 2], no. 48a.

[138] On 21 October colliery waste had engulfed houses and a school in Aberfan, killing over 100 people, mainly children.

[139] LBJ Library, NSF, Head of State Correspondence File, Box 10, United Kingdom: Prime Minister Wilson Correspondence, Volume 5 [1 of 2], no. 46.

[140] See 164.

[141] LBJ Library, NSF, Head of State Correspondence File, Box 10, United Kingdom: Prime Minister Wilson Correspondence, Volume 5 [1 of 2], no. 43.

[142] Johnson had a growth in his throat removed in early November 1966 (Robert E. Gilbert, 'The Political Effects of Presidential Illness: The Case of Lyndon B. Johnson', *Political Psychology*,

exceptionally important and busy moment, to have to take time off for this. Please accept my warmest wishes for its complete success and for your very speedy return to full strength.

I have read with the greatest interest accounts of your Asian trip. You must have found it a fascinating and encouraging experience.

167. Message from Johnson to Wilson, 12 November 1966[143]

Many thanks for your kind thought which I greatly appreciate.[144] It is frustrating to be tied up like this but my doctors assure me that it will only be for a few days.

The Asian trip was fascinating and we were pleased with the results of the Manila Conference.[145] I believe we are on the right track although there is still much to be done in Vietnam and in Asia. Above all, I am convinced a vital new Asia will rapidly emerge if we see it through in Vietnam.

Averell[146] tells me he had a good go-around with you.

168. Message from Wilson to Johnson, 11 November 1966[147]

I have asked Pat Dean to give you the full text of what I said yesterday in the House of Commons about our new approach to the problem of British entry into the Common Market. I hope this speaks for itself. But there are two points that I should like to underline to you personally.

Before doing this, however, perhaps I could explain briefly how I see this whole operation. As you know, I have never been one of the little band of so-called "Europeans." I believe that the way our predecessors set about things five years ago was the wrong way: the failure of their attempt was inevitable: and no government under my leadership is going to get into a similar situation. Moreover, it always seemed to me doubtful—and I never hesitated to make this clear in public—whether the six left to themselves were likely to develop into a community dedicated to a concept over ever-widening and freer trade:

16, 4 (1995), 768.

[143] LBJ Library, NSF, Head of State Correspondence File, Box 10, United Kingdom: Prime Minister Wilson Correspondence, Volume 5 [1 of 2], no. 38.

[144] See 166.

[145] The Manila Conference, held on 24–5 October 1966, brought together representatives from Australia, New Zealand, South Korea, South Vietnam, the Philippines, Thailand and the United States.

[146] Averell Harriman.

[147] LBJ Library, NSF, Head of State Correspondence File, Box 10, United Kingdom: Prime Minister Wilson Correspondence, Volume 5 [1 of 2], no. 34.

or whether the trend would not be towards a tight little inward-looking group of countries concerned essentially with their own affairs. I am bound to say that in their attitude towards agriculture and on the whole towards the Kennedy Round,[148] they have sometimes seemed to justify doubts of this kind. This tendency represents a real danger for all of us. And, as I made clear yesterday, George Brown and I intend to emphasize during the probing visits we shall be making to European capitals that a forthcoming attitude by the six towards the Kennedy Round will be significant earnest of their desire for British membership in a joint enterprise with them.

On the other hand and this is perhaps the main reason why I feel that our present initiative is right—I believe that the situation in Europe has changed pretty fundamentally since 1962 and is continuing to change: that the prospects of building a new and wider community including, as well as ourselves, a number if not all of our EFTA partners, are now much more promising than they were: and that if we can build such a community, it will greatly strengthen not only Britain and Europe, but the West as a whole. Obviously this concept of an outward looking European community, designed to play the constructive role in world affairs that each of us individually is now finding too difficult, is bound to raise once more the fundamental issue of our own relationship with the United States which stuck in de Gaulle's gullet last time. The prophets of gloom say that this remains as total an obstacle to our present approach as it proved for our predecessors. We shall see. My own belief is that the General has not changed one iota in his general view of the world or of our own relationship with yourselves. But, as I say, Europe and the world are changing around him and so is the situation in France itself. In 1962 de Gaulle was on the crest of the political wave. I am sure his power in France is still absolute. But I am equally sure that his subordinates are now thinking very deeply about the future of France without de Gaulle and that a great many of them realize how necessary to France in that period partnership with Britain must be—as well as a close partnership between the two of us and Germany. Clearly, our talks in Paris will be far the most difficult and delicate of any we shall have. But if I despaired of them, I would not have said what I did yesterday.

This is the background against which I wish you to see my personal commitment to the policy I explained to the House yesterday. The two points that I mentioned at the outset and on which I want you to be clear in your mind beyond peradventure are, first the firm determination of my colleagues and of myself that there shall be no change in the fundamental relationship between our two countries and in our own basic loyalty to and belief in the Atlantic concept. As I have suggested earlier in this message, I am convinced that

---

[148] The Kennedy Round, named after President Kennedy, were multilateral trade talks held in Geneva between 1964 and 1967.

British membership of the right kind European community—conscious of its responsibilities to the rest of the world and not simply concentrating on its own narrow interests—and British membership of that type of community, which is the objective of our present approach, far from being incompatible with the Atlantic concept will be, on the contrary a means of strengthening and enriching it. Secondly, the key to this whole exercise rests in the words at the end of the paragraph in my statement where I speak or our clear intention and determination to enter EEC if, as we hope, our essential British and Commonwealth interests can be safeguarded. Those words are "We mean business."[149] We are going into this in the firm belief—and the Cabinet are united with me in agreement on this—that the sort of European concept I have outlined above is the right one and that our efforts to achieve it shall succeed.

I confidently believe that our discussions during the coming months will confirm the sincerity of our approach and strength of support for it among our potential partners in Europe. I am convinced that, with this support, we shall succeed together in what I personally regard as an historic initiative.

169. Message from Johnson to Wilson, 15 November 1966[150]

I am immensely heartened by your courageous announcement about joining the EEC.[151] Your entry would certainly help to strengthen and unify the West. If you find on the way that there is anything we might do to smooth the path, I hope you will let me know.

The report from John McCloy on the trilateral talks is encouraging, despite the real difficulties we still face. Thomson made an excellent contribution. I am hopeful that we can get a genuine return from this exercise—militarily, politically and financially.

The immense snag, which Carstens confirmed, is the inevitability of delay on the German side. While they can fruitfully continue to work with us in the trilateral group, it would be impossible for them to reach a responsible government position on these matters in time to keep the present schedule. We should surely give the Germans a chance to get themselves a government.

I know we agree that we must move together in order to maintain NATO as a credible deterrent and as a stabilising influence, especially in Germany. Your

---

[149] *Parliamentary Debates (Hansard): House of Commons, 1966–67: Volume 735*, 10 November 1966, col. 1540.

[150] LBJ Library, NSF, Head of State Correspondence File, Box 10, United Kingdom: Prime Minister Wilson Correspondence, Volume 5 [1 of 2], no. 30.

[151] See 168.

presence in Germany is as important to us as your presence in the East, which I assume remains as we last discussed it.

I understand, as you know, the importance to you of being able to justify a change in your announced program, in view of the pressures inherent in your difficult but promising policies of economic adjustment. Would it help if I placed in the United Kingdom in the near future $35 million in orders beyond those already agreed to? I think I could do so on assurance from you that you will stay with us and the Germans in completing this fundamental review of the military, political and financial basis for the US-UK presence in Germany, making no change in your troop and supply dispositions there until after the completion of the review, and then that you will concert with us on any such changes in the light of that review. This procurement would supplement the accruals of dollars to you associated with the recent shift of our forces and installations to Britain from the continent.

I must get some heat from Congress on this, and cannot move definitively until I have talked it over with some of my people on the Hill. I think I can persuade them to go along on the basis outlined here.

McCloy and our government officials are working on plans to handle deficits that result from the presence of our troops abroad through a multilateral clearing arrangement that should help neutralize balances, and contribute to an ultimate resolution of the monetary problem. That may take some time to negotiate. If successful, such an arrangement should help to satisfy some of our critics in Congress, and move the Germans to accept their own proper responsibilities.

I cannot stress too strongly the need for progress towards more equitable patterns for dealing with the various responsibilities we all bear throughout the world. As we both know, some of the criticism I get here on the subject is justified. And, as you can imagine, the new Congress will not be easier to persuade than its predecessor.[152]

I very much hope that the arrangements proposed here will help you join us in keeping this exercise on the tracks. Let us keep in close touch on this.

170. Message from Wilson to Johnson, 17 November 1966[153]

We are all delighted to hear that things have gone so well. I send you my best wishes for your speedy return to full activity. But equally, we all hope that you

---

[152] Although still enjoying a majority in both the Senate and House of Representatives, Johnson's Democrats had suffered significance losses in the mid-term elections held on 8 November 1966.

[153] LBJ Library, NSF, Head of State Correspondence File, Box 10, United Kingdom: Prime Minister Wilson Correspondence, Volume 5 [1 of 2], no. 5.

will seize this opportunity of taking things easy, if only for a very short while. You have rightly deserved a few days off.

Warmest regards,
   Harold Wilson

171. Message from Wilson to Johnson, 18 November 1966[154]

Thank you for your generous message of 15 November[155] and for the characteristically imaginative and sympathetic way in which you approach our problems.

I share your hope that we shall get a genuine return from this exercise. However, despite the good atmosphere in which these talks have taken place, I am bound to say I am most disappointed that so little real progress has been made. My position, which I have made clear to you and you yourself have recognised from the day you first proposed these trilateral talks, is that our needs are pressing. While I fully share your view of the need to maintain the credibility of NATO and the stability of Germany, it is absolutely vital to our ability to contribute to these aims that we should have a really satisfactory balance of payments surplus next year. It is in fact critical to all our policies that we should succeed in this. To achieve this we must reduce the drain from our overseas military expenditure. Delay in the trilateral talks puts in jeopardy the saving of foreign exchange in Germany. We have as you know demanded severe deflationary sacrifices from our own people. It is not easy to maintain the pressure on the domestic economy while this expenditure continues in Germany.

This is the background which I must look at all these questions. Before I can comment usefully on your proposals I would clearly need to know what orders you have in mind, what the timing of them would be and how far they are additional to orders which would have been placed and been offset against our purchases of the F111. I shall also be very glad to have further details of the multilateral clearing arrangements on which you say your people are working. We must of course be wary of doing anything which might ease the pressure on the Germans to accept what you rightly call their proper responsibilities. But we shall welcome all proposals for bringing to an end our foreign exchange losses in Germany next year.

Would I be right in thinking that on your side Gene Rostow would be competent to enter into details of your ideas? If so, I suggest that we should

---

[154] LBJ Library, NSF, Head of State Correspondence File, Box 10, United Kingdom: Prime Minister Wilson Correspondence, Volume 5 [1 of 2], no. 26a.

[155] See 169.

use the opportunity of his visit to London next week to go into all this very thoroughly with him, so that you and I may then communicate again.

172. Message from Johnson to Wilson, 19 November 1966[156]

Thank you for your message of the 18th.[157] Gene Rostow will be prepared to discuss with you and your people our thinking on the question you raise. In the meanwhile I do not want to assure you that we fully intend that the $35 million would be additional to the total of purchases to which we are already committed under the F-111 arrangement. Further, Bob McNamara tells me that he can actually make payment of the extra $35 million before December 31, 1967.

You will understand, of course, that before I can finally confirm the above arrangement, I will have to talk to my senior people on the Hill and to assure them that, on your side, you will find it possible to go along with the propositions in my message of the 15th.[158]

173. Message from Wilson to Johnson, 29 November 1966[159]

I am most grateful for your second message of November 19[160] explaining the terms of your offer of 35 million dollars to make easier our task in the tripartite talks. My talk with Gene Rostow was also extremely valuable and fruitful, as I am sure he will have told you. I entirely share your wish to see tripartite agreement on these difficult problems as a contribution to holding NATO together at this difficult time. You yourself, of course, fully understand the needs for us to achieve a balance of payments surplus if we are to go on making our contribution to the common cause in NATO and elsewhere, including the Far East. We also have to consider the effect on our other NATO allies if the tripartite talks go on too long.

Nevertheless, given especially the difficulty for the Germans in taking effective decisions for some little time, I am sure it is right that we should accept your helpful offer of 35 million dollars and I am glad to know that payment can actually be made before December 31, 1967 at the latest, even if definite orders have not been placed by then. I talked to Gene Rostow about the exact

---

[156] LBJ Library, NSF, Head of State Correspondence File, Box 10, United Kingdom: Prime Minister Wilson Correspondence, Volume 5 [1 of 2], no. 22.

[157] See 171.

[158] See 169.

[159] LBJ Library, NSF, Head of State Correspondence File, Box 10, United Kingdom: Prime Minister Wilson Correspondence, Volume 5 [1 of 2], no. 20.

[160] See 172.

terms of the offer. My understanding is that we for our part would make no changes in our troop and supply dispositions in Germany before the end of June 1967: but that this would not be held to prevent us from making savings in the personal expenditure of our troops and other administrative economies not affecting their combat capability. Nor would it be designed to prevent us from rotating our troops in the normal way or preparing in the United Kingdom for any withdrawals which may subsequently prove necessary. Meanwhile we should continue with the tripartite talk and do our utmost to reach the earliest possible agreement on the military and financial questions at issue, so that we may then as you say concert any moves together. I sincerely hope that we can achieve this early next year. But if, by the end of June 1967, agreement has still not been reached, then, as Jim Callaghan and I were at pains to make clear to Gene Rostow, we should have to regard ourselves as free to take whatever measures seemed necessary to us to cover in full the balance of the foreign exchange costs of our forces in Germany in 1967/68, remaining after payments by Germany and your payment of 35 million dollars.

As regards the orders which you will place here, I would only say two things at this stage. First, they must make a real contribution to our balance of payments problem and employment in this country. This means, for example, that the purchase of fuel with a high import content would not meet our needs, so we shall have to look for hardware purchases. Second, I was glad to have your assurance, and its clarification by Rostow, that these orders would be additional to the F.111 arrangement and to the current and prospective dollar accruals from the United States forces stationed in the United Kingdom. I assume that Bob McNamara will arrange for his people to discuss with ours in detail the orders to be placed, the payment arrangements, and the mechanism for ensuring additionality.

I understand from Gene Rostow that, with regard to the Far East, which you mentioned in your message of November 19 you would wish us to make no dramatic change in our force dispositions there within the six months period we are considering. I can certainly assure you that apart from the changes resulting from our defence review and our economy measures of July, which we have already discussed together, we have nothing in mind for that period.

I take it that you will now want to take soundings on the Hill. We must then consider how to tell the Germans the arrangements made between us, without giving them any cause to think that there is any less reason for them to meet your and our foreign exchange costs to the fullest extent they can. We must also consider how to tell the rest of NATO, who will undoubtedly need reassurance at the prospect of the tripartite talks lasting longer than they thought at first. In this context, we must clearly try to reach tripartite agreement on a report to NATO which will allow them to give the fullest possible guidance to the military authorities, so that NATO's consideration of strategy and force levels can go forward in parallel with our own tripartite exercise.

Finally, we must consider together the terms and timing of a public announcement which, for my part, I should like to see not later than the NATO Ministerial meeting in December and the adjournment of Parliament for the Christmas recess.

Many thanks again for all your help in this difficult but, for us, absolutely crucial matter.

174. Message from Wilson to Johnson, 29 November 1966[161]

I want you to know, for the strictly personal information of yourself and Dean Rusk at this stage, that I hope to be able to tell the House of Commons tomorrow that the Commonwealth Secretary and I will be meeting Ian Smith later this week. If he agrees to this, it will be a final showdown between us. Our prolonged probings of his position, culminating in Bowden's visit this last weekend, coupled with Smith's developing realisation of the pressures building up on him—our Commonwealth undertakings, the threatened UN action, South African representations to him (and I am confident Vorster has done this) and even signs of possible division within the Rhodesia front—all these things have, I believe, at last brought him to recognise that he stands now at the brink. And, as he gazes at the abyss ahead, I believe too that he is, perhaps for the first time since November of last year, seriously thinking that he must come to terms with us, because he understands how much worse for him and for Rhodesia any alternative course would be.

This, at all events, is the conclusion that my colleagues and I have drawn from the attitude he took last weekend with the Commonwealth Secretary. I need not trouble you with the details. He has not come all the way to meet us—far from it. The gulf is still wide between us. And, if it is to be bridged, the initiative must come from him. We shall stand firm on our six principles, on a return to legality and on guarantees both against any fresh IDI[162] and on unimpeded advance to African majority rule. But Smith has said enough to make it clear to me that I could not justify, to my country or my conscience, a break with him now and the implementation of paragraph 10 of the communiqué, with all the consequences that would flow for Rhodesia, for Britain and for the world as a whole, without one last personal effort to bring this narrow, obstinate, but not, I think, fundamentally dishonorable man to face up to the realities. If I fail,

---

[161] LBJ Library, NSF, Head of State Correspondence File, Box 10, United Kingdom: Prime Minister Wilson Correspondence, Volume 5 [1 of 2], no. 17.

[162] Wilson evidently means UDI.

that will be that, and we shall go ahead as undertaken at the Commonwealth Conference. If I succeed, this will, I know, be only the beginning of many further difficulties—with the African Commonwealth, at the United Nations—and with some of our own supporters here. But there will be no agreement with Smith that does not meet our stated requirements and that I can not therefore with honour defend to Parliament. So I am prepared to face up to these difficulties and see them through, as the inevitable but acceptable price of a favourable settlement.

I do not want to make this message any longer. But you have given us such staunch support throughout this Rhodesian business, and despite the misgivings that I know many of your people have felt, that I wanted you to have this advance warning of our plans. Joe Garner can fill in the State Department on some of the background. And I shall of course keep you posted of progress—if any. This is a very crucial moment. But we are going into it with clear heads and no illusions. If I was a betting man, I should wager against a settlement. But the odds are not so steep that the gamble is not worth taking: and the stakes, for all of us, are high.

175. Message from Wilson to Johnson, 30 November 1966[163]

We have not been able to announce today the proposed meeting with Ian Smith on which I wrote to you yesterday.[164] But this is simply because Smith asked for a little extra time to consul [sic] his colleagues. He has now confirmed his willingness to come and plans are going ahead satisfactorily. Our meeting later this week seems likely only to be delayed by a few hours. I would not at this stage modify the estimate of the likely chances that I gave you yesterday. But on the basis of what we have heard from Salisbury, I believe the odds may be shortening a shade.

176. Message from Wilson to Johnson, 4 December 1966[165]

I write this to you in the plane on my way back from one more of these strangely tantalizing and—yet again—ultimately disappointing meetings with Smith. I say tantalizing because, after two days (and nights) of argument, discussion

---

[163] LBJ Library, NSF, Head of State Correspondence File, Box 10, United Kingdom: Prime Minister Wilson Correspondence, Volume 5 [1 of 2], no. 15a.
[164] See 174.
[165] LBJ Library, NSF, Head of State Correspondence File, Box 10, United Kingdom: Prime Minister Wilson Correspondence, Volume 5 [1 of 2], no. 10a.

and very plain speaking, it seemed by yesterday evening that an honourable agreement was at last within our grasp.

I need not trouble you with details. We discussed the three main issues—indissolubly related in our minds: to be dissociated so far as possible in his: the independence constitution: the prior return to legality and the formation of the interim government: and the essential external guarantees of the eventual settlement. By late yesterday we had hammered out a document which gave Smith a better deal in all three respects than he conceivably deserves: and on which my two colleagues and I had to reflect very carefully before we decided that this was something we could with honour recommend to Parliament. On the text itself, argued over line by line, paragraph by paragraph, there seemed in the end to be agreement between us.

Why then have we had to make the indecisive short statement today which will have been shown to you? The answer I am afraid, is that we are dealing with a very devious and schizophrenic personality. Smith agreed to meet us on the absolutely clear understanding, to which he specifically assented that each of us came with full powers from our respective colleagues to settle. But on Friday he recanted on this and insisted that he could not go further than agree with us a text which he would recommend to his colleagues as acceptable. By Saturday evening we had such a text. But then he recanted again: he would go no further than take it back and think over whether or not to recommend its acceptance.

This was intolerable. But we were so resolved that the chance of a settlement should not slip through our fingers through any fault of ours that we have, as you see, given him till noon tomorrow to give us a plain yes or no to the document, without any modification whatever. I think there is still an outside chance that he, or some of his colleagues will come to their senses. Before he left late last night, I spoke to him in rougher and more brutal terms than ever before of the appalling dangers for himself, for Rhodesia and for the whole of Southern Africa which were bound to be the consequence of a refusal. I may have shaken him (I certainly shook his colleagues). But what still sticks in his gullet as he put it, is the idea that he must return to legality before there can be the test of Rhodesian opinion in the new constitution.

If he could not remove this bone on board the Tiger, I doubt if he will in Salisbury. At all events, by noon tomorrow the die will be cast, one way or the other. If, by then, he has not said yes to our text, we shall go straight ahead with the programme of action we promised to the Commonwealth in September. Garner has reported on the extremely helpful and thorough talks which he had with your people last week. I am sure that we must continue to act in the closest concert as we go forward to this next stage, fraught as it is with so many difficulties and I am glad to know that there is such close understanding between us.

It is clear to us from our exchange with the South African Government that they have been leaning pretty heavily on Smith to reach a settlement. We have informed them of the content of the text we worked out with Smith, in the hope that even at this eleventh hour they may be able to exert some further pressure. I hope you may be willing to consider most urgently whether, by saying anything to them today, you too might help persuade them to try their hand again in Salisbury before noon tomorrow.[166]

177. Message from Johnson to Wilson, 5 December 1966[167]

Many thanks for your thoughtful message about my operation.[168] It went remarkable [sic] well. My doctors are satisfied. More important, I feel fine.

I was glad to get you last message on the tripartite schedule.[169] I am delighted that we have been able to arrive at an understanding that will allow the three of us until the end of June, if necessary, to complete our review and to make our decision.

Bob McNamara will be in touch with your people to arrange for $35 million of orders and payments. I accept your point about oil; we will do our best to place $35 million of purchases that will meet your needs. These purchases will definitely be additional those under the F-111 agreement and will be subject to the understandings governing that agreement. They will not be expenditures which are now in prospect for U.S. forces in Britain—including the forces recently transferred from the Continent.

On the terms and timing of the public announcement, we will be glad to meet your convenience. From our point of view—unless it is important to you—it might be better not to mention the exact amount. In any case, I think we should move fairly quickly to avoid leaks. Your people can work out the details with David Bruce in London.

I assume you will inform the Germans before any public announcement.

---

[166] Johnson subsequently authorized Rusk to send a message to the South African Foreign Minister, urging the South Africans to use their good offices to encourage a settlement. Rusk's message to Muller of 4 December is reproduced in *FRUS, 1964–1968*: Volume XXIV, *Africa* (Washington, DC: US Government Printing Office, 1999), pp. 929–30.

[167] LBJ Library, NSF, Head of State Correspondence File, Box 10, United Kingdom: Prime Minister Wilson Correspondence, Volume 5 [1 of 2], no. 3a.

[168] See 170.

[169] See 173.

178. Message from Johnson to Wilson, 31 December 1966[170]

As we begin the New Year, Mr. Prime Minister, I extend to the British people and to you my warmest personal regards and best wishes for a prosperous and happy 1967.

During the past our two countries have cooperated closely, as friends and allies, in the cause of world peace. I know that we shall continue this work together in the years ahead.

Lyndon B. Johnson

179. Message from Wilson to Johnson, 2 January 1967[171]

I send you my sincere thanks, Mr. President, for your kind New Year message.[172] Please accept my own warm good wishes for the people of the United States of America and for yourself. I, too, look forward to a continuation of the close and friendly relationship between our two countries that has been such a valued source of mutual strength and counsel to our alliance in the past.

---

[170] LBJ Library, NSF, Head of State Correspondence File, Box 10, United Kingdom: Prime Minister Wilson Correspondence, Volume 6 [2 of 2], no. 109.

[171] LBJ Library, NSF, Head of State Correspondence File, Box 10, United Kingdom: Prime Minister Wilson Correspondence, Volume 6 [2 of 2], no. 106b.

[172] See 178.

Chapter 3

The Wilson–Kosygin Talks, Crisis in the Middle East, the Defence Review, and the Devaluation of Sterling, January–December 1967

180. Message from Wilson to Johnson, 12 January 1967[1]

I want you to know that, as I have told David Bruce privately, I am seriously concerned at a matter which is, I think, pretty fundamental to our relationship.[2] David [Bruce] will of course be reporting about it but, as I told him, I feel that I should send you this personal word about it.
Best regards.

---

[1] TNA, PREM 13/1917.
[2] In November 1966, Washington had failed to inform London of a mission by the Polish member of the International Control Commission, Lewandowski, to explain to Hanoi the terms under which the United States would cease bombing North Vietnam. During a conversation with David Bruce on 10 January, Wilson complained that 'it was most unsatisfactory that the Poles should have known what was going on whereas the Foreign Secretary was "put in to bat" in Moscow without complete knowledge' (Record of conversation between the Prime Minister and the United States Ambassador at No. 10, Downing Street at 12.10 p.m. on Tuesday, 10 January 1967, TNA, PREM 13/1917). Wilson went on to say that 'this raised a major issue of confidence in relations between the Foreign Secretary and himself and the President and Mr. Rusk' (ibid). With Kosygin's impending visit to Britain, Wilson recorded in his memoirs that 'there could be no repetition of the Lewandowski affair' (Harold Wilson, *The Labour Government, 1964–1970: A Personal Record* (London: Wiedenfeld and Nicolson, 1971), p. 345). He therefore requested Johnson to send a representative 'in whom he had confidence' to put him 'fully in the picture' before Kosygin's arrival (ibid., p. 346). Chester Cooper was subsequently sent to London with details of Johnson's proposals for ending the bombing and starting negotiations.

181. Message from Johnson to Wilson, 21 January 1967[3]

I trust your talk with David Bruce and Cooper settled the questions you raised earlier with David and put you in a knowledgeable position to deal with Kosygin.

182. Message from Wilson to Johnson, 21 January 1967[4]

Many thanks for your message.[5] Yes indeed, Chet Cooper has given an admirably full briefing to George Brown and myself[6] and I am glad to feel that we are now fully in possession of the facts. I am grateful to you for responding so promptly and helpfully and for letting Cooper come to talk to us in this way.

As I told him, I think it essential that I should be completely up to date when Kosygin arrives here on February 6. I hope you will feel able to let me have any further briefing this may require shortly before that date. If Cooper could pay us another short visit, that would be admirable.

183. Message from Wilson to Johnson, 28 January 1967[7]

I am greatly distressed at the news of the tragic death of the three officers in the Apollo spacecraft. Please accept this expression of deep sympathy at the loss of these brave men.

184. Message from Johnson to Wilson, 6 February 1967[8]

I am sending these thoughts to you on the question posed as to whether the U.S. could stop the bombing of North Viet Nam in exchange for an indication that Hanoi would enter into talks without any military acts of de-escalation on their side.

---

[3] LBJ Library, NSF, Head of State Correspondence File, Box 10, United Kingdom: Prime Minister Wilson Correspondence, Volume 6 [2 of 2], no. 100.

[4] LBJ Library, NSF, Head of State Correspondence File, Box 10, United Kingdom: Prime Minister Wilson Correspondence, Volume 6 [2 of 2], no. 98.

[5] See 181.

[6] See Record of a conversation between the Prime Minister and Mr. Chester Cooper in the Prime Minister's room in the House of Commons at 6.00 p.m. on Wednesday 18 January 1968, TNA, PREM 13/1917.

[7] LBJ Library, NSF, Head of State Correspondence File, Box 11, M.O.D. 1967, no. 6.

[8] TNA, PREM 13/1808.

It is important to recall that the Poles said to us in the first part of December that Hanoi would be prepared to hold discussions with us on the basis of a Polish summary of what the Poles understood our position to be. Discussion of mutual de-escalation, including a cessation of the bombing, would be part of those talks. We promptly agreed to such talks but found that Hanoi (so the Poles told us) was unwilling to proceed with such talks because of certain bombing actions which occurred on 13–14 December. Although we had seen no real move toward talks before that date, we nevertheless removed that obstacle (if that was the obstacle) by informing Hanoi that we were refraining from bombing within a radius of 10 nautical miles of the center of Hanoi – restrictions which have been in effect for more than a month. We took this action without conditions but did state that we would be impressed by any corresponding action by Hanoi. This was an important military move on our part. We have seen neither a corresponding military step on their side nor a use of existing channels to get on with discussions. In contacts with Hanoi since December 23 Hanoi received messages from us but we have not had any replies from Hanoi on any points of substance. Indeed, the Burchett interview[9] represents a step backward from Hanoi's position in December if the Poles were accurately reporting to us.

We have recently informed Hanoi directly that we would be prepared to take additional military measures of de-escalation similar to the limitation of bombing within the Hanoi perimeter, on similar terms. We have had no reply to that suggestion.

We are ready and willing to hold discussions with Hanoi through any feasible process – publicly or privately, directly or indirectly. We are inclined to the view that better progress could be made if such talks were private and direct.

If we are asked to take military action on our side, we need to know what the military consequences will be, that is, what military action will be taken by the other side. We have noted that a suspension of the bombing has been termed by the other side as unacceptable and that we must accept an unconditional and permanent cessation of bombing. That makes it all the more necessary to know what military action Hanoi would take if we in fact stopped the bombing.

We are prepared to take up with Hanoi steps of mutual de-escalation and are prepared to have the most private preliminary conversations with them on arrangements for serious discussions of a final settlement.

---

[9] Johnson is referring to an interview with the DRV foreign minister, Nguyen Duy Trinh conducted by Australian journalist, Wilfred Burchett. Nguyen remarked: 'If it [the United States] really wants talks, it must first halt unconditionally the bombing raids and all other acts of war against the DRV. It is only after the unconditional cessation of U.S. bombing and all other acts of war against the DRV that there could be talks between the DRV and the United States' (George C. Herring, *The Secret Diplomacy of the Vietnam War: The Negotiating Volumes of the Pentagon Papers* (Austin: University of Texas Press, 1983), p. 424).

Specifically, we are prepared to and plan, through established channels, to inform Hanoi that if they will agree to an assured stoppage of infiltration into South Viet Nam, we will stop the bombing of North Viet Nam and stop further augmentation of U.S. forces in South Viet Nam. We would welcome your joint advocacy of this position.

Further, or alternatively, you should know we would recommend to the South Vietnamese authorities that they discuss with North Vietnamese military authorities a prolongation of the Tet ceasefire.

For your own information, you should be aware of my feeling that, in all of our various contacts with Hanoi, we have had no impression from them as to the substance of the issues which must be resolved as a part of a peaceful settlement. They have received repeated statements from us about our views. They have reiterated their four points[10] and the Liberation Front's five points[11] with varying degree of vagueness as to their status, but they have not replied to our suggestions for a revision of their point three of their four points or a readiness to hold preliminary discussion looking towards agreed points as a basis for negotiations.

In sum, I would suggest that you try to separate the political processes of discussions from military action. We will participate fully in any political process including discussions of de-escalation. We are prepared to move immediately on major steps of mutual de-escalation, as indicated above. What we cannot accept is the exchange of guarantee of a safe haven for North Vietnam merely for discussions which thus far have no form or content, during which they could continue to expand their military operation without limit.

I doubt very much that Kosygin expected to resolve this matter on his first evening in London, and it would be helpful if you could fully explore just what Kosygin is willing or able to do. If he has counter-proposals to my major suggestion of mutual military de-escalation, we will give them immediate attention.

If Kosygin is seriously worried about China, as he told you he was, we would hope that he would exert himself to help bring peace to Viet Nam and allow North Viet Nam to participate in the peaceful development of Southeast Asia.

Finally, I would strongly urge that the two co-chairman not suggest a stoppage of bombing in exchange merely for talks, but, instead, appeal to Hanoi to consider seriously the reasonable proposals we are putting before them, which would take us not merely into negotiation but a long step toward peace itself.

---

[10] See 84, footnote 168.

[11] Towards the end of 1966, the NLF produced a five-point peace plan which called for a place for NLF members in the Vietnamese government, greater provincial autonomy, recognition of the NLF as a legitimate political party, incorporation of NLF officers and troops in to the Vietnamese army, a withdrawal of US and North Vietnamese troops.

185. Message from Wilson to Johnson, 7 February 1967[12]

I am very grateful to you for arranging that Chet Cooper should be here to brief me before these talks with Kosygin and to be available for consultation. For my part I have felt it right that he should be personally briefed by me on all that has happened in my talks with Kosygin and I have in fact had two long sessions with him this evening. I have given him a complete account of my talks and have entrusted him with details which I have not so far given to my colleagues. These briefings cover first a private talk I had for an hour with Kosygin this afternoon with no officials present except interpreters, second our plenary discussions and third a further private talk with only a British interpreter present at the end of a dinner I gave for Kosygin.

Chet Cooper will no doubt be reporting to you and I have asked him to ensure, as I know you will do, maximum security for these reports.

What I do know is that on everything Kosygin has said to me, there has been a significant change in the Soviet attitude. He is obsessed with Chinese behaviour and is anxious to see an end to the Vietnam War because on his account the continuance of the war strengths the hands of the Chinese in Vietnam and more widely. Whereas in the past he has always argued that this is no affair of his and that he has not been asked to intervene by the North Vietnamese authorities, he appears to be moved by a great sense of urgency and a great desire, I quote his words, to 'assist in reaching a settlement', and puts the highest importance on a direct contact between you and North Vietnam. He knows all that is going on. He is in close touch with Hanoi and admitted to me that he had been in touch with them both before and after his talks with me today: and that they have endorsed what he said to me today.

All our experts feel that there is a great deal of movement and movement in the right direction. Properly handled this could lead to an increasing engagement of the Russians in the process which would lead to a political settlement instead of slogging it out. Settlement by negotiations is now Kosygin's aim and he says that Hanoi are now prepared to accept such a settlement. But so far he has not gone further than suggesting an agreed Anglo/Russian approach to you based on the statement of the North Vietnamese foreign minister to Burchett[13] which Kosygin says he is prepared to underwrite personally though not as yet publicly. It will be extremely difficult to push him further than this although we are pressing for some more definite guarantees involving some clear sign of de-escalation during Tet and/or constructive negotiations in good faith. So far Kosygin is dismissing this pressure on the grounds that the North Vietnamese foreign minister is offering negotiations that he himself will underwrite the sincerity of

---

[12] TNA, PREM 13/1808.
[13] See 184, footnote 9.

this offer and that this should be enough. This of course is unacceptable to us as it would be to you. Nevertheless Kosygin is on the move and I am very anxious to know how far you would be prepared to go at this critical time, ie exactly what you would be prepared to accept in the form of a sign from North Vietnam sufficient to bring about a cessation of bombing.

At our third meeting tonight Kosygin was pressing me to get in touch with you urgently on the telephone: and he has promised to give me tomorrow the draft of a message to you indicating the lines on which he would like me to press you to meet the North Vietnamese offer. It is therefore important that I should know in good time for our Tuesday afternoon session beginning at 10.45 Washington time, the lines of an alternative proposal which I should know in advance would be acceptable to you.

Kosygin has not so far raised the question of extending Tet beyond four days. This may prove to be necessary: but for the moment we are anxious to cash in on his present sense of urgency and his feeling that the matter should be settled this week. We have stressed to him the paramount urgency of ensuring that nothing provocative is done by Hanoi during Tet and indeed the need, if at all possible, for a constructive sign during this period which would be helpful to you. The corollary is of course an equal restraint by your own people.

I hope that when you have received Chet Cooper's more detailed report of our talks you will give us the necessary tool to help you finish this job.

186. Message from Johnson to Wilson, 10 February 1967[14]

On behalf of the families of the three astronauts and of the American people, I express deep gratitude for your thoughtful message[15] of sympathy on the tragic accident at Cape Kennedy. Grissom, Chaffee and White were envoys of mankind in the exploration of space. The continuation of the work they did so much to advance – the exploration of our common space environment for the mutual benefit of all peoples on earth – will be a fitting memorial for these brave men. Sincerely,
Lyndon

---

[14] LBJ Library, NSF, Special Head of State Correspondence File, Box 56, United Kingdom [3 of 4], no. 90b.

[15] See 183.

187. Message from Wilson to Johnson, 11 February 1967[16]

You will have been kept in close touch through David [Bruce] and Chet Cooper with the progress of our talks with Kosygin. You should know that yesterday, Thursday, in a long private session with him I rejected the proposal he has been urging privately and publicly that we should join with him in the communiqué in asking you to stop the bombing unconditionally so that the DRV foreign minister's statement to Burchett[17] could become effective. As things are at present (and the formal talks end today) the communiqué may contain no more than a formal statement of our disagreement on the Vietnam issue.

You will know that the foreign secretary yesterday handed a note to Kosygin trying to push the Russians into activation of the Geneva machinery but, unless Kosygin strongly reverses his position, this will not be accepted.

But Kosygin and I in our private talk yesterday morning both agreed about the urgency of the problem, particularly in view of the Tet timing. And in a pre-lunch talk today he showed himself a little more forthcoming and very fully seized of the urgency. At this meeting I was able to tell him that the United States Government would go along with either the foreign secretary's proposal mentioned in my preceding paragraph: or your earlier two-phase proposal. But knowing your own preferences as between these two proposals, I made it clear to him that the first was our own and not yours; and that you were very concerned that nothing should be said by him to Hanoi which implied that you were going back on your acceptance of the secrecy of the assurances you would receive under your own two-phase proposal or that you were trying to impose some sort of public position on the North Vietnamese which they might construe as an attempt to make them lose face or cause them any other embarrassment. Kosygin took this point very clearly and he bit more firmly than hitherto on the two-phase proposal as a whole. At his request I therefore gave him this evening a further piece of paper, setting out in writing our understanding of your position on the two proposals: and I subsequently sent him the revised version that we received from Rostow, indicating to him that this was the authentic statement of the American position on the two-phase proposal and should be substituted for the version I had given him earlier in the evening. Apart from a reception I am attending at the Soviet Embassy this evening (Friday) we shall not be meeting again until early Sunday evening: and we have agreed to look at the Vietnamese situation again then in the light of any response from Hanoi during the interval and against the background of a Tet timetable.

---

[16] TNA, PREM 13/1808. The message was drafted on 10 February, but actually despatched at 1.30am on 11 February.

[17] See 184, footnote 9.

Incidentally, when I told Kosygin about the tremendous build up in waterborne traffic from North Vietnam during the first part of Tet and of the difficulties with which this would confront you in considering extending the bombing pause, he showed distinct signs of constructive interest – though whether he will actually do anything with the North Vietnamese about it I cannot, of course, judge.

In this connection I think it is important that you should let me know before Sunday evening of any developments which might have taken place, particularly in relation to the fate of the message that you have communicated to Hanoi. Kosygin is in close touch with Hanoi and will know the latest form by Sunday. You can rely on our continuing in all our dealings with him to stand absolutely firm on the lines set out in your telegram to me[18] and repeatedly stated since then by me to Kosygin. This will remain our position even if, this means recording a total disagreement on this issue with all that that will mean for me in terms of domestic politics, which I don't need describe to you. But although the political position here will be extremely difficult – and I know equally the tremendously difficult position you are facing with many pressures of a very different kind – I am standing by the line in your last message to me, above all because I believe it is right.

It is clear to me that the next 48 hours will be crucial particularly the period from 5.00 pm to midnight GMT on Sunday when Kosygin is with me at Chequers. We shall do everything in our power to get a settlement. But want you to know and you can rely on this absolutely, that during that period as throughout this past week we shall make no commitments or proposals as to the terms of settlement for Vietnam which do not square one hundred per cent with what we know to be your policy. Kosygin knows that. You can rely on it too.

I shall be sending you another message on Saturday about two different subjects which have come up in our discussions here and which may be included in the communiqué.

188. Message from Wilson to Johnson, 11 February 1967[19]

I told you that I would be writing to you about two topics other than Vietnam[20] that are likely to be referred to in the communiqué at the end of the Kosygin visit. These are the Russian proposal for an Anglo-Soviet Treaty of Friendship, Non-Aggression and Co-operative Development: and the question of a

---

[18] See 184.

[19] LBJ Library, NSF, Head of State Correspondence File, Box 10, United Kingdom: Prime Minister Wilson Correspondence, Volume 6 [2 of 2], no. 96a.

[20] See 187.

European security conference which as you will remember was plugged in the communiqué at the end of the Warsaw Pact meeting last summer.

On the first, you may have seen that Kosygin has now twice suggested in public speeches here and has also of course raised the question with us in our meetings, that there should be a bilateral treaty of this kind between us. I need not trouble you with his arguments.

As I have argued to him, treaties of this kind may have some formal merit but are of no real substantive value unless the partners are agreed on the major issues affecting their relations. And certainly we shall not allow him to use it to drive a wedge even the thinnest wedge between us and our allies. But George Brown and I see no particular harm in concluding a treaty of friendship and co-operation though clearly we shall need to scrutinise the potential content very closely and to steer clear of the numerous pitfalls that Muscovite drafters are no doubt already busy preparing. But equally the notion of a patient reconstruction of relations with Russia and Eastern Europe and that this can best be done on a bilateral rather than a multilateral basis is one which I know we both share and which the Russians themselves profess to accept. There could thus, I believe, be some political advantage to be gained from formally enshrining this in a treaty, if that is what they want: and the treaty itself could provide a useful framework within which we could operate our future bilateral relations with the Russians, cultural, economic and commercial. At all events we have decided that we should go along with their desire to announce in the communiqué our willingness in principle to enter into such a treaty. But I wanted you to know of this before hand and to know in particular that we are going into it with our eyes even wider open than usual.

We shall watch the drafting of the communiqué very carefully on the proposal for a draft treaty. And in my statement to Parliament after Kosygin's return I shall make quite clear that this treaty involves no derogation from our loyalty to and obligations under existing treaties, particularly NATO. I intend also to make a Ministerial television broadcast on all channels to the British people on the communiqué and shall again emphasise this fact. I intend to refer back to a statement I made when leader of the opposition on Moscow television that we have our friends and allies just as the USSR have theirs. And that, while because of historic ties between Britain and the Soviet Union we shall always be ready to offer our hand in friendship to them, we shall always do so from a position foursquare within the Western Alliance, and our other international commitments, including the United Nations Charter. I repeated this phrase many times since and will present to the British people the proposed Anglo-Soviet friendship treaty in this light.

You should know, incidentally, that Macmillan, when he visited Russia in 1959, prepared a joint Anglo-Soviet declaration in response to Khrushchev's proposal for a treaty of non-aggression, but he equally made the necessary reservations about loyalty to NATO etc. Nothing came of this owing to failure to agree about the terms of the declaration. But I presume that Macmillan cleared his line with your predecessors.

Secondly, the European Security Conference. Here again, we are fully aware of the political purposes that underlie the Russian approach. But we do not believe that a reference to this in fairly general terms in the communiqué will do any damage to Western relationships; and, again the notion of breaking down barriers between Eastern and Western Europe inherent in the notion of such a conference is one that now commands widespread sympathy in this country and, I believe, throughout the West. We have made it abundantly clear to the Russians that we are not prepared to accept such a conference unless it is clearly understood that the United Sates, because of its major political and security interests and associations in Europe, should be present and we have told them that in our view the conference will be meaningless without long and careful preparation beforehand and without agreement amongst the potential participants on what is to be discussed. In fact without any prompting from us Kosygin, although he had referred to an all European conference suggested that there should be a preparatory commission to prepare the way for the conference and that this might deal with the question of United States participation. But so far as we are concerned, the United States would have to participate in the preparatory commission itself. These requirements in effect would probably put the thing off to the Greek Kalends.[21] Given that, we see no reason not to refer to it in general terms in the communiqué. But here again I wanted you to know our thinking before you read the communiqué.

189. Message from Wilson to Johnson, 11 February 1967[22]

I am sorry to bombard you with all these telegrams about the Kosygin talks but 20 or 30 hours of consecutive discussion has thrown up a great deal of Soviet thinking.

I have been struck by the great contrast between his private utterances and his public speeches and there is a warning here for the Kremlinologists employed by the press of our two countries who write such learned pieces on the basis of public speeches by Soviet leaders.

In public he took a hard line on Vietnam and on all the sinful enormities of American policy, and a very gentle line of denunciation on China. In private he was less tough on Vietnam, more sensitive in his criticism of America and quite

---

[21] A time indefinitely remote.
[22] Bodleian Library, Oxford, Wilson Papers, MS. Wilson c. 1585, folios 195–6.

uninhibited about China. But on Germany he was pretty tough both in public and in private.

The basic fact about the whole week is that Kosygin is obsessional about the Chinese problem. Although he is cool, reserved and given to understatement I have never heard any statesman talk in such terms about another country. China has gone mad. China is in chaos. China is an organised military dictatorship with no ideological principles. China's aim is not only to enslave Vietnam but also the whole of Asia. The trouble with the United States is that they have not yet perceived the full extent of the Chinese menace. These are only a few selections from the tirades I have had, always in private conversation. I have given David [Bruce] and Chet [Cooper] a fuller account of what he has said.

He described to me the state of economic warfare between the Soviet Union and China and I have given David these details. He gave me a rocket because we sent a computer to China. Personally I think this is a bit hard. I got a rocket from you and now from Kosygin on the same point. He complained of the firms, particularly in Japan but also in Germany, Italy and less seriously, as yet, Canada, who are supplying or being asked to supply, electronic and other equipment which the Chinese will use for their nuclear military development. He indicated he was preparing a black list of these firms to ensure that they got no Soviet orders. His present restrictions on general trade with China are approaching the higher forms of economic warfare. Whatever the subject he was tempted to come back to his Chinese obsession with Pavlovian predictability. And without temptation for example in a dinnertime conversation with my wife he would suddenly turn to me and say he wanted to tell me about China. And he did for a half hour without stopping. He said they had stopped all house-building to concentrate on military development and no child above fifth grade was receiving any schooling in order to train them in military and political techniques. All in all I gather you are a disappointment to him for your failure to recognise the extent of the Chinese menace.

The other thing about which I am glad to say he was absolutely clear was his desire that we should maintain the closest relations with the United States. In my first tete a tete conversation on Monday afternoon in the Vietnam context, while he first said I should not be afraid of the United States or accept any monopoly dictation, he was careful to add in the strongest terms that he did not want us to break or even strain our relations with the United States to which he obviously attached the greatest importance. Several times during the week he was anxious to know that we were in touch with the United States. I am sure that he does not know that Chet Cooper has been here or that I had regular meetings with him and David. If he did know, I feel he should have been reassured by the fact. More than once he has anxiously asked whether I would be on the telephone to you obviously hoping that I should be. In the Vietnamese context he wanted to be sure of American authenticity of any proposals that we put to him but it was not only on this subject that he wanted to be assured that our Transatlantic lines were in full working order.

190. Message from Wilson to Johnson, 12 February 1967[23]

T.30/67. You will realise what a hell of a situation I am in for my last day of talks with Kosygin. My immediately following telegram[24] sets out what seems to have happened over the past week as I understand it but I want to concentrate here on the immediate way ahead. I have to re-establish trust because not only will he have doubts about my credibility but he will have lost credibility in Hanoi and possibly among his colleagues.

I propose to be pretty frank with him and to tell him that the present situation arises in my view from the deep American concern about intensive North Vietnamese movements during the Tet period. I shall say that I warned him at the beginning of the week that there should not be provocative DRV movements during Tet and remind him that on Friday at lunch on the basis of a message from you people I told him that certain movements in the first two days of Tet had been on a shocking scale.

Nevertheless, I think he will feel, because his own position has been weakened, that we cannot make any definitive progress towards a settlement in the next few days. I have got to get him into as relaxed a posture as possible and tell him that his position and mine must be not to concern ourselves with military activities but to concentrate on the longer term political situation.

On the vitally important question of whether as I have told him a cessation of bombing depends on a prior secret assurance by Hanoi that infiltration will stop or as now seems to be the case from your recent messages, will only take place after infiltration has stopped on this question I face very great difficulties. You must realise that at lunchtime on Friday he suddenly bit hard on what I said to him, namely that all that was required was a private assurance that infiltration would stop. He bit on this because he clearly knew as I did not, that your message to Hanoi was the tougher version which required a prior stopping of infiltration before bombing could cease. He thought I was telling him something new. I thought I was merely repeating what I had told him earlier with as I thought your authority.

As soon as I repeated this offer, he asked for it in writing, and he said he would transmit it at once to Moscow for Hanoi. In the evening he told me he had reported this to Brezhnev who had supported his action. At that moment peace looked like being within our grasp. I think this was David's view at that time.

---

[23] TNA, PREM 13/1918.
[24] See 191.

I can only now get out of this position if I say to him either that I am not in your confidence or that there was a sudden and completely unforeseeable change in Washington which as a loyal satellite I must follow. I cannot say either. George and I have discussed this dilemma for some three hours with Chet and David. My decision as to how to proceed is of course mine and not theirs, but I have fully taken into account all they have said.

I am standing by, as I must, the document which I handed to Kosygin at 7:00 p.m. GMT on Friday before I received Rostow's message for transmission to Kosygin. Both Kosygin and I know that as of today we cannot accept this.

The only thing I can do is to say to Kosygin if he will go along with this one and press it on Hanoi, I will similarly press it on you. In this I am slightly encouraged, if that is a word I can use on a day like this, by the last sentence of Rusk's telegram which David has shown me this evening.

If I do get Kosygin to agree, then I must press our line on you and if it is impossible for you to accept, we shall have to reason together about the situation which will then arise.

More generally it will be my attempt to get Kosygin into a position where he and I accept joint responsibility for trying to assist the parties concerned in the fighting to reach agreement. This is going to be very difficult particularly when bombing restarts. I shall not of course say anything to Kosygin about bombing or any other military question. But all week he has asserted a position very different from his previous posture. He no longer says this question has nothing to do with him, but is a matter for Hanoi. He now says he and I must do all we can to get a settlement. I want to nail him to this position despite his disappointment that nothing happened during Tet. I have thought since November that he chose the date of this week to coincide with Tet and he will be bitterly disappointed as indeed am I.

I do not know whether I can nail him to this in the communiqué. I hope I can. But he and I have got to move to a slightly more central position, each of us loyal to our respective allies but each slightly more capable of taking a detached view which if they and if we could agree we will then press on our respective friends. He agreed with an analogy I used earlier in the week that in one sense he and I were lawyers representing our respective clients, and that because they were at war they could hardly be expected to come together and that we must try to get a settlement out of court ad referendum to the two clients. I must now nail him down to a continuing acceptance of this position.

I assure you our fees will be low, and I am only too conscious of the infinitely heavier price you are paying in this matter.

I am conscious how much depends on the five hours or so I shall have with Kosygin at Chequers on Sunday evening. You should know that Chet Cooper will be in close proximity but no-one will know that. All necessary arrangements have been made for teleprinter and if necessary telephone communication to the

White House whether for use by me or by Chet who will of course be in touch with David.

If I can get him to accept a continuing responsibility in these matters that is probably the best I can hope for. There could I suppose be a dramatic change on his side though this is unlikely. If it is, we must be ready to react.

But if I do nail him down to a continuing responsibility, it would be very helpful if, for example, after the communiqué, you were able to make some public reference to the value of a continuing joint effort by him and me.

Perhaps you and I are so close to this problem now—and of course most of the difficulties have arisen on an issue which must remain secret—that it is difficult for us to realise the impact which bombing resumption must make. But also on opinion in our two countries, particularly on Kosygin whom I certainly cannot warn in advance. I think I can handle the political opinion and party pressures in Britain though this is becoming increasingly difficult.

But in view of the clear breakdown in communication and understanding which has occurred this week, and the need for the fullest understanding in the future, we ought to meet very soon.

191. Message from Wilson to Johnson, 12 February 1967[25]

T. 31/67. This is a background telegram about the reasons for our present difficulties which you may or may not wish to study and in any case I think that David or Chet may be filling in the detail.

The main difficulty is this. On Tuesday I outlined to Kosygin the basic American position based on paragraph 14 of Dean Rusk's detailed letter to George Brown before George's Moscow visit.[26] It was given more specific content by the briefing I received just before Kosygin's arrival from Chet Cooper whom you had sent in response to my appeal. I was further reinforced in this by the relevant paragraph of your telegram no CAP 67038.44.[27]

I did not at that time know that the message you were sending to Hanoi was in a different and tougher form and in terms of the sequence of timing was different from the Rusk/Brown exchanges of November, different from the

---

[25] TNA, PREM 13/1918.

[26] Rusk had informed Brown that 'as one way of saving Hanoi's face, you may wish to explore on your own initiative the possibility of a package deal which in its totality represented what both we and Hanoi would agree to as a reasonable measure of mutual de-escalation, but which would have two separate phases in its execution. Phase A would be a bombing suspension, while Phase B, which would follow, would see the execution of all the other agreed de-escalatory actions' (Message from Rusk to Brown, 16 November 1966, cited in Herring, *The Secret Diplomacy of the Vietnam War*, p. 34).

[27] See 184, paragraph 7.

more detailed Cooper briefing and indeed appears to be inconsistent with your 14th Point.[28]

Kosygin was interested and he told me he had been in touch with Ho Chi Minh between the end of the formal meetings and my dinner with him that evening.

I was surprised on Friday when I went over this ground again with him that he was highly excited by my formulation which only repeated my Tuesday statement.[29] Obviously the reason for this as I can now appreciate was that Hanoi had told him what they had heard from Washington and my account of Friday naturally seemed to be more acceptable to them. This is why he asked me to put it in writing and why he told me he was transmitting it forthwith. You can imagine the shock he must have had on boarding his train for Scotland when he got Rostow's message late on Friday night British time.

You will forgive me if I say what I cannot understand is this. My statement to him on Tuesday originally oral but followed up by a written repetition, was communicated at once to Washington. It is now clear to me that it differed from the Washington/Hanoi message referred to in your telegram under reference. If my message was going to be repudiated, as indeed it was on Friday night by Rostow's telegram,[30] I cannot understand why I was not told earlier. Kosygin will find it even more difficult to understand.

You will I am sure appreciate Kosygin's position as I understand it. For a long time he has been trying to put pressure on Hanoi and there have been

---

[28] This point of the Fourteen Points statement of January 3 maintained: 'We have said publicly and privately that we could stop the bombing of North Viet Nam as a step toward peace although there has not been the slightest hint or suggestion from the other side as to what they would do if the bombing was stopped' (*FRUS, 1964–8*: Volume V, *Vietnam, 1967* (Washington, DC: United States Government Printing Office, 2002), p. 142, footnote 6).

[29] On 7 February, Wilson had informed Kosygin that 'the United States are willing to stop the build-up of their forces in the South if they are assured that the movement of North Vietnamese forces from the North to the South will stop at the same time. Essentially therefore the two stages are kept apart. But because the United States Government know that the second stage will follow, they will therefore be able first to stop the bombing, even if there is a short period between the first stage and the actions to be taken by both sides in the second stage. There would be balanced concessions in the second stage; the first stage would be carried out by the United States alone; but the United States would only carry out the first stage because they would know that the second stage would follow within a short period of time' (*FRUS, 1964–8*: Vol. V, Vietnam, 1967, attachment to document 41, p. 95).

[30] Noting that the formulation had been cleared 'at the highest level', Rostow stated: 'The United States will order a cessation of bombing of North Vietnam as soon as they are assured that infiltration from North Vietnam to South Vietnam has stopped' (Telegram from Rostow to Bruce and Cooper, 10 February 1967, cited in *FRUS, 1964–8*: Vol. V, *Vietnam, 1967*, p. 115).

undoubtedly those there who did not want any truck with a peaceful settlement. He climbed out on a limb trusting in my confident assertion of where you stood. Now his enemies in Hanoi and perhaps in Moscow will be saying he was wrong to be misled by me.

I hope I can quickly reestablish trust with Kosygin. As you know, I have known these Russians for 20 years and this week I have been trying to cash the cheque I have painfully built up over this time. I hope past credit will stand me in good stead tomorrow. Above all I am passionately keen to get him associated with me for the future in the political operation we all know is necessary.

I know you understand my difficulties. I see little purpose in an inquest into the events of the past week. We must look to the future. And I feel the sooner we can meet the better, provided that the meeting is related to the continuing Anglo Russian responsibility for a political settlement and does not seem to be merely in response to any military developments in these next few days.

192. Message from Johnson to Wilson, 12 February 1967[31]

CAP 67043. I have carefully read and considered your two messages bearing on your talks later today with Kosygin.[32]

I would wish to leave these thoughts with you on the present position.

I really do not believe that the matter hangs on the tense of verbs. Moscow had from George Brown in November the Phase A-Phase B formulation. Hanoi also had it from the Poles. Hanoi has shown no flicker of interest for more than two months. Meanwhile their build-up continues and they have used 3 periods of no bombing (Christmas, New Year's and Tet) for large scale movement and preparation of their forces for further military action.

I want to emphasize that we have had nothing yet from Hanoi. They receive our messages—but thus far it has been a one-way conversation. Many intermediaries have attempted, from time to time, to negotiate with us. Everyone seems to wish to negotiate except Hanoi. I wish someone would produce a real live North Vietnamese prepared to talk.

Understandably your present preoccupation is Kosygin's attitude. But thus far, Kosygin has not transmitted one word from Hanoi except to endorse their Foreign Minister's interview with Burchett[33] in his own press conference.

From an operational point of view, we can not stop the bombing while three (possibly four) divisions dash south from the DMZ before their promise is to

---

[31] TNA, PREM 13/1918.
[32] See 190 and 191.
[33] See 184, footnote 9.

take effect. I hope you will see the importance of this for the men out there who are doing the fighting.

We do not accept the view that our statement to you of our position on February 7[34] is inconsistent with either our message to Hanoi[35] or our formula for you and Kosygin of February 10.[36] We asked on February 7 for an "assured stoppage" of infiltration. In your version of an A–B formula it was transmuted to an assurance that infiltration "will stop." This, in our view, is a quite different matter. We so recognized promptly on receipt of your formula and telephoned Burke Trend that we were drafting and would transmit our response shortly.

The problem of substance is that no formula can be satisfactory to us—and perhaps to Hanoi—unless there is clarity about two matters:

—The timing of a cessation of bombing, cessation of infiltration, and no further augmentation of forces.

—How assurance in the matter of infiltration will be established. You have correctly pointed out that the cessation of bombing and the stoppage of augmentation by us will necessarily be public.

I would not expect Kosygin to come in at Chequers with anything firm and definitive by way of a positive response. In that case we can take stock and see where we go from here on the diplomatic track. If he does respond positively and constructively, we can then proceed to the clarifications that both sides will surely require.

Hanoi has received our messages and has just today informed us that a direct response to us from Hanoi will be forthcoming. We suppose that we shall not hear from them until your talks are concluded. There is importance, then, in our staying together. We must not let them play one position off against another.

Let me add that I much appreciate your dedicated effort during this week—and will, of course, express publicly our thanks. I'm always glad to know that you are in my corner but I would have some difficulty, in view of my responsibilities and problems here, in giving anyone a power of attorney. I hope for peace more than you can possibly know and will be much interested in what happens at Chequers.

---

[34] See 184. The message was actually sent on 6 February.

[35] Johnson had declared that 'I am prepared to order a cessation of bombing against your country and the stopping of further augmentation of US forces in South Viet-Nam as soon as I am assured that infiltration into South Viet-Nam by land and by sea has stopped' (Letter from Johnson to Ho Chi Minh, 7 February 1967, cited in *FRUS, 1964–8*: Vol. V, *Vietnam, 1967*, pp. 92–3).

[36] See 191, footnote 30.

193. Message from Wilson to Johnson, 12 February 1967[37]

T. 33/67. Thank you for your message CAP 67043[38] which I have carefully studied.

I fully take your point about the grave danger that if there were an interval between the cessation of bombing and the stoppage of infiltration, Hanoi might rush three or four divisions through the DMZ into South Vietnam before their promised stoppage of infiltration took effect. This I agree could happen even if the interval between Phase A and Phase B were only two or three days.

I have been turning over in my mind an alternative way of securing the required guarantee, namely that the prior two-way assurance should contain a timetable if possible underwritten by or communicated through the Russians. What might be provided is that you would agree in advance to stop the bombing in return for their prior assurance that they would stop the infiltration, say six hours afterwards, or an even shorter timetable if that was considered necessary. I'm not asking you to comment on this at this stage but if the conditions are right tonight I might see what mileage I can get out of it with Kosygin. It would of course be aired as a possible idea without committing you in any way. Indeed I would make it clear I have not attempted to ascertain your views on it. I'll let you know of course how things go.

By the way. You misunderstood me I think about a power of attorney. Clearly that would be out of the question. That was not my phrase. The key words were ad referendum, repeat ad referendum.

We will keep you informed on how things go this evening.

194. Message from Johnson to Wilson, 12 February 1967[39]

CAP 67045. As I pointed out early this morning,[40] the A–B offer has been outstanding now for about three months. I gather from Cooper that as of the time you went into dinner tonight, you had no reply from Kosygin. We have had no reply from Hanoi.

Nevertheless, you have worked nobly this week to bring about what all humanity wants: a decisive move towards peace. It is an effort that will be long remembered. I feel a responsibility to give you this further chance to make that effort bear fruit. We will go more than half way. I am prepared to go the last mile in this week's particular effort: although none of us can regard a failure tonight as the end of the road.

---

[37] TNA, PREM 13/1918.
[38] See 192.
[39] TNA, PREM 13/1918.
[40] See 193.

I must, of course, also bear in mind my responsibility to our men who are fighting there, to our allies, to the people of South Viet Nam who are counting on us to bring about an honorable peace consistent with our commitments to them.

Therefore, I agree with you that you should go forward and try once again with Kosygin saying to him:

If you can get a North Vietnamese assurance—communicated either direct to the United States or through you—before 10:00 am British time tomorrow that all movement of troops and supplies into South Viet-Nam will stop at that time, I will get an assurance from the US that they will not resume bombing of North Viet-Nam from that time. Of course the US build up would also then stop within a matter of days.

This would then give you and me the opportunity to try to consolidate and build on what has been achieved by bringing the parties together and promoting further balanced measures of de-escalation.

With this deal consummated, we would, of course, be prepared to move promptly to a neutral spot to engage in unconditional negotiations designed to bring peace to the area.

Herewith some further observations.

It is significant that Kosygin reflects no further word from Hanoi. Our own private line with Hanoi remains silent. Actually, Kosygin may prefer that any final deal come bilaterally after he leaves London in view of his China problem.

Presumably the two co-chairmen would continue to be in touch with each other. It would be helpful if communiqué could express support of two co-chairmen for 1954 and 1962 Accords and agreement that any differences arising out of these accords should be settled by peaceful means.

195. Message from Johnson to Wilson, 13 February 1967[41]

We have considered the case for further delay to receive a message from Hanoi beyond 10:00 A.M. British time, which you suggested.

I have gone into this with my senior advisers and, after carefully considering your suggestion, the problems you presented, and the problems here—including the morale of our uniformed men—we are extending the time by 6 hours. This is as long as we believe is advisable.

I am sure you would want to know that our Joint Chiefs, CINCPAC, and General Westmoreland have unanimously opposed the Tet and other truces and extensions thereto—not only on the grounds of troop morale but because of the cost in human lives. We will wait, then, for information that may be forthcoming

---

[41] TNA, PREM 13/1918.

until 11:00 A.M. Washington time—4:00 P.M. your time. Military operations against the North will be permitted to resume between 11:00 A.M. and noon our time.

In making this decision I bore in mind Moscow's and Hanoi's problems of transmittal two ways. But I also was conscious of the fact that they have had the possibility of responding to essentially this message for the 3 months since we gave it to the Poles and you gave it to the Russians; and the 5 days since it was transmitted direct to Hanoi and also given by you to Kosygin.

If there is any interest in some such A–B proposition, there has been—and still is—ample time for them either to agree or to come back with a counter-proposal.

Your gallant last minute effort—which I consented to—is one on which they must move. On receiving it they must be either ready to make a response or not. A few hours either way cannot be significant. Bear in mind that the offer for a reciprocal de-escalation has not been withdrawn. It can be accepted any moment they may desire to do so, even though operations are in effect. They could be suspended momentarily. The channels for discussions on these or other lines will remain open.

Right now supplies and weapons are moving down from the North at a high rate. While bearing in mind the safety of more than a half million of our men, I feel I should, nevertheless, go as far as possible to meet your suggestion and, therefore, am stretching the beginning of military operations by another 6 hours.

Considering all the time and conversation that has gone on before, this allows added time for talk if they are really serious.

I hope you have a good chance to catch up on sleep after this arduous and interesting week which, I am inclined to believe, will prove in the end to have been most constructive.

196. Message from Wilson to Johnson, 21 February 1967[42]

As you know, George Brown and I returned last week from our visit to Bonn, the fourth in the round of exploratory talks with the six on the prospects of our joining the EEC. This prevented me from sending earlier any general impressions on the Kosygin visit. But on the whole this delay is quite useful, since so much of what said to us in Bonn outside the purely common market context is related to what passed in our talks with Kosygin last week, and vice versa.

I need not tell you how disturbed the Germans are at the prospects of the conclusion of a non-proliferation treaty. I am reasonably confident that only a minority follows Strauss in the argument that, without the option in the

---

[42] TNA, PREM 13/1857.

treaty of transferring control to an association of states, German prestige and German security will both be irreparably impaired. He argued this with us at length and with passion, even threatening to withdraw from the government if it tried to sign the treaty. But while, as I say, I do not take this kind of extreme view too seriously, there are other – and perhaps both more genuine and more respectable – German considerations which could, and I am sure should, be met. This is not to suggest changes in the draft treaty. But I believe we both still have a big job of explanation and education to do with the Germans. Kiesinger and Brandt both assured us of their support for the concept of non-proliferation, and of their continuing rejection of any national nuclear ambitions. Indeed they told me privately that Strauss was not, emphatically not, speaking for the government. But they have a political problem on their hands and we must try to help with what is the real point, namely their fear that they would be prejudiced in developing the civil use of atomic energy. In this context, they keep on referring to a case where salesmen for an American group have told the potential purchaser that a competing German bid was useless since the Germans would not be able to supply the necessary materials. On the scientific and technical level, they welcomed any suggestion that Solly Zuckerman should visit their experts and go much more fully with them than has been done before into some of the arguments about 'industrial espionage', controls, safeguards, etc. where I believe there is a genuine misunderstanding or lack of knowledge on their part. We have also stressed that British entry to the Communities or merged Community would enable us to make a reality of EURATOM which has hardly got off the ground.

I lay emphasis on the urgency of trying to carry the Germans more fully with us on non-proliferation for two reasons: first because we were encouraged by the vigour with which Kosygin expressed his support of the treaty, and his confidence that it would be concluded before long: and secondly because German opposition to the treaty could make difficulties for us in our present approach to the EEC. You know how much we welcome the progress made by your people and the Russians in hammering out the text over these past months – the extent of the help and support we have given speaks for itself. I am convinced that the sooner we can get this treaty finally negotiated and signed the better for all of us and for mankind as a whole.

But, while I personally give the treaty top priority, we must clearly do all we can to ensure that we do not, through any failure on our part to explain its purposes, or misunderstanding by our friends of its likely implications, contribute to further tensions within the Alliance or to a slowing down in the process of growing detente between the countries of Eastern and Western Europe.

Here the Kosygin visit and our trip to Bonn have disclosed what the Russians would call both negative and positive elements. On the negative side is the A.B.M. question. We argued strongly with Kosygin that the deployment of

A.B.M.s would give a new twist to the arms race and serve the security interests of neither side. He was noncommittal on the substance but developed with great passion the thesis that A.B.M.s, though costly, were purely defensive and therefore fully justified. This and the exchanges on neo-Nazism in Germany were really the only tough and rather unpleasant passages we had with him. And he argued that the only reason you and Bob McNamara were reluctant to deploy A.B.M.s was because it would be much cheaper for you to increase your deployment of 'offensive' missiles. We disputed this, having in mind particularly your own remarks about this in your State of the Union message. But we failed to shift Kosygin one inch and I am personally rather apprehensive of a firm Soviet decision to deploy A.B.M.s. But you may have even more recent evidence about this in the light of Ambassador Thompson's talks with Kosygin.

In Bonn, though German ministers other than Strauss did not speak to me about the A.B.M. question, I gathered that there is a trend of opinion which holds that, since Soviet and U.S. deployment of A.B.M.s is inevitable, Europe must have its own system. The divisive potential of this kind of thinking is all too clear. The fact that it is, in my view totally unrealistic does not unfortunately mean that it necessarily lacks a certain political appeal. But we surely don't want any more 'hardware solutions' of this kind in Europe.

However, I am not suggesting that his particular negative point outweighs the more positive aspects of the Kosygin visit for future European relationships. I dare say that events in China (and you will have seen my earlier message[43] giving the account of Kosygin's obsessional concern with the Chinese) are to some extent responsible for his obvious desire to develop closer Anglo-Soviet relations, for his private insistence on the need for continuing good US/UK relations and for the greater receptiveness he also showed to a discussion of relationships within Europe as a whole.

There is however, one disquieting development in Kosygin's thinking. On some subjects eg Vietnam, what he said to me privately was much more relaxed than his public statements. But not on Germany. This may be because his priority is Vietnam and he cannot be even moderately accommodating on two major subjects at the same time, especially if one is the great obsession, Germany. What worried me is his insistence on linking, first in a private talk with me and later in a public speech, what he calls the growth of Nazism in Germany, which he takes very seriously, and the Chinese problem. This was incomprehensible to me until it emerged that he has decided that Mao is a fascist military dictator. It is a turn up for the book that he feels that the US government does not take the Chinese threat seriously enough. But he has now apparently reached the classic stage where he sees Chinese communists under every bed, even in Germany. We tried of course repeatedly but ineffectively to convince him that the 'Nazi threat'

---

[43] See 189.

was nothing like so great as he said and that NATO and British entry to EEC would be powerful guarantees against it.

I should tell you that we are well pleased with bilateral aspects of the visit. Quite apart from such intrinsic benefits as these may bring us on the national level (and past experience naturally makes one cautious about this, though I equally believe that great deal has changed in Soviet attitudes towards trade, technological cooperation etc.) I do not think it wholely [sic] fanciful to conclude that the Russians wanted to demonstrate their readiness to discuss, negotiate and cooperate with Britain, the avowed associate of the United States and supporter of so many theses they dislike, to no lesser degree than with France which has chosen to follow a very different path and one that should superficially seem more attractive to the Soviet Union.

My view has always been that the Soviet relationship with France is useful to the Russians because the French play the Soviet propaganda game particularly in agreeing to communiqués attacking you, on Vietnam and more generally. But the Russians are realists and attach more importance to better relations with you, subject to the limitations imposed by their competition with China for world communist support. The evident desire of the Russians to have a more active relationship with Britain, and the support that Kosygin expressed for our ideas on the need for closer bilateral contacts between Eastern and Western countries as the best means of breaking down tensions, are relevant not only as supporting the line you, we and our allies are discussing in NATO but also in the context of our current approach to Europe, and particularly in that of our latest visit to Bonn. I made it very clear to Kiesinger that the last thing we wanted was to disrupt his relations with France, or to imply that a good Anglo-German relationship was incompatible with a good Franco-German relationship. But equally, it has been clear for months that Paris hoped to attract Bonn amongst other things by presenting itself as the honest broker with Moscow. To the extent that Moscow recognises publicly that relations with London are just as important to it as relations with Paris, the political attractions of a close association with Britain may become more evident in Bonn. I felt that I detected an understanding of this in my talks with Kiesinger and Brandt, as well as support from them for our general concept that political tensions can be eased by the wider European unity that is our current objective: and that, as a result, their own problems with the Russians might be eased. I for my part made it clear that, in speaking to Kosygin, we had supported the German concept of increasing bilateral contacts with the countries of Eastern Europe and that, while Kosygin's basic attitude towards Germany remained apparently quite unchanged, welcomed this method of gradually improving relations between East and West.

On the whole, therefore, I regard the balance sheet of our discussions during these past ten days as reasonably encouraging. I have tried here to single out one or two of the problems that we shall need to watch. They are certainly not unmanageable. In Bonn we naturally touched on the off set problem and you will have seen that Strauss, largely I believe for reasons of internal politics, has touched off a fine little flurry about it since we left. But at least we were able to deal with this as an issue separate from the question of our common market approach: and, on the latter, the Germans spoke as firmly in support of our entry as they did in their declaration of policy in December. How firmly they will be prepared to speak in Paris is another matter. But here again, the fact that we were able to give them a very frank and complete account of the Kosygin talks and to fit these into a wider pattern of European and world relationships will I hope have had a helpful and instructive effect.

197. Message from Wilson to Johnson, 16 March 1967[44]

I sent you on February 21 a fairly full account of my impressions from the Kosygin talks and from the talks George Brown and I had with the German Government in Bonn.[45]

But as you will have known from the messages I sent you during the Kosygin visit and from what David Bruce will have told you then, I was worried during and after the visit about a deeper, underlying problem. I did not go into this in my message of the 21st because Walt Rostow was due here and I wanted first to discuss the whole issue with him. He will have reported to you about our lengthy talk and the anxieties I expressed to him.[46] I found this talk very helpful. But it did not resolve these anxieties, which continue to cause me serious concern.

I have now discussed all this fairly fully with Pat Dean. In the light of that and of my talk with Walt, I believe that there is still an unresolved problem between us. I will not take up your time now by seeking to discuss this in greater detail.

---

[44] LBJ Library, NSF, Head of State Correspondence File, Box 10, United Kingdom: Prime Minister Wilson Correspondence, Volume 6 [2 of 2], no. 91a. Foreign Secretary George Brown had initially questioned the good sense in sending Johnson a further piece of correspondence relating to the Wilson–Kosygin talks on the grounds that 'it would be better not to run the risks of unnecessarily irritating L.B.J. or his advisers now by sending a message on this aspect of the problem' ('Vietam', Minute from Brown to Wilson, PM/67/31, 14 March 1967, TNA, PREM 13/2458). Wilson rejected this advice with the remark: 'whether or not a message will irritate the President, I want him to be in no doubt of the fact that we also are worried at the way things went during that week' (Minute from Wilson to Brown, M 24/67, 15 March 1967, TNA, PREM 13/2458). In the end, the message sent on 16 March was somewhat shorter than the original draft (Draft message to Johnson from the Prime Minister, undated, TNA, PREM 13/2458).

[45] See 196.

[46] See Record of a conversation between the Prime Minister and Mr. Walt Rostow at No. 10 Downing Street at 5.30 p.m. on Friday, 24 February 1967, TNA, PREM 13/1918.

But when Pat Dean returns to Washington at the end of this month, I should be grateful if you could arrange for him to call on you to discuss the problem as I see it and to examine what can be done to resolve the misunderstanding that arose between us and to make sure that there is no question of a similar situation arising in the future. I am, of course, most grateful for the invitation conveyed by Walt Rostow to visit you in Washington around the end of May and I much look forward to this. But it is still some way ahead and much can happen between now and then. This is why I think it would be useful for you to have a word with Pat Dean on his return, as I suggested.

Meanwhile, I should be grateful also for your confirmation of one point. Could you please let me know whether, in your view, the message which you sent to me to hand to Kosygin late on the night of February 12,[47] still represents the position as you see it, however dark immediate prospects may look.

198. Message from Johnson to Wilson, 22 March 1967[48]

I need not tell you that I shall be happy to see Pat Dean upon his return and to go over with him any misunderstanding which might have arisen.

We had a good meeting at Guam.[49] The press tried to turn it into a meeting which we told them from the beginning it would not be and the same press turned around and complained because we did not do what we told them in Washington we had no intention of doing. Specifically, we did not take up such questions as troop levels or specific military measures or matters of that sort.

One by-product of the Guam meeting was the conclusion of the new constitution in Viet-Nam and its approval both by the constituent assembly and the military directorate. If the South Vietnamese succeed, as I am beginning to believe they will, in establishing an elected constitutional government in the midst of all the violence, it will be a most extraordinary performance. The Viet Cong will bitterly oppose the process and there will be many cynics in other parts of the world. We anticipate elections for village councils in early April and for hamlet chiefs running into June: a president and a senate will be elected at the end of August or early September followed by elections a month later for the lower house.

We do not have a very clear view as to just why Ho Chi Minh made public out [sic] exchange of letters. It's possible that the action was taken as a part of the Moscow–Peking debate, because of rumors which might be affecting the morale

---

[47] See 194.
[48] LBJ Library, NSF, Head of State Correspondence File, Box 10, United Kingdom: Prime Minister Wilson Correspondence, Volume 6 [2 of 2], no. 89.
[49] Johnson met South Vietnamese leaders on the island of Guam on 20–21 March.

of the National Liberation Front or for still some other reason. I'll be glad to hear anything which your people pick up as to Ho Chi Minh's motivation. My impression is that he well [sic] not respond constructively to U Thant and we have seen no indications of anything of interest developing on any bilateral contact with us or between Hanoi and Saigon.

As to your concluding question, the offers we made during your meeting with Kosygin remain open.

I am glad that the Vice President[50] will have a chance to visit London in the course of his European trip. I think you would find him helpful in talking to some of your people in the House of Commons.

199. Message from Wilson to Johnson, 23 March 1967[51]

Many thanks for your latest message.[52] I shall see Pat Dean again before he returns and am glad that you will be able to have a good talk with him.

I am also glad to have your confirmation that the offers made during our talks with Kosygin remain open. Our people will, of course, be ready to exchange impressions with yours about current North Vietnamese intentions.

I am greatly looking forward to seeing the Vice President. He can rely on receiving a warm welcome here.

200. Message from Johnson to Wilson, 29 March 1967[53]

I have followed with concern the courageous efforts to limit damage to your beautiful southern coast.[54] We should like to be of help. I have asked my people to explore what we might do, and to stay in touch with your Government.

Please convey my warm greetings and those of my countrymen to the people of Southern England.

---

[50] Hubert Humphrey.
[51] LBJ Library, NSF, Head of State Correspondence File, Box 10, United Kingdom: Prime Minister Wilson Correspondence, Volume 6 [2 of 2], no. 87.
[52] See 198.
[53] LBJ Library, NSF, Head of State Correspondence File, Box 10, United Kingdom: Prime Minister Wilson Correspondence, Volume 6 [2 of 2], no. 85.
[54] The supertanker, *Torrey Canyon*, carrying 100,000 tons of crude oil, ran aground on rocks off the Cornish coast on 18 March 1967.

201. Message from Wilson to Johnson, 31 March 1967[55]

Thank you most sincerely for your very kind message[56] which I have passed on to the people in the areas damaged and threatened by the floating oil. We are all most grateful for your generous offer of help, and our people are in close touch with yours to see what can best be done.

202. Message from Johnson to Wilson, 12 May 1967[57]

Dean Rusk has reported to me his exchange with George Brown and Bob McNamara his exchange with Denis Healey on your east of Suez problem.

It is of the utmost importance that we have an opportunity to talk before decision is finally made.

I look forward to seeing you in early June.

203. Message from Wilson to Johnson, 12 May 1967[58]

Thank you for your message.[59] As I told you when we saw each other in Bonn, we shall take no final decision until you and I have had an opportunity to discuss all this on 2 June. I too greatly look forward to that meeting.

204. Message from Wilson to Johnson, 25 May 1967[60]

I have not been in touch with you direct so far about the Middle East situation[61] because our people have been in such close and continuous touch and particularly because George Thomson has himself been in Washington discussing all this

---

[55] LBJ Library, NSF, Head of State Correspondence File, Box 10, United Kingdom: Prime Minister Wilson Correspondence, Volume 6 [2 of 2], no. 83a.
[56] See 200.
[57] LBJ Library, NSF, Head of State Correspondence File, Box 10, United Kingdom: Prime Minister Wilson Correspondence, Volume 6 [2 of 2], no. 81c.
[58] LBJ Library, NSF, Head of State Correspondence File, Box 10, United Kingdom: Prime Minister Wilson Correspondence, Volume 6 [2 of 2], no. 79a.
[59] See 202.
[60] LBJ Library, NSF, Head of State Correspondence File, Box 10, United Kingdom: Prime Minister Wilson Correspondence, Volume 6 [2 of 2], no. 77.
[61] On 22 May, Egyptian President Nasser announced the closure of the Gulf of Aqaba to Israeli shipping precipitating an Arab–Israeli crisis which culminated in the Six Day War (5–10 June 1967).

with Dean Rusk. But we have taken stock today in the Cabinet in the light of what we have heard from George Brown in Moscow (which I am bound to say is not so far particularly encouraging on this front): of George Thomson's report: of my own talk yesterday with Eban (you will have had an account of this via George Thomson): and, finally, in the light of de Gaulle's proposal that this should be handled, at least initially, on a four power basis.[62]

The French have told us – and no doubt yourselves – that they are thinking in the first instance of a meeting of the four permanent representatives in New York. Their approach rests as you know on the basic proposition that, if any good is to come out of the Security Council, it can only result from some four power understanding. It is not at all clear to me how far de Gaulle has thought through this proposition. His political purposes are, of course, fairly transparent in terms of French influence and of seeking to avoid French involvement in any exclusively Western approach. (Eban told me that de Gaulle advised him strongly not to get too closely involved in any exclusively Western tie-up).

But the fact that this approach may be designed to enhance French standing and, perhaps, to cut down to size some of the General's Western allies need not, in my view, prevent our recognising its intrinsic merits. It seems to us to have two potential advantages. First, if we can get the Russians into four power discussion – and as far as I am concerned I would be glad for this to happen either at ambassadorial level in New York as at present suggested by the French, or eventually at a much higher level somewhere else (summit if necessary) in view of the terrible dangers involved – this could mean that they are clear-headed enough to see the immense dangers of a major confrontation with the West in a part of the world where neither side can confidently expect to control the passions or reactions of the local participants. In that situation, there might be a prospect of reaching agreement with them. Secondly, if the French initiative peters out because the Russians will have nothing to do with it, the French can hardly then just fold their hands and play no further part. The prospect of drawing them into a wider Western operation should be somewhat enhanced. Either way, the prospects for peace should be a little brighter.

These are the reasons why we decided today to announce our support for the French proposal – and I dare say that in authorising Arthur Goldberg's statement of support for the idea, which I saw last night, your government had the same kind of considerations in mind.

Meanwhile, we have, as you will have heard, agreed that George Thomson should continue to work out with Dean Rusk the terms of any eventual approach to the other maritime powers and of the draft declaration for which we might

---

[62] Britain, France, the US, and the Soviet Union.

canvass their support. When the Cabinet discussed this this morning,[63] it was clear to us, from the reports already received from our ambassadors in a number of key maritime countries, that we should not get the kind of support that is required for any such declaration until all efforts to get something constructive out of the Security Council have demonstrably failed. In these circumstances, and given the intrinsic value of the French proposal anyway, we felt that before we could finally decide on the terms and method of proposing the joint approach to the maritime powers, we must give the French four-power approach a chance to prove itself.

As I write this, I learn that by the time it reaches you, you will probably have talked with Mike Pearson. I need not to say how much I welcome this meeting. Canada has a key role to play in all this and we shall of course be keeping in the closest touch with them too. This is indeed a further reason why I am very glad that I shall be able next week to see both Mike and yourself. Clearly we shall have to give a good deal of time to the Middle East situation. I hope things there will be a lot clearer by the time we meet – and I hope even more that there will not have been a major explosion there – but I am sure you share my own desire that, overshadowed as events may be for the time being by the Arab–Israel crisis, we shall be able to have a good talk about the other important issues on our agenda.

If, meanwhile you can let me know how you see things, especially in the light of your talk with Mike [Pearson], I shall welcome this.

205. Message from Johnson to Wilson, 25 May 1967[64]

I had a good talk today with Mike Pearson. He can, evidently, talk for himself. But it is my impression that he wishes us all to stay together in this Middle East crisis: First, to see if anything useful can be accomplished in the UN; and then to work out something along the lines that you have suggested and about which George Thomson has been talking with our people in Washington. I have the impression that—if it comes to the point—the Canadians will join the party.

We had hoped—and still hope—that this track will keep the Israelis steady; but I should report to you that Eban came in this afternoon to Dean Rusk, on a very urgent basis, with the following.

He reported that a message from his Prime Minister indicates they fear an early general attack on Israel by the UAR and Syria. What they have asked for in this situation is immediate application of the U.S. commitment, backed up by

---

[63] See Cabinet Conclusions, 25 May 1967, CC (67) 32nd conclusions, TNA, CAB 128/42 Part 2.

[64] LBJ Library, NSF, Head of State Correspondence File, Box 10, United Kingdom: Prime Minister Wilson Correspondence, Volume 6 [2 of 2], no. 75.

a public declaration as well as practical actions. They would like a statement by us that an attack on Israel is equivalent to an attack on the U.S. They also want this announcement accompanied by an instruction to U.S. forces in the area to coordinate action with the Israeli Defense Force against any possible attack.

Our own intelligence estimate does not back up their statement, and we are not inclined to be as alarmed as they appear to be. We are taking the line with them here that our own knowledge does not coincide with their estimates. We are also pointing out that as far as the U.S. is concerned, the President and the Congress must proceed together in dealing with this problem, and on a multilateral basis.

We are also urging upon Eban the real danger of any pre-emptive action by the Israelis which would create an impossible situation in the Middle East as well as in the U.S. It would, we fear, create real difficulty in getting the support of other countries, to say nothing of Congressional support in the U.S.

I will see Eban tomorrow, as I feel I must. I plan to follow the same line with him Dean Rusk is taking tonight.

I would be interested to know whether your intelligence people share our judgment that the Israeli assessment is overdrawn; and, indeed, what your estimate of Nasser's intentions is.

I should also like you to know directly my own view about the notion of four-power meetings outside the United Nations. I am against them, for reasons we can discuss when we meet on June 2. I am, of course, quite content to have the permanent representatives of the members of the Security Council meet in New York; but I do believe it would be unwise now to encourage quadripartitism outside that framework.

I must say that the initiative you have showed in this crisis thus far has been greatly appreciated here where our capacity to act hinges so greatly on some of us at least being able to move together.

206. Message from Wilson to Johnson, 28 May 1967[65]

Many thanks for your message.[66] I'm grateful too for the very full account we have had of Eban's talks with yourself and others in Washington. I warmly welcome the insistence with which you urged caution on the Israelis. But I am addressing you now because I fear that, despite all your efforts and ours, there must be a serious likelihood that, after the Israeli Cabinet has met tomorrow (correction – today) to consider Eban's report, you and we will find ourselves

---

[65] LBJ Library, NSF, Head of State Correspondence, Box 10, United Kingdom: Prime Minister Wilson Correspondence, Volume 6 [2 of 2], no. 73.

[66] See 205.

confronted with what could amount to an Israeli ultimatum – that, if we do not give them even more categorical assurances than both of us have given so far about the right of passage through the Straits of Tiran, they will feel obliged to assert those rights by force, in whatever manner and at whatever time seem most appropriate to them. This is the vital issue. Closure of the Straits is what Nasser has gained. It affects a vital Israeli interest.

George Thomson and your people made good progress this week and now the military are following this up urgently. It is clear that we shall soon have a workable scheme, though I know you agree with me that it is vitally important that we should plan to develop this though the United Nations, if possible, and in any case on the widest possible basis of international co-operation (even if you and we are going to have do most of the donkey work). But I am gravely concerned at the time factor. An Israeli ultimatum (or something like it) on the lines I have suggested would open up a dramatic prospect of great power confrontation in an area where, as I said to you the other day, none of us can hope to control the local combatants,[67] except perhaps by such direct military involvements on one side or the other as to constitute an unavoidable challenge to the other side. The potential dangers of that happening are such as to make it essential that everything is done to avoid it. I have in mind particularly the need to avoid a situation in which it could seem to the world – and, even more important, the Soviet Union would be enabled to claim – that the United States and Britain were taking sides militarily in the Arab–Israeli conflict. In fact we have made it clear that our commitment is addressed to the principle of freedom of passage through the Straits as an international waterway: and, given a workable scheme, this is what we should do with you and any others we can persuade to join us. But, as I said in my earlier message, we can be under no illusion that we shall easily get them to do so unless we have demonstrably exhausted the United Nations possibilities. And part of this effort at going into this with our eyes open, knowing full well that French and Soviet estimates are [sic] of the possibilities are likely to be different from our own. But we believe that we must exploit the intrinsic merits in the fourpower approach, which is to get the Russians to face up to their responsibilities to prevent a really dangerous confrontation. We may not succeed: probably we shall not. But our public opinion will not, I believe, understand or support what we may to do hereafter if we cannot show convincingly that we have tried.

Accordingly, I want you to know that I have tonight sent a personal message to Kosygin urging on him the dangers of this situation and inviting him to get Federenko [sic] to join with Goldberg, Seydoux and Caradon, in the context of the present meeting of the Security Council, to see whether it really is impossible for them to hammer out something which could make sense in this crazy Middle

---

[67] See 204.

East situation. One of the main reasons I have done this was because George Brown had come back from Moscow convinced that the Russians are beginning to realise the gravity of the situation for which they themselves are so largely responsible and are really concerned to avoid an escalation into a major confrontation. I am not so naïve as to believe that this means that they will cooperation [sic] with us in New York. But I believe it is our duty to try. If we fail and if the Security Council likewise fails then I believe that there are enough countries in the world with the sense to realise that world peace is more important even than trying to go on working through an impotent United Nations, and with the guts to stand up and be counted. In those circumstances, we should I believe get the broad basis of support that we want for our declaration and for any eventual enforcement action – who knows, perhaps even France might agree?

I need not say that in addressing Kosygin I have had much in mind your own reservations about fourpower action outside the United Nations framework: and I have said nothing to him about any fourpower activity anywhere else or at any level.

I am of course informing de Gaulle as well. We have heard today from the French that they still have no reply from the Russians. And they seem content simply to sit tight and wait for it to turn up, as if delay were what they really wanted. But the French clearly can have no objection to my urging Kosygin to support a French initiative.

Since I wrote this, we have heard from Pat Dean of the Russian approach to you. I note that you will be sending a message to Eshkol. I do not think I need send him any further message since our ambassador in Israel was instructed this afternoon (in the light of a somewhat ominous remark to George Thomson by the Israeli ambassador here) to make a further urgent approach to the Israeli government urging them to maintain their present policy of restraint while international efforts to find a solution continue.

I think this latest news adds force to the approach I have made to Kosygin as described in this message.

207. Message from Johnson to Wilson, 3 June 1967[68]

My good friend:
It was very good to see you again.[69] As always, our talks together were most helpful. Your friendship, and that of the British people, is a great comfort in these troubled times.

---

[68] LBJ Library, NSF, Head of State Correspondence File, Box 10, United Kingdom: Prime Minister Wilson Correspondence, Volume 6 [2 of 2], no. 71.

[69] Wilson visited Washington on 2 June 1967.

Mrs. Johnson joins me in wishing you and Mrs. Wilson a pleasant journey home.
Sincerely,
Lyndon B. Johnson

208. Message from Wilson to Johnson, 3 June 1967[70]

Very many thanks for your message.[71] I too was so glad to be with you again and to be able to discuss together in depth the great issues that challenge us both. Our sense of common purpose was indeed heartening.

My wife and I thank Mrs. Johnson and yourself most gratefully for your kindness and great hospitality. Our warmest regards to you both.
Harold Wilson

209. Message from Wilson to Johnson, 5 June 1967[72]

I remember that in our last talk together before we left the White House on Friday night, you expressed your sombre belief that war between Israel and the Arabs could not be avoided, despite the efforts we had been making and discussing together earlier that day. This morning's news appears to confirm your estimate.[73] I have just discussed the situation with George Brown and Denis Healey. We all agree on the paramount importance of our two Governments keeping in the closest concert. George has already seen Philip Kaiser and I know you and your people will be in constant touch with Pat Dean.

The first thing we can try to do, I suggest, is to avoid the Security Council becoming hopelessly bogged down in sterile argument about which side is the aggressor. What we need is a clear demand from the Council for a cease fire: after which a fresh attempt to thrash out a longer term settlement might be made.

The French attitude is important in all this and we shall do our best to make them face up to their responsibilities as a permanent member and not simply back the situation both ways.

But of course we have no particular illusions. It seems unlikely that the Security Council will succeed in reaching an agreed view and we shall probably need to plan jointly for other possible contingencies. This underlines the value

---

[70] LBJ Library, NSF, Head of State Correspondence File, Box 10, United Kingdom: Prime Minister Wilson Correspondence, Volume 6 [2 of 2], no. 69a.

[71] See 207.

[72] LBJ Library, NSF, Head of State Correspondence File, Box 10, United Kingdom: Prime Minister Wilson Correspondence, Volume 6 [2 of 2], no. 66b.

[73] The Six Day War broke out on 5 June.

of meeting last week. I am indeed glad that you and I were able to go over the ground so exhaustively so that, in this situation of confusion and uncertainly, we at least are clearer in our minds about each other's attitude.

Many thanks again for all you did to make our visit so interesting and memorable.

210. Message from Johnson to Wilson, 5 June 1967[74]

Dear Harold:
I appreciate your comments on the unfortunate developments in the Near East.[75] We had feared that someone might feel compelled to strike. We had no advance indication that a decision had been taken. We believed, in fact, we had at least a clean week for diplomacy.

Arthur Goldberg has had a difficult time in the Security Council. Like you, we had hoped for a quick cease-fire resolution. But we have had to deal with a determined effort to have the Council call for a withdrawal of forces in terms which would legitimize Nasser's action at the Strait of Tiran[76] a subject on which we have both taken unequivocal positions.

We have done everything we could to get an even-handed Security Council pronouncement. We shall work with your people in New York to encourage helpful UN action. If the Soviets, and the French, are more forthcoming than they have been, both of us will want to build on that development to work toward a satisfactory settlement.

Meanwhile, I hope we can keep in closest touch as the military situation develops and put the best minds available to both of us to work on the contingencies that may arise and the constructive possibilities that may unfold.

I think you know the deep satisfaction I derived from our discussions.
Sincerely,
Lyndon B. Johnson

211. Message from Wilson to Johnson, 15 June 1967[77]

It looks as if we must expect a Soviet-inspired debate in the United Nations General Assembly about the Middle East and, to judge from Gromyko's letter

---

[74] LBJ Library, NSF, Head of State Correspondence File, Box 10, United Kingdom: Prime Minister Wilson Correspondence, Volume 6 [2 of 2], no. 60.
[75] See 209.
[76] The narrow sea passage separating the Gulf of Aqaba and the Rea Sea.
[77] LBJ Library, NSF, Head of State Correspondence File, Box 10, United Kingdom: Prime Minister Wilson Correspondence, Volume 6 [2 of 2], no. 58.

to U Thant, Kosygin himself and possibly some of the other top Soviet brass may go to it. The Russians are obviously preparing a full-scale propaganda and diplomatic effort to retrieve their friends and themselves from the disaster of the past week.

George Brown tells me that Dean Rusk and he had a good talk about this in Luxemburg. Naturally Dean was not in a position to commit himself but I understand their feeling was that if this debate takes place and Kosygin (or someone of equivalent standing and not simply Gromyko) attends on the Soviet side it would be a mistake for you or me to dignify their efforts by attending ourselves. I think this is right but I shall be glad to know your views about it.

Equally, I think we can assume that, if the debate takes place, a great many Arab foreign ministers, no doubt Eban and probably the foreign ministers of many other countries are likely to be there. In that case, George and I feel that it would be right for him to go: and we hope you would agree that Dean should also attend. I would then do what I could with de Gaulle on Monday to get him to do the same as we do – not that we have any particular hopes of much help from that quarter, but we feel that they ought at least to get their feet wet.

If the Russians finally decide to leave Gromyko to play the hand and its seems likely that few foreign ministers of interest are to attend, it becomes a much more open question whether we should not leave Arthur Goldberg and Hugh Caradon to play it on our side.

If Kosygin goes there might be an outside chance, whatever he said in public, of making some progress with him on substance, outside the U.N. If Gromyko goes however, it is unlikely that even this outside chance would exist. However, assuming that foreign ministers from other countries and particularly Arabs turned up we might be able to persuade some of them to see the Western part in the events of the last three weeks in its true colours.

I hope you can let me know what you feel about all this and also whether you yourself are likely to wish to have a fuller exchange at some point with Kosygin, if he goes to the United States. If there were a question of some kind of summit I think it would be useful for this to be on a wider basis.

212. Message from Wilson to Johnson, 16 June 1967[78]

David Bruce told me last night that you would probably not decide until today how to handle the Special Assembly of the United Nations and what to do about any possible meeting with Kosygin. I was grateful for this very prompt response

---

[78] LBJ Library, NSF, Head of State Correspondence File, Box 10, United Kingdom: Prime Minister Wilson Correspondence, Volume 6 [2 of 2], no. 62a.

to our enquiries and shall of course be glad to know your plans as soon as they are reasonably firm.

For my part, I remain broadly of the view expressed in my message of yesterday.[79] But my final decision is bound to be affected by de Gaulle's talk today with Kosygin. The General may be urged to attend the session in person with perhaps the bait of a four power summit dangled before him. If he decides to go, I shall do likewise. He asked our ambassador in Paris yesterday whether the Special Session of the Assembly was likely to affect my plans for my talk with him on Monday. I have sent him a short reply saying that this must clearly depend to some extent on the conclusions he draws from his talk today with Kosygin. If he decides in the light of that, that he wishes to go at once to New York, then clearly I shall go too and shall either have my talk with him there or try to fit it in on our eventual return. But I have said that that my present disposition is to stick to the timetable for Monday. The Assembly will probably go on for days, and if at any point it looks as if there is a prospect and a need for a top level four power meeting, then he and I can go over at that stage to meet with yourself and Kosygin. Nothing is more risky than to predict how the old man will handle a tactical situation. But my slight hunch is that he and I will meet as planned at the Trianon[80] on Monday.

213. Message from Johnson to Wilson, 16 June 1967[81]

Your messages of the last two days[82] have been helpful, as always.

None of us can predict what situations may arise in the days ahead, but my present thinking is this.

First, at the moment I doubt that anything useful can come from my personal participation in the General Assembly.

Second, from the beginning of this crisis I have not looked with favor on a four-power meeting outside the U.N. Security Council. It is something of an illusion that the four powers have the capacity to design and impose successfully a peace plan on the Near East. The states of the area have made it abundantly clear that they are not subject to effective control from outside. What the major powers can do is to try to create a climate in which the nations of the area themselves might gradually settle their affairs on a peaceful basis. But I am not confident that a four-power session is the best way to do this.

---

[79] See 211.

[80] Part of the Palace of Versailles.

[81] LBJ Library, NSF, Head of State Correspondence File, Box 10, United Kingdom: Prime Minister Wilson Correspondence, Volume 6 [2 of 2], no. 56.

[82] See 211 and 212.

Moreover, I should think both of us would wish to avoid the possibility of having the four of us split or otherwise be strained in such a session.

I hope we can keep in close contact in the days ahead as the situation evolves, and we might wish to counsel together shortly after the smoke clears to assess the situation and see what is required to move things forward towards our common objective of stable peace in the area.

214. Message from Wilson to Johnson, 22 June 1967[83]

Pat Dean will be able to give Dean Rusk, and of course yourself if you wish, an account of the five and a half hours of talks that I had with de Gaulle on 19 and 20 June. But I thought you would like to have a few highly personal impressions. I know you will treat them with particular care and for your personal eye only.

The General was in a more gloomy mood than I have seen him. I think that he found his talk with Kosygin last Friday pretty shattering. I am not clear exactly what he hoped to get out of it – presumably agreement to a four-power summit. In practice, Kosygin seems to have twisted his arm pretty hard to give straight support to the Soviet line and the General (who dislikes having his arm twisted) left him, as he told me, in uncertainty about France's attitude. But, I think that the talk with Kosygin, and the whole Middle East situation as a whole, have forced him to face up to the realities of France's lack of effective influence in world affairs and to ask himself what his foreign policy has so far achieved.

In his heart I believe he realises that it has led him to something of a dead end. But he is too old, and I think physically too weary, to work out a new approach. In any event, this has never been something he does very readily. Given this reluctant recognition that France cannot fundamentally influence affairs, his response is a sad reflection of the old Maginot Line approach – sitting behind his Force de Frappe, watching the world move towards Armageddon.

The general theme that ran through the whole discussion was that, as he put it at one point, the United States which was now the greatest power in the world behaved (as France and Britain had done in their hey-day) exclusively in her own interests. The only way for a medium-sized power like France, (or, in his view, Britain) to conduct their affairs in such a situation was to disengage and to make it clear that America's quarrels are not our quarrels and their wars will not be our wars. All this was of course related primarily to Vietnam and the Far Eastern situation and to the danger of world war arising from it. You will have seen the way he has now publicly linked the Middle East with Vietnam in condemnation of yourself. This was his line with me – that there was no hope

---

[83] LBJ Library, NSF, Head of State Correspondence File, Box 10, United Kingdom: Prime Minister Wilson Correspondence, Volume 6 [2 of 2], no. 64a.

of a Middle East settlement while the war in Vietnam continued to poison the world scene, and he gave as the main reason for France's withdrawal from NATO his determination to keep his hands free in this cataclysmic situation.

Britain's involvement with the United States made it inevitable that we should be dragged into your wars. It also affected us damagingly in such areas as the Middle East, where we were now suffering because we were regarded by the Arabs as indistinguishable from the pro-Jewish Americans. I rubbed it into him very hard that, in the thermo-nuclear age, it was unrealistic to think that France could avoid involvement and that, far from being disengaged, he and we should try to be engaged in a positive exertion of influence.

This led on naturally to our European discussion. We had a useful run over the ground on technological and industrial co-operation and on the lesson that political influence is related to economic strength. Here again his constant theme was our involvement with yourselves and the danger that if we came in, all the weaker brethren in the six (the poor Italians, the poor Belgians, the Germans, exposed to constant temptation, and the Dutch already on our side anyway) would follow our lead and the whole thing would become an American-dominated Atlantic arrangement. It was to prevent this that France was in the Community.

Painted this way, the picture looks pretty sombre for our E.E.C. prospects. And so, on the basis of what he actually said, I suppose it is. But in practice, I believe this to have been a useful visit and I think that I shook him a little out of his complacent gloom. In the broader context, he seemed genuinely attracted at the possibility of Britain, France and Europe generally playing a more effective role in the world – and, particularly in the European context, he showed unmistakable interest in what I told him about our willingness to co-operate (if we got in) in the advanced technologies.

There is something strangely sad about this lonely old man obsessed in his fatalistic way by a sense of real impotence (a word he used twice with me). For our European venture, on the other hand, I feel moderately encouraged. The General does not want us in and he will use all the delaying tactics he can (though, incidentally the word association was not once mentioned, nor anything like it). But if we keep firmly beating at the door (as I told him unequivocally we should) and do not falter in our purpose or our resolve I am not sure that he any longer has the strength finally to keep us out – a dangerous prophecy, as prophecy always is with the General. But that is my personal impression, for what is worth it.

All this took place against the astonishing background of the reconstituted imperial splendour of the Grand Trianon. As a tourist, I warmly recommend it (though the tone in which the General spoke of your failure ever to consult him – while admitting that he never consulted you – was perhaps not too encouraging in this respect). But, as a politician, I felt that it all underlined the kind of regal isolation into which the General has withdrawn. He could not have been a more kindly or genial host, and, incidentally, he was at pains on a number of occasions to emphasise that his policies implied no hostility either to the United States or to Britain. But in France today one has a distinct sense of the beginning of the end of an era.

215. Message from Johnson to Wilson, 24 June 1967[84]

I thought you would wish to know that my first discussions with Kosygin were friendly in tone and businesslike.[85] He listened but did not move from known Soviet positions.

As you would expect, we concentrated on major issues in the fields of arms control and Southeast Asia as well as the Middle East.

I shall be in touch with you again on Monday. I am greatly in your debt for the portrait of de Gaulle,[86] which I shall not easily forget.

216. Message from Johnson to Wilson, 26 June 1967[87]

The public statement made after my second meeting with Kosygin accurately reflect [sic] the lack of movement forward on specific matters, and his stiffness, in particular, on the Middle East.

It seemed probable to me that his instructions were to hold the line until he could return home and take stock with his colleagues.

It will take time, therefore, before we know whether Soviet policy will shift from its present familiar tracks.

I found it useful to talk directly with him.

---

[84] LBJ Library, NSF, Head of State Correspondence File, Box 10, United Kingdom: Prime Minister Wilson Correspondence, Volume 6 [1 of 2], no. 44.

[85] Johnson and Kosygin held talks on 23 and 25 June 1967 at Glassboro State College in Glassboro, New Jersey. For a record of the discussions, see *FRUS, 1964–8*: Volume XIV, *Soviet Union*, pp. 514–25, 528–31, 538–43, 544–56.

[86] See 214.

[87] LBJ Library, NSF, Head of State Correspondence File, Box 10, United Kingdom: Prime Minister Wilson Correspondence, Volume 6 [1 of 2], no. 42.

217. Message from Johnson to Wilson, 6 July 1967[88]

Dear Prime Minister:
We are now in the process of mopping up after Mr. Kosygin's onslaught in the General Assembly. You will have seen the results of the voting yesterday from which we can conclude that the Russians and the more extreme Arabs will not be able to get the United Nations to favour a return to the previous state of belligerence. Ambassador Dobrynin asked Ambassador Goldberg earlier today for a 48-hour delay in the General Assembly to permit some further reconciliation of views. More significantly, he added that Mr. Gromyko needed that additional time for consultations with Moscow. I have some doubt that another 48-hours can significantly narrow the gap between the two principal resolutions before the Assembly. My doubt is based principally upon the scepticism that the Russians would be willing to go very far beyond the Arab point of view. Although there are some signs that second thoughts are taking hold among some of the Arabs, they may require a little more time before they dare to be reasonable. However, we are inclined to give the Russians their additional 48-hours, as a matter of comity, in view of Dobrynin's remarks. The most likely prospect is that the Middle East will go back to the Security Council, where it belongs, and that results will have to be negotiated out behind the scenes.

I continue to be much preoccupied with your East of Suez decision. The ASPAC countries are now meeting in Bangkok with the prospect that they will register a growing sense of solidarity among the free nations of Asia. Hanoi seems to be calling home a number of its key ambassadors: whether this means a policy review, we do not know. Meanwhile Burma is under new pressures from China which continues in turmoil.

Tonight Bob McNamara and Nick Katzenback [sic] go off to Saigon. On their return we shall face here – and among our fighting allies – some difficult and critical manpower decisions.

It just does not seem to me that this is the time for Britain to make or to announce a decision that it is sharply reducing its presence in Southeast Asia. I do hope that you can find some way to put this matter off for a time and not take a step which would be contrary to your and our interests and to the interests of the free nations of Asia.

The stakes are very high in the Western Pacific these days and it is most important that we all try to stay steady on course.
Cordially yours,
　　Lyndon B. Johnson

---

[88] LBJ Library, NSF, Head of State Correspondence File, Box 10, United Kingdom: Prime Minister Wilson Correspondence, Volume 6 [2 of 2], no. 54a.

218. Message from Wilson to Johnson, 13 July 1967[89]

Thank you for your message of July 6.[90]

As you know, the General Assembly has been having a week's breathing space in which to see whether agreement can be reached on any form of words.[91] But all the signs so far bear out your doubts about the likelihood of any significant closing of the gap between the two positions taken in the Assembly on the main issue. I have found it reassuring that a substantial part of the membership—and notably the Latin Americans—insisted on a balanced resolution (providing for an end to the state of belligerency as well as Israel's withdrawal), or none. The Soviet Union and the less reasonable Arabs have certainly been given good cause for reconsidering, though I also agree with you that it may be a little time before any shift becomes discernible. But at least the atmosphere is now very different from what it was when the slanging match first began. It is also a good sign that the Security Council have now agreed to permit U Thant to arrange with the Israelis and Egyptians for United Nations troops to be stationed along the sides of the canal. This agreement should be used as a first step towards establishing a U.N. presence elsewhere in the area. It is a hopeful sign too that U Thant has now appointed a Swede to pursue the refugee problem. A really determined and imaginative effort by the international community is now needed to solve this problem. We ought perhaps to examine what part a comprehensive development plan might play in all this. In general I think we should go on concentrating through the Security Council, on discussion of practical matters, pressing particularly for the appointment of a representative of the Secretary General, on developing the UN presence in the area and tackling the issues affecting freedom of passage through the water-ways.

As regards the Far East we have, as I am sure you know, been giving very earnest and deep consideration to this problem since I saw you last month. We have discussed it here with Harold Holt, Marshall from New Zealand, Harry Lee from Singapore and, most recently, with the Tunku. All have expressed their concern about our longer-term intentions and, while the considerations that you and they have in mind differ in many respects from country to country (as one would expect), we fully understand the fundamental concern that is shared in common by you all. And, as I explained to you we not only understand this but we sympathise with it and wish to do everything we can to mitigate it. We have planned to phase our withdrawal over a period of years so as to reduce the

---

[89] LBJ Library, NSF, Head of State Correspondence File, Box 10, United Kingdom: Prime Minister Wilson Correspondence, Volume 6 [1 of 2], no.52d.
[90] See 217.
[91] Wilson to referring to UN consideration of the Middle East following the Six-Day War.

likelihood of any lasting setback to the economies of the countries in the area; and our mitigating aid coupled with their own determination to help themselves will contribute positively to the kind of self-reliant future at which the whole area should aim.

The British Government have had to reach their decisions, after the fullest consultation with their friends and allies and taking due account of their views, on the basis of their own best judgment of what is politically and economically right for this country. The decision we have now taken has been reached in the light of the best assessment we can make of the likely development of political relationships in the area in the second half of the next decade; and of the economic requirements if Britain is to play any continuing part there at that time. We in this country will be unable to play any such part—or indeed any effective part in world affairs as a whole—unless we get our economy straight now; and to do this we have no option but to bring our defence spending into line with our resources, while making full use of these resources to achieve our political objectives. If this is to be achieved, it requires long-term decisions about the overall shape of our forces and about weapon systems which we must take now. I repeat that the views that you and the heads of the Commonwealth governments concerned have expressed to us have been taken into the fullest account and we are grateful for the frankness, and also for the spirit of friendly understanding in which they have been expressed. My colleagues and I have decided that it is politically and economically right for us to reduce our forces in Singapore and Malaysia to about half the current levels by 1970–71 and to plan on leaving the mainland of Southeast Asia entirely by the middle seventies. But because we are equally resolved that Britain shall have a continuing part to play in the area, though one that must be commensurate with our resources, we shall also plan to retain a sophisticated military capability for use if required in the Far East after that time. For it really is nonsense for us to offer to provide independently ground troops to defend Asian countries who have it in their power to train and provide their own. What we can do and intend to do is to maintain a military capability for use in the area which provides the sophisticated sea-air support which they cannot afford to provide as an assurance against external aggression. In the further round of consultations just completed, the Commonwealth Prime Ministers have, I think, been impressed by the likely scale and character of this capability.

Now that we have taken this decision, the question arises—again in the light of what you and our Commonwealth colleagues have said—whether we can avoid announcing it publicly at this time. The fact is that so much has appeared publicly in various parts of the world about our long-term intentions (and this was certainly not something that we either wished or accept responsibility for) that it is simply impossible for us now to avoid giving some public indication of what they are. Otherwise there is a real risk that it may be believed that we are planning a more rapid rundown than is in fact the case. In any event, we must in all fairness give our armed forces some idea of their long term size, shape and equipment when the process is completed in the middle 1970s, particularly as the careers of many are involved. This is difficult unless we indicate the major premise on which our planning is based. In any case, as the process gets under way in the coming months our long term intentions are bound to become known. Even if we ourselves attempted to disguise them, other governments concerned might not be able to avoid some disclosures in order to kill rumours and speculation and to explain the consequential adjustments to their own policy. I believe a continuation of the present uncertainty would be damaging to us all. But we are anxious to do all we can to meet your concern by avoiding anything too specific.

Accordingly, in the Defence White Paper that we shall be presenting to Parliament shortly, we propose to say that, while we plan to withdraw altogether from our bases in Singapore and Malaysia in the middle 1970s, the precise timing of our eventual withdrawal will depend on progress made in achieving a new basis for stability in Southeast Asia and in resolving other problems in the Far East.

I know that this will be unwelcome news to you. But these decisions have been taken for reasons which seem right to us, and after the most prolonged consideration and consultation. I am convinced that, if this country is in the future to be the same kind of effective partner for her friends and allies in the world as she has, I hope, been in the past, the political and economic realities must be faced and not fudged; and, in particular, that our essential objective of building an unshakeable economic base for Britain is the right one not only for this country but for all our allies as well. I believe that, in deciding and announcing now our intention to maintain a military capability for use in the Far East after the mid 1970s, we are demonstrating our continued interest in the area.

The two Asian governments most directly concerned[92] have demonstrated an impressive steadiness in this new situation. They have recognised the inevitability of change: they take the point I have made above about the need for them to make the contribution to their own defence that best accords with their own resources, while we help with a more sophisticated capability: and they have shown a readiness to co-operate with us in effecting an orderly transition to the new basis for stability in Southeast Asia which is our aim. The fact that it is very much in their interest that they should do so does not detract from the value or significance of the wise way in which they have reacted to our new policy. I am sure that we can count on the same degree of understanding and positive co-operation from our other allies.

---

[92] Malaysia and Singapore.

I have gone into all this at considerable length and detail because of the frankness and straightforward approach that has always characterised the exchanges between us. But you will realise how essential it is to hold this information very tight until our White Paper is published. I know I can rely on your total discretion here.

219. Message from Johnson to Wilson, 14 July 1967[93]

I take pleasure in presenting to you, on behalf of the American people, this collection of photographs made by the Astronauts who participated in the Gemini Flights III, IV and V. The flights took place in March, June and August of 1965.

I believe you will find these photographs of startling beauty, and also of great scientific interest to those concerned with topography, geography, hydrology and cartography and other earth sciences.

Our hope is that space will always be a region of peaceful international cooperation. The men who venture there go, not as representatives of one nation, but as ambassadors of all mankind. In that spirit, and in the hope that these photographs will contribute to a greater knowledge of our earth, we send you this book.

With best wishes,

Lyndon B. Johnson

220. Message from Wilson to Johnson, 26 July 1967[94]

I understand that the State Department have told our embassy in Washington that permission cannot be given for the sale by British Aircraft Corporation of 5 of the 6 Canberra aircraft the Peruvian Government wish to buy. I am told this decision was reached in the light of a general directive from you that arms sales of this type should be discouraged in Latin America.

I know you want to do everything you can to prevent anything in the nature of an arms race in Latin America. I also do not contest the right of the U.S. Government to withhold permission in this case, since these aircraft are partly M.D.A.P.-funded. I do not believe that the sale of these aircraft would in fact have the kind of effect you fear, and would very much hope that the decision can be reconsidered. The matter is urgent since the contract negotiated in good

---

[93] TNA, PREM 13/3012.

[94] LBJ Library, NSF, Head of State Correspondence File, Box 10, United Kingdom: Prime Minister Wilson Correspondence, Volume 6 [1 of 2], no. 48b.

faith was due to be signed over the last weekend in Lima. If the British Aircraft Corporation's representative in Lima is not to sign it, he will have to explain frankly to the Peruvians that U.S. permission has not been given.

My main reasons for asking you to agree to this sale are these:

The Peruvians already have Canberra aircraft. To supply them with the additional number they wish to buy would not represent a new departure, and would therefore be most unlikely to trigger off an arms race:

The Peruvians will not be prevented from obtaining aircraft of comparable type elsewhere if they are prevented from buying Canberras: they will no doubt turn to e.g. the French, who are likely to press on them less suitable aircraft.

Indeed, in his present mood, de Gaulle might regard this as an excellent opportunity to make trouble for and between us: and of course, between yourselves and the Peruvians. The State Department already have the detailed arguments.

I do not underestimate the strength of feeling in Congress on these matters, and would not have addressed you personally had it not seemed to me that this was a case in which a negative decision might be totally counter-productive and simply make the Peruvians and others in the area less amenable to advice and more ready to turn to less desirable sources of supply for still more sophisticated weapons. Surely this is not in either of our interests.

221. Message from Johnson to Wilson, 28 July 1967[95]

I have reviewed your request on the sale of Canberras to Peru[96] with the greatest care. I appreciate your consulting with us on this matter and the cooperation we have had from your government on military sales to Latin America.

Congressional feeling on the acquisition of unnecessary military equipment by under-developed countries receiving economic assistance from us has reached such a point that the whole foreign aid program is threatened.

Peru is at present seeking substantial economic assistance. Were they to use scarce foreign exchange on military procurement at a time when we are furnishing dollars to tide them over financial difficulties, the Congressional and public reaction would be so strong that our ability to continue supporting the Alliance for Progress[97] would be seriously endangered. Earlier this week our ambassador in Lima informed President Belaunde of our willingness to conclude

---

[95] LBJ Library, NSF, Head of State Correspondence File, Box 10, United Kingdom: Prime Minister Wilson Correspondence, Volume 6 [1 of 2], no. 46.

[96] See 220.

[97] Established by President Kennedy in 1961, the Alliance for Progress aimed to promote economic cooperation between the US and Latin America.

a sizeable loan provided we could agree, among other things, on a total level of military spending, with special attention to costs of major equipment purchases such as aircraft.

President Belaunde understands that the purchase of French Mirage aircraft would make it impossible for us to go forward with the loan. Unfortunately the Canberras also fall within our general conditions to Peru about levels of military spending, and we could not successfully explain to Congress why under such circumstances we had given consent to sell Canberras to Peru.

I feel that I must do all that I can at this time to meet widely and deeply held Congressional objections to unnecessary arms expenditures by countries such as Peru. This includes equipment of United States origin. Certain influential Congressmen have for the moment expressed their concern about supersonic military aircraft, because it is the supersonic Mirage that has been the major problem. But I am sure that if I did consent to the sale of the sub-sonic but medium-range Canberra, Congressional reaction would be equally strong.

For these reasons, and with full understanding of the embarrassing position in which the British aircraft representatives in Lima will find themselves, I must conclude that we cannot alter the negative decision on the proposed sale.

I realize that the United Kingdom Group will have to tell the Peruvians why the Canberra sale cannot go forward, and I have no objection to their doing so. While there is some added risk that the denial of Canberras might of itself trigger a Peruvian decision to spurn American assistance and buy Mirages, I have some doubt that this would occur. It seems to me that it is a risk which we will have to take, given our major problems with the Congress with our foreign aid programs.

222. Message from Wilson to Johnson, 3 August 1967[98]

I greatly appreciate your kind thought in sending me with your letter of 14 July[99] the collection of photographs by the Astronauts who participated in Gemini Flights III, IV and V. I found them fascinating. They are most beautiful, especially in the colours which they show, and are also of great interest.

I share your hope that space will always be a region for peaceful co-operation between nations.

With best wishes,
    Yours very sincerely,
    Harold Wilson

---

[98] LBJ Library, NSF: Special Head of State Correspondence File, Box 56, United Kingdom [3 of 4], no. 73a.
[99] See 219.

223. Message from Wilson to Johnson, 7 August 1967[100]

I am very gratified by the progress which has been made under the F.111 offset arrangement for the purchase by your armed forces of equipment from Britain. You will remember that in my message of 17 February, 1966,[101] I said that we hoped we could sell you communications aircraft: at that time it seemed likely that your first requirement in this field would be for an aircraft of the same type as our HS 125 Executive Jet. You were kind enough to tell me in reply that when the time came to replace your present communications aircraft, careful consideration would be given to the HS 125. In the event other requirements of the US Air Force have come to the top before this one and a competition for a casualty evacuation aircraft is now in its concluding stages. We entered the BAC 1-11 for this and I am sure that our entry was given very full and fair consideration, but I understand that we have not been successful this time. I understand that the next US Air Force Competition is for a smaller and less sophisticated aircraft of a type for which British Handley Page JETSTREAM might be very suitable. This aircraft has already been ordered by a number of users and we think its economics will prove particularly attractive. I should therefore be very grateful if the JETSTREAM could receive the same consideration as you have told me will be given to the HS 125.

224. Message from Wilson to Johnson, 31 August 1967[102]

I send you may [sic] greetings and very best wishes for a happy birthday and many happy returns. I am at the moment just finishing a very enjoyable change at my holiday cottage in the Isles of Scilly. I hope you will be managing to take a break at your home for your birthday.

---

[100] LBJ Library, NSF, Head of State Correspondence File, Box 10, United Kingdom: Prime Minister Wilson Correspondence, Volume 6 [1 of 2], no. 39b.

[101] See 94. The message was actually dated 16 February.

[102] LBJ Library, NSF, Head of State Correspondence File, Box 10, United Kingdom: Prime Minister Wilson Correspondence, Volume 6 [1 of 2], no. 35.

225. Message from Johnson to Wilson, 31 August 1967[103]

Thank you for your kind message of congratulations on my birthday.[104] I am glad your brief holiday has been pleasant and send you and Mrs Wilson my warmest personal regards.
Sincerely,
    Lyndon B. Johnson

226. Message from Johnson to Wilson, 6 September 1967[105]

I have looked into the questions that you raised in your message of August 7[106] about the Handley-Page Jetstream Aircraft. The Department of Defense has received the Handley-Page bid, is familiar with the aircraft, and will give it full and fair consideration in the light of the competition from other producers.
    Lyndon B. Johnson

227. Message from Johnson to Wilson and George Brown, 5 October 1967[107]

I want you both to know how heartened I was by your success in holding the line so well at Scarborough.[108] With what I confront every day, it wasn't hard for me to reconstruct what you faced. I think you understand how much it matters that the government of the country which means most to us, aside from my own, is lending its support for what we all know is right, despite the storms around us.

---

[103] LBJ Library, NSF, Head of State Correspondence File, Box 10, United Kingdom: Prime Minister Wilson Correspondence, Volume 6 [1 of 2], no. 35.
[104] See 224.
[105] LBJ Library, NSF, Head of State Correspondence File, Box 10, United Kingdom: Prime Minister Wilson Correspondence, Volume 6 [1 of 2], no. 33.
[106] See 223.
[107] LBJ Library, NSF, Head of State Correspondence File, Box 10, United Kingdom: Prime Minister Wilson Correspondence, Volume 6 [1 of 2], no. 31.
[108] The annual Labour Party conference was held in Scarborough between 2 and 6 October. Conference rejected the Labour leadership's position on Vietnam (Wilson, *The Labour Government, 1964–1970*, p. 436).

228. Message from Johnson to Wilson, 8 October 1967[109]

I was saddened to learn of the death of Lord Attlee who in a long life served his country and the cause of freedom so faithfully and so well. Please accept my deepest sympathy and that of the American people in your loss.[110]

229. Message from Wilson to Johnson, 30 October 1967[111]

I want you to know that there is not a word of truth in the fantastic stories that have been flying around Europe this weekend about possible reappraisals of fundamental issues of British foreign policy, in the light of a hypothetical French veto on our membership of the E.E.C. I will not dignify these by analysing their origins beyond saying that they derive from a series of misrepresentations and in certain cases downright falsehoods put out after a totally informal seminar-type discussion between Alun Chalfont and a group of British correspondents. Most of the wild ideas originated with the correspondents and I have seldom seen a more blatant example of a minister's trust being abused.

I was particularly sorry to see the scandalous allegation that you and I had been in some kind of consultation beforehand about all this.

Our position in this matter is of course, and will remain, as George Brown and I have stated it publicly, most recently in George's full statement to the House, last Thursday, made with the approval of the united Cabinet. To sum up, we are not taking no for an answer and we are not thinking in terms of alternatives, still less of fundamental reappraisals of British policy. I intend to make this abundantly clear in my speech tomorrow in the House.

We of course left Kiesinger in no doubt of our position during the extremely useful and forthcoming exchanges we had with him last week. You will have seen the helpful statement he made at the end of his visit, before leaving London. We naturally made clear to him also how vital it is for the Germans and ourselves to reach satisfactory agreement on the offset problem. But we did this firmly in the context of our desire for membership of the European communities, making clear what an important element it represented in our general economic approach. As we said to him, we should be much better placed to deal with Couve's arguments about British balance of payments if we did not have an offset burden of the

---

[109] LBJ Library, NSF, Head of State Correspondence File, Box 10, United Kingdom: Prime Minister Wilson Correspondence, Volume 6 [1 of 2], no. 29.

[110] Wilson expressed his appreciation for Johnson's message through the British Ambassador, Sir Patrick Dean (Letter from Dean to Johnson, 13 October 1967, LBJ Library, NSF, Head of State Correspondence File, Box 10, Volume 6 [1 of 2], no. 27a.).

[111] LBJ Library, NSF, Head of State Correspondence File, Box 10, United Kingdom: Prime Minister Wilson Correspondence, Volume 6 [1 of 2], no. 25.

current order. But all this, of course, has nothing whatsoever to do with the reports of our alleged attitude with which this message is concerned.

I am sure that you and your people did not give any credence to what a German spokesman has rightly described as a lot of rubbish. But, in view of the reports linking your name with these stories I felt I owed it to you to let you have this short personal message.

Warmest regards,
    Harold Wilson

230. Message from Wilson to Johnson, 17 November 1967[112]

This is a very secret message for your own eyes alone. But I did want to let you know personally, at the earliest opportunity, that the Cabinet have decided to devalue the pound this weekend. I will not waste your time with the technicalities, beyond saying that we have chosen the new rate very carefully in order, amongst other things, to cause the minimum disturbance for the dollar. Your people will be explaining all the details to you. This message deals with the politics in the widest sense of the word. I think that is what you will be mainly concerned about, as indeed I have been throughout the long, deep and difficult examination I have had to give this very fundamental problem.

You know from all our exchanges how resolutely I have sought to avoid taking this step, if this could be done consistently with the basic objectives we had set ourselves for Britain, at home and abroad. You know, too, of the series of hard and unpopular decisions we have had to take since we came to office, landed with a £800,000,000 (repeat pounds sterling) deficit. These were designed not only to hold the pound but also, and more fundamentally, to transform the economy and technological and industrial base of British society.

What very few people yet realise, I think, is how far the country have begun to move along this road – and this in part because, at every stage, our efforts have apparently been frustrated, usually through events over which we could exert little or no control, by recurring periods of uncertainty leading to intense pressure on sterling.

By this summer we were in fact practically in balance, and ready to move into surplus, when the ground was cut from under us by events in the Middle East. This disrupted our trade and surcharged our imports, through the high cost of the extra transport needed in a volatile tanker market – the denial of traditional oil supplies, based on the great lie of Anglo-American involvement in the fighting – the price of having to replace that oil from high cost areas – and the temporary loss of Middle Eastern markets. Serious though these consequences

---

[112] TNA, PREM 13/1854.

were, they were exaggerated in their effects by a continuous wave of speculation against the pound, which was aggravated by the disproportionate impact of the dock strikes here and the general rise in world interest rates.

The latest resultant sterling crisis, over the past weeks, has also been amongst the gravest, as your people will have explained to you. In resolving to deal with it in this way, we have tried to make an act of decisive choice between two available options. It is possible that our friends, under the impulse of your own warm-hearted response to our difficulties, might once again have helped us over the relatively short term though, in saying this, I am bound to add that the reluctance of certain of the Europeans to give the kind of backing that was needed, coupled with the barely disguised political motivations of certain others, has made us feel that this was not an option on which we could rely with any confidence.

The government came unanimously to this conclusion. But, in choosing the alternative, distasteful as this has been, we have tried to do something more than merely reject the softer of two options. Each of us, I suppose, must at times have suffered the misery of the abscess which breaks out, is temporarily healed, then breaks out again. Each of us has shrunk from having the tooth pulled out. Relief is not simply an illusion. The removal of a certain poison from the system purges the whole system itself.

This rather crude image is as frank a way as I can think of for explaining how my colleagues and I have reached this momentous decision. We all realise that it will have to be accompanied by an exceptionally ghoulish package of further measures, designed not only to hold the world's confidence in the new exchange rate for sterling, but even more to switch resources in Britain towards the thrust for greater exports and for the leaner but more muscular industrial base on which the future of this country depends.

A similar package would of course have been necessary if we had chosen the softer of the two options I have mentioned. But you as a politician – and also I believe as someone who really comprehends the spirit of the British people – will understand that the government, our supporters in Parliament, and the ordinary men and women of this country have become sick and tired of the feeling that the world outside regarded us as living beyond our means and content to rely on the continuing financial support – however generous and well-intentioned – of our friends abroad. To have got them to accept a continuation of this situation coupled with a further disinflationary package would, I believe, not only have been wrong on the merits, but also out of the question politically.

Of course, our people will dislike what we shall now have to ask them to accept. But the way we have decided to do it will, I believe, present them at long last with the challenge to which I am confident they will respond.

This is a long message. But I wanted you, who have been so generous in your help and encouragement over these past three years and who yourself face such immense difficulties and problems, to have the full picture of the political decisions we have been obliged to make.

There are two other things I want also to say in the same connection. First, I know that this decision will cause you concern. I am truly grateful for what you and your people have tried to do to avert it. But I believe it to be right and that, as the result of it, we in Britain will be better able to pursue the kind of foreign policy that we – and you – believe to be right. Secondly, I must admit that there have been moments during these past weeks when I doubted whether, in taking the measures necessary to put our economy to rights, we could possibly avoid some really damaging effects on our posture in the world outside.

The essence of the domestic package we have decided on is the release of resources from the home market to make possible full deployment of resources on increased exports. The underlying philosophy will be the need to trim our home market economy so as to live, and be seen to be living, within our means. But, after all our people have had to take in the past 18 months, and this has had a pretty debilitating effect on national morale, not only politically, I would have found it impossible to ask for further belt tightening without meeting a strong riposte from our own people, right, left and centre, that the first belts to be tightened should in their view, be those of the military. With the best will in the world a week ago, I could not see how this could be achieved without major changes in our defence posture both in Europe and East of Suez, going far beyond the decisions announced in our defence White Paper four months ago. And I was only too well aware of what this would have meant for the Alliance and for the fulfilment of the common purpose which you and I have often proclaimed, particularly if this meant having to withdraw much earlier than planned from Singapore or even possibly to make savage troop reductions in Europe.

I am happy to say that this is not the case and I can assure you that, provided, as we confidently believe, the pound can now again become a strong currency and our economy forge ahead in the new circumstances, we shall be able to maintain, both in Europe and East of Suez, the policies set out in our defence White Paper as I explained them to you at our last meeting.

What is more, I believe that our decision can prove a significant factor in helping us move forward in our European policy, which I know to enjoy your support. The option we have chosen should go far towards disposing of one of the major objections which has been raised against our application to join the European Communities. Of course, I have no illusions about this. We know perfectly well the intense political motivations that underline French opposition to our entry. But at least what we are doing now should undermine one major line of French attack. They will then, I have no doubt, fall back on others. We shall do our best to undermine those too. And I remain confident that we shall succeed.

This brings me to my final point. There is no doubt that part of our recent difficulties on the monetary front has resulted from a calculated policy designed to take advantage of our difficulties in order to attack you. Because, as we both know, any attack on the pound tends to be merely the prelude to an attack on the dollar. The way we are handling our problem now is, as I have explained, designed to leave the dollar as little exposed as possible. Nevertheless, each of us may well face major political problems in the weeks ahead. I need not spell these out to you. But I believe that certain of them will be of fundamental political importance to ourselves and to the Alliance, and that concerted policies founded on the identity of purpose of our two countries can be decisive in dealing with them.

I am sure therefore that it will be useful for us to meet again quite soon. Meanwhile I am greatly looking forward to my talks with Hubert Humphrey later this month. Perhaps we could have another look at the situation in the light of those talks.

231. Message from Wilson to Johnson, 18 November 1967[113]

Pat Dean has told me of the characteristically open-hearted way in which you responded to my message[114] and to the account he was able to give you of the background to it. I just want to say how greatly I appreciate this. It will be a source of strength for me over the coming difficult days.

I hope we can indeed arrange to meet soon, though I fully realise your many pre-occupations at present. Of course I entirely agree with you that, if we can find a naturally convenient time, it should be announced and treated as a meeting to discuss world problems as a whole.

Many thanks and best regards.
    Harold

232. Message from Johnson to Wilson, 23 November 1967[115]

I have read several times your courageous message of 17 November.[116] I think I know how hard your decision was, especially because in the first half of the year things went so well. If it is a comfort to you, I can tell you that my faith is deep

---

[113] LBJ Library, NSF, Head of State Correspondence File, Box 10, United Kingdom: Prime Minister Wilson Correspondence, Volume 6 [1 of 2], no. 20.

[114] See 230.

[115] LBJ Library, NSF, Special Head of State Correspondence File, Box 56, United Kingdom [3 of 4], no. 62c.

[116] See 230.

that the British people have the will and the means both to pay their way and to continue to play the part they must in the world.

This faith is in my blood and in my life's experience with Britain.

As for yourself, I understand what is to absorb the shock of all this and, at the same time, try to set your people on a sound if painful course.

Our prayers are with you and with the men and women of your land: for it is somehow just wrong for Britain to be off balance this way.

As for ourselves, we shall be helping in the IMF and elsewhere to make a success of the new sterling rate. And we shall do whatever is necessary to defend the dollar.

Immediately on hearing the news from you, I turned to the task of trying to get a tax increase and an expenditure cut from the Congress as soon as possible. Unless our deficit is cut quite sharply, our borrowing requirements in the capital markets are likely to push interest rates through the ceiling with grave effects here and elsewhere. And we shall also, of course, have to deal with the speculators already working against the dollar.

I was much impressed by the response around the world in the wake of the devaluation of the pound. There are strong currents of international understanding and good will. And there ought to be, especially for those like you and me who lived through the Great Depression after 1929 and who also lived through the other great tragedy when Britain saved us all.

It will be difficult to hold each of the major nations on a steady course but this is the only way to maintain and strengthen the international monetary system. That is clearly our duty. I shall do everything I can to fulfil it. And I know we shall be shoulder to shoulder.

As Pat Dean told you, I look forward to our taking stock together here at any period when the time is right for you.

233. Message from Wilson to Johnson, 24 November 1967[117]

I am greatly moved by your message.[118] It is indeed heartening to feel the depth of your understanding for the action we felt it right to take.

Pat Dean will be in touch with your people shortly about the best time for us to meet. I greatly look forward to it.

---

[117] LBJ Library, NSF, Head of State Correspondence File, Box 10, United Kingdom: Prime Minister Wilson Correspondence, Volume 6 [1 of 2], no. 15.

[118] See 232.

234. Message from Johnson to Wilson, 5 December 1967[119]

I know you share my deep satisfaction that we have avoided war over Cyprus.[120] There is no doubt that the strong cooperation so generously given by you and your government was a major factor in the ultimate success of Cyrus Vance's mission.[121] I know that in particular he valued, as did I, the active efforts of your ambassadors in the respective capitals. Your letter to President Makarios at the time of the final negotiations in Nicosia was particularly helpful.
With best regards,
Sincerely,

235. Message from Wilson to Johnson, 6 December 1967[122]

Many thanks for your kind message about Cyprus.[123] I do indeed share your satisfaction that we have avoided war in the Eastern Mediterranean. It is good of you to say that the part played by our representatives in the three capitals was useful and that my own message to Makarios may also have helped. But the main credit must go Cyrus Vance. He has done a magnificent job. As you may have heard, George Brown has already asked Dean Rusk to pass on to Vance his and George Thomson's warmest congratulations.

I am sure we must continue to work very closely together on the difficult problems that still lie ahead of us over Cyprus.
Best regards,
As ever
    Harold

---

[119] LBJ Library, NSF, Head of State Correspondence File, Box 10, United Kingdom: Prime Minister Wilson Correspondence, Volume 6 [1 of 2], no. 12a.

[120] Fighting erupted between Turkish Cypriots and Greek Cypriot police and National Guard units on 15 November 1967. The following day, the Turkish Government demanded that Greek Cypriots end their attacks or face military intervention.

[121] Johnson despatched former Under Secretary of Defense Cyrus Vance to serve as his envoy to the area on 23 November 1967. Between November 23 and December 4, Vance travelled between Ankara, Athens, and Nicosia to broker a peaceful resolution to the crisis. For Vance's own account of his mission, see Transcript, Cyrus Vance Oral History Interview II, 12/29/69, by Paige E. Mulhollan, LBJ Library.

[122] LBJ Library, NSF, Head of State Correspondence File, Box 10, United Kingdom: Prime Minister Wilson Correspondence, Volume 6 [1 of 2], no. 10a.

[123] See 234.

236. Message from Johnson to Wilson, 25 December 1967[124]

Dear Harold:

The sadness of my Australian visit[125] was eased by sharing the occasion with you.

I was heartened to have the chance of another candid exchange with the partner who brings strength to my purpose and brightness to the prospect of peace. Whatever burdens we are forced to bear now, they will be sooner lifted because we carry them in mutual faith and understanding.

I think you will share my feeling that this international tribute to Harold Holt gave further evidence of the emergence of a New Asia. The course of its change will be affected in no small way by the encouraging presence of Prince Charles and yourself in Melbourne.

The leaders and people of Asia share my gratitude. It is our faith and belief that the British presence in Asia will be vital to the hopeful future, in one good way or another.

May the New Year bring you all joy and success to you and your fine family.
Sincerely,
Lyndon B. Johnson

237. Message from Wilson to Johnson, 27 December 1967[126]

Dear Lyndon,

Many thanks for your kind message sent since we met in Australia.[127] I too greatly appreciated the talk we were able to have, despite the sadness of the circumstances that made it possible. As I told you, I wanted to indicate by my personal attendance at this last tribute to Harold Holt not only the sympathy we all felt with his family at a very sad occasion, but also the real solidarity that exists – and will, I am confident, continue – between Britain and Australia within the world-wide Commonwealth association that is of such enduring importance to this country.

My very best New Year wishes to you and yours. I so look forward to the opportunity of a longer and more relaxed exchange with you early in February.

---

[124] LBJ Library, NSF, Head of State Correspondence File, Box 10, United Kingdom: Prime Minister Wilson Correspondence, Volume 6 [1 of 2], no. 8.

[125] Johnson and Wilson were attending the funeral of Australian premier Harold Holt who had died in mysterious circumstances on 17 December 1967.

[126] LBJ Library, NSF, Special Head of State Correspondence File, Box 56, United Kingdom [2 of 4], no. 60w.

[127] See 236.

238. Message from Johnson to Wilson, 31 December 1967[128]

Dear Harold:

We are at the end of a difficult year, and both our countries have much unfinished business to carry forward. It is encouraging to recall, nonetheless, that it has been a year in which our close consultation and collaboration have helped produce a number of memorable achievements—the maintenance of security arrangements in Europe, the agreement of the new reserve unit in the IMF, the completion of the Kennedy Round, to recall a few. We are not yet out of the woods in the Middle East, but we have certainly made progress, with the passage of your Resolution in the Security Council.[129]

We can take heart also from the success we have had through our joint efforts and through the cooperation of the other financial powers in meeting the critical problems of November and December and in restoring a sense of confidence and order to the world's financial system.

The speculative fever of these weeks has severely tested our methods of cooperating on economic problems; but, we have continued to work together effectively in a financial world suddenly beset by fear and disorder. We have, thus far, met and repelled a serious threat to the foundations of the international monetary system, which, in turn, could also have undone the accomplishments of the Kennedy Round[130] and the unity of the system of international commerce.

Meanwhile, the agreements at London and Rio on a plan to supplement existing reserve assets are a further reason for solid satisfaction, as we look to the longer future.

In both of these achievements—the long-range improvement of our international monetary system and the recent defense of the existing system—James Callaghan at the Treasury and Leslie O'Brien at the Bank of England have played important and indeed vital roles. I know that they have contributed much to the recent efforts to preserve order in the gold and foreign exchange markets. I am reassured by our mutual determination to exert a constructive force in the world financial system. This I know reflects a clear common understanding of the importance of international monetary cooperation in creating that environment of safety and opportunity which is required for the continued growth and stability of our nation's [sic] economies.

As you know, we, as well as our trading partners, have been concerned about the balance of payments position of the United States. This concern has been increased by the events of recent weeks. As a result, I am announcing on January

---

[128] LBJ Library, NSF, Head of State Correspondence File, Box 10, United Kingdom: Prime Minister Wilson Correspondence, Volume 6 [1 of 2], no. 3.
[129] Security Council Resolution 242 (1967), adopted 11 November 1967.
[130] See 168, footnote 148.

1, 1968, a new and vastly strengthened program to reduce our deficit and guarantee the continued viability of the international monetary system.

In the program, I will press for tax increase to restrain excessive demand in the United States and to reduce our budget deficit to manageable proportions. I hope that this bill will soon become law. This, in itself, should be a helpful factor in our balance of payments and should demonstrate to the world that we will keep our own economic house in order. And the Federal Reserve has already made clear its determination to use monetary policy to this end.

But much more needs to be done; and we propose to do much more. Our balance of payments actions are designed to improve both our current and our capital accounts.

These actions will be painful to the United States and, to some degree, to our international partners. They are designed to avoid as far as possible adverse effects on the developing areas of the world. We hope they will result more in the reduction of surpluses than in the shift or increase of deficits. And we have kept very much in mind the views of other countries and the international economic institutions.

In this effort we wish to proceed within the spirit and the letter of the recent resolution of the OECD Ministerial Council that the adjustment of the American deficit and the European surplus is a matter of common concern to be handled cooperatively. Surpluses in international payments are the mirror image of deficits. Thus, both surplus and deficit countries must strive to reach balance and act cooperatively to this end. This is no less true in the 1960s than it was in the late 1940's and '50's, when we carried the responsibilities of a surplus nation. This concept was definitively developed by our best economic and financial experts in a carefully prepared OECD report on "The Adjustment Process" in August 1966.

Our deficits have been the net result of a current account surplus, including a trade surplus, inadequate to support foreign exchange costs of our external capital flows, foreign aid programs, and military expenditures for the common defense. During the period of the "Dollar Gap", these deficits helped redistribute the world's monetary reserves—the time has come, we all agree, to bring them to an end.

As we see the problem, we need to act to improve our current account, reduce capital outflows, and neutralize more fully our net foreign exchange expenditures in the common defense. Our new program is designed to move us strongly towards equilibrium. But full success will require the understanding and cooperation of our partners. It seems axiomatic to us, and basic to our view of the OECD Resolution, that those in strong reserve positions, or in surplus, should avoid actions that increase surpluses, should not take off-setting action to preserve their surpluses—indeed, that it will be necessary for them to take positive action to move toward balance. Otherwise, the only result will be to shift the adjustment burden to those who can least bear it or to make it more difficult for us to achieve balance. In our judgment—and, I believe, in your judgment—it is important for the United States to move decisively toward balance with the least possible dislocation to the world's system of trade and finance. Our mutual security and collective well-being, which rest upon the continuing strength and unity of the international economic system, are at stake.

It is against these fundamental objectives, which I am sure are common objectives, that I hope you and your Government will judge our new and strengthened balance of payments program. I have asked Ambassador Bruce to call on you to explain our new program more fully. I have also asked Under Secretary Katzenbach to visit with you in London to review further both this program and the entire scope of our mutual cooperation. I trust you and your key ministers will support this program and, thereby, help preserve confidence in the system we have built so diligently together over the past twenty years. I am looking forward to seeing you in February.

Sincerely,

Lyndon B. Johnson

Chapter 4

Withdrawal from East of Suez, Wilson's Visit to Moscow, Gold and Monetary Crises, Vietnam Peace Initiatives, and the End of the Johnson Presidency, January 1968–January 1969

239. Message from Wilson to Johnson, 1 January 1968[1]

Thank you so much for your letter,[2] with which you sent me an advance summary of the measures to improve the United States balance of payments which you are announcing in Washington today. I can assure you that we understand the need for the strong and resolute action which you are taking. We are glad that in view of our balance of payments situation you have been able to mitigate the effects on us of your restrictions on direct investment by giving favoured treatment to the United Kingdom as compared with the rest of Western Europe. It is satisfactory also that you have been able to give special treatment both to the developing countries and to a number of other countries which are particularly dependent on an inflow of capital investment from the United States. We have not been able to assess fully what the effects of your measures on our balance of payments are likely to be. Clearly there will be some adverse effect. But we fully recognise that, if the United States is to restore its payments to balance, other countries must be ready to accept some worsening of their position. In particular, as you rightly say, surplus countries must be willing to accept the consequences of your action without taking offset measures.

We are very much looking forward to seeing Nicholas Katzenbach and Fred Deming tomorrow. I am asking Roy Jenkins to go thoroughly into the whole matter with them.

---

[1] LBJ Library, NSF, Head of State Correspondence File, Box 10, United Kingdom, Prime Minister Wilson Correspondence, Volume 7, no. 69a.
[2] See 238.

I was very glad to have the opportunity of a meeting with you in Melbourne.[3]
I am greatly looking forward to my visit to Washington next month.

I extend to you my warmest best wishes for the New Year.

240. Message from Johnson to Wilson, 11 January 1968[4]

Dear Harold:

I have just learned from Dean Rusk of your plans for total British withdrawal from the Far East and the Persian Gulf by 1971.

I know you are close to a final decision and that there is not much time for reconsideration. I also can guess at what soul-searching you and your colleagues have been going through in trying to find the means for restoring the health of the British economy and still carrying as much as possible of the financial burdens which you have so courageously borne thus far.

This having been said, I cannot conceal from you my deep dismay upon learning this profoundly discouraging news. If these steps are taken, they will be tantamount to British withdrawal from world affairs, with all that means for the future safety and health of the free world. The structure of peace-keeping will be shaken to its foundations. Our own capability and political will could be gravely weakened if we have to man the ramparts all alone.

Although the decision must, of course, be your own, I can only wonder if you and all of your associates have taken fully into account the direct and indirect consequences.

While the hour is late, I urge you and your colleagues once more to review the alternatives before you take these irrevocable steps. Even a prolongation of your presence in the Far East and the Persian Gulf until other stable arrangements can be put in place would be of help at this very difficult time for all of us.

With warmest personal regards,
Sincerely,
   Lyndon B. Johnson

---

[3] See 236 and 237.

[4] LBJ Library, NSF, Head of State Correspondence File, Box 10, United Kingdom, Prime Minister Wilson Correspondence, Volume 7, no. 67a.

241. Message from Johnson to Wilson, 15 January 1968[5]

The question of Britain's future in the world, about which I wrote you the other day,[6] continues to be very much on my mind. I know that you and your colleagues will be making crucial decisions on this question in the coming hours.

The London press this morning carries reports that the Cabinet has in fact decided to cancel the F-111. Though I know how unreliable the press can be, I have decided to communicate to you my extreme concern about this matter in particular.

As Dean Rusk and Bob McNamara explained to George [Brown] during his recent visit,[7] and as I stated in my recent letter to you, the announcement of accelerated British withdrawal both from its Far Eastern bases and from the Persian Gulf would create most serious problems for the United States Government and for the security of the entire free world. Americans will find great difficulty in supporting the idea that we must move in to secure areas which the United Kingdom has abandoned.

It has been our hope that a demonstrated ability of United Kingdom military forces speedily to deploy to these areas from its own bases might alleviate somewhat the strong reaction which will inevitably take place. The F-111, because of its range and overall capability, would demonstrate this rapid deployment ability.

But if you decide to forego the acquisition of the F-111, everyone here will regard this as a total disengagement from any commitments whatsoever to the security of areas outside Europe and, indeed, to a considerable extent in Europe as well. Moreover, it will be viewed here as a strong indication of British isolation which would be fatal to the chances of cooperation between our countries in the field of defense procurement. Both Dean [Rusk] and Bob [McNamara] made it clear to George Brown that financial penalties will have to be applied if there is a decision to cancel the F-111 contract. Politically, we have no choice. Appreciable as these penalties would be in monetary terms, however, they would be far less serious than the reciprocal actions which in all likelihood would follow. Retention of the present offset arrangements would become out of the question. Pressures for domestic procurement could no longer be resisted. These would almost inescapably lead to complete cancellation of recent awards of military contracts to British firms.

---

[5] LBJ Library, NSF, Head of State Correspondence File, Box 10, United Kingdom, Prime Minister Wilson Correspondence, Volume 7, no. 65a.
[6] See 240.
[7] See Memorandum of Conversation 11 January 1968, *FRUS, 1964–8*: Volume XII: *Western Europe* (Washington, DC: United States Government Printing Office, 2001), pp. 603–8.

But even these severe economic effects would be overshadowed by the foreign policy consequences of an F-111 cancellation. Many in this country, including influential members of Congress, would bring the strongest pressures to bear on us to sacrifice international security interests to ease our present financial problems. Our ability to maintain substantial forces in Europe, while fighting a difficult and costly war in Southeast Asia, would be greatly endangered.

As I indicated in my last letter to you, I recognize fully that a decision on this question is one that the British Government alone can make. I hope that it will do so with full consideration of all the factors involved. And I wanted you to know how important I consider it to be that the United Kingdom and the United States maintain their understanding on the F-111 in all essential respects and continue to at least try to defend freedom in this hectic and unsettled world in which we live.
Sincerely,
Lyndon B. Johnson

242. Message from Wilson to Johnson, 15 January 1968[8]

I laid both your messages[9] before my Cabinet colleagues today[10] and they were carefully read before our final deliberations and decisions on the range and extent of the swingeing cuts in public expenditure, at home and overseas, that I shall be announcing to Parliament tomorrow. I should like to say at the outset how grateful I am to you for setting out with such restraint and understanding what I know to be your powerfully-held views on the measures we are having to take.

I need hardly tell you how profoundly my colleagues and I regret the necessity for our decisions. As you will see when you receive a copy of my statement—and I will do my best to get this to you as early as possible—some of the decisions we have taken on the home front strike at the very root of principles to which many of us have been dedicated since we first went into politics. They are bitter decisions for us to have to make; and only our conviction that they are vital in the long-term interests of Britain, and that the British people will accept them as such, has made it possible for us to stomach them.

The heavy sacrifices at home would have been pointless without drastic retrenchment abroad. I ask you to believe that this is not, as some journalists and even some Commonwealth statesmen have been saying, simply a matter

---

[8] LBJ Library, NSF, Head of State Correspondence File, Box 11, M.O.D. 1968, no 5.
[9] See 240 and 241.
[10] See Conclusions of a meeting of the Cabinet, 15 January 1968, CC (68) 7th conclusions, TNA, CAB 128/43.

of party politics—of keeping some kind of "balance" to force the unpleasant home medicine down the throats of our party supporters. Of course politics is involved here—what is politics all about anyway? But this is much wider than party politics—the politics of the nation and the sense of purpose of the British people as a whole are deeply involved.

At the time of devaluation, I told you that the British people were sick and tired of being thought willing to eke out a comfortable existence on borrowed money. As your people may have told you, there has been over the past weeks an astonishing assertion of this kind of spirit throughout the nation and irrespective of party. At the root of this is a still rather confused groping for the real role that Britain ought to be playing in the world; and it has been striking to observe, in polls and other tests of public opinion, not only the extent to which people are prepared to accept drastic sacrifice at home but also their demand that we must no longer continue to overstrain our real resources and capabilities in the military field abroad.

This does not mean, as you suggest, a British withdrawal from world affairs. Of course there are always, in any country, those who in moments of storm prefer to bury their heads in the sand. But the spirit that has been running through this nation in recent weeks is not that of "Little England." I believe it to be a blend of exasperation at our inability to weather the successive economic storms of the past twenty years and determination, once and for all, to hew out a new role for Britain in the world at once commensurate with her real resources yet worthy of her past. There is at last a nation-wide realisation that this can not be done on borrowed time and borrowed money.

I shall not attempt to list here all the measures which will be set out in my statement tomorrow. But just as you were able to give me brief forewarning[11] of the dramatic steps you felt it necessary to take on New Year's Day to protect even the vast economic strength of the United States, so I wish you to know now the two decisions that are most directly relevant to this country's international posture and thus to our own working relationship; and those to which your two messages were addressed.

First, the Far East and the Gulf. As I shall be explaining tomorrow, it is absolutely clear to us that our present political commitments are too great for the military capability of the forces that we can reasonably afford, if the economy is to be restored quickly and decisively; but without economic strength, we can have no real military credibility. If there is any lesson to be learned from the sombre way we have found ourselves obliged to lurch from one defence review to another in recent years, it is that we must now take certain major foreign policy decisions as the prerequisite of economies in our defence expenditure. Put simply, this only amounts to saying that we have to come to terms with our

---

[11] See 238.

role in the world. And we are confident that if we fully assert our economic strength, we can, by realistic priorities, strengthen this country's real influence and power for peace in the world.

This was what underlay the intention, conveyed to Dean Rusk by George Brown, to withdraw our forces from the Far East and the Middle East by the end of the financial year 1970/71. But, as George explained, we fixed this deadline subject to reconsideration in the light of the account he brought back of your government's views and what George Thomson returned to tell us of the views of the Commonwealth governments in the area. We also, as you may have seen, sent the Minister of State in the Foreign Office to discuss our intentions with the heads of government and others concerned in the Middle East. In the light of your message to me, of the reports from our other colleagues and of our deep and searching discussion with Harry Lee, who flew to London this weekend, we have decided to defer our withdrawal for a further nine months, i.e. to the end of 1971. I know that this will still seem too soon to yourself and to many others. But, in the face of the appallingly difficult decisions we are having to take over home expenditure, I believe that it is a significant contribution to the time needed to help those in the areas concerned prepare for the day when we shall no longer have a military presence there—for, believe me, it is only of our military presence that we are speaking. We know that its withdrawal involves risks. We believe that there is no option but to run them. But we intended to continue our aid programmes to the best of our ability, and of course to maintain our political, trading and economic interests there.

Secondly, the F111. Again, I ask you to believe that my colleagues and I have spent many hours of discussion and heart-searching on this problem at three separate meetings and gave the fullest weight to the considerations advanced in your message. But we have come to the reluctant conclusion that the only way we can achieve the really decisive economies that are essential in the hardware budget of the Royal Air Force, while still keeping effective and sophisticated capabilities in all three services, is to cancel the order for the 50 F111 aircraft. I hope you are wrong in assessing that this decision will be interpreted abroad as a disengagement from any commitments to the security of areas outside Europe or indeed largely in Europe as well. And you are certainly wrong if you take the view you mentioned that it is "a strong indication of British isolation." In fact, I believe both these views to be wrong. As I shall be explaining tomorrow, we intend to make to the alliances of which we are members, a contribution related to our economic capability; we shall not be withdrawing from our three major alliances; and the general capability that we shall retain in this country and on the continent can also be deployed overseas and will still thus enable us to continue to give assistance to our international partners and other allies concerned, if the circumstances so demand.

Against this background and having regard to what you yourself said in the second of your two messages, I nevertheless hope that Denis Healey and Bob McNamara, for whose helpful efforts in these matters we are all most grateful, can reach an early agreement in broad terms about continued credit facilities for the unchanged Phantom and Hercules programmes and for appropriate adaptation of the offset arrangements.

Believe me, Lyndon, the decisions we are having to take now have been the most difficult and the heaviest of any that I, and I think all my colleagues, can remember in our public life. We are not taking them in a narrow or partisan spirit. We are taking them because we are convinced that, in the longer term, only thus can Britain find the new place on the world stage that I firmly believe the British people ardently desire. And when I say "the world stage" I mean just that.

Warm regards,
 Harold Wilson

243. Message from Wilson to Johnson, 23 January 1968[12]

I am dictating this note to you in secure conditions in Moscow. I have asked Pat Dean to bring to you very urgently a note I have just dictated of a number of things said to me by Kosygin throughout the second act of Carmen.[13] He was very much concerned to get this across to me. I dictated the note in the presence of my Downing Street and Foreign Office colleagues without any idea of sending it to you, just as it came out of my memory. But without any amendment I would like you to see it as an addition to the facts which you ought to have in the developing Vietnam situation. You will realise that this onslaught left me somewhat non-plussed because, in all my talks in Moscow, extending over many hours, I have stuck absolutely to the line which Bill Bundy so admirably described and the suggestions he made to us on Saturday.

I think you ought to have Kosygin's statements. I should like to have your comments very urgently, because we are at present dead-locked with the Russians on the communiqué so far as Vietnam is concerned—though I strongly suspect that the Russians concerned with its drafting not be fully apprised of what Kosygin felt it right to say to me. Kosygin seemed to want me to make contact with the North Vietnamese Embassy in Moscow—indeed this may have been lined up. I am not doing so. One of the possibilities we have to take into account is that there are a number of lines into Hanoi: that the Soviet Union know your line and don't like it: and that the DRV Ambassador in Moscow may

---

[12] TNA, PREM 13/2459.
[13] See 244.

be a very different line. In view of what Bill Bundy said to me we are anxious to do nothing which might prejudice the very delicate contacts you have, so I am not responding to the clear hint which Kosygin gave me. But I am beginning to wonder how much the Russian position is due to sheer obstruction and, after what Kosygin said to me, how much to sheer ignorance.

You will realise I also am not fully in the picture after my talk with Bundy. He made it very clear to us that he was under firm instructions not to inform me of the nature of the channel of communication and I therefore did not press him. I am not (repeat not) asking you now to tell me the channel: but I want you to realise that I am in considerable difficulty on concerting a helpful communiqué with the Russians, since they appear to be throwing doubts on the reality of contacts of which Bundy was instructed to tell us and about which he said that they would know exactly the same as he told us—no more and no less. The Russians may be trying to drive a wedge, but I must be sure in my own mind that their doubts are ill-founded if I am to press them on the communiqué which might be helpful to your purposes. I meet them again to discuss this at 4am your time, 24 January.

244. Note by the Prime Minister of a talk with Mr. Kosygin, the Soviet Prime Minister, during the second act of the opera Carmen in Moscow on Tuesday evening, 23 January 1968[14]

Kosygin gave me his figures of the destruction of American bombers in Vietnam, attributing most of it to conventional anti-craft, less to Migs and missiles than I would have expected. He then plunged into the political situation. He said he could not understand us. What did I mean by saying to him and Brezhnev that contacts were going on. He felt there was a lot of self-delusion in this. I said "you knew exactly as much as we know on this matter. It is not for you and us to discuss this." I reminded him that last year talks were going on, as he then knew, and we preferred then to use the phrase "under a palm-tree." He said "If the Americans have told you that there are significant talks going on now, under a palm-tree or anywhere else, they are lying."

I thought these remarks not only significant, whatever their motive, but worth probing. I said that I presumed he was in touch with Hanoi on these questions so he must know what was going on. He replied that everything Hanoi had told him suggested that there was nothing that could really be called contacts of the type I had described in my talks with him and Brezhnev.

He then asked me what President Johnson's aim was. Did he really want a settlement or was it not true that he was playing election politics. I said I knew

---

[14] TNA, PREM 13/2459.

Johnson as well as I knew most people and I was absolutely convinced he was sincere in wanting a settlement. It was true that many people in America were taking a hard line, including very many of Johnson's electorate, and I thought it therefore implied courage to be going for a settlement which could be misused by any politician to the right of him. Kosygin said for the nth time this week that he could not understand this because everybody he met in America wanted peace and denounced Johnson. I told him for the nth minus tenth time (having stood this politely for the nth minus ninth time) that those were the sort of people he would meet or who would meet him. I told him he misread American public opinion if he thought it was easy for Johnson to take great risks in going for peace this time; but this I was convinced he was doing.

At this point he stopped to applaud the Toreador song.

He then came back, shifting his ground, and said he thought Johnson would probably win the election if he did get peace in Vietnam. I said I thought Johnson would take exactly the same line on this in 1968 as he would in any other year, election or not, in today's circumstances as they were facing him.

He then came back to the contacts and again said that nothing significant was going on. People might think there were. People might tell other people there were. But from what he knew this was not so. I then said that I knew he had contacts with Hanoi. He cut in to say that they were direct and not based on palm-trees or unsatisfactory intermediaries. I said was he really saying to me that when we had said that there were significant talks going on, this was not true. He said "This is a question which I can neither confirm nor deny."

He said "All this suggests to us and to our (and he slightly underlined our, if that means anything) friends in Hanoi that the Americans are not sincere in a bid for peace. Certainly we do not know anything which would justify us in thinking they are, or in accepting what you have very strongly urged upon us."

I said that I was disturbed to hear this and I must think hard on what he had told me. I then pressed him again, to make sure I had not misunderstood or that there had been any error in translation. He said "If the Americans were sincere in their contact—and I do not deny there are probings—they would not proceed in this way. All that is going on is just probing." He then went on to indicate that he had no confidence in them. "But we would like to know whether the Americans really mean business in following up the Trinh declaration.[15] If they

---

[15] On 1 January 1968, Radio Hanoi broadcast a statement made by DRV Foreign Minister Nguyen Duy Trinh in which he declared: 'If the American government really wants conversations, as clearly stated in our declaration of January 28, 1967, it must first unconditionally cease bombing and all other acts of war against the Democratic Republic of Vietnam. After the cessation of bombing and all other acts of war against the Democratic Republic of Vietnam, the DRV will start conversations with the United States on relevant problems' (*FRUS, 1964–8*: Volume VI: *Vietnam, January–August 1968* (Washington, DC: United States Government Printing Office, 2002), p. 1).

do, they could either approach us direct and give us a formulation to pass on to Hanoi or they could give it to you to give to us to pass to Hanoi. When are you going to Washington?"

I said "In a fortnight's time."

I then tried to press him on all the things he had said. But by this time he felt that the Opera demanded some attention and I could get no more than a repetition of this. (I think it was at this time he conceded the word "probing"). He was at pains to let me know that they were in close touch with Hanoi, in better touch than the Americans; and in answer to a question I put to him he suggested that what might be happening was that the Americans were closely in touch with someone who claimed to be in touch with significant people in Hanoi, but that his own contacts in Hanoi discounted the contact. He was clear about this as about anything he said; and he again repeated that his contacts with Hanoi were clear and definite and that if there had been significant contacts he would have known—hence his puzzlement at my repeated references to this.

Then he threw another question at me. He said "If you really believe what you are being told"—and at this point he started doubting American sincerity, casting some doubts on the competence of their contacts—he said "Why don't you ask Hanoi? On your last visit Lord Chalfont talked to the North Vietnamese Embassy."

I said it had occurred to me that on this occasion we might want to have a direct talk with the Embassy and that indeed Mr. Harold Davies,[16] with his North Vietnamese contacts, might well have talked with them. But I had judged that in this very delicate situation this would be wrong. Indeed, it might be extremely embarrassing to the Soviet Government as well as to others. He said that this would not present any embarrassment. I said this was really a matter which I want to think carefully about.

The following questions arise:

Who is taking whom for a ride? Has Hanoi sold Moscow a bum steer? Is Kosygin trying to sell me one, or is he for some reason trying to persuade me that the Americans have sold me one? If so, why; and who will come unstuck, on the evidence available?

I have stated the facts as well as I remember them in a very colourful Second Act. I think I have put the right questions to the answers. Now I would like to hear from the professionals the answers to the questions.

---

[16] Davies had led an unsuccessful mission to Hanoi in July 1965.

245. Message from Johnson to Wilson, 24 January 1968[17]

We have given a careful reading to your record of the current discussion[18] and much appreciate your letting us see it.

We are a bit puzzled about just what Kosygin has in mind. Over a year ago Secretary Rusk asked Gromyko for advice about which of the capitals in reasonably friendly relations with Moscow would be the most appropriate and reliable contact with Hanoi. Gromyko quite categorically stated "Moscow. The others are of no value." In the most recent period, however, it has been our very strong impression that Moscow was not interested in working seriously in Hanoi for a peaceful settlement. If that was their view, we thought we ought to accommodate them.

One can never be sure about contacts involving third parties. In this instance, however, we have every reason to believe that we are in such contact with Pham Van Dong and Trinh, the Foreign Minister. This derives both from internal evidence in what has allegedly been said and from external evidence in the consistency between what has been said privately, what has been said publicly by Hanoi and by reasonable interpretations of a great deal of diplomatic gossip in a number of capitals involving Hanoi's representatives.

It is probable that Moscow knows the channel and does not particularly like it. After all, Moscow's own prestige could be involved. It may be that Hanoi is somewhat evasive with Moscow because of Hanoi's problem with Peking. There is always the possibility, whatever the intermediary might be, that we are being hoodwinked. But we are protecting ourselves against being hoodwinked. For example, the bombing has not been stopped.

It is curious that Kosygin seems to feel strongly about the channel but has nothing to say on the substance. We have had nothing from your talks with him or with Brezhnev indicating what Moscow is prepared to do on the assumption that we are prepared to stop the bombing within the framework of the San Antonio formula.[19]

We have followed our own contact closely, know where he is and when he will get back. We expect to see him or hear from him again before the end of the

---

[17] LBJ Library, NSF, Head of State Correspondence File, Box 10, United Kingdom, Prime Minister Wilson Correspondence, Volume 7, no. 61.

[18] See 243 and 244.

[19] On 29 September 1967, Johnson told the National Legislative Conference in San Antonio, Texas, that 'The United States is willing to stop all aerial and naval bombardment of North Vietnam when this will lead promptly to productive discussions. We, of course, assume that while discussions proceed, North Vietnam would not take advantage of the bombing cessation or limitation' (*FRUS, 1964–8*: Volume V: *Vietnam, 1967* (Washington, DC: United States Government Printing Office, 2002), p. 837).

month. We have even done one or two little things as a contribution to his safety and comfort while on his mission.

If Kosygin, unexpectedly, wishes to talk about the issues in substance we would be glad to know what he has in mind. He knows our own view, he knows our address and we have had nothing from him.

We concur in your judgment that perhaps you yourself should not see the North Vietnamese Ambassador in Moscow but we have no particular problem about your Ambassador, or indeed our Ambassador, seeing this individual to listen although we would not ourselves wish to direct any message through that channel at the present time. We say this because we have tried on other occasions and have gotten nothing but bruises for our efforts.

Trying to answer your specific questions, we don't know who is taking whom for a ride except that we don't intend to be the victim. It is possible that Hanoi is dealing somewhat at arm's length with Moscow because of the Peking problem. It is entirely possible that Kosygin is trying to sell you something and it would be habitual for him to try to persuade you that we are trying to sell you something. In this case, I have no doubt that he would like to get a tender morsel on Viet-Nam in the communiqué. What is perhaps more ominous is that Moscow may be playing a spoiling game in Hanoi because of their irritations with the present procedure.

Our inclination would be to play our hand out on the present line to see where we get. If that gets nowhere and Moscow is ready to play the next chapter, we won't object if they smirk a bit and say "we told you so." I do hope that you can keep your position as co-chairman intact when it comes to the communiqué because there will be a lot of people engaged in defending South Viet-Nam who need to have confidence that at least one of the co-chairmen is playing it straight.

246. Message from Wilson to Johnson, 24 January 1968[20]

I was most grateful for your very prompt reply[21] to my message last night from Moscow. It arrived just in time to arm me for what proved a classic Kremlin battle over the passage on Vietnam in the communiqué.[22]

I will try to let you have, before our own meeting next month, some considered thoughts about the Moscow trip and especially about the attitude

---

[20] LBJ Library, NSF, Head of State Correspondence File, Box 10, United Kingdom, Prime Minister Wilson Correspondence, Volume 7, no. 59a.
[21] See 245.
[22] A copy of the communiqué can be found in LBJ Library, National Security File, Head of State Correspondence: United Kingdom: Prime Minister Wilson Correspondence, Volume 7, no. 59b.

on Vietnam. But meanwhile I want you to have straight away the background to what we managed to agree in the communiqué (which will of course be available to you). After our officials had battled for several hours yesterday, Kosygin and I argued about it for nearly three hours this morning and early afternoon.

The significance lies in what he was determined if he could to get in, and in the passages we wanted which he was equally resolved to keep out. This text was of course for public consumption so I do not suggest that one need draw too firm conclusions about his real attitude to your current attempts. But all the same I did not find it—or the subsequent private talks I had with him at our very delayed lunch—entirely encouraging. Briefly he (and a platoon of ministers and officials, including Poliansky and Gromyko at his most rigid) fought with total intransigence for a formula which would have had us denounce outside (i.e. American) interference and declare that any settlement should be based on the right of the local peoples to solve their internal affairs without it. They also refused to consider including a good passage we had drafted, trying to tie them as well as us to support for your current efforts, in the light both of San Antonio[23] and of Trinh.[24] I made it clear that there was nothing doing on interference and that we were not going to base ourselves on Soviet double talk, and in the end we agreed to drop both the contentious passages.

On the other hand I got a good reference to the Geneva agreements and the co-chairmanship. I was also determined despite Kosygin's strong opposition to commit him to acting with us in support of a negotiated political settlement, and, in return for securing this, we finally found a form of words which he wearily conceded (against Gromyko's more or less vertical eyebrows) which, after the reaffirmation of the Geneva principles, says that such a settlement must respect the rights of the locals to manage their own affairs.

These are just some hasty first impressions. As I say, I shall want to reflect more carefully on the talks as a whole before I try to give you a considered view.

247. Message from Wilson to Johnson, 29 January 1968[25]

I promised you some further thoughts about my Moscow trip.[26] I shall in fact want to think about it pretty carefully over the next 10 days, so as to discuss

---

[23] See 245, footnote 19.
[24] See 244, footnote 15.
[25] LBJ Library, NSF, Head of State Correspondence File, Box 10, United Kingdom, Prime Minister Wilson Correspondence, Volume 7, no. 56a.
[26] See 246.

it with you personally when we meet, as part of the background to our wider discussions. But meanwhile the following are just a few further reflections to those I sent to you on the evening of my return.

The main exchanges of course were with Kosygin. You will already have had an account of my first long talk with him on the afternoon of my arrival and you also know about our full-blown exchange in competition with the toreadors.[27] As you will have seen, my main job was to try to convince him of the sincerity of your position as set out at San Antonio[28] and in the State of the Union message.[29] I am afraid that Dobrynin had not succeeded in conveying the point that Averell Harriman had made so clearly to him—namely that you were not insisting on knowing the outcome of any eventual negotiations, before agreeing to halt the bombing (which would of course have been a nonsensical position): but that what you needed was to be assured that, if the bombing stopped, not only prompt but meaningful talks would follow and that North Vietnam would not take any unfair military advantage of the pause. I made this point clear beyond possibility of doubt separately to Kosygin, to Brezhnev and to Podgorny. And I think I got it across.

I was interested to find that Kosygin was throughout much more rigid during the formal meetings when he had Polyansky at his elbow than when we were on our own, in the car, at meals or at the opera. Of course, this is partly because, when he is speaking for the record, he sticks more closely to the official line. But there is a baleful quality to Polyansky's glance, and a certain brash impertinence of his occasional interventions which made me feel (rightly or wrongly) that Kosygin was uneasily aware that little brother was keeping a close eye. Gromyko was his usual sardonic self and, though he said little, what he said, particularly at the drafting session, was hard line stuff.

But, on thinking it over, I feel that my talk with Brezhnev was—perhaps not surprisingly—the most revealing about basic Soviet thinking on Vietnam. I need not go into the details—Pat Dean will be giving your people an account of what was said. On the personal plane, he was much more relaxed, friendly and quiet in tone than when I last saw him two years ago, when he did his best

---

[27] See 244.

[28] See 245, footnote 19.

[29] In the course of his State of the Union message on 17 January 1968, Johnson had remarked: 'Our goal is peace—and peace at the earliest possible moment … . We believe that any talks should follow the San Antonio formula that I stated last September, which said: The bombing would stop immediately if talks would take place promptly and with reasonable hopes that they would be productive. And the other side must not take advantage of our restraint as they have in the past. This Nation simply cannot accept anything less without jeopardizing the lives of our men and of our allies' (*Public Papers of the Presidents of the United States: Lyndon B. Johnson, 1968–69: Book I* (Washington, DC: United States Government Printing Office, 1970), p. 25).

to put me through the wringer. This time we had a perfectly normal exchange and I think I made some impact on him in terms of San Antonio. But it also confirmed my more general impression of a kind of schizophrenia in Moscow about Vietnam.

I cannot help feeling that their real dilemma is how to strike a satisfactory balance in their own minds between, on the one hand, the requirements of their global relationship with yourselves and their determination not to get involved in a conflict with you: and, on the other hand, a blend of gut-reaction against (as they would see it) any attempt by the capitalist world to eliminate a socialist state and of plain fear that any open let up on their part will weaken their effort to retain leadership of the world communist movement. Brezhnev could never admit that there was any contradiction between his saying at two points in the same conversation that all that was needed to stop the war was for your shameful aggression to end: and, at the same time and knowing perfectly well what our position was, his contention that Britain and the Soviet Union should singly and jointly do everything they could to help end the war. We saw the same process of self-contradiction in evidence throughout the appallingly long argument over the Vietnam section of the communiqué. But, as you know, they finally conceded not only a reference to the co-chairmanship, but also, though with infinitely greater difficulty, the phrase about the two sides having the firm intention to take singly or jointly all actions within their power to achieve a political settlement.

On balance I was not discouraged by my exchanges. Let us leave it at that until we meet. In any case, you have other things on your mind at present. I know how deeply concerned and troubled you must be: and send you my warm and sympathetic wishes.

248. Message from Wilson to Johnson, 9 February 1968[30]

I am writing to confirm what I told you this morning, mainly that Her Majesty's Government have decided to make a substantial contribution to releave [sic] the distress of the civilian population in South Vietnam. We believe that the best way of doing this will be to step up urgently the strength and deployment of the British Medical Team already working in Saigon. Accordingly the Government are despatching one of their senior medical advisers immediately to Saigon to examine, with the British Medical personnel already there and with others concerned, how best this extra effort can be applied and to report urgently.

---

[30] LBJ Library, NSF, Head of State Correspondence File, Box 10, United Kingdom, Prime Minister Wilson Correspondence, Volume 7, no. 55a.

You might also like to know that, in addition to this Governmental effort in Britain, non-Governmental societies are also responding urgently to the needs of this situation. In particular the Red Cross and associated societies are launching a Nation-wide appeal tonight on television and I am confident that the people of Britain will respond generously to it.

249. Message from Message from Johnson to Wilson, 10 February 1968[31]

The following are extracts from the memorandum that we discussed earlier today:

"You may give the following message:

"The United States is willing to stop the aerial and naval bombardment of North Vietnam if this will lead promptly to productive discussions between representatives of the US and the DRV looking toward a resolution of the issues between them.

"The United States is prepared to negotiate either openly or secretly. It would seem, however, that a total cessation of the bombing is inconsistent with keeping secret the fact that negotiations are taking place. Accordingly, the DRV may prefer to consider the alternative of a cutback in the magnitude or scope of the bombing while secret negotiations are in progress.

"We would assume that, while discussions proceed either with public knowledge or secretly, the DRV would not take advantage of the bombing cessation or limitation. Any such move on their part would obviously be inconsistent with the movement toward resolution of the issues between the US and DRV which the negotiations are intended to achieve.

"The US is ready to have immediate private contact with the DRV to explore the above approach or any suggestions the DRV might wish to propose in the same direction."

250. Message from Wilson to Johnson, 10 February 1968[32]

This is to bring you briefly, but with heartfelt warmth and sincerity, my thanks and deep appreciation for the cordiality of your welcome and for the openhearted way in which, as always, you developed your thinking. My thoughts and wishes go out to you for the difficult days that lie ahead. Many

---

[31] LBJ Library, NSF, Head of State Correspondence File, Box 10, United Kingdom, Prime Minister Wilson Correspondence, Volume 7, no. 53.

[32] LBJ Library, NSF, Head of State Correspondence File, Box 10, United Kingdom, Prime Minister Wilson Correspondence, Volume 7, no. 51a.

thanks again and warmest regards to Mrs. Johnson and yourself. I shall be acting in London on suggestions you made at our short final talk yesterday,[33] and will be in touch with you further about it.

Harold

251. Message from Wilson to Johnson, 13 February 1968[34]

George Brown and I have spent a pretty disheartening two and half hours today with U Thant. George took him first for three-quarters of an hour at the Foreign Office and then brought him round here for a very small working lunch. As George arrived he said to me, 'This man is wet, repeat wet.' He was. Pat Dean can give your people the details of our exchanges. In this message I want to give you our personal impressions: and the line I felt obliged to take with him. Briefly, he claims to have put a number of questions in Delhi to the new DRV Consul General, deriving from the account of your position allegedly given to him by Arthur Goldberg (between ourselves we got the impression either that this was a slightly out-of-date briefing or that he had not fully taken aboard whatever Goldberg had said to him). The Hanoi man was naturally unable to answer his questions and promised him a reply either in Moscow or subsequently. The answers have now turned up in Paris, as you will see from a later paragraph in this message. But what thoroughly disturbed us both was the pathetically weak-kneed and biased posture of U Thant. The Russians have clearly put him through the wringer in Moscow. He is still quivering gently from the after-effects of his interview with Brezhnev. He told me Brezhnev had told spoken to him in such violent terms about yourself and the whole American position that he hesitated to dictate it to his secretary—I asked 'Woman or man?' and he said 'Man.' I told him that this was nothing less than he should expect from Brezhnev. My own first interview with the latter two years ago had been very similar: even on my

---

[33] Johnson had asked Wilson to impress upon the Russians with respect to Vietnam that 'the Americans were dug in and determined, and were going to see this thing through' (Harold Wilson, *The Labour Government, 1964–1970: A Personal Record* (London: Wiedenfeld and Nicolson, 1971), p. 502). With reference to the USS *Pueblo* which had been seized by North Korea, he also asked the British premier to remind the Russians of their 'interest in seeing this issue peacefully settled' and to urge them to 'use their influence with North Korea to prevent it from getting out of hand' (ibid.). Ambassador Dean subsequently informed Johnson that Wilson had sent messages to Kosygin on Vietnam and the *Pubelo* on the lines agreed in Washington (Letter from Dean to Johnson, 15 February 1968, LBJ Library, NSF, Head of State Correspondence File, Box 10, United Kingdom: Prime Minister Wilson correspondence, Volume 7, no. 47a.).

[34] LBJ Library, NSF, Head of State Correspondence File, Box 10, United Kingdom, Prime Minister Wilson Correspondence, Volume 7, no. 49b.

latest visit, as you know, we had had a tough exchange. But I had taken a good deal of the steam out of it by telling Brezhnev at the outset that I saw no point in us both simply re-stating our known positions. If he had taken the same line he might have fared better. At all events, the upshot of this is that, even before he receives Hanoi's answers to his questions and despite his evident desire to help, Thant is again ruling himself out as an interlocutor by the total one-sidedness of his approach. We had a long theological exposition from him at lunch of Hanoi's view that, because the North Vietnamese were not bombing the United States, thereby balancing your bombing of North Vietnam, it was perfectly reasonable that they should expect you to stop the bombing unconditionally without the slightest hint from Hanoi that there would not immediately be a further military build-up in the South. We then had some pretty sick-making criticism of the last South Vietnamese elections because, for reasons beyond his understanding, Communists and neutralists (to say nothing of Big Minh[35]) had been forbidden to stand. At this point I thought it desirable to have a reasonably controlled burst of temper. And I put, in terms more forceful than I have ever before used with him, three main points. First, that, while we were all sitting around a well loaded table, innocent people were dying daily: and that the task of all of us who wished to work for peace was not to indulge in public and one-sided appeals for an unconditional end to the bombing (the position which he had just said he would feel obliged to take) but to pursue discreetly, objectively and in private all possible ways of narrowing the gap between the two sides. Secondly, that I was unaware that the Conservatives, Liberals or Democratic Socialists had ever been permitted to stand for election in North Vietnam, or in other communist countries, and that if he adopted double standards of the kind he had implied he was destroying his own credibility either as a mediator or a world statesman. Finally, if it were correct, as he had claimed, that Ho Chi Minh really wanted to be independent of Peking, but that every day the war continued increased his dependence, the sooner all concerned got down from the pulpit and around the negotiating table the better. Moreover, if he really wished to play a helpful part in fruitful secret exchanges—and without such exchanges one could hardly see the way forward at all—it was thoroughly counter-productive to emerge from secrecy at intervals to make ex cathedra statements setting out of a view point on which his mind was already made up before he had begun secret talks. He did not like any of this, but I hope he took the point. As I said, he now has an answer to his questions awaiting him with the North Vietnamese representative in Paris. But you will be interested to know how we learned of this. Harold Davies, my Parliamentary Private Secretary, who, as you will remember, carried out an exploratory mission to Hanoi for me in 1965 and has many Vietnamese

---

[35] Duong Van Minh, popularly known as 'Big Minh,' was a Vietnamese general and politician who served briefly as President of the Republic of Vietnam, 1963–64.

contacts, was telephoned early this morning by one of the North Vietnamese 'journalists' in London, who have kept in touch with him from time to time to ask where they could find U Thant to let him know that an answer to his questions was available if he cared to go to Paris and collect it. Since U Thant's address in London was public knowledge, we must conclude that Hanoi were concerned to keep us in the picture on this exchange, and I find this mildly encouraging. We of course put them in touch with Thant at once, and offered to put a plane at his disposal to fly him to Paris this afternoon. He had in the end decided to stay here overnight and fly to Paris tomorrow morning to see the DRV man before going to New York. We will do our best to de-brief him in Paris or New York. For our part, we are considering how far we might try discreetly to pump the North Vietnamese in London since they are clearly, to some extent at least, in the know.

Meanwhile, I now intend to follow up with Kosygin as you suggested. I am sure that the best way of doing this is, at least at this stage, to discount U Thant completely—the Russians have given him the works and it would only be counter-productive to play their game—and to address Kosygin along the lines you and I agreed. I will let you know the outcome.

252. Message from Johnson to Wilson, 15 February 1968[36]

Lady Bird and I want to say again how much we appreciated the gifts which you and Mary presented during your recent visit.

The marvellous prints, together with the beautifully etched glasses and fascinating books on famous British houses and gardens, will be such pleasant reminders of your thoughtfulness and friendship.

With our warmest good wishes,
Sincerely,
    Lyndon B. Johnson

---

[36] Bodleian Library, Oxford, Wilson Papers, Ms. Wilson c. 1586, folio 30.

253. Message from Wilson to Johnson, 1 March 1968[37]

It was very kind of you to write about the presents.[38]

Mary and I got back last week after a most enjoyable visit to Boston with our son at M.I.T. She and I would like Lady Bird and yourself to know again how much we appreciated all the kindness you both showed to us during our stay and how grateful we are for the splendid presents you gave us.

The golf clubs, in particular, are doing wonders for my game.[39] It was truly thoughtful of you to find such a particularly welcome reminder of our meeting.

Mary joins me in sending our warmest regards to Lady Bird and yourself.

254. Message from Wilson to Johnson, 14 March 1968[40]

I have just heard the import of the talks between the heads of our two central banks up to the point when Martin was seeing you. I fully recognise the need for you to take urgent action almost certainly tonight, not only in your interests but in ours and indeed of the world. What is important is that the action taken must be one which holds our two nations together.

We must both realise that we may tonight have reached the situation you foresaw when you showed me, in the White House last month, the short document you had received, envisaging a remorseless development of events which could land us back in 1931. At that time you thought it might come through the weakness of sterling, in fact it has come through the scramble for gold.[41]

---

[37] LBJ Library, NSF, Head of State Correspondence File, Box 10, United Kingdom, Prime Minister Wilson Correspondence, Volume 7, no. 45a.

[38] See 252.

[39] Ambassador Bruce recorded that 'The President gave the PM a luxurious set of golf clubs. We had done research for this present at the Embassy, being instructed to find out what might be appropriate in the way of shaft lengths, and color of bag' (John W. Young and Raj Roy (eds), *Ambassador to Sixties London: The Diaries of David Bruce, 1961–1969* (Dordrecht: Republic of Letters, 2009), p. 359).

[40] LBJ Library, NSF, Head of State Correspondence File, Box 10, United Kingdom, Prime Minister Wilson Correspondence, Volume 7, no. 43.

[41] The decision of holders of sterling balances to diversify into gold created in March 1968 potentially the most severe test for sterling in the post-war period with repercussions for the US financial system as it struggled to maintain the principle established at Bretton Woods in 1944 that the US would exchange gold for dollars at $35 an ounce (see Arran Hamilton, 'Beyond the sterling devaluation: The gold crisis of March 1968,' *Contemporary European History*, 17, 1 (2008): 73–95; Robert M. Collins, 'The Economic Crisis of 1968 and the Waning of the "American Century"', *American Historical Review*, 101, 2 (1996),

Of the various choices before you, there may be one or two alternative schemes which could temporarily relieve your situation, but at the almost certain cost of catastrophic damage to the pound. If this were to happen, the dollar would be at risk. The decision therefore is vital to us both.

If in the interests of urgency and speed you take a decision which puts us in immediate risk it is vital that we are covered by you during the days immediately ahead. Otherwise both currencies will go.

Alternatively we would have to take urgent action to protect ourselves which could only have the effect of dumping the whole speculative burden back on the dollar. I hope we can keep close together tonight.

255. Message from Johnson to Wilson, 15 March 1968[42]

Dear Harold:
Joe Fowler has been in touch with Roy Jenkins since seeing me and Bill Martin has talked to Leslie O'Brien. By now, you will know how we propose to proceed.

I understand there may be a special immediate jeopardy to sterling. That is a matter of concern not only for you and me but also for the countries associated with us in the gold pool. It is right for the bankers meeting this weekend in Washington to consider how they can overcome that danger. I gather our central banks have made some swap arrangements for Friday.

My people are preparing ideas, not only on how to overcome the short-term risks, but also how we use our present decisions to move towards a more sensible way of handling international money. I should say two things here. First, it is essential that Britain stay in this game: none of us should make any move that could jeopardize the meeting this weekend. Second, you will understand it if I say that in any future arrangements a change in the official price of gold would be unacceptable to me.

You are right to say that we must act in a way which holds our two nations together,[43] but as in so many other matters that require loyalty to principles which will engage around us a large group of friends.

396–422; Scott Newton, 'Sterling, Bretton Woods, and Social Democracy, 1968–1970', *Diplomacy and Statecraft*, 24, 3 (2013), 439–40).

[42] LBJ Library, NSF, Head of State Correspondence File, Box 10, United Kingdom, Prime Minister Wilson Correspondence, Volume 7, no. 41.

[43] See 254.

256. Message from Wilson to Johnson, 17 March 1968[44]

As you will guess, I have been personally following every move in the discussion in Washington this weekend and I share what I know will be your satisfaction that we have all been able to reach an agreed solution.[45] As you know, from the outset the British delegation joined with yours in rejecting any solution based on a change in the price of gold. We support you completely in this matter, and this has never been in doubt.

I believe that the agreement announced tonight is the best that could be achieved in present circumstances. We must hope that it will carry sufficient conviction in the world financial arena to stop the nonsense which has been going on in these past weeks. It is impossible to be certain, because we are dealing with a degree of irrationality which I have today described as Gadarene Dementia. In addition there have been the signs of a hidden hand in operation against the dollar and the pound—and not all that hidden either.[46]

In a rational world this clear evidence of determination should be decisive. But we must, even at this stage, reckon with the possibility that the irrational elements with which we have to deal may take charge. If this is so, the attack will switch more directly from the gold markets to the foreign exchange markets and will be directed against the two reserve currencies. Our continental colleagues have responded well to the dangers which we all face and I welcome the special consideration given to the position of sterling. Sterling has been, and still is, in

---

[44] LBJ Library, NSF, Head of State Correspondence File, Box 10, United Kingdom, Prime Minister Wilson Correspondence, Volume 7, no. 39.

[45] The Governors of the Central Banks of Belgium, Germany, Italy, the Netherlands, Switzerland, the UK and the US met in Washington on 16 and 17 March 1968 to examine the operations of the gold pool, to which they were all contributors. The resulting communiqué stated: 'The Governors agreed to cooperate fully to maintain the existing parities as well as orderly conditions in their exchange markets in accordance with their obligations under the Articles of Agreement of the International Monetary Fund. The Governors believe that henceforth officially-held gold should be used only to effect transfers among monetary authorities and, therefore, they decided no longer to supply gold to the London gold market or any other gold market. Moreover, as the existing stock of monetary gold is sufficient in view of the prospective establishment of the facility for Special Drawing Rights, they no longer feel it necessary to buy gold from the market. Finally, they agreed that henceforth they will not sell gold to monetary authorities to replace gold sold in private markets. The Governors agreed to cooperate even more closely than in the past to minimize flows of funds contributing to instability in the exchange markets, and to offset as necessary any such flows that may arise. In view of the importance of the pound sterling in the international monetary system, the Governors have agreed to provide further facilities which will bring the total of credits immediately available to the U.K. authorities (including the IMF standby) to $4 billion' (*The Department of State Bulletin*, Vol. LVIII, No. 1502, 8 April 1968).

[46] Wilson is referring to President de Gaulle.

the front line, but in a very real sense we all stand together. This stood out from the message you sent me on Thursday night.[47]

That was in response to the message[48] in which I said that, if we had to protect ourselves, we should be forced to take action which could have a grave effect on all other currencies. Since I sent you my Thursday message, this has been reiterated by my colleagues and our determination is absolute.

Let us hope that what is happening in Washington means that the attack will now spend itself. But if it does not, we must urgently consult together to agree what further collective action can be taken in order to avert the danger that we may be driven apart. Should we reach this point, we shall not propose a change in the gold price, but there are other policies that might have to be urgently considered between us. It is too early to canvass the various arguments, though we should prefer an arrangement providing for an embargo on the buying and selling of gold to anything which gave the enemy the prize for which they are contending, namely an increase in the gold price. We must keep in close touch if necessary on a day-to-day basis this week, though again, I hope that what has been achieved in response to your lead on Thursday night may exorcise once and for all the danger we have been facing together.

257. Message from Johnson to Wilson, 30 March 1968[49]

As you know, we have been giving the most careful thought to the Vietnam situation and to our next moves. I have reached the conclusion that we must prepare to take certain very limited additional military actions involving the sending of an additional 13,500 forces to Vietnam over the summer. These would be support forces designed to round out combat elements that we sent in February after the Tet offensive began.[50]

At the same time, in light of the depleted condition of our strategic reserve for world-wide use, I have become convinced that we must replenish that reserve—for all purposes—by calling up additional reserves amounting to 45,500 men.

I expect to announce these measures on Sunday night, or Monday including with them a lengthy discussion of the vital importance of increased effectiveness by the South Vietnamese as our first priority, and making clear once again that

---

[47] See 255.
[48] See 254.
[49] LBJ Library, NSF, Head of State Correspondence File, Box 10, United Kingdom, Prime Minister Wilson Correspondence, Volume 7, no. 37.
[50] Launched at the end of January 1968, the Tet offensive saw communist forces attacking every major city and military base in South Vietnam.

our military objective is solely to help provide a shield behind which the South Vietnamese can develop.

Yet, in deciding on these actions, it has become totally clear to me that I should not take them unless at the same time I announce a really clear move toward peace. Accordingly, I expect to announce at the very forefront of my speech that we are cutting back the bombing of the North to the area roughly south of the 26th parallel. This would leave out Hanoi and Haiphong, and indeed all the major populated areas in North Vietnam.

I shall announce this action without specifying what Hanoi should do in response, and without time limit. At the same time, I shall say that Hanoi's actions could offer a basis for our making the reasonable assumption stated in the San Antonio formula[51]—that they would not take advantage of the situation if we stopped the bombing altogether. I shall say that we would be prepared for any response, and would specifically hold Governor Harriman and Ambassador Thompson instantly ready for discussions with Hanoi in any quarter.

I would wish you to know of these actions in any case. But I am particularly anxious to have your judgment on additional language—now before me—which would call upon the United Kingdom and the Soviet Union, 'as co-chairmen of the Geneva Conference and as Permanent Members of the Security Council,'—to exert their influence so that movement toward peace may result from this act of de-escalation on our part.

I do not need to say that we have never had the slightest doubt that you and your government would do all in your power in any event. The purpose of the passage is to put the pressure on the Soviets—where it rightly belongs in the light of their whole responsibility and particularly their major supply contribution to Hanoi's current offensive. In the description of the two nations, the Geneva aspect is of course paramount; at the same time, reference to the Security Council membership would have a useful effect here, even though we fully recognise that Hanoi's total rejection of UN competence—(plus the present composition of the Security Council) make it most unlikely that the Council as such can act.

I now plan to make the whole of this announcement on Sunday or Monday night.[52] I hope that it will meet your full approval, and that you might be prepared to make a responsible statement promptly thereafter. I do not know how Soviets will handle this, but we will keep you very closely posted and may have further suggestions.

I count on you to hold this absolutely tight until announcement is made.

---

[51] See 245, footnote 19.

[52] See *Public Papers of the Presidents of the United States: Lyndon B. Johnson, 1968–69: Book I*, pp. 469–76. Johnson also famously announced that 'I shall not seek, and I will not accept, the nomination of my party for another term as your President'.

258. Message from Wilson to Johnson, 30 March 1968[53]

I was very glad and encouraged to get your message.[54] Of course we shall do all we can to help without delay. I agree at once to make a prompt response in support of this initiative.

We are scratching our heads hard about how we can build on what you are announcing, particularly in the Russian context you mention. Michael Stewart and I are meeting urgently on Sunday morning to go into this more fully and I shall let you know in good time tomorrow our ideas about this, and my considered view on the wording on which you have asked my judgment.

259. Message from Wilson to Johnson, 31 March 1968[55]

Before sending you, in my immediately following message,[56] our considered assessment of what should now be done following you [sic] statement tonight[57] I should like to give you my personal assessment of the value of your initiative.

I wholeheartedly indorse [sic] your proposals and am content with the wording which you suggest for the reference to the Geneva co-chairmen, etc.[58] I believe that what you propose is a wise and generous move, which ought to convince any reasonable person that the United States is anxious for peace on a just basis. Moreover, I see the importance of your initiative as affecting public opinion in both our countries. From the point of view of our common objective of achieving an honourable peace in Vietnam the political reaction in the

---

[53] LBJ Library, NSF, Head of State Correspondence File, Box 10, United Kingdom, Prime Minister Wilson Correspondence, Volume 7, no. 35.

[54] See 257.

[55] LBJ Library, NSF, Head of State Correspondence File, Box 10, United Kingdom, Prime Minister Wilson Correspondence, Volume 7, no. 33a.

[56] See 260.

[57] In his address to the nation, Johnson announced that 'Tonight, I have ordered our aircraft and our naval vessels to make no attacks on North Vietnam, except in the area north of the demilitarized zone where the continuing enemy buildup directly threatens allied forward positions and where the movements of their troops and supplies are clearly related to that threat. The area in which we are stopping our attacks includes almost 90 percent of North Vietnam's population, and most of its territory. Thus there will be no attacks around the principal populated areas, or in the food-producing areas of North Vietnam' (*Public Papers of the Presidents of the United States: Lyndon B. Johnson, 1968–69: Book I*, p. 470).

[58] Johnson stated: 'And tonight, I call upon the United Kingdom and I call upon the Soviet Union—as cochairmen of the Geneva Conferences, and as permanent members of the United Nations Security Council—to do all they can to move from the unilateral act of deescalation that I have just announced toward genuine peace in Southeast Asia' (ibid.).

United States is clearly more important than the reaction in Britain. It is not for me to interpret what you are doing in terms of the internal political situation in America, though I can well understand it. What I want you to know also is that, while this must be your responsibility I believe that from the point of view of a peaceful settlement it is of the first importance that the whole world, but particularly Hanoi, must be clear that we are carrying public opinion with us both in your country and to a lesser extent in ours.

We have, of course, to recognise that there are some who are wilfully hostile and will not be convinced that your offer is genuine. And I must confess that I doubt whether Hanoi will in fact respond to it. There are too many signs that they are playing American politics. They are counting on a great peace movement developing and a loss of determination by the American people. To the extent that they think this they will of course be more intransigent and less likely to respond to any initiative however reasonable, however generous. Nevertheless, even if the only result of your current initiative is to bring home to Western public opinion generally that you have done everything in your power to get this issue transferred from the battle field to the conference chamber, this will be important not only in terms of our Western politics but, more important in bringing home to Hanoi the firm resolve of all of us, a resolve which your initiative could help to consolidate in terms of popular support.

I agree with you that it is of great importance to try and get some movement out of the Soviet government. This is relevant, as you say, both in the Geneva and in the Security Council context. We propose the make a speedy move towards the Russians. But, as you know, the Russians are cautious and difficult about this and, in the Hanoi context, not their own masters and we ought not, therefore to try to tie them to an exact framework of moves, particularly to meeting at Geneva within the ambit of the 1954 agreement. Neither of us underrates the difficulties of getting the Russians to move. But when I was in Moscow two months ago I was able to give effect in the communiqué to your hopes that we could get some agreement with the Russians on our joint responsibilities as Geneva co-chairman. Clearly we must now exploit this as far as we can, and in my following message I am suggesting how we might set about it in terms of the successive moves we should now take over the next 24 hours as regards both our public response and the approach to the Russians. Among other things it is very important to distinguish between Moscow's acceptance of the joint responsibility to which I think we can hold them and any suggestion that the Geneva agreement as the context for a conference provides the next step toward any settlement.

Naturally, before taking any final decisions about what we would propose successively to do in the 24 hours following your statement which I understand will be at 3am London time and 5 am Moscow time, we shall want to have your views on what we shall be proposing, and I shall be grateful for your early reactions.

I repeat, we welcome the initiative and we shall make clear both publicly and in our contact with the Russians, that it has our full support. Even if it leads to no immediate response I believe its value will be in convincing public opinion of Western sincerity in these matters and this of itself could have an effect over the months on Russia, even on Hanoi, and therefore on the achievement of peace.

260. Message from Wilson to Johnson, 31 March 1968[59]

This is my message about the practical steps to be taken following your statement tonight.

The action which we have in mind would follow a time table starting at 7am B.S.T. on Monday, April 1 which would be 1am Washington and 9am in Moscow. At that point I propose to issue from No. 10 a short statement warmly welcoming and supporting what you have said.

A little later—just sufficiently later to indicate that we have thought about your statement—I shall send a preliminary message to Kosygin which will be designed merely to make the point that we attach great importance to your statement and intend to follow it up with them as rapidly as possible.

Later in the day the Foreign Secretary will be answering questions in the House of Commons. He has 12 questions on Vietnam, and this will provide a convenient opportunity to reaffirm in Parliament that we welcome your statement and intend to give it our full support in whatever way we can. The Foreign Secretary will also say that we have already made contact with the Soviet government and that he intends to follow it up with the Soviet ambassador later in the afternoon. He will avoid going further at this stage, particularly as regards the mechanics and substance of subsequent more detailed discussions with the Soviet ambassador.

Thereafter the Foreign Secretary will see the Soviet ambassador probably about 5pm B.S.T. From this point onwards we shall have to play the thing by ear to some extent. Our inclination at the present is that Michael Stewart should ask Smirnovsky to convey to Moscow the suggestion that we should follow up the communiqué issued at the end of my visit to Moscow in January. As you will remember, this confirmed our intention to take singly or jointly all actions within our power to achieve the goal of a political settlement of the Vietnam conflict. There is also the oral message about personal contacts which Smirnovsky gave me when handing me Kosygin's reply to my last message on Vietnam. The

---

[59] LBJ Library, NSF, Head of State Correspondence File, Box 10, United Kingdom, Prime Minister Wilson Correspondence, Volume 7, no. 33b.

Foreign Secretary would suggest that, since he himself has only recently returned to this post, he would in any event have wished to renew personal contact with Gromyko in the near future, and what more suitable occasion could there be for doing so than your own statement?

It is here that the real difficulties may begin. Our ability to suggest possible times and places for such a meeting and still more to suggest a possible agenda for discussion will depend on what you and we think we can do in practical terms in the light of the first reactions of Moscow and Hanoi. I do not think that we can afford to be too optimistic about the outcome unless the proposition put to them is reasonably hard and definite and amounts to something which both Moscow and Hanoi feel that they cannot justifiably refuse in the light of their public statements. It is here that I am a little unclear about the crucial phrase in your message that Hanoi's actions could offer a basis for our making the reasonable assumption stated in the San Antonio formula[60]—that they would not take advantage of the situation if we stopped the bombing altogether.[61] Even if genuinely interested in your offer (and this can be no more than an assumption), Moscow and Hanoi are likely to say to themselves that they are still prepared to talk if you stop the bombing unconditionally and altogether: that they think they can see a hint in your statement that this could be achieved: but that they cannot understand what it is they have to do in order to bring this about. If we are to go into action with Moscow on your behalf we must have some answer to this question which will be in their minds. In other words what is the real nature of the proposition we are try to sell to Moscow?

In addition, we shall always have need to bear in mind that the word Geneva has two special meanings for the Russians. They have made it clear to me on a number of occasions—and have implied it publicly—that the Geneva co-chairmanship is for them a valid relationship carrying responsibility. But they have made it equally clear that they regard a conference under Geneva auspices as one of the later stages after the parties have agreed on negotiations, not a preliminary step. One reason for their reluctance about a Geneva Conference is the worry that the Chinese might press their claim to be there. But the main point is that they are not going to move, above all, in public, beyond what Hanoi wants at any moment.

---

[60] See 245, footnote 19.

[61] In his address to the nation of 31 March, Johnson declared: 'Tonight, I renew the offer I made last August—to stop the bombardment of North Vietnam. We ask that talks begin promptly, that they be serious talks on the substance of peace. We assume that during those talks Hanoi will not take advantage of our restraint' (*Public Papers of the Presidents of the United States: Lyndon B. Johnson, 1968–69: Book I*, p. 470).

261. Message from Johnson to Wilson, 1 April 1968[62]

I am heartened and grateful that you are prepared to seize with both hands on my initiative of tonight.

Your proposed schedule of action is constructive.

We shall be getting to you soon a response to the questions you raise in your last two paragraphs.[63]

You may wish to know that I have just finished briefing ambassador Dobrynin underlining the responsibility Moscow bears as co-chairman and as a major arms supplier to Hanoi.

262. Message from Johnson to Wilson, 2 April 1968[64]

As promised last night,[65] I would send our further thoughts on the specific question raised in your detailed message of yesterday[66] about the actions by Hanoi which could lead us stop the bombing entirely.

The relevant sentences in my speech of yesterday were: 'Even this limited bombing of the north could come to an early end—if our restraint is matched by restraint in Hanoi. But I cannot in conscience stop all bombing so long as to do so would immediately and directly endanger the lives of our men and our allies. Whether a complete halt becomes possible in the future will be determined by events.'

What you might tell Moscow is that the question of which party should take the first deescalatory step towards peace has now been answered by the unilateral and unconditional action of the U.S. The United States has stopped bombing the area which contains almost 90 percent of the population of North Vietnam, and is restricting its bombing to the military targets in the less populated southern portion of North Vietnam where such bombing is tactically necessary to protect the lives of U.S. and allied troops. The next move in trying to bring about peace talks and a reduction in the level of violence is now clearly up to Hanoi, and the world will be watching to see how Hanoi responds.

You might add that the USG will be examining Hanoi's military moves with greatest care in the period ahead, and will be looking for any indication that Hanoi too is willing to take steps to decrease the level of violence. Obviously we

---

[62] LBJ Library, NSF, Head of State Correspondence File, Box 10, United Kingdom, Prime Minister Wilson Correspondence, Volume 7, no. 29.

[63] See 260.

[64] LBJ Library, NSF, Head of State Correspondence File, Box 10, United Kingdom, Prime Minister Wilson Correspondence, Volume 7, no. 27.

[65] See 261.

[66] See 260.

would be concerned with any major new attacks or efforts to increase the already abnormally high levels of infiltration of men and supplies.

Obviously we will also be interested in any communication indicating Hanoi's thoughts about how to move towards peace, in particular any indication of what Hanoi's military actions would be if the US stopped all bombardment of North Vietnam.

You might also wish to indicate to Moscow that it is your personal belief that if Hanoi rejects this latest American initiative, the U.S. would be under heavy pressure to take additional military action.

I would be grateful to receive your reaction to my suggestions.

263. Message from Wilson to Johnson, 4 April 1968[67]

Thank you for your message[68] and useful guidance it contained.

The statement issued this afternoon by Hanoi[69] changes the situation. You will have seen the short statement we have issued publicly welcoming Hanoi's decision to talk: and I have been glad to see your own comments. This is a response which I am sure you are right to take up, despite the offensive verbiage in which it is wrapped.[70] Even though Hanoi continue to insist on the unconditional cessation of the bombing and all other war-like acts against the DRV they are at least now willing for the first time to meet and talk.

With this latest development it is not absolutely clear how we and the Russians can best help at present. Your people will have had a full report on Michael Stewart's talk with the Soviet ambassador when he passed a message to Gromyko suggesting an early meeting. We for our part stand ready, as always, to play our part, both as co-chairman and as a Permanent member of the Security Council, as you asked in your first message,[71] and, in short, to do anything we can to be of help.

---

[67] LBJ Library, NSF, Head of State Correspondence File, Box 10, United Kingdom, Prime Minister Wilson Correspondence, Volume 7, no. 25a.

[68] See 262.

[69] Wilson is referring to the North Vietnamese response on 3 April to Johnson's offer of peace talks. The DRV declared its 'readiness to appoint its representative to contact the U.S. representative with a view to determining with the American side the unconditional cessation of the U.S. bombing raids and all other acts of war against the Democratic Republic of Vietnam so that talks may start' (*FRUS, 1964–8*: Volume VI: *Vietnam, January–August 1968* (Washington, DC: United States Government Printing Office 2002), p. 510).

[70] Hanoi characterized Johnson's 31 March statement as a 'defeat and at the same time a shrewd trick' (ibid.).

[71] See 257.

I know you will tell me when you think the time has come when we can weigh in again to help you. Meanwhile you have our heartfelt good wishes in the very difficult and delicate discussions which certainly lie ahead.

264. Message from Wilson to Johnson, 6 June 1968[72]

I have heard with a sense of deep sadness of the death of Senator Robert Kennedy. This act of senseless violence comes as another tragic blow to a family which has already suffered so much. The people and government of Britain share with the people and government of the United States their feelings of horror and sorrow. Our people's heartfelt sympathy will go out to Senator Kennedy's widow and children, and to his parents, at this sad time.

265. Message from Wilson to Johnson, 20 August 1968[73]

The Soviet ambassador delivered an oral message to the Minister of State at the Foreign Office at 1.30am approximately GMT informing me personally that the government of Czechoslovakia had appealed to the Soviet Union [and] its allies for direct assistance including armed forces assistance. In view of this the Soviet government and the governments of their allies have decided to render all necessary assistance and accordingly Soviet military units had been instructed to enter Czechoslovak territory.

I assume you have received a similar message and would be grateful to know whether you intend to communicate direct with the government of the Soviet Union.

266. Message from Johnson to Wilson, 22 August 1968[74]

I am grateful for your quick message of Tuesday night.[75] Our only response thus far to Moscow's communication to us was given orally by Dean Rusk to Dobrynin. As you doubtless know, the details of what Dean said were outlined to minister Tomkins at about midnight.

---

[72] LBJ Library, NSF, Special Head of State Correspondence File, Box 56, United Kingdom [1 of 4], no. 38.
[73] LBJ Library, NSF, Head of State Correspondence File, Box 10, United Kingdom, Prime Minister Wilson Correspondence, Volume 7, no. 23a.
[74] LBJ Library, NSF, Head of State Correspondence File, Box 10, United Kingdom, Prime Minister Wilson Correspondence, Volume 7, no. 21.
[75] See 265.

We should continue to keep in close touch as the situation develops.

267. Message from Wilson to Johnson, 7 October 1968[76]

Your people will have told you of my plans for a further meeting with Ian Smith to see if we cannot at last thrash out together an honourable settlement of this tragic Rhodesian business. We shall not announce it until early tomorrow afternoon (our time) because, although my senior colleagues principally concerned are naturally at one with me in the enterprise, I have to seek the endorsement of the full Cabinet at our meeting tomorrow, the first that has been possible since our conference last week.

Assuming, as I hope and believe, that my colleagues endorse this action, I plan to meet Smith in Gibraltar on Wednesday afternoon, on board a warship and to allow as much time as may be needed during the next week or so to negotiate an agreement.

I need not trouble you with the detailed background to our position. Your people will know it. In this message I only want to say two things.

First I am determined that, if no settlement can be agreed, this will not be through lack of goodwill, patience or resolution on our side. This conflict has been a tragedy not only in the relationship between Britain and Rhodesia but also for the development of our Commonwealth ties and, more widely, for the international community as a whole. Its continuation not only threatens the future peace and prosperity of the Rhodesian Africans but also causes the danger of a wider and continuing conflict throughout southern Africa. I know what difficult problems it has raised for you and I have been most grateful for the support and understanding that you have so consistently displayed.

Secondly, if a settlement can be achieved, I am equally resolved that it shall not represent a sacrifice of the rights and interests of the peoples of Rhodesia—and especially the African peoples. We have made absolutely clear to Smith that for us certain points are not negotiable—and these points relate essentially to the protection of the rights of the African majority and to the need to ensure that substantial change of circumstances in Rhodesia which, as I have said repeatedly, will be essential before there can be any question of our going back to the Commonwealth to re-open our commitment on no independence before majority rule.

I will not pretend that I am optimistic. Long experience in dealing with this problem—and in dealing with Smith personally—has made me too wary for that. But recent developments in Rhodesia, the pressures of sanctions (and other

---

[76] LBJ Library, NSF, Head of State Correspondence File, Box 10, United Kingdom, Prime Minister Wilson Correspondence, Volume 7, no. 19b.

pressures too: I am sure for example that South Africa would like us to settle), coupled with the way Smith has handled some of his own right wing extremists have all created a situation in which, once again I am convinced that we should be wrong not to try. I am confident that I can count on your good wishes for our success: and this will be a source of encouragement to me throughout the difficult and delicate discussions that lie ahead.

268. Message from Wilson to Johnson, 1 November 1968[77]

You have taken a courageous step and one which the whole world will applaud.[78] We have watched with admiration your steadfast refusal to make the decision pressed upon you from so many quarters until there was a real possibility that it could contribute to progress. We all pray that what you have done will meet with the right response.

I am grateful for the way you have kept us so closely informed: and we have tried to help by damping down speculation here during the most crucial periods.

If there is any way you think we can help in the future I know you will tell us. But in the hard negotiations which lie ahead, I and my colleagues know that it is the United States which will have to play the hand. You will know how much all our thoughts and good wishes are with you.

269. Message from Wilson to Johnson, 18 November 1968[79]

I am sure we ought to act closely together in dealing with the present disturbances in the foreign exchange markets.[80] We understand that the French definitely intend to devalue, possibly within the next few hours, and that they may do so by as much as 15 percent unless the Germans can be persuaded to revalue at the same time. If the Germans were to revalue by (say) 5 percent, the French devaluation might only be 10 percent. I must warn you that a French devaluation, unless it

---

[77] LBJ Library, NSF, Head of State Correspondence File, Box 10, United Kingdom, Prime Minister Wilson Correspondence, Volume 7, no. 16.

[78] On 31 October, Johnson informed the American people that he had 'ordered that all air, naval, and artillery bombardment of North Vietnam cease as of 8a.m. Washington time, Friday morning' (*Public Papers of the Presidents of the United States: Lyndon B. Johnson, 1968–69: Book II* (Washington, DC: United States Government Printing Office, 1970), p. 1100).

[79] LBJ Library, NSF, Head of State Correspondence File, Box 10, United Kingdom, Prime Minister Wilson Correspondence, Volume 7, no. 12.

[80] The 'disturbance' stemmed from the weakness of the French economy by comparison with the German, and the consequent movement of funds from the franc to the mark.

were to be accompanied by a simultaneous German revaluation, might well make it impossible for us to continue to hold our rate and this situation could develop rapidly. This is because it would be believed that the position was unstable and that an early upwards movement in the German rate could not be avoided. We have already had heavy reserve losses through speculation on this account. No statement by the German authorities that revaluation has been rejected can prevent these losses being repeated, and once the French have devalued there is likely to be a further massive and insupportable move out of sterling into Deutschmarks. If further heavy speculation against sterling, and inevitably the dollar continued, then Roy Jenkins has told Joe Fowler of the serious decisions we should have to contemplate. I believe your people think great damage would also be done to the dollar. The chances of reestablishing stability in the world monetary system in the short term would then be slim indeed.

2. My understanding is that there is no chance of our being able to persuade the French not to devalue. They have had heavy losses, and are not prepared to accept any more.

It is therefore essential in all our interests that the Germans should be persuaded to revalue at the same time as the French devalue. The Bundesbank are in favour of an appreciation of at least 5 percent, but think German ministers will be resistant even to this. 5 percent would certainly help, though there is no doubt the D.M. is greatly undervalued and seven and a half or ten percent would be more realistic change.

3. Roy Jenkins and Joe Fowler discussed all these possibilities when the latter was in London, and I understand there is no difference between us on what should be done. In the week since they met things have developed at a dangerous rate and new decisions look like being taken—or possibly, in the case of Germany, not being taken—within the next few hours. I am therefore very glad to hear that Joe is on his way to Bonn, where no doubt he will do everything possible to persuade the Germans to accept their responsibilities. We shall be urging on them the importance of revaluing, of doing so at the same time as the French move, and of doing so by as much as possible.[81] The most powerful factor in helping the German ministers, who are meeting in Cabinet this afternoon, to take decisions without which international monetary chaos will be almost inevitable, would undoubtedly be your own personal intervention . I hope you will be able to make your own views known to the Germans as soon as possible,

---

[81] On 20 November, Ambassador Bruce recorded in his diary: 'The suggestion has been widely offered that the Germans revalue their mark. One London newspaper, with customary tactlessness about the Germans, stated "This is the only decent thing the Federal Republic can do." In other words, they are being asked to sacrifice a part of their own prosperity and stability to support the failing economies and finances of less well managed economies' (John W. Young and Raj Roy (eds), *Ambassador to Sixties London: The Diaries of David Bruce, 1961–1969* (Dordrecht: Republic of Letters, 2009), p. 418).

and that we can keep in the closest touch dealing with this latest problem together as we have so often in the past four years.

270. Message from Johnson to Wilson, 18 November 1968[82]

I have instructed Fowler in my name to make recommendations to Kiesinger urging multilateral and cooperative solutions for present situation. He has done so with great vigour, and will stay in Europe to lead effort to persuade Germans to revalue and to prevent large unilateral French devaluation. German position strongly against revaluation at this time, proposing instead reducing border taxes on imports and lessening some export rebates. We do not believe this approach would work, or contain French devaluation to reasonable level.

Our tentative approach would be to work for something like 10 percent German revaluation and 5 percent French devaluation, with small corresponding moves by Italy and the Netherlands. To confirm this approach, we are considering G-10 meeting in Europe with Schweitzer present as soon as possible. We assume you will wish to cooperate fully in this approach and will not wish to move in any way pending the outcome of these efforts.

271. Message from Wilson to Johnson, 19 November 1968[83]

Many thanks for your helpful response to my message of yesterday.[84] Roy Jenkins has heard from Fowler and we greatly welcome the vigorous effort you are making to persuade the Germans to act constructively.

2. We are fully in accord with the approach set out in your second paragraph. If the Germans respond to it satisfactorily, a high level meeting may not prove necessary. But if they do not, the speculative pressures upon us are such as to make it imperative that the meeting should be held not later than tomorrow, Wednesday, preferably in Bonn. We understand that this is also Fowler's view, but he will need all the backing you can give him. Roy Jenkins will attend the meeting in person.

3. We certainly wish to co-operate fully with you. But it is essential for these efforts to be brought to fruition very quickly indeed.

---

[82] LBJ Library, NSF, Head of State Correspondence File, Box 10, United Kingdom, Prime Minister Wilson Correspondence, Volume 7, no. 14.

[83] LBJ Library, NSF, Head of State Correspondence File, Box 10, United Kingdom, Prime Minister Wilson Correspondence, Volume 7, no. 10.

[84] See 269 and 270.

272. Message from Wilson to Johnson, 19 November 1968[85]

We have of course accepted the invitation to the meeting of the group of ten in Bonn tomorrow. But we see grave risks in this meeting now that the Germans have announced what is apparently a firm decision not to revalue the DM. If there is to be a satisfactory outcome in our opinion it is vital for all of us to concentrate on getting the Germans to do much more than they have so far indicated. The only satisfactory solution is a revaluation of the DM. We shall not achieve this unless we are prepared to use all the pressures open to your several departments, I repeat several departments, so that not only financial and economic pressures are invoked. I am myself seeing the German Ambassador in a few minutes' time, midnight our time. If we allow ourselves to be distanced from this objective by consideration of what is after all the second problem of the French, which however objectionable you and we can contain, we shall run grave risks. A conference built up as this has been must not be allowed to fail. If it does, not only will our situation in the United Kingdom be highly precarious but the whole international monetary structure including the dollar will be in danger.

A secondary but not unimportant question is the problem of closing the markets while the group of Ten Meeting takes place. The proposal that the New York market should be closed for dealings in sterling, French Francs and DMs only, seem dangerous to us. It would be infinitely preferable if you would ensure the closure of the market for dealings in all the currencies of the group of ten countries.

273. Message from Wilson to Johnson, 20 November 1968[86]

I have just seen the German Ambassador. Michael Stewart and Roy Jenkins were with me. We spoke to him in the sternest language about the inadequacy of the measures announced tonight by the German Government and expressed our strongly held view that the right answer would be a substantial revaluation of the Deutsche Mark. We said that if there were really no question of the German Government reconsidering their decision against revaluation, it seemed to us that the alternative measures they had announced would need to be strengthened at least threefold if they were to have the required effect, in terms of a correction in the underlying imbalance of payments and thus stemming the

---

[85] LBJ Library, NSF, Head of State Correspondence File, Box 10, United Kingdom, Prime Minister Wilson Correspondence, Volume 7, no. 7a.

[86] LBJ Library, NSF, Head of State Correspondence File, Box 10, United Kingdom, Prime Minister Wilson Correspondence, Volume 7, no. 5.

flow of speculation. I described the German decision of today as inadequate and irresponsible in free world terms; and said that we could not accept it as final. We pointed out the inevitability, if continuing doubt about the German position persisted, of an escalation in international speculation. And the Chancellor made it clear to him that if this happened we might well be unable to sustain our rate and have to float, with the gravest consequences not only for Britain but for the other major currencies.

We pointed out to the Ambassador that, in these circumstances, and despite our continuing conviction of the immense importance to us of the North Atlantic Alliance, we should be obliged, if events developed as we feared they might in view of the inadequacy of the present German measures, to reappraise our present contribution to the Alliance, though this was the last thing we should wish to do. We reminded the Ambassador of the reference in the latest N.A.T.O. communiqué to the relationship between the solidarity of the Alliance and cooperation between members in alleviating the burdens arising from balance of payments deficits resulting from defence expenditure: and said that, while we had no intention of deserting our duty, the issue, if the situation deteriorated on the lines we had foreshadowed, would not be what we or others might wish to do but what it would be possible for us to do.

We thus left the Ambassador in no possible doubt of the extreme gravity with which we viewed the inadequacy of the action proposed by the German Government: and I tell you this because you too will wish to be entirely clear about our position.

Blankenhorn was of course without instructions and had simply heard on the radio of his Government's intentions. But he was clearly shaken by the interview and undertook to report immediately by telephone to Brandt and Schiller and to ensure that Chancellor Kiesinger was also informed of what we had said.

In short, what we were concerned to make clear to the Germans was that failure to deal with the economic imbalance would have consequences for us all going far beyond the economic sphere, grave though the economic effects in themselves would be.

274. Message from Johnson to Wilson, 24 November 1968[87]

1. I concluded last night that it would be right for me to send a message to President de Gaulle as he faced this lonely and difficult moment. I thought the message might have some favourable effect on the program he announced to back his decision against devaluation and on the kind

---

[87] LBJ Library, NSF, Head of State Correspondence File, Box 11, United Kingdom, Prime Minister Wilson Correspondence, Volume 8, no. 1.

of cooperation that would be needed in the weeks and months ahead in any case.
2. We shall all shortly know what de Gaulle's program is. We have no knowledge of it before the event.
3. I know, also, that the decisions you had to take after the Bonn meeting were painful and difficult. We have all learned how hard it is to keep both domestic balance and an international environment which permits world trade to continue to expand and the monetary system from falling apart. Thus far we have been successful; and if we stay with it, I believe we can make it to the other side.
4. You know you can count on our help and support, as always.

275. Message from Wilson to Johnson, 25 November 1968[88]

Thank you for the message which you sent to me through David Bruce.[89]

I greatly welcomed your generous and timely message to President de Gaulle.[90] In the same spirit Roy Jenkins has made it clear in today's debate that we admire French courage in deciding not to devalue and that we wish them well.

We must hope now that the decisions reached will give us a period of greater calm in the money markets, though it will clearly be necessary to watch developments very carefully in the days ahead. I am grateful to you for the assurance of your continued help and support. I am sure that it remains as important as ever that you and we should keep in closest touch on this matter.

276. Message from Wilson to Johnson, 27 December 1968[91]

My warmest congratulations on the Apollo 8 mission. This voyage is an important contribution to the expansion of mankind's knowledge of the universe and, because we have been able to follow it on television, it has added a new dimension to our appreciation that this is indeed one world. Please convey

---

[88] LBJ Library, NSF, Head of State Correspondence File, Box 10, United Kingdom, Prime Minister Wilson Correspondence, Volume 7, no. 3a.

[89] See 274.

[90] On 24 November, Johnson told de Gaulle: 'I have read today of the decision you have taken. I know that the American people will wish me to tell you of the common hope that your course of action will be successful and that we are ready to cooperate in any way we can to achieve your objective consistent with our national purposes' (*The Department of State Bulletin*, Vol. LIX, No. 1535, 25 November 1968).

[91] LBJ Library, NSF, Special Head of State Correspondence File, Box 56, United Kingdom [1 of 4], no. 32a.

my personal congratulations to the crew of Apollo 8, whose great courage and skill we have all admired, and to all who have been associated with this historic achievement.

277. Message from Johnson to Wilson, 29 December 1968[92]

Dear Mr. Prime Minister:
Thank you for your message on Apollo 8.[93]

As we make the turn into the New Year, we have, I believe, reason for confidence that the clouds may be lifting a bit in Southeast Asia, the Middle East, and in the affairs of Western Europe.

It has been a year of some difficulty for both of us: but our continued ability to stay close and work together when the going gets tough has been a source of strength to our nations, to the West, and to the cause of peace and international cooperation.

I believe you know how much I have treasured our ability to communicate with candor and confidence over these years. No problem was so grave that its burden was not eased by a back-channel message from the Prime Minister.
You have my best wishes in the time ahead—for the British people and yourself.
Sincerely,
Lyndon B. Johnson

278. Message from Wilson to Johnson, 17 January 1969[94]

Dear Lyndon,
I was indeed grateful for the generosity and friendship expressed in your New Year message.[95] As you hand over to your successor, I want you to know how much confidence and strength I have derived from the exceptionally close and cordial relationship that you and I have enjoyed over the past four years and more. I have felt the warmth of your welcome on each of my six visits to Washington and the depth and frankness of our talks at those times have been of inestimable value to me, as I hope to you also.

Your departure from the White House after more than five years of dedicated service to your nation there, and indeed to our common cause of world peace and

---

[92] LBJ Library, NSF, Special Head of State Correspondence File, Box 56, United Kingdom [1 of 4], no. 30.
[93] See 276.
[94] LBJ Library, NSF, Special Head of State Correspondence File, Box 56, United Kingdom [1 of 4], no. 9b.
[95] See 277.

stability, will be viewed with sadness by all your many friends in this country. But you leave with accomplishments behind you of which you can be justly proud. I have greatly admired your determination at all times to ensure that, in spite of the difficulties, the United States should make her full and rightful contribution to freedom and prosperity throughout the world. I believe too that the hopes and designs you have presented to your people for a just society, for the solution of America's urban problems, and for the attainment of racial harmony and understanding—and particularly the successful passage of your wise legislation on this subject—all these will equally be remembered and treasured. I recall that when I first met you in the White House before I became Prime Minister I asked you if you regarded yourself above all as a follower and disciple of Roosevelt. The concept of the great society and your own personal contribution to it is truly in the great Roosevelt mood. In this spirit too was the grandure [sic] and scope of your last State of the Union message—and the fact that characteristically, you chose to deliver it in person.

Britain too has had to face many grave problems, both economic and political. It has been a constant source of encouragement to know that we could always count on your support and understanding. These past five years have been difficult times for us all. But I agree with you in feeling that, in the last few months, there has been a perceptible brightening of the international scene. Your own steadfastness and courage have greatly contributed to this.

In particular I share what I know will be your great satisfaction that the procedural log jam has now been broken in Paris and that substantive talks about Vietnam are to go ahead. Your part in laying the foundations for this will go down in history.

We for our part have also drawn hope from our latest meeting of Commonwealth heads of government. You will not expect an account of this here. But it is, of course, in the nature of things that the press account of our discussions could not be complete nor indeed give a really accurate impression of the real achievements of this meeting—and they were very real. Of course we had our differences, deep differences, continuing differences, over problems such as Rhodesia. But there was also a very wide measure of agreement going far beyond individual problems. I believe that no one should under-rate an association which will bring 24 busy heads of state and government not only to meet together in London but also—and here lies the true lesson—to agree on the value of the association and on their determination to keep it in being, in the interests of their own countries and of the world as a whole. I was also encouraged by the wisdom and statesmanship displayed by a number of our new colleagues. John Gorton of Australia, whom you know, struck me as an impressive figure. But it was not only from older Commonwealth countries that these qualities of leadership emerged. It was striking, during the relatively easy discussion of our long communiqué (which you will already have seen) to note the increasing sophistication and common-sense shown on such issues as Vietnam, China and Czechoslovakia by the prime ministers of small countries whose governments one might not, on past form, have expected to be as aware of the issues as they showed themselves to be. Here again, I think, is one of the great values of these Commonwealth meetings. Not only do they bring us all together. They educate and inform as well. I was personally much heartened by this latest meeting and I believe that you and your country can take heart from it too.

As you know, I would have greatly liked to have had a final meeting with you before you left office but, since this was not possible, may I now take this opportunity to wish you and all your family every possible future happiness? I would like to say, too, that I know that many will continue to turn to you in the days to come for the benefit of your wisdom and wide experience: and that, when the real history is written, you will be shown to have been one of the great innovators among United States Presidents and one whose contribution to the American people has been second to none.

With my warm and affectionate good wishes,
Yours
   Harold

279. Message from Johnson to Wilson, 18 January 1969[96]

Dear Mr. Prime Minister:
As I leave the White House, I again express my thanks to you and your colleagues for the cooperation, assistance, and understanding you have given me and my associates during my Presidency.

Our personal association has been a source of special gratification to me. We have achieved much together, and what we have not finished we have started in the right direction. The qualities of friendship and trust that have done so much to cement Anglo-American relations over the years will continue to keep our two countries close together in the future.

As the enclosed photographs of the recent lunar flight of Apollo VIII suggest, we live on a small and shrinking globe. In such a world there is little room and no rational place for the animosities between nations that have for so long frustrated mankind's search for universal peace. I know that both our countries will continue their efforts to secure world peace in freedom.

Despite my retirement from the Presidency, my interest in the United Kingdom's role and my friendship for its people will remain strong and undiminished, as will my dedication to the goals which both our countries share.

---

[96] LBJ Library, NSF, Special Head of State Correspondence File, Box 56, United Kingdom [1 of 4], no. 17.

280. Message from Johnson to Wilson, 19 January 1969[97]

Your warm and interesting message and report of the Commonwealth conference[98] was a fitting conclusion to our official exchanges. As I have said before, they—and our face-to-face talks—have been a source of strength and comfort to me in times which have not always been easy for either of us.

Over these years there has been no single joint enterprise for us to conduct as Roosevelt and Churchill had to conduct during the Second World War. There are places in the world where the policies of your country and mine threatened to diverge—as in Vietnam. We have had to deal—both of us—with a Western Europe frustrated by others from moving down the path of unity which both of us know is right. We have both been hampered by balance of payments problems in a world which has not yet created a kind of cooperative international monetary system which it needs. But through all this—and crises from the Middle East to Dominican Republic, from Czechoslovakia to Rhodesia—we have managed to understand one another, to help one another whenever it was possible, to make it as easy as possible for one another when circumstances did not permit complete accord.

And so I shall always treasure our connection and continue to believe that the special ties between Great Britain and the United States will survive and retain their value as we struggle to build the structure of stable peace.

I shall be looking for you in the days ahead—at the Ranch and on the podium at the University in Austin. In the meanwhile, you will know that I shall be cheering you on as you continue to bear the heavy burdens of responsibility.

281. Message from Wilson to Johnson, 4 February 1969[99]

Dear Lyndon,

I am writing to thank you for your generous message of January 18[100] and the fine photographs from the Apollo VIII flight which you enclosed.

Freedom for individuals and nations to think and act as conscience dictates is never easily achieved; once achieved it is a very special possession and must be continually defended. I believe that the cause of freedom is always best served when the Americans and Britons work closely together. The friendship for the United Kingdom which you have shown so consistently during your term

---

[97] LBJ Library, NSF, Special Head of State Correspondence File, Box 56, United Kingdom [1 of 4], no. 7.
[98] See 278.
[99] TNA, PREM 13/3006.
[100] See 279.

in office has therefore not only brought great satisfaction to me but has also made for a close and fruitful relationship between our two Governments. This friendship has made a vital contribution to the search for peace and stability in the world which, however peaceful it may have seemed to the distant watchers in Apollo VIII, is torn by dissension and distrust.

History will record your dedicated efforts in the cause of peace and understanding between peoples; and future students will recognise the great contribution you personally have made.

I will treasure the photographs you sent.
Yours,
Harold

282. Message from Johnson to Wilson, 12 February 1969[101]

Dear Harold,
As rancher no less than as President, I count it a rewarding day which brings a good letter from you.[102] Thank you so much for the fine message I just received.

I believe the work we did together to strengthen the bonds between our two Nations will long endure. I will always be proud of that joint effort, and of the firm personal friendship which united us. I will always be hopeful that our partnership advanced the cause of peace and progress in the world.
With warm regards.
Sincerely,
Lyndon Johnson

---

[101] TNA, PREM 13/3006.
[102] See 281.

Dramatis Personae

UNITED KINGDOM

Attlee, Lord
British Prime Minister, 1945–51

Bowden, Herbert
Secretary of State for Commonwealth Affairs, 1966–67

Brown, George
Foreign Secretary, 1966–68

Callaghan, James
Chancellor of the Exchequer, 1964–67

Caradon, Lord
Permanent UK Representative at the UN, 1964–70

Chalfont, Lord
Minister of State at the Foreign Office, 1964–70

Davies, Harold
Parliamentary Private Secretary to Harold Wilson, 1967–70

Dean, Sir Patrick
British Ambassador in Washington, 1965–69

Douglas-Home, Sir Alec
Foreign Secretary, 1960–63, 1970–74; Prime Minister, 1963–64

Eden, Anthony
Foreign Secretary 1951–55; Prime Minister, 1955–57

Garner, Sir Saville Joseph (Joe)
Permanent Under-Secretary, Commonwealth Relations Office, 1962–68

Healey, Denis
Secretary of State for Defence, 1964–70

Heath, Edward
Leader of the Opposition, 1965–70; Prime Minister, 1970–74

Hennings, John Dunn
British High Commission, Residual Staff, Salisbury, Rhodesia, 1966–68

Hogg, Quintin
Leader of the House of Lords, 1960–63; Lord President of the Council, 1960–64

Jenkins, Roy
Chancellor of the Exchequer, 1967–70

MacDonald, Malcolm
Governor-General, Kenya, 1964–65; British Special Representative in East and Central Africa, 1966–67

Macmillan, Harold
Prime Minister, 1957–63

Noel-Baker, Philip
Chairman, Foreign Affairs Group, Parliamentary Labour Party, 1964–70

O'Brien, Leslie
Governor of the Bank of England, 1966–73

Roll, Sir Eric
Economic Minister at the British Embassy and Head of the UK Treasury delegation in Washington, 1963–64; Permanent Secretary, Department of Economic Affairs, 1964–66

Stewart, Michael
Foreign Secretary, 1965–66, 1968–70; First Secretary of State, 1966–68

Thomson, George
Minister of State, Foreign Office, 1964–66, 1967

Tomkins, Edward
Minister, British Embassy, Washington, 1967–70

Trend, Sir Burke
Cabinet Secretary, 1963–73

Walker, Patrick Gordon
Foreign Secretary, 1964–65

Watson, (Noel) Duncan
Assistant Under-Secretary of State, Commonwealth Relations Office, 1964–67

Wilson, Harold
Prime Minister, 1964–70, 1974–76

Wright, (John) Oliver
Private Secretary to the Prime Minister, 1964–66

Wright, Rear-Admiral Noel
Entered Royal Navy, 1908; Fleet Supply Officer, Mediterranean and Levant 1942–43; Command Supply Officer Western Approaches, 1944–45

Zuckerman, Solly
Chief Scientific Adviser, HM Government, 1964–71

UNITED STATES

Ball, George
Under Secretary of State, 1961–66

Bator, Francis
Senior member, National Security Council staff, April 1964–September 1967; Deputy Special Assistant to the President for National Security Affairs, October 1965–September 1967

Bruce, David, K. E.
US Ambassador in London, 1961–69

Bundy, McGeorge
National Security Adviser, 1961–66

Bundy, William P.
Assistant Secretary of State for East Asian and Pacific Affairs, 1966–69

Cooper, Chester (Chet)
Special Assistant to Ambassador at Large W. Averell Harriman

Deming, Fred
US Under Secretary of the Treasury for Monetary Affairs

Dillon, Douglas
US Secretary of the Treasury, 1961–65

Eisenhower, Dwight D.
US President, 1953–61

Fowler, Henry H. ('Joe')
US Secretary of the Treasury, 1965–68

Freeman, Orville
US Secretary of Agriculture, 1961–69

Fulbright, J. William
Chairman of the Senate Foreign Relations Committee, 1959–74

Gilpatric, Roswell L.
US Deputy Secretary of Defense, 1961–64

Goldberg, Arthur J.
US Permanent Representative to the UN, 1965–68

Gordon, Kermit
Director of the United States Bureau of the Budget, 1962–65

Harriman, W. Averell
US Ambassador at Large, 1965–69

Johnson, Lyndon Baines
President, 1963–69

Jones, Howard P.
US Ambassador to Indonesia, 1958-65

Kaiser, Philip
Deputy Chief of Mission, US Embassy, London, 1964–69

Katzenbach, Nicholas
US Under Secretary of State, 1966–69

Kennedy, Robert
US Senator, New York, 1965–68

Mann, Thomas (Tom)
US Under-Secretary of State for Economic Affairs

Martin, William McChesney, Jr
Chairman of the United States Federal Reserve Bank, 1951–70

McCloy, John J.
Former High Commissioner for Germany and Representative to the trilateral offset negotiations

McNamara, Robert (Bob) S.
Secretary of Defense, 1961–68

Rogers, Bernard
Military Assistant and Executive Officer to the Chairman of the Joint Chiefs of Staff, 1962–66

Roosevelt, Franklin D.
US President, 1933–45

Rostow, Eugene (Gene)
Under-Secretary of State for Political Affairs, 1966–69

Rostow, Walt W.
Special Assistant to the President, 1966–69

Rusk, Dean
US Secretary of State, 1961–69

Stevens, John
Economics minister, US Embassy London

Stevenson, Adlai
Chief US representative to the UN, 1961–65

Thompson, Llewellyn E.
US Ambassador to the Soviet Union, 1967–69

Westmoreland, William C.
Commander, Military Assistance Command, Vietnam, 1964–68

Woods, George
President of the World Bank, 1963–68

OTHER COUNTRIES

Abubakar
See Balewa, Alhaji Abubakar Takawa

Ayub Khan, Mohammad
President of Pakistan, 1958–69

Balewa, Alhaji Abubakar Takawa
Prime Minister, Nigeria, 1957–66

Beadle, Sir (Thomas) Hugh
Chief Justice, Rhodesia, 1961–77

Belaunde, Fernando
President of Peru, 1963–68

Bhutto, Zulfikar Ali
Founder of the Pakistan Peoples Party; President of Pakistan, 1971–73

Blankenhorn, Herbert
West German Ambassador to the UK, 1965–70

Brandt, Willy
Vice-Chancellor of the Federal Republic of Germany and Foreign Minister, 1966–69

Brezhnev, Leonid
General Secretary of the Central Committee of the Communist Party of the Soviet Union, 1966–82

Campbell, Evan
High Commissioner in London for Southern Rhodesia, 1964–65

Carstens, Karl
Secretary of State in the German Ministry of Defence, 1966–68

Couve de Murville, Maurice
French Foreign Minister, 1958–68

De Gaulle, Charles
President of France, 1958–69

Dobrynin, Anatoly
Soviet Ambassador to the United States, 1962–86

Eban, Abba
Israeli Foreign Minister, 1966–74

Erhard, Ludwig
Chancellor of West Germany, 1963–66

Eshkol, Levi
Israeli Prime Minister, 1963–69

Fedorenko, Nikolai
Permanent Representative of the USSR at the UN, 1963–68

Gandhi, Indira
Prime Minister of India, 1966–77

Gorton, John
Prime Minister of Australia, 1968–71

Gromyko, Andrei
Soviet Foreign Minister, 1957–85

Hallstein, Walter
President of the European Commission, 1958–67

Ho Chi Minh
President of the Democratic Republic of Vietnam, 1945–69

Holt, Harold
Australian Prime Minister, 1966–67

Holyoake, Keith
Prime Minister of New Zealand, 1960–72

Kaunda, Kenneth
President of Zambia, 1964–91

Kenyatta, Jomo
President of Kenya, 1964–78

Kiesinger, Kurt Georg
Chancellor of West Germany, 1966–69

Kosho Ogasa
Special Japanese envoy to Jakarta

Kosygin, Alexei
Soviet Prime Minister, 1964–80

Ky
See Nguyen Cao Ky

Lee Kuan Yew ('Harry Lee')
Prime Minister of Singapore, 1959–90

Makarios III
President of Cyprus, 1960–74

Margai, Albert
Prime Minister of Sierra Leone, 1964–67

Marshall, John Ross ('Jack')
Deputy Prime Minister, New Zealand, 1960–72

Menzies, Robert (Bob)
Prime Minister of Australia, 1949–66

Mikoyan, Anastas
Member of the Politburo, 1935–66

Muller, Hilgard
South African Foreign Minister, 1964–77

Nasser, Gamal Abdel
President of Egypt, 1956–70

Nehru, Jawaharlal
Prime Minister of India, 1947–64

Nguyen Cao Ky
Prime Minister of the Republic of Vietnam, 1965–67

Nguyen Duy Trinh
DRV Foreign Minister, 1965–80

Nkomo, Joshua
Leader of the African National Congress, Southern Rhodesia, 1952–59; leader of the National Democratic Party, 1960–61; founder of the Zimbabwe African People's Union (ZAPU), 1961

Nkrumah, Kwame
President of Ghana, 1960–66

Nyerere, Julius
President of Tanzania, 1964–85

Obote, A. Milton
Prime Minister of Uganda, 1966–71

Pearson, Lester Bowles ('Mike')
Prime Minister of Canada, 1963–68

Pham Van Dong
Prime Minister of the DRV, 1955–76

Podgorny, Nikolai
Chairman of the Presidium of the Supreme Soviet of the Soviet Union, 1965–77

Poliansky (Polyansky), Dimitrii
First Deputy Chairman of the Council of Ministers of the Soviet Union, 1965–73

Pompidou, Georges
Prime Minister of France, 1962–68

Ronning, Chester
Retired Canadian Foreign Service officer who met with North Vietnamese leaders in March and June 1966

Rueff, Jacques
French economist and adviser to the French Government

Sato, Eisaku
Prime Minister of Japan, 1964–72

Schiller, Karl
Minister of Economic Affairs, Federal Republic of Germany, 1966–72

Schröder, Gerhard
German Foreign Minister, 1961–6

Schweitzer, Pierre-Paul
Managing Director, International Monetary Fund, 1963–73

Senghor, Leopold
President of Senegal, 1960–80

Seydoux, Roger
French Permanent Representative to the United Nations, 1962–67

Shastri, Lal Bahadur
Prime Minister of India, 1964–66

Shelepin, Alexander
Member of the Politburo, 1964–75

Sihanouk, Prince Norodom
Chief of State of Cambodia

Sithole, Ndabaningi
Founder of the Zimbabwe African National Union

Smirnovsky, Mikhail
Soviet Ambassador to the UK

Smith, Ian
Prime Minister of Rhodesia, 1964–79

Souvanna Phouma
Prime Minister of Laos, 1962–75

Strauss, Franz Josef
Federal Minister of Finance, West Germany, 1966–69

Subandrio
First Deputy Prime Minister of Indonesia and Minister Coordinator of Foreign Affairs and Foreign Economic Affairs until July 1966

Sukarno
President of Indonesia, 1945–67

Tunku Abdul Rahman
Prime Minister of Malaya/Malaysia, 1957–70

U Thant
Secretary-General of the United Nations, 1961–71

Verwoerd, H.F.
Prime Minister of South Africa, 1958–66

Von Hassel, Kai-Uwe
German Minister of Defence, 1963–66

Vorster, B. J.
Prime Minister of South Africa, 1966–78

Further Reading

Bartlett, C. J., *'The Special Relationship': A Political History of Anglo-American Relations since 1945* (London and New York: Longman, 1992)

Boyle, Kevin, 'The Price of Peace: Vietnam, the Pound, and the Crisis of the American Empire', *Diplomatic History*, 27, 1 (2003): 37–72

Brands, H. W., *The Wages of Globalism: Lyndon Johnson and the Limits of American Power* (New York and Oxford: Oxford University Press, 1995)

Brown, George, *In My Way* (London: Victor Gollancz, 1971)

Burk, Kathleen, *Old World New World: The Story of Britain and America* (London: Abacus, 2009)

Castle, Barbara, *The Castle Diaries, 1964–70* (London: Weidenfeld and Nicolson, 1984)

Colman, Jonathan, 'Harold Wilson, Lyndon Johnson and Anglo-American "Summit Diplomacy", 1964–68', *Journal of Transatlantic Studies*, 1, 2 (2003): 131–51

———, 'The London Ambassadorship of David K. E. Bruce during the Wilson-Johnson years, 1964–68', *Diplomacy and Statecraft*, 15, 2 (2004): 327–52

———, *A 'Special Relationship'? Harold Wilson, Lyndon B. Johnson and Anglo-American Relations 'at the Summit', 1964–68* (Manchester and New York: Manchester University Press, 2004)

———, '"Dealing with Disillusioned Men": The Washington Ambassadorship of Sir Patrick Dean', *Contemporary British History*, 21, 2 (2007): 247–70

———, '"What now for Britain?": The State Department's Intelligence Assessment of the "Special Relationship", 7 February 1968', *Diplomacy and Statecraft*, 19, 2 (2008): 350–60

———, 'Britain and the Indo-Pakistan Conflict: The Rann of Kutch and Kashmir, 1965', *Journal of Imperial and Commonwealth History*, 37, 3 (2009): 465–82

———, *The Foreign Policy of Lyndon B. Johnson: The United States and the World, 1963–1969* (Edinburgh: Edinburgh University Press, 2010)

———, 'Lost crusader? Chester Cooper and the Vietnam War, 1963–68', *Cold War History*, 12, 3 (2012): 429–49

Cooper, Chester L., *The Lost Crusade: The Full Story of U.S. Involvement in Vietnam from Roosevelt to Nixon* (London: MacGibbon & Kee, 1971)

Crossman, Richard, *The Crossman Diaries: Selections from the Diaries of a Cabinet Minister, 1964–1970* (London: Hamish Hamilton and Jonathan Cape, 1979)
Dickie, John, *"Special" No More: Anglo-American Relations: Rhetoric and Reality* (London: Weidenfeld and Nicolson, 1994)
Dimitrakis, Panagiotis, *Failed Alliances of the Cold War: Britain's Strategy and Ambitions in Asia and the Middle East* (London: I.B. Tauris, 2012)
Dobson, Alan P., *The Politics of the Anglo-American Economic Special Relationship 1940–1987* (Brighton: Wheatsheaf, 1988)
_____, 'Labour or Conservative: Does it Matter in Anglo-American Relations?', *Journal of Contemporary History*, 25, 4 (1990): 387–407
_____, *Anglo-American Relations in the Twentieth Century: Of Friendship, Conflict and the Rise and Decline of Superpowers* (London: Routledge, 1995)
_____, 'The USA, Britain, and the Question of Hegemony', in Geir Lundestad (ed.), *No End of Alliance: The United States and Western Europe: Past, Present and Future* (Macmillan: Basingstoke, 1998)
_____, 'Anglo-American Relations and Diverging Economic Defence Policies in the 1950s and 1960s', in Jonathan Hollowell (ed.), *Twentieth-Century Anglo-American Relations*, (Basingstoke: Palgrave, 2001)
Dockrill, Saki, *Britain's Retreat from East of Suez: The Choice between Europe and the World?* (Basingstoke: Palgrave Macmillan, 2002)
Dumbrell, John, *A Special Relationship: Anglo-American Relations in the Cold War and After* (Basingstoke: Macmillan, 2001)
_____, 'Personal Diplomacy: Relations between Prime Ministers and Presidents', in Alan P. Dobson and Steve Marsh (eds), *Anglo-American Relations: Contemporary Perspectives* (London and New York: Routledge, 2013)
_____, and Sylvia Ellis, 'British Involvement in Vietnam Peace Initiatives, 1966–1967: Marigolds, Sunflowers, and "Kosygin Week"', *Diplomatic History*, 27, 1 (2003): 113–49
Dyson, Stephen Benedict, 'Alliances, Domestic Politics, and Leader Psychology: Why Did Britain Stay Out of Vietnam and Go into Iraq?', *Political Psychology*, 28, 6 (2007): 647-66
Ellis, Sylvia, 'Lyndon Johnson, Harold Wilson and the Vietnam War: A Not So Special Relationship?', in Jonathan Hollowell (ed.), *Twentieth-Century Anglo-American Relations* (Basingstoke: Macmillan, 2001)
_____, *Britain, America, and the Vietnam War* (Westport, CT: Praeger, 2004)
_____, 'A Foreign Policy Success? LBJ and Transatlantic Relations', *Journal of Transatlantic Studies*, 8, 3 (2010): 247–56
Ellison, James, 'Dealing with de Gaulle: Anglo-American Relations, NATO and the Second Application', in Oliver Daddow (ed.), *Harold Wilson*

and European Integration: Britain's Second Application to Join the EEC (London: Frank Cass, 2003)

_____, *The United States, Britain and the Transatlantic Crisis: Rising to the Gaullist Challenge, 1963–68* (Basingstoke: Palgrave, 2007)

Fain, W. Taylor, *American Ascendance and British Retreat in the Persian Gulf Region* (New York: Palgrave Macmillan, 2008)

Fielding, Jeremy, 'Coping with Decline: US Policy toward the British Defense Reviews of 1966', *Diplomatic History*, 23, 4 (1999): 633–56

Hamilton, Arran, 'Beyond sterling devaluation: The gold crisis of March 1968', *Contemporary European History*, 17, 1 (2008): 73–95

Hathaway, Robert M., *Great Britain and the United States: Special Relations since World War II* (Boston: Twayne Publishers, 1990)

Herring, George C., *The Secret Diplomacy of the Vietnam War: The Negotiating Volumes of the Pentagon Papers* (Austin: University of Texas Press, 1983)

Johnson, Lyndon Baines, *The Vantage Point: Perspectives on the Presidency, 1963–1969* (London: Weidenfeld and Nicolson, 1971)

Jones, Matthew, *Conflict and Confrontation in South East Asia, 1961–1965: Britain, the United States, and the Creation of Malaysia* (Cambridge: Cambridge University Press, 2002)

_____, 'A Decision Delayed: Britain's Withdrawal from South East Asia Reconsidered, 1961–68', *English Historical Review*, 117, 472 (2002): 569–95

Jones, Peter, *America and the British Labour Party: The 'Special Relationship' at Work* (London: Tauris Academic Studies, 1997)

Kaiser, Philip M., *Journeying Far and Wide: A Political and Diplomatic Memoir* (New York: Charles Scribner's Sons, Maxwell Macmillan International, 1992)

Kandiah, Michael and Gillian Staerck, '"Reliable Allies": Anglo-American Relations', in Wolfram Kaiser and Gillian Staerck (eds), *British Foreign Policy, 1955–1964: Contracting Options* (Basingstoke: Macmillan, 2000)

Kunz, Diane B., 'Cold War Dollar Diplomacy: The Other Side of Containment', in Diane B. Kunz (ed.), *The Diplomacy of the Crucial Decade: American Foreign Relations During the 1960s* (New York: Columbia University Press, 1994)

_____, '"Somewhat Mixed Up Together": Anglo-American Defence and Financial Policy during the 1960s', *Journal of Imperial and Commonwealth History*, 27, 2 (1999): 213–32

Lankford, Nelson D., *The Last American Aristocrat: The Biography of David K. E. Bruce, 1898–1977* (Boston: Little, Brown and Company, 1996)

Louis, Wm. Roger, 'The Dissolution of the British Empire in the Era of Vietnam', *American Historical Review*, 107, 1 (2002): 1–25

McGarr, Paul M., *The Cold War in South Asia: Britain, the United States and the Indian Subcontinent, 1945–1965* (Cambridge: Cambridge University Press, 2013)

O'Hara, Glen, 'The Limits of US Power: Transatlantic Financial Diplomacy under the Johnson and Wilson Administrations, October 1964–November 1968', *Contemporary European History*, 12, 3 (2003): 257–78

Ovendale, Ritchie, *Anglo-American Relations in the Twentieth Century* (Basingstoke: Macmillan, 1998)

Parr, Helen, *Britain's Policy towards the European Community: Harold Wilson and Britain's World Role, 1964–1967* (London: Routledge, 2006)

Petersen, Tore T., *The Decline of the Anglo-American Middle East, 1961–1969* (Brighton: Sussex Academic Press, 2006)

Pham, P. L., *Ending 'East of Suez': The British Decision to Withdraw from Malaysia and Singapore, 1964–1968* (Oxford and New York: Oxford University Press, 2010)

Pimlott, Ben, *Harold Wilson* (London: BCA, 1992)

_____, 'Courting the President: Wilson and Johnson in the 1960s', in Antoine Capet (ed.), *The "Special Relationship": La Relation Speciale" entre le Royaume-Uni et les Etats-Unis* (Rouen: University of Rouen, 2003)

Pine, Melissa, *Harold Wilson and Europe: Pursuing Britain's Membership of the European Community* (London: Tauris Academic Studies, 2007)

Priest, Andrew, *Kennedy, Johnson and NATO: Britain, America and the Dynamics of Alliance, 1962–68* (London: Routledge, 2006)

Roth, Andrew, *Sir Harold Wilson: Yorkshire Walter Mitty* (London: Macdonald and Jane's, 1977)

Roy, Rajarshi, 'The Battle for the Pound: The Political Economy of Anglo-American Relations, 1964–1968', PhD thesis, London School of Economics, 2000

_____ and John W. Young (eds), *Ambassador to Sixties London: The Diaries of David Bruce, 1961–1969* (Dordrecht: Republic of Letters Publishing, 2009)

Sandbrook, Dominic, *White Heat: A History of Britain in the Swinging Sixties* (London: Abacus, 2006)

Schwartz, Thomas Alan, *Lyndon Johnson and Europe: In the Shadow of Vietnam* (Cambridge, MA: Harvard University Press, 2003)

Spelling, Alex, '"A Reputation for Parsimony to Uphold": Harold Wilson, Richard Nixon and the Re-Valued "Special Relationship"', *Contemporary British History*, 27, 2 (2013): 192–213

Staerck, Gillian, 'The Role of the British Embassy in Washington', *Contemporary British History*, 12, 3 (1998): 115–38

Steininger, Rolf, '"The Americans are in a hopeless Position": Great Britain and the War in Vietnam, 1964–65', *Diplomacy and Statecraft*, 8, 3 (1997): 237–85

Stoddart, Kristan, *Losing an Empire and Finding a Role: Britain, the USA, NATO and Nuclear Weapons, 1964–70* (Basingstoke: Palgrave Macmillan, 2012)

Subritzky, John, *Confronting Sukarno: British, American, Australian and New Zealand Diplomacy in the Malaysian-Indonesian Confrontation, 1961-5* (Basingstoke: Macmillan, 2000)

Tomlinson, Jim, *The Labour Governments 1964–70*: Volume 3: *Economic Policy* (Manchester: Manchester University Press, 2004)

Watts, Carl P., 'The United States, Britain, and the Problem of Rhodesian Independence, 1964–1965', *Diplomatic History*, 30, 3 (2006): 439–70

Wilson, Harold, *The Labour Government 1964–1970: A Personal Record* (London: Weidenfeld and Nicolson, 1971)

Young, John W., 'Britain and "LBJ's war", 1964–68', *Cold War History*, 2, 3 (2002): 63–92

———, *The Labour Governments, 1964–70*: Volume 2: *International Policy* (Manchester: Manchester University Press, 2003)

———, *Twentieth-century Diplomacy: A Case Study of British Practice, 1963–1976* (Cambridge: Cambridge University Press, 2008)

———, 'Ambassador David Bruce and "LBJ's War": Vietnam viewed from London, 1963–1968', *Diplomacy and Statecraft*, 22, 1 (2011): 81–100

———, 'David K. E. Bruce, 1961–69', in Alison R. Holmes and J. Simon Rofe (eds), *The Embassy in Grosvenor Square: American Ambassadors to the United Kingdom, 1938–2008* (Basingstoke: Palgrave Macmillan, 2012)

———, 'The US embassy in London and Britain's withdrawal from East of Suez, 1961–69', in John W. Young, Effie G. H. Pedaliu, and Michael D. Kandiah (eds), *Britain in Global Politics*: Volume 2: *From Churchill to Blair* (Basingstoke: Palgrave Macmillan, 2013)

———, *David Bruce and Diplomatic Practice: An American Ambassador in London, 1961–9* (New York and London: Bloomsbury, 2014)

Ziegler, Philip, *Wilson: The Authorised Life* (London: Weidenfeld and Nicolson, 1993)

Index

Abubakar 64, 98, 103, 104
Aden 68, 115 n 190
ANF 53, 57, 92
Anglo-American relations 7–11, 23, 28, 29, 30–2, 38, 62–3, 194, 296 (see also special relationship)
Anglo-Soviet Treaty of Friendship Non-Aggression and Co-operative Development 202–03
Apollo 196
Apollo 8 292–3, 295, 296
Asian Development Bank 89–90
Attlee, Lord 243
Ayub Khan, Mohammed 15, 85–9

Ball, George 2, 75, 82, 84, 89, 146, 176
BAOR (see British Army on the Rhine)
Bartlett, C. J. 9
Bator, Francis 8 n 54, 168
Beadle, Sir Hugh 102, 138, 139, 142
Belaunde, Fernando 239–40
Bhutto, Ali 86, 87, 89
Blankenhorn, Herbert 291
Bowden, Herbert 190
Boyle, Peter 20
Brandon, Henry 6
Brands, H. W. 7
Brandt, Willy 215, 217, 291
Brezhnev, Leonid 120, 122, 206, 262, 265, 268, 269, 271–2
British Army on the Rhine 19, 173, 177
Brown, George 5, 11, 20, 26, 170, 176, 179, 181, 182, 196, 203, 207, 210, 218 n 44, 222, 226, 227, 229, 243, 249, 257, 260, 271
Bruce, David 1, 5, 7, 13, 24, 28, 31–2, 196, 201, 205, 207, 229, 253, 288 n 81

Bundy, McGeorge 13, 28, 55–6, 80 n 110
Bundy, William 24, 261, 262
Burchett, Wilfred 197, 201, 210
Bustamante, Alexander 38 n 19
Butler, R. A. 28

Callaghan, James 189, 251
Cambodia 155, 156, 165
Campbell, Evan 141
Caradon, Lord 225
Carstens, Karl 185
Castle, Barbara 6
Chalfont, Lord 114 n 185, 121, 125, 131, 132, 243, 264
China 116, 205 (see also Mao Tse-tung; Sino-Soviet relations)
Churchill, Winston 6, 28, 44, 296
Clifford, Clark 7–8
Colman Jonathan 6, 8
Commonwealth 65, 98, 103–4
Commonwealth Prime Ministers' conference (1965) 64–5
'confrontation' 13, 46, 47–50
Cooper, Chester 20, 21, 22, 195 n 2, 196, 199, 201, 205, 208–9
Couve de Murville, Maurice 243
Crossman, Richard 4
Cyprus 25, 249
Czechoslovakia 285

Davies, Harold 264, 272
de Gaulle, Charles 10, 16, 19, 57, 60–2, 127, 133–6, 150, 154, 171, 173, 184, 222, 226, 229, 230, 231–3, 291–2
Dean, Sir Patrick 18, 23–4, 25–6, 31, 218–19, 226, 227, 247, 248

Dell, Edmund 5
Deming, Fred 255
devaluation 8, 9, 25, 31, 244
Dickie, John 9
Dillon, Douglas 38
Dobrynin, Anatoly 234, 268, 283, 285
Dobson Alan 4, 9
Dockrill, Saki 7
Douglas-Home, Sir Alec 28, 41, 70, 124
Dumbrell, John 5, 8, 27

East of Suez 7–8, 9, 10, 24–5, 25–6, 27, 30–1, 83, 234
Eban, Abba 222, 224, 229
Eden, Anthony 72, 124
EEC (see Johnson, Lyndon: EEC; Wilson, Harold: EEC)
EFTA 38 n 19, 57, 58, 59, 143, 150, 184
Eisenhower, Dwight D. 28, 124
Ellis, Sylvia 2–3, 8, 13, 18, 23
Ellison, James 10
Erhard, Ludwig 16, 57–8, 59, 60, 91–2, 97, 135, 146, 147, 148, 148–50, 151, 171, 173, 177, 178
Eshkol, Levi 226

F111 aircraft 115 n 190, 126, 187, 188, 189, 193, 257–8, 260
Fedorenko, Nikolai 225
Fowler, Henry H. ('Joe') 68, 275, 288, 289
France (see de Gaulle, Charles; Johnson, Lyndon: French devaluation; Wilson, Harold: France)
Freeman, Orville 112
Fulbright, William J. 110, 111

Gandhi, Indira 136–7, 138
Garner, Joe 191, 192
Geneva conference 14, 61, 69, 113, 114, 117, 119, 164, 279, 280, 282
Germany 16, 19, 91–2, 97, 118–19, 121, 122, 133, 135, 146, 147, 149–5, 151, 171, 173, 185–6, 187, 189, 217, 289, 290–1
Gibraltar 55

Gilpatric, Roswell 82, 83, 84–5
gold crisis (1968) 29, 274, 275, 276–7
Goldberg, Arthur 81, 94, 97, 222, 225, 228, 234, 271
Gordon, Kermit 61
Gorton, John 294
Gromyko, Andrei 119, 131, 132, 228, 234, 265, 267, 284

Halls, Michael 22
Hallstein, Walter 59
Harriman, Averrell 19 n 100, 94, 119, 183, 268, 278
Hathaway, Robert 4
Healey, Denis 12, 108, 115, 120, 126, 227, 261
Heath, Edward 124
Hennings, John Dunn 138
Herter, Christian 134 n 29
Ho Chi Minh 111, 209, 219–20
Hollyoake, Keith 73
Holt, Harold 235, 250
Hong Kong 144
Hughes, Thomas L. 31
Hull 109 n 174
Humphrey, Hubert 247

India 15, 63, 86, 87, 137, 138 n 40
Israel 223–4

Jenkins, Roy 255, 275, 288, 289, 290, 292
Johnson, Lyndon
  Aberfan 182
  Africa 151
  aircraft sales 239–40, 243
  Apollo 8 293, 295
  Asian Development Bank 90
  Attlee, Lord 243
  Ayub Khan 89
  Baltimore speech (1965) 64
  Belaunde, Fernando 239–40
  Britain, attitude towards 32, 39, 62–3, 242, 247–8, 295, 296, 296–7
  Britain's world role 26, 256, 257
  British Army on the Rhine 19, 173, 177

Index

British economy 256
British General Election (1964) 34
British General Election (1966) 136
Cambodia 156, 165
China 120, 234
Churchill, Winston, 44, 296
Commonwealth Prime Ministers' meeting (1965) 66
Cuba 28
Cyprus 25, 249
Czechoslovakia 285–6
de Gaulle, General Charles 127, 146, 171, 173, 233, 291–2, 292 n 90
devaluation 25, 247–8
'dissociation' 19 n 100, 156
dollar 248, 251
East of Suez 24–5, 27, 31, 221, 234
EEC 16, 19, 151, 185
Erhard, Ludwig 91–2, 146, 147, 151, 171, 173, 177, 178
F111 257–8
Far East 256, 257
French devaluation 289
Gandhi, Indira 136–7
Gemini Flights 238
Geneva conference 114, 119, 278, 279 n 58
Germany 16, 59–60, 91–2, 118–19, 126, 132, 146, 147, 151, 171, 173, 185–6
gold crisis (1968) 275
Guam meeting (1967) 219
health 77, 182–3, 193
Honolulu conference (1966) 112
India 137
Indonesia 44–6
Israel 223–4
Kaunda, Kenneth 103
Kennedy Round 251
Kiesinger, Kurt 289
Kosygin, Alexei 165, 196, 198, 210–11, 213, 220, 233, 234, 265–6
Malaysia 46, 53, 54, 74
Manila conference (1966) 183

Middle East crisis (1967) 223, 228, 230–1, 234
MLF 53
Nasser, Gamal Abdel 224, 228
NATO 131–2, 147, 171, 173, 174, 178, 185
nuclear weapons 41, 59, 80–1, 91–2, 117–19
Pearson, Mike 223
Persian Gulf 256, 257
Peru 239–40
Phase A-Phase B 210–11, 212, 214
Rann of Kutch 63
relationship with Harold Wilson 2–7, 18, 21, 23–4, 25, 26–7, 27–8, 29, 33–4, 39, 42, 43, 51, 74, 90, 92, 109, 113, 120, 126, 129–30, 136, 169, 193, 194, 214, 226–7, 242, 250, 273, 282, 292, 293, 295, 297
Rhodesia 15, 19, 66, 76, 77–8 n 103, 78 n 105, 84–5, 100, 103, 140–1, 151, 157, 180
San Antonio formula 265, 278
Singapore 74
Smith, Ian 76, 80, 101, 180
South Africa 180
Soviet Union 118–19, 125, 132, 164–5, 228, 233, 278
State of the Union messages 268 n 29, 294
sterling 19, 37, 40, 129, 173, 275
Stevenson, Adlai 66–7
Surveyor I 155
Torrey Canyon 220
trilateral/tripartite talks 177, 193
US economy 251–3
USS *Pueblo* 271 n 33
Vietnam 13–14, 16, 17, 18, 22, 27, 29, 52, 53, 55–6, 66, 67–8, 93–4, 96, 105–7, 109–10, 112–13, 114–15, 141, 151, 156–7, 183, 196–8, 213, 219–20, 265–6, 270, 271 n 33, 277–8, 279 n 57, 282 n 61, 283–4, 287 n 78, 296
Wilson-Kosygin deal 22

Zambia 84, 100
Jones, Howard P. 45
Jones, Matthew 9
Jones, Peter 3

Kaiser, Philip 2, 227
Kashmir 63 n 60, 85, 87, 88
Katzenbach, Nicholas 234, 253, 255
Kaunda, Kenneth 15, 82–3, 104
Kennedy, John F. 5, 10, 41, 45, 62 n 56, 119 n 198, 239 n 97
Kennedy, Robert 285
Kennedy round 59, 184, 251
Kenyatta, Jomo 82, 103
Kiesinger, Kurt 215, 217, 243, 289
Kosho Ogasa 49
Kosygin, Alexei 18, 20–21, 23, 56, 119, 120, 122, 153, 163, 164, 165, 172, 179, 199–200, 201–2, 202–3, 204–5, 206–8, 210–11, 213, 215–16, 219, 220, 226, 229, 230, 231, 233, 234, 261–2, 262–4, 265–6, 267, 268, 273, 281

Lee Kuan Yew 235, 260
Lewandowski 20, 195 n 2

MacDonald, Malcolm 82, 101
Macmillan, Harold 5, 10–11, 41, 119 n 198, 124, 203–4
Makarios 249
Malaysia 13, 24, 46, 47–50, 65, 72, 236
Manila conference (1966) 183
Mann, Tom 83
Mao Tse-tung 216
Margai, Albert 103
Marshall, John Ross 235
Martin, William McChesney 274, 275
McCloy, John 177, 178, 185, 186
McGarr, Philip 2
McNamara, Robert 82, 83, 115, 120, 126, 151, 152, 162, 188, 193, 234, 257, 261
Menzies, Robert 64, 66, 100
Mikoyan, Anastas 122

MLF 53, 57, 91–2
Muller, Hilgard 181

Nasser, Gamal Abdel 221 n 61, 224, 225, 228
NATO 10, 16, 19, 70–1, 81, 118–19, 131–2, 133–6, 147, 148, 150, 171, 173, 174, 177, 178, 179, 185, 187, 188, 189–90, 203, 232, 291
Nehru, Jawaharlal 87
Neustadt, Richard 3, 7
Nguyen Cao Ky 112
Nguyen Duy Trinh 197 n 9, 263 n 15, 265
Nixon, Richard 5
Nkomo, Joshua 78
Nkrumah, Kwame 64, 103
Noel-Baker, Philip 111
Nuclear Planning Working Group 97, 126
nuclear weapons 40–1, 80–1, 91–2, 97–8, 117–19, 121, 122
Nyerere, Julius 83, 103

Obote, A. Milton 83
O'Brien, Leslie 251, 275
Ovendale, Ritchie 3–4

Pakistan 15, 63, 138 n 40
Palliser, Michael 4, 20
Pearson, Mike 100, 223
Persian Gulf 26, 256, 257, 259
Petersen, Tore 9
Pham Van Dong 105 n 168, 265
Pimlott, Ben 9–10
Pine, Melissa 2
PKI 45, 48
Podgorny, Nikolai 268
Poliansky, Dimitrii 267, 268
Pompidou, Georges 154, 157
Priest, Andrew 11

Rann of Kutch 15, 63, 65, 88
Read, Benjamin 22, 23 n 120, 144 n 55
Rhodesia 11, 15 (see also Johnson, Lyndon: Rhodesia; Smith, Ian; Wilson, Harold: Rhodesia)

UDI 78, 79, 80, 81 n 115, 181
Rogers, Bernard 17, 152
Roll, Sir Eric 37, 40
Ronning, Chester 158, 159, 162
Roosevelt, Franklin D. 294, 296
Rostow, Gene 187, 188, 189
Rostow, Walt 11, 17, 22, 23, 207, 209, 218
Roth, Andrew 23
Roy, Rajarshi 4
Rueff, Jacques 57
Rusk, Dean 2, 31, 146, 153–4, 155, 156, 158, 179, 208 n 26, 222, 229, 249, 256, 257, 260, 265, 285

San Antonio formula 265, 267, 268, 278, 282
Sato, Eisaku 45
Schiller, Karl 291
Schröder, Gerhard 150
Schwartz, Thomas 10
Schweitzer, Pierre-Paul 289
SEATO 156, 157, 158
Seitz, Raymond 5
Selma 58–9
Senghor, Leopold 157
Seydoux, Roger 225
Shastri, Lal Bahadur 87
Shelepin, Alexander 95, 96, 105
Sihanouk, Prince 163
Singapore 24, 72, 236
Sino-Soviet relations 95, 167, 199, 204–5, 216, 282
Sithole, Ndabaningi 78
Six Day War 221 n 61, 227
Smirnovsky, Mikhail 281
Smith, Ian 15, 75, 78, 79, 80, 83, 98, 99, 100, 101, 102, 138–40, 142, 145, 175, 176, 180, 181, 190, 191–3, 286–7
South Africa 99, 142, 175, 176, 180, 181, 192, 287
Souvanna Phouma 105
Soviet Union (see Johnson, Lyndon: Soviet Union; Sino-Soviet relations; Wilson, Harold: Soviet Union)

special relationship 4, 7, 10, 11 (see also Anglo-American relations)
Spelling, Alex 5
sterling 12, 19, 25, 37, 39–40, 124, 128, 129, 244–5, 274 n 41, 276–7
Stevens, John 168
Stevenson, Adlai 66–7
Stewart, Michael 81, 108, 150, 158, 170, 279, 281, 284, 290
Stoddart, Kristan 11
Strauss, Franz Josef 214–15, 216, 218
Subandrio 47
Subritzky, John 8–9
Sukarno 13, 44–6, 47–50, 52
Syria 223

Test Ban Treaty (1963) 119
Thompson, Llewellyn E. 278
Thomson, George 146, 149, 178, 222–3, 225, 226, 249
Tomkins, Edward 285
Tomlinson, Jim 3
Trend, Sir Burke 68
Trinh (see Nguyen Duy Trinh)
Tunku Abdul Rahman 49, 50, 235

U Thant 88, 229, 235, 271–3
United Arab Republic 223

Vance, Cyrus 249
Verwoerd, H. F. 138
Viet Cong 56, 95, 106, 109, 219
Vietnam 3, 8, 13–14, 16–17, 28–9 (see also Johnson, Lyndon: Vietnam; Wilson, Harold: Vietnam)
Von Hassel, Kai-Uwe 97
Vorster, B. J. 180, 181, 190

Walker, Patrick Gordon 61
Watson, Duncan 142
Watts, Carl P. 7, 11
Western Peace Plan (1959) 134
Westmoreland, General William C. 213
Wilson, Harold
   Aberfan 182

ABMs 215–16
Aden 68
aircraft sales 238–9, 241
ANF 53
Apollo 196
Apollo 8 292–3, 296
Asian Development Bank 89–90
Ayub Khan 85–9
Bhutto, Ali 86, 87, 89
Brezhnev, Leonid 120, 122, 268, 269, 271–2
Britain's world role 259–61
British economy 35–7, 68, 123, 143, 168, 169–70, 236, 244–6, 259
Canada 223
character 2
China 116
Churchill, Winston 46–7
Commonwealth 65, 98, 99, 236, 250, 294–5
Commonwealth Prime Ministers' meeting (1965) 64–5
Cooper, Chester 196, 199, 207–8, 208–9
Cyprus 25
Czechoslovakia 285
de Gaulle, Charles 60–2, 130, 133–6, 150, 154, 222, 226, 229, 230, 231–3, 292
defence expenditure 108–9
devaluation 25, 244
disarmament 165–6, 167
'dissociation' 3, 17, 148, 153, 155, 159
dollar 247, 275
East of Suez 24–5, 25–6, 30–1, 83, 246
Eban, Abba 223–4, 229
EEC 2, 16, 183–5, 214, 215, 232, 243, 246
Erhard, Ludwig 57–8, 97, 135, 148
escalation of Vietnam War 52
F111 241, 260
Far East 235, 259–60
France 61–2, 217, 222, 226, 246, 287–8
Gandhi, Indira 138

Gemini Flights 240
General Election (1966) 16, 123–5
Geneva conference 113, 117, 119, 267, 279, 280, 282
Germany 16, 57–8, 97, 121, 122, 124, 130, 133, 135, 149–50, 168, 172–3, 187, 189, 205, 214–15, 217, 243, 287–8, 289, 290–1
Gibraltar 55
gold crisis (1968) 274, 276–7
Hong Kong 144
India 86
Indonesia-Malaysia confrontation 47–50
Israel 224–5
Kashmir 85, 87, 88
Kaunda, Kenneth 82–3, 101–2, 104
Kennedy, Robert 285
Kenyatta, Jomo 83, 103, 104
Kosygin 23, 119, 120, 122, 153, 163, 164, 165, 166–7, 172, 179, 199–200, 201–2, 202–3, 204–5, 206–8, 209–10, 215–16, 220, 226, 229, 230, 261–2, 262–4, 267, 268, 273, 281
Malaysia 68, 72, 74, 236
Middle East crisis (1967) 221, 224–5, 227, 228–9, 235, 244
MLF 53, 122
Nasser, Gamal Abdel 225
NATO 133–6, 148, 150, 172, 173, 179, 187, 188, 189–90, 203, 291
nuclear weapons 40–1, 57, 69–72, 97–8, 119, 121–3
Nyerere, Julius 83
Pakistan 85–9
Persian Gulf 259–60
Peru 238
Phase A-Phase B 212
Rann of Kutch 63, 65, 88
relationship with Lyndon Johnson 2–7, 18, 28, 29–30, 33, 38, 42–3, 73, 77, 84, 90, 91, 117, 138, 155, 166, 169, 172, 174, 186–7, 194, 195, 206, 208, 218–19, 227, 228, 241, 247,

248, 250, 256, 271–2, 274, 292, 293–5, 296–7
Rhodesia 15, 19, 64–5, 75, 76, 77–80, 82–3, 98–9, 100, 101, 104, 124, 143, 145, 174–5, 190–1, 286–7
Selma 58–9
Singapore 72, 74, 236
Smith, Ian 75, 76, 78, 79, 83, 98, 99, 101, 102, 138–40, 142, 145, 175, 176, 181, 190, 191, 286–7
South Africa 175, 176, 181, 192, 287
Soviet Union 120–3, 134, 166–7, 179, 182, 202–3, 216, 217, 225, 269, 280, 285
Spain 55
sterling 39–40, 68, 124, 128, 244–5, 274–5, 276–7
Stevenson, Adlai 66
Sukarno 47–50
Surveyor I 152
Thailand 153
trilateral/tripartite talks 172, 178, 187, 188, 189
U Thant 271
UDI 181, 190

US economy 255
US Presidential election (1964) 38, 73
Vietnam 3, 13–14, 16–17, 20–21, 23–4, 28–9, 55, 61, 64–5, 69, 93, 94–6, 107–8, 110–111, 113–14, 117, 120–1, 143–4, 148, 152–3, 161, 199–200, 212, 220, 261–2, 262–4, 266–7, 268–9, 272–3, 279–81, 281–2, 284, 287, 294
Washington 21–2
White Paper on Defence (1966) 115, 149
White Paper on Defence (1967) 237, 238, 246
Zambia 82–3, 98, 99, 101–2, 104
Woods, George 137
World Bank 137
Wright, Noel 62, 62–3 n 58
Wright, Oliver 138, 139, 140, 142

Young, John 3, 4, 9

Zambia 82–3, 84, 98, 99
Zuckerman, Sir Solly 215